BLACKS IN THE DIASPORA

Editors

Herman L. Bennett
Kim D. Butler
Judith A. Byfield
Tracy Sharpley-Whiting

THAT
THE BLOOD
STAY PURE

AFRICAN AMERICANS, NATIVE AMERICANS, AND
THE PREDICAMENT OF RACE AND IDENTITY IN VIRGINIA

ARICA L. COLEMAN

INDIANA UNIVERSITY PRESS

Bloomington & Indianapolis

This book is a publication of

INDIANA UNIVERSITY PRESS
Office of Scholarly Publishing
Herman B Wells Library 350
1320 East 10th Street
Bloomington, Indiana 47405 USA

iupress.indiana.edu

Telephone orders 800-842-6796
Fax orders 812-855-7931

♾ The paper used in this publication
meets the minimum requirements of
the American National Standard for
Information Sciences–Permanence of
Paper for Printed Library Materials,
ANSI Z39.48–1992.

*Manufactured in the
United States of America*

*Library of Congress
Cataloging-in-Publication Data*

Coleman, Arica L.
  That the blood stay pure : African
Americans, Native Americans, and the
predicament of race and identity in Vir-
ginia / Arica L. Coleman.
    pages cm. — (Blacks in the diaspora)
  Includes bibliographical references
and index.
  ISBN 978-0-253-01043-8 (cl : alk. paper)
— ISBN 978-0-253-01050-6 (ebook)
  1. African Americans—Virginia—
History. 2. Indians of North America—
Virginia—History. 3. African Americans
—Relations with Indians. 4. Virginia—
Ethnic relations—History. 5. Racism—
Virginia—History. I. Title.
  F235.N4C65 2013
  305.8009755—dc23

2013011321

1 2 3 4 5   18 17 16 15 14 13

In memory of Lillian, Leighton, and Jack

I found that to tell the truth is the hardest thing on earth, harder than fighting in a war, harder than taking part in a revolution. If you try it you will find at times sweat will break upon you. You will find that even if you succeed in discounting the attitudes of others to you and your life, you will wrestle with yourself most of all, fight with yourself, for there will surge up in you a strong desire to alter facts, to dress up your feelings. You'll find that there are many things you don't want to admit about yourself and others. As your record shapes itself, an awed wonder haunts you. And yet there is no more exciting adventure than trying to be honest in this way. The clean, strong feeling that sweeps you when you've done it makes you know that.

—RICHARD WRIGHT

CONTENTS

FOREWORD

With this timely and important new book, Arica L. Coleman extends discussions first opened by the pioneering work of scholars and activists who challenged the way Native American–African American interactions have been depicted in academic literature, political struggles, and popular culture. As she notes, scholarship using Black–Indian relations as an entry point, thus challenging the legal foundations of racialized thinking at both the federal and state levels, has proliferated over the last twenty or so years. We could even argue, convincingly, that problematizing the relationships between African Americans and American Indians has provided the most important new conceptual approaches to the study of race, identity, and place. Sadly those openings, though promising, have not produced the paradigm shifts that, if followed to their logical conclusions, would have fundamentally altered the way we study African Americans and American Indians. By extension, we would also have seen a transformation and perhaps fruitful expansion of various fields of study both disciplinary and interdisciplinary, including African American, American Indian, cultural studies, and almost every area of the social sciences and humanities. Fortunately, it is these kinds of contradictions that attract the interest of the new cadre of scholars of Black–Indian relations.

Coleman's work, which sits comfortably among new critical studies of Black–Indian lives, does not sidestep the many contradictions, conflicts, and questions that complicate the history of Black–Indian relations. In particular, the genesis and evolution of Virginia's racial state demands this kind of scrutiny as it remains one of the states that has always had a difficult time dealing with its less-than-inspiring history around matters of race. The sham science that buttressed the state's racialized statutes on marriage, identity, and property ownership went beyond the intended purpose of policing bodies and containing an imagined "contagion." It also fixed and reified a historical trajectory that saw racial separation as natural if not desirable. In the minds of its citizens, particularly its White citizens, notions of privilege associated with one's race must have been difficult to reject. So difficult in fact, that when private citizens, legal advocacy organizations, and the federal government stepped in to challenge the most repugnant of Virginia's racial hierarchy laws, in many small communities and in some entire counties, White citizens engaged in their own special form of socio-civil disobedience. It is from the experience of Virginia that we learned about "massive resistance" and other such actions that encouraged the wholesale and complete withdrawal from schools and other public venues that might see the social mixing or social commerce between Black and White people. In the midst of this turmoil and the virtual damning of Black folk, what would an Indian do? We do know, up until a certain point, what they were forced to do, as Coleman tells us in the unfolding of her thesis. They would have chosen from several very limiting choices. They could accept the state's binary logic, which divided the state into two distinct communities: one White and on top and the other Black and consigned—or condemned if we choose the more appropriate term—to an inviolable lower, caste state. I use the term "state" because the condition of Blackness in this historical period was designed to designate all elements of Black existence as sanctioned. It was a physical, psychic, and even spiritual banishment whose indiscriminate aspects ensnared Indians as well. How did they resist? How did they resist and recapture their identities, or the semblance of their identities, that they'd fought to preserve for over 400 years? Some were able to pass through a legal loophole that Coleman relates in the text. Bloodlines were important when seeking escape from the Black–White binary system. It does not take much research to understand that the proximity to either Whiteness or Blackness was more important than any other legacy or genealogical justification that might be offered up. More importantly, one could not necessarily declare against all evidence that one was White, but under no circumstance would it be wise to tout your closeness to a Black past.

Fortunately, in *That the Blood Stay Pure* Coleman amplifies discussions of narrative strategy, identity, and identity formation, and the roles of the state of Virginia's race and racializing practices. The discussion throughout this text helps us to develop the needed critical perspectives on epistemic privilege and sovereignty, the broader implications of racialist strategy, and the ways these abstract notions affect the lives of members of both of these diverse and complex communities.

This text arrives at a difficult moment in Black–Indian relations in Virginia as conflicts over identity and belonging burdens interactions that may have, under different circumstances, been less strained. In recent years, "identity" (i.e., tribal and familial affiliation) for Virginia's native peoples has not only arbitrated actual and perceived notions of "belonging," it has also arbitrated rights within the tribe or tribal nation-place.

Fortunately Coleman's interests reach beyond these disputes, and she succeeds in challenging us to consider whether 500 years of joint histories and historical interaction should be reduced to, or be understood only in the context of, recent debates about tribal membership. This issue has captured the imagination of scholars from many fields as well as the popular press for many reasons beyond concern for either community. Within the arguments of both those who claim the right to determine tribal membership and those Freedmen descendants who assert their rights of inclusion are echoes of historical debates over "blood" and race, place, and rights to land. This is why this text is so important. Coleman takes a long and critical look at the making of Virginia's Indian and African American peoples and the construction of various counter narratives that, despite the prevailing social order, succeed in several cases, most notably the Nottoway, in defining ideas about community and identity built upon concepts such as adoption, inclusion, and non-racial identities.

By critically engaging the many challenges described here, Coleman arrives at a powerful and principled critique of Virginia's history and the lack of inclusion of non-White narratives in telling the story of the making of the state. She also engages in a broader exploration of the consequences, associated with identity formation and preservation of privilege, of the persistence of racialized thinking.

—*Joseph F. Jordan*
University of North Carolina Chapel Hill

PREFACE

In *That the Blood Stay Pure,* I trace the history and legacy of Virginia's effort to maintain racial purity and the consequences of this almost four-hundred-year effort for African American–Native American relations and kinship bonds in the Commonwealth. This book is an interdisciplinary history supported by a number of fields including race, ethnic and identity studies, law, anthropology, and literature. It also includes contemporary case studies that highlight the continued efforts to maintain the racial integrity of tribal communities. This book is not a survey of the cultures of Virginia Indians nor is it a compendium of tribal histories. In writing it, my goal is to tell, what has been until now, the neglected story of the social impact of Virginia's racial purity campaign from the perspective of those who were disavowed and expelled from tribal communities due to their affiliation with people of African descent or physical attributes that linked them ancestrally to people of African heritage. This history is also told from the perspective of those within tribal communities who reject the notion that Indian identity hinges on the absence of Blackness.

My interest in Black–Indian relations in Virginia came as the result of a conversation I had about my family's history in 1997 with my great-aunt Mary Jones (my maternal grandmother's sister) who informed me that her grandmother, Alethea Garnett Gray, from Caroline County, Virginia, was an Indian woman or at least had American Indian ancestry. Initially, I was dismissive of her claim and had no interest in exploring Black–Indian ancestral connections. I had grown up hearing numerous African Americans assert, "We got Indian in our family." This was the first time, however, that I had heard one of my relatives claim Indian ancestry. *Really?* That was my outward response. Inwardly, I thought, *Whatever.* I was a firm believer in what is now popularly referred to as "the one-drop rule," a concept invented by racial purity advocates to justify proscriptions against racial intermarriage with people of African descent. The myth that one-drop of Negro "blood" made a person Black was so inculcated in the African American community that the old folks would say, "Black blood is like the blood of Jesus—one drop makes you whole." Consequently, I wanted nothing to do with this "we part Indian" business. Besides, now that we were at the dawn of the twenty-first century, what did it matter? There were no more Indians in Virginia, right? Yet, my own curiosity began to get the better of me. My late stepfather, Leighton Sylvester Kyler, Jr., was Black (from his father's side) and Indian (from his mother's side). His mother, Lillian Grooms, a woman with caramel-colored skin, a hawk-shaped nose, and snow-white hair that extended to the small of her back, had ancestral roots in Virginia. The Kyler family was one among many African-American families with American Indian relatives "hidden" in plain sight.[1] Despite my own misgivings, I decided to give the matter some consideration.

I not only soon learned that there were still Indians in Virginia—at the time there were eight state-recognized tribes and numerous others seeking recognition—but I also learned that tracing American Indian ancestry in Virginia was difficult and in many cases impossible. The federal census from 1790 to 1860 did not include the term Indian as a racial category. Therefore, American Indians were classified as Negro, mulatto, or free people of color—terms also used to identify a range of people of color including those of African descent. Despite the addition of an Indian category in 1870, the tendency to group American Indians and African Americans into the single racial category "colored" continued for much of the twentieth century, particularly in the eastern United States. The same pattern was followed on vital records such as birth and death certificates, which Virginia maintained from 1853 to 1896 and then again from 1912 to the present. By the late nineteenth century and during much of the twentieth century, various tribal communities, mostly remnants of the former Powhatan Confederacy within the Tidewater Region, were engaged in cultural revitalization efforts to reassert their Indian identity. However, supporters of Virginia's 1924 Racial Integrity

Act, underscored by the American Eugenics Movement, which only recognized two racial categories (White and colored), vehemently resisted
any effort to recognize "Indian" as a third racial category. Opponents to
the addition believed that the purpose of those claiming to be Indian was
to subvert racial purity laws that forbade Whites from intermarrying
with "Negroes." As far as the state was concerned, Indians were Negroes
not only because of their shared historic racial designation with people
of African descent, but also because of the historic familial ties shared by
the two peoples. In the words of Booker T. Washington, "the product of
every sort of racial mixture between the black man and any other race is
always a Negro and never a white man, Indian or any other sort of man."[2]

Virginia Indians fought tenaciously against being racially classified
with African Americans because they desired to maintain a separate
racial identity and they did not want to be subjected to Jim Crow laws.
A large portion of the tribal community embraced the myth of the one-
drop-rule; they also embraced a second myth invented by racial purists
that alleged Black "blood" resulted in racial contamination and wanted
to distance themselves from this stigma. During my preliminary research it became clear that racial purity, as it was defined by Whites
and later adopted by Virginia Indians, meant the absence of Blackness.
Consequently, the anti-Black sentiment that began to take hold within
tribal communities during the late nineteenth century became codified
within twentieth-century tribal policy—a policy adhered to by most of
the state-recognized tribes to this day. While many have dismissed the
anti-Black sentiments within Virginia's tribal communities as a necessary and inconsequential effort to maintain a distinctly racial and
cultural identity, I contend that racism is never necessary or inconsequential. I began to wonder how the consequences were reflected in the
social phenomena of Black–Indian relations, Black–Indian familial ties,
and Afro-Indian identity as a result of the Powhatan tribal community's
effort for state recognition. To what extent did racial purity ideology affect tribal membership and state recognition policy? And in what ways
did the history of Virginia's racial purity efforts inform contemporary
realities regarding Black–Indian relations in the Commonwealth?

My curiosity regarding this angle of the story was piqued in 2003
during an informal gathering hosted by Hugh and Anita Harrell in their

home in Hampton, Virginia. I had come to Virginia to attend a program organized by the Weyanoke Association of Red/Black History and Culture, an organization founded by the Harrell's in 1993. The small group that gathered after the program initially engaged in small talk; however, it was not long before someone steered the conversation toward the subject of Blacks, Indians, and the politics of racial purity. I sat quietly in an artfully carved, wooden, African lazy chair as one person after the other recounted his or her story of rejection from tribal membership or of refusal to be acknowledged by tribal members because a parent or grandparent had married an African American. In particular, one young woman's story deepened my commitment to pursuing this avenue of inquiry. With tears streaming down her, prominent cheeks, she recounted an incident in which her "Indian" cousin refused to speak to her when they encountered each other at a local supermarket a few weeks prior. "We are first cousins," she snapped. "Our grandfathers are brothers. Same mother, same father. But one is Indian and the other Black. My grandfather married a Black woman so they disowned him. They said he was no longer an Indian because he married my grandmother. So, they don't want anything to do with us." It was at this point that I began to search in earnest to further understand the effect of Virginia's racial purity campaign on Black–Indian relations and familial ties. It was also at this point that I began to understand why my written inquiries to a local tribal chief regarding my own Afro-Indian heritage and the history of Black-Indian encounters in Virginia had gone unanswered.

My approach to this work is straightforward: I aim to highlight the legacy of Virginia's racial purity campaign and its effects on Black–Indian relations, familial ties, and state recognition policy by providing a historical context by which to examine these contemporary issues. In this work I focus on the development of racial purity ideology in relation to African American–Native American kinship ties as espoused by eighteenth-century thinkers; the influence of this ideology on the changing relations between these two peoples during the nineteenth and twentieth centuries; how racial purity ideology came to underscore the historiography and state recognition policy regarding Virginia Indians; and highlight three case studies which examine the continued impact of racial purity ideology regarding Black and Indian identity in the present state of Virginia. To complete this narrative history, I have relied on primary and secondary sources such as personal papers, newspaper articles, census data (United States and Canada), vital records, recorded symposium and meeting sessions, meeting minutes, books, journal articles, and personal interviews.

Regarding terminology, I have chosen to follow the late historian Peggy Pascoe and depart from the conventional use of lower case letters when referring to the racial terms "Black" and "White." I concur that capitalizing these terms demonstrates the pervasiveness of racial categories, denotes Black Americans as a group possessing a wide range of skin colors and backgrounds rather than as a single physical descriptor, and marks "White" as a category that has historically denoted aspiration as well as entitlement. I use the terms "American Indian" and "Native American" as well as the terms "Black" and "African American" interchangeably. I have chosen to use the term "Afro-Indian," to denote people of mixed African American–Native American heritage; and the term "colored" to denote people and communities of unidentified mixed race origin. Finally, I have chosen to place the word "blood" in quotation marks where it is coupled with racial terms (i.e., Indian "blood"). Although theories of separate biological races have been long debunked, race as a scientific reality continues as a pervasive myth in American society. With the uncritical acceptance of recreational commodities such as ancestry DNA, this myth will remain unabated for some time to come. Nevertheless, as cultural critic Stuart Hall has argued, "When thinking about race, think less about biology and more about politics."[3]

The consequences of Virginia's racial purity campaign have been the focus of numerous studies that have detailed, for example, the forced sterilization of Carrie Buck (*Buck v. Bell*, 1927), a poor White woman deemed feeble-minded by the state despite her apparent intelligence; the temporary banishment of the White/Afro-Indian couple Richard and Mildred Loving (*Loving v. Virginia*, 1967) because they defied anti-miscegenation statutes; and the terrorization of Virginian citizens such as Atha Sorrells (*Sorrells v. Shields*, 1924) as well as tribal groups that dared to proclaim an Indian identity despite the state's insistence on maintaining a two tier racial system. Taken together, these studies demonstrate that the effects of racial integrity extended to every corner of the Commonwealth. Yet, the silence regarding the consequences of racial purity policies for Black–Indian relations and Afro-Indian peoples in Virginia remains. This silence is largely due to its controversy and the intense emotion surrounding the subject. For certain, this book will spark bitter debate. Some will cheer its publication, while others will bemoan it. Some will hail it as indisputable truth, while others will denounce it as a despicable lie. In other words, this will be a difficult dialogue. Difficult dialogue notwithstanding, the silence regarding the historic and contemporary relations of Black and Indian peoples in Virginia indeed must be broken. And the time for that silence to be broken is now.

ACKNOWLEDGMENTS

This project began over a decade ago and true to the old African proverb, it indeed took a village to bring this book to completion. I am indebted to the staffs of many great libraries and archives including the Library of Virginia, University of Virginia Special Collections, Cornell University Special Collections, Boston Public Library, the Library of Congress, the National Archives, the National Anthropological Archives, the American Philosophical Society, the Delaware State Archives, and especially the University of Delaware Morris Library and Interlibrary Loan.

There are a number of people who were instrumental to this work and who read portions of the manuscript, granted interviews, or provided the moral support I needed to successfully complete this project. I wish to offer many, many thanks to the late Jack D. Forbes, to whom this book is dedicated; Hugh and Anita Harrell and the Weyanoke Associate of Red/Black History and Culture; Richard and Marian Bowman and the many citizens of Charles City County and other Virginia communities who willingly shared their stories; Sherida Bradby; Lynette and Allard Allston, and the Nottoway Indian Tribe of Virginia, Inc.; Adele Logan Alexander; Joanne Gabbin; Joseph F. Jordan; Gary Lemons; Beverly Guy-Sheftall; Lee D. Baker; David Lazarus Jones; Frederic Gleach; Erik McDuffie; Peter Wallenstein; Robert Pratt; the late Manning Marable; Howard Johnson; Alvina Quintana; Erica Armstrong Dunbar; and Wunyabari Maloba.

I would also like to thank Bob Sloan and the wonderful staff at Indiana University Press for believing in this project and making my dream of its publication a reality.

Last and certainly not least, I wish to thank my family—my daughter Julienne (thanks for lending Mommy your proofreading skills), my son Manny, and especially my husband Tracy, whose support and long-suffering (literally) sustained me throughout this process.

THAT THE BLOOD STAY PURE

Introduction

While nothing can be said against racial integrity, much can
be said against the un-Christian, un-democratic, and inhumane
methods too often employed in its attainment . . .

—GORDON BLAINE HANCOCK, 1944

In February 2004, the Rappahannock Indian Baptist Church was en-
gulfed in the flames of controversy when a married couple, Lori and
Jasper Battle, were denied membership. The Battles attempted to join the
"tidy brick church in this hamlet at the convergence of King and Queen,
Essex and Caroline County" and did not foresee a problem.[1] They visited
the pastor, Rev. Clayton Custalow, a member of the Mattaponi Tribe
located in King William County, Virginia. According to a *Richmond
Times-Dispatch* article the Battles were cordially received by Rev. Custalow. The Reverend prayed with the couple and thought their decision to
join the church was a good idea. However, not everyone agreed. Shortly
after the Battles met with Rev. Custalow, they had another meeting, this
time with Deacons John Fortune, Jr., and Daniel Fortune of the Rappahannock Tribe. According to Lori Battle, during a closed door meeting
the Fortunes "told me they did not want us to join the church because
I had married outside of my race."[2] Lori, a Rappahannock Indian, was
married to Jasper, an African American.

To marry outside of your race is code for marrying Black. While serving in the capacity of tribal chairman of the United Rappahannock Tribe, Daniel Fortune amended the membership criteria in 1981 to state that, "Any person who is not [of] American Indian descent in whole or part Indian and White and who applies for membership will not be accepted in the United Rappahannock Tribe." But membership was extended to "Any person of American Indian descent, in whole or in part Indian and White, who marries a Rappahannock and applies for membership, will be accepted into the Tribe."[3] While marrying White does not jeopardize one's tribal status, marriage or even a common law relationship with an African American is a different matter altogether. An African American spouse or significant other endangers one's tribal status and has forced many to forfeit tribal membership despite having close relatives in leadership roles. As one Rappahannock informant stated, "Some of these folks being refused tribal cards have parents, grandparents and other relatives who have served as tribal council members. Yet, because they married outside of their race, they are no longer seen as Rappahannock. I think that's wrong."[4]

The same racialized policy that controls tribal membership also controls church membership. According to Susie Fortune, one of the church's founders, there had never been a Black member in the entire forty-year history of the church. The church's constitution, while not forbidding people of other races to attend services, limits membership to those of Indian descent. The constitution states that members "do not believe in stressing integration or segregation. We welcome into our worship services all who have a longing to study, to learn of and bring praise unto our Lord. *We encourage all races of people to join and support the local church built and supported by their own race of people.*" (italics mine)[5] In fact, the church indeed stressed segregation. The purpose of its organization in the early 1960s was to establish an exclusively Indian worship community separate from its African American counterpart, St. Stephen's Baptist Church, where many of its members had previously attended. The Rappahannock Tribe was the last of the tribes that would become a part of the state-recognized tribal community to establish its own church as a part of the Indian cultural revitalization effort, which began during the waning years of the nineteenth century. Although, the church's constitution encourages membership along racial lines, the Rappahannock Indian Baptist Church extends membership to Whites. As Lori Battle contended, "If you're not going to let black people in the church, you're not going to let white people in the church, right? Well they got white people in the church."[6]

This issue concerning the racial disparity of church membership continued to be a point of contention when on April 4, 2004, a White couple, James and Ann Tignor, stepped forward during a Sunday service desiring to become members. The request "prompted some open and awkward discussion that highlighted the confusion and division among the body."[7] But, James Tignor stood firmly before the congregation, addressed the controversy and refused to withdraw his request for membership. Prior to the Tignor incident, church members held a meeting on March 3, 2004, to vote on a constitutional amendment banning membership based on race. The majority of the congregation voted in opposition to the amendment. Chief Anne Richardson, though not an active member of the church, joined opponents by casting her vote in opposition to the amendment.

Pastor Custalow initially seemed to display ambivalence towards the mounting conflict and did not attend the meeting pertaining to the constitution. Concerning his absence from the meeting Custalow asserted, "I know that a person who is a pastor is called to lead . . . I wanted to give the people of this fellowship the freedom to make a decision without feeling the pastor was taking sides."[8] Yet the Pastor had taken sides. Not only had he encouraged the Battles' membership during their initial meeting, Custalow also resigned from the pastorate in protest because he considered the overwhelming opposition to amend the constitution an endorsement of racism. Custalow told his congregation, "I must make it clear: I am not in favor of racism."[9] As a member of one of the eight state-recognized tribes, Custalow's position on the matter was rare. Anti-Black racism was/is dominant among the majority of Virginia's state recognized tribes. Custalow's firm stance against racism was an exception to the rule. Nonetheless, those who opposed the Battles joining the church, according to Custalow, viewed it not so much as racism, but "as a preservation of identity."[10] Tammy Hayes, another church member, asserted that those in opposition to the Battles' membership desired "the Indian identity to stay pure."[11]

FIG. 0.1. Jasper and Lori Battle standing in front of the Rappahannock Indian Baptist Church on March 30, 2004. Photo by the Associated Press. Used by permission.

The above episode provides a glaring example of the legacy of Virginia's long obsession with racial purity, which culminated in the 1924 *Act to Preserve Racial Integrity* also known as the *Racial Integrity Act* (RIA). This unprecedented legislation, signed into law on March 20, 1924, codified a two-tier racial hierarchy in which residents could only fit within the rigid racial categories of either White or colored. The legislation was a full-throated endorsement of eugenics, the pseudo-science of good breeding that lent credence to the pathology of White supremacy, much like the theories of scientific racism promoted during the previous century. The purpose of the RIA was to define Whiteness in the strictest of terms so as to prevent non-"Caucasian blood" from entering into the "White" gene pool and thereby preserve the integrity of the "White" race. To this end, the law called for the state and local registrars to create a registration certificate for the purpose of collecting racial data on every citizen of the Commonwealth born prior to June 14, 1912, the date Virginia's Office of Vital Statistics was created. Registration certificates were to provide information regarding, "the racial composition of any individual, as Caucasian, Negro, Mongolian, American Indian, Asiatic Indian, Malay, or any mixture thereof, or any other non-Caucasic strains, and if there be any mixture, then, the racial composition of the parents and other ancestors, in so far as ascertainable, so as to show in what generation such mixture occurred. . . ."[12]

Race mixing, commonly referred to as miscegenation, a term adopted during the Civil War era, was the cause of much hyper-anxiety among racial purists who believed the consequence of Whites marrying non-Whites would be the degeneration of the White race, resulting in racial suicide.[13] Hence, Virginia's racial integrity law became the twentieth century's vanguard of anti-miscegenation legislation. A modification of the original draft of the law known as the "Pocahontas Exception" was made in the case of people of mixed White and American Indian ancestry, due to claims among the White elite that they were descendants of the Indian princess Pocahontas and the English colonist John Rolfe. As a result, the definition of a White person as one of exclusive Caucasian ancestry was revised to include those of White–Indian ancestry.

> It shall hereafter be unlawful for any white person in this State to marry any save a white person, or a person with no other admixture of blood than white and American Indian. For the purpose of this act, the term "white person" shall apply only to the person who has no trace whatsoever of any blood other than Caucasian; but persons who have one-sixteenth or less of the blood of the American Indian and have no other non-Caucasic blood shall be deemed to be white persons.[14]

White elites were able to use their influence to narrowly escape being reclassified as colored; but what about the approximately 900 residents identified as Indian on the 1920 census? Did they as indigenous people possess the power of influence similar to their White elite counterparts? The answer, in a word, is no. They were powerless against the racialized political forces of the Commonwealth and were, therefore, reclassified as colored and subjected to Jim Crow laws. Racial reclassification of Virginia Indians further demonstrated the Commonwealth's paranoia of miscegenation and adherence to the myth of racial hygiene. Racial purists characterized Virginia's Indian population as racial contaminants due to historic Black–Indian marriages and cohabitations, which began almost immediately upon the arrival of peoples of African descent to the Virginia colony. The threat of racial reclassification resulted in what anthropologist Helen Rountree has dubbed "the racial integrity fight"—a battle between the state and the American Indian population that raged on for much of the twentieth century. Consequently, many tribal communities unabashedly disavowed all familial relations and associations with anyone whose phenotype betrayed Black admixture. Despite the triumph of the Supreme Court decision in *Loving v. Virginia,* which rendered anti-miscegenation laws unconstitutional in 1967, and the repeal of the RIA in 1975, the absence of Blackness continues to be the sine qua non of Virginia Indian identity. Hence, without apology, the Rappahannock Indian Baptist Church felt justified in its decision to accept as members James and Ann Tignor and to reject Jasper and Lori Battle.

Carter G. Woodson, recognizing that race relations in the United States were not limited to Black–White encounters, stated in 1920, "One of the longest unwritten chapters of the history of the United States is that treating of the relations of the Negroes and the Indians."[15] His statement may now appear somewhat of a cliché; nonetheless, it has been recognized as the catalyst responsible for the plethora of works now available on the subject, covering numerous states and regions from coast to coast. What these studies have highlighted are the ways in which African Americans and Native Americans have struggled to maintain their own communities as independent, self-defining peoples. They also, however, highlight the complex realities of intermarriage, conflict, and shared histories nurtured within the crucible of a racialized hierarchy that simultaneously helped forge alliances and foster animosity between the two groups. Much of the scholarship on Black–Indian intersections has focused on the so-called Five Civilized Tribes (Cherokee, Creek, Seminole, Chickasaw, and Choctaw), which were forced out west as a result of Andrew Jackson's 1830 Indian Removal Act. While the miscegenation of Whites among the tribes produced Indians, people of mixed Black–Indian ancestry produced Black Indians or simply Blacks.[16]

This racialized identity of Indianness versus Blackness has further complicated Du Bois's concept of double consciousness and codified the position of Indians with African ancestry as "other" even within this marginalized group. Indian Country has not been a haven from racism for people of African and Afro-Indian descent, as some would suppose.

For example, during the Allotment Era of the late-nineteenth century, tribal leaders lobbied the Dawes Commission to minimize the number of freedmen—former slaves of Indian nations—to be included on the Dawes Rolls, which entitled them to receive land allotments as citizens of sovereign Indian nations. Because the rolls were segregated by degree of Indian "blood" with no blood quantum listed for the freedmen, their racial identity "fixed them forever" as Black and "guaranteed that 'black Indian' would become an impossible identity."[17] It also guaranteed that the freedmen's right of citizenship in the Indian nations that once enslaved them would be continually contested. Numerous attempts have been made to dis-enroll the freedmen, despite proof of their ancestors' names on the rolls, because they were viewed by many within the nation as not being "blood" Indians. Recent manifestations of this practice can be found among the Seminole and Cherokee nations that attempted to dis-enroll the freedmen within the last decade.[18] Anti-Black racism, resulting from the internalization of the colonial imposition that defined Indians by race rather than culture, has been well documented as it pertains to a diverse number of tribes in the western, northeastern, and southeastern parts of the United States. Nevertheless, Woodson's assertion continues to hold true, as Black and Indian relations in Virginia remain one of the longest, unwritten chapters of the history of the Commonwealth.[19]

The subject of Black–Indian relations in Virginia remains highly controversial and deemed taboo by many in the academic and tribal communities within the Commonwealth. The lack of serious scholarly treatment of the subject is comparable to the treatment once afforded to the Thomas Jefferson–Sally Hemings controversy in that "The historiography," to borrow the words of Annette Gordon-Reed, "displays a carelessness with the lives" of African American people. It demonstrates a blatant disregard "for their sensibilities and a concomitant willingness to safeguard the interest of those" within and without Indian communities whose contempt for African American and Afro-Indian peoples both reify and internalize the racist value system which they claim to abhor.[20] Twentieth-century scholarship on Virginia tribes, with the exception of the works of Jack D. Forbes and Frederic Gleach, downplayed or outright denied contacts between Blacks and Indians in a deliberate effort to construct a White–Indian only historicity and as a means to validate the racial integrity of recognized Virginia Indian tribes.[21] Consequently, the representation of the struggle of Virginia Indians against the ethnocidal efforts of the state, to once again borrow from Gordon-Reed, lent credence to "our distorted racial values," which "promote and protect error, irrationality and unfairness." The perpetrators of this gross distortion "presented themselves and were accepted as models of accuracy, rationality and fairness."[22] Examining Virginia's racial purity campaign through the lens of Black–Indian relations, however, makes for a complicated and more nuanced history. It not only challenges prevailing notions of the absence of Blackness within tribal communities, but it also substitutes the representation of Indians as people of agency for Indians as helpless victims. From this vantage point Indians are viewed as both victims of and partners to the very racial oppression they fought tenaciously against. As Jack D. Forbes, capturing the complexity of the matter, aptly noted:

> in Virginia, a Pamunkey family might well have been viciously shattered in this [twentieth] century by the state law which allowed "Indians" living on the Pamunkey Reservation to have up to one-thirty-second African ancestry and still be "Indian." But if they moved to Richmond or just across the reservation boundary, they would become "colored" if they had any African blood whatsoever. Moreover, those who had more than one-thirty-second African blood could not remain on the reservation as "Indians," even though they might have lived there all of their lives. . . . We can speculate that families were permanently split, in some cases, and that those persons with visible African blood were placed under great pressure to move away and to drop connections.[23]

While Forbes based the above speculation regarding the Pamunkey Tribe on precedents set in early twentieth century Oklahoma, in this book I will provide a preponderance of evidence to demonstrate that enforcement of Virginia's racial integrity law indeed permanently split families, communities, churches, and friendships as a means to achieve the illusion of racial purity. In this work I will chronicle Black-Indian relations from the colonial era to the present to highlight the ways in which the racial integrity doctrine shaped the historical and contemporary realities of Black–Indian relations in general and Afro-Indian identity in Virginia in specific.

As with much of the indigenous population from coast to coast, Virginia Indians have been in an intense struggle to maintain their status as indigenous people. In the early days of the Commonwealth, they intermarried with Blacks (in addition to Whites and other tribal peoples) and formed alliances. However, Black–Indian relations in Virginia became increasingly antagonistic in the nineteenth century as alliances with Blacks proved a liability to Indians whose ethnic authenticity and land rights were challenged by local Whites and resulted in reservation loss, detribalization, and ethnic reclassification. The Gingaskin Tribe located along Virginia's Eastern Shore, for example, was declared no longer Indian, but free Negroes, and dispossessed of their reservation land in 1812. By the close of the nineteenth century, the Powhatan remnants on the mainland enacted anti-miscegenation laws that forbade intermarriage and association with Blacks. But if Virginia Indians thought discontinuing relations with Blacks safeguarded them from White persecution, they were sorely mistaken. With the enactment of the 1924 Racial Integrity Act, and its subsequent challenge by residents whom racial purists labeled "negroid Indians," the state registrar of Virginia changed the vital records of anyone listed as Indian to colored. Midwives were forbidden to classify anyone as Indian on birth certificates and clerks were forbidden to issue marriage licenses to anyone attempting to marry a White person under the pretense of being an Indian.

Several years prior to the establishment of the RIA, renowned anthropologist Frank Speck began working among some of the remnant tribes in Virginia's Tidewater Region. Speck, echoing the sentiments of his predecessor James Mooney, believed their Indian claim to be authentic despite their racial mixture. Speck so infuriated the lobbyists responsible for the enactment of the RIA that they attempted to have his books on Virginia Indians banned from the state. Lobbyists also sent law officials to intimidate Speck at his office at the University of Pennsylvania. Undaunted, Speck remained a fierce advocate for the Virginia tribes. The tribes also found allies among a number of prominent citizens and other scholars willing to validate their claim as American Indians with only White admixture. These advocates were determined to save the Indians and therefore encouraged the tribes to disassociate themselves from African Americans, even those with whom they had familial ties. Tribal leaders were also advised to expel any member whose phenotype displayed any trace of Negro ancestry. This divided African Americans, Native Americans and Afro-Indian peoples. As Charles City County historian Richard Bowman stated, "It split families, sister against brother, brother against sister."[24]

Despite the disruption to the Native community and its continuing repercussions for Black–Indian relations, the purging effort gained eight tribes—the majority of the former Powhatan Confederacy, state recognition during the 1980s. The prevailing narrative of a decisive Indian victory against ethnocide and the self-congratulatory sentiments purported by Virginia Indian advocates for their assistance in that victory, however, proves misleading. The casualties resulting from the racial integrity fight, in both the African American and American Indian communities as well as those of Afro-Indian ancestry, continue to be treated with blatant disregard. The debris of broken friendships, disrupted kinship ties, deep-seated animosities, and their contemporary effects on Black–Indian relations in Virginia, have been placed, as W. E. B. Du Bois once eloquently stated, "within the veil."[25] In *That the Blood Stay Pure*, I step "within the veil, raising it that you may view faintly its deeper recesses."[26] This will not only demonstrate that the respective threads of African American and American Indian peoples indeed intertwined, but will also demonstrate that the efforts of American Indian opponents and advocates alike served the purpose of maintaining racial purity and White supremacy.

The book is comprised of two parts: Part 1, Historicizing Black–Red Relations in Virginia, consists of a Prologue and chapters 1–4, which provide a historical context for Black–Indian relations, Afro-Indian identity and the RIA.

The prologue, "Lingering at the Crossroads: African–Native American History and Kinship Lineage in Armstrong Archer's *A Compendium on Slavery*," examines the unusual 1844 anti-slavery pamphlet *A Compendium of Slavery* by Armstrong Archer. A short portion of the pamphlet is comprised of a brief narrative in which Archer identified himself as a descendant of an African King from Guinea and the famous Indian chief Powhatan. While the claim to African royalty was/is common for American Blacks, as in the adage "We descended from kings and queens," and the claim to Native American ancestry often conjures up relations to an Indian princess (Archer's mother was a descendant of Pocahontas's sister Powcanoe) or Indian chief, Archer is unique in that he asserts a blended identity claim of Afro-Indian royalty. His narrative is perhaps the earliest and only remaining nineteenth century document which stakes a pre-Civil War claim to Afro-Indian identity and serves as metaphor for the confluence of African–American Indian history, the changing relations of Blacks and Indians in Virginia as well as the manipulation of race and identity within America's racial hierarchy.

Chapter 1, "Notes on the State of Virginia: Jeffersonian Thought and the Rise of Racial Purity Ideology in the Eighteenth Century," explores the foundations of racial purity ideology within Virginian politics by critically analyzing Thomas Jefferson's *Notes* with a focus on his racial comparisons of Africans and Indians as well as his ambiguity regarding miscegenation. Jefferson's *Notes* may well contain the most disparaging remarks regarding people of African descent ever written. Among Jefferson's remarks outlining his supposed suspicions of the innate inferiority of people of African descent lays the vicious myth of Black contamination. Due to his deep paranoia of Black–White amalgamation (later referred to as miscegenation) Jefferson advocated for the removal of African Americans from the United States immediately upon emancipation as a solution to the "Negro problem." In contrast, Jefferson believed that American Indians were equally endowed in mind and body as Whites, and so he proposed a different course of action for the "Indian problem." His solution for them was voluntary amalgamation with the settler class. However, the offer of voluntary amalgamation was only extended to the frontier Indians, which Jefferson and others proposed in order to advance their own self-interest: the acquisition of coveted lands. On the other hand, Jefferson viewed the Virginia Indians as the wretched of the earth, unfit for amalgamation with Whites because they were no longer racially pure due to Black intermixture. As Jefferson saw it, they were no longer authentic Indians. He, therefore, advanced a second myth that Black–Indian amalgamation equaled the depletion of "Indianness." Jefferson's eighteenth-century theories not only informed the twentieth-century theories of the eugenics movement, as well as Virginia's legislative campaign to preserve the integrity of the White race, but they are also the foundation for the ideological justification for the anti-Black racism among some Virginia Indian Tribes, which persists to this day.

Chapter 2, "Redefining Race and Identity: The Indian–Negro Confusion and the Changing State of Black–Indian Relations in the Nineteenth Century," examines African–Indian relations during the antebellum years following the lines of Black and Red through both the slave and free populations. Slavery has been so thoroughly contextualized within an African framework, that it has largely eclipsed the American Indian slave trade which began with the indigenous population's first contacts with Europeans. In fact, the first North American slaves were Indians. Similar to the African slave trade, which bought slaves from the African continent to South and Central America, the Caribbean, then on to North America, so too the American Indian slave trade, which obtained slaves by war as well as by kidnapping, traded Indians from one colony to the other, from one continent to the other and sold them at auction like their African counterparts. As a result, American Indians were bought, and sold, and forced to labor side by side with Blacks. This phenomenon occurred throughout the English colonies including Virginia which received Indian slaves from the Caribbean, the mainland interior such as the North Carolina region, the western plains region as well as from the Virginia colony itself. To trace "the Red in Black slavery" to use the words of Tiya Miles,[27] this chapter examines Virginia legislation which first sanctioned and then condemned Indian slavery; however, the overturning of Indian slave laws did not lead to the mass emancipation of Indian slaves as late eighteenth and early nineteenth-century court cases bear out. In addition, slave narratives and runaway slave notices are examined, providing further evidence of Indian slavery in Virginia as well as evidence of kinship relations between the two groups.

In addition to tracing the Red in Black slavery, this chapter traces the Red in the free "Negro" population as well. Racial definitions and terminology were often used inconsistently resulting in the racial obscurity of the free "colored" population. Terms such as "colored," "mulatto," "free person of color," and "free Negro" were not exclusively used to describe

Africans or people of part African descent resulting in much confusion over racial identity. This too is borne out in judicial court cases in which numerous people found their racial identity on trial.[28] The criterion in determining who was White, Black or Indian was not applied with any consistency. This was largely due to amalgamation, which was more widespread among peoples of African and American Indian descent than some modern scholars wish to admit. For this reason, I have depended largely on nineteenth- and early twentieth-century scholarship as well as on Jack D. Forbes's extensive late-twentieth-century work on the language of race to unravel the threads of Red and Black in antebellum Virginia. I also examine the changing relations of Black-Indian peoples as the threat of racial reclassification placed a strain on the once amiable relations between the two groups, which resulted in increased animosities as the racial purity campaign intensified.

Chapter 3, "Race Purity and the Law: The Racial Integrity Act and Policing Black–Indian Identity in the Twentieth Century," follows the evolution and subsequent modifications of the 1924 Racial Integrity Act (RIA), which was rooted in eugenics—the pseudoscientific dogma of "good breeding" that gained popularity in the United States in the early twentieth century. The RIA was the brain child of the renowned classical musician John Powell of Richmond, Virginia, an ardent supporter of eugenics. Powell's efforts were supported by ethnologist Earnest Sevier Cox and Walter Ashby Plecker, the Virginia State Registrar. These men were staunch believers in hereditarianism, a nineteenth century theory which advocated that it was one's heredity and not one's environment which determined one's character and intelligence. This concept gained increasing popularity during the early years of the twentieth century as a result of the rediscovery of Mendel's Law. Gregor Mendel was a Moravian monk who in the 1860's formulated principles based on breeding experiments he conducted on garden peas. Mendel determined that cross-fertilized pure breed plants were both dominant and superior to cross-fertilized hybrid plants. The theories formulated by Mendel, resulting from his experiments with plants, were adopted by American eugenicists to explain human heredity. Eugenics adherents such as Powell, Cox, and Plecker believed one's morality, intelligence, and social adaptability could be fundamentally traced back to heredity.

They invoked the rhetoric of blood to promote notions of purity and to advance a campaign to guard against so-called racial suicide and mongrelization.

Yet, quite early on, Virginians began to resist such efforts. White elites managed to have the Pocahontas Exception inserted into the racial integrity law. Many interpreted this exception, however, to mean that Whites and anyone of White–Indian ancestry did not fall under the anti-miscegenation statute. However, when Atha Sorrells, an Amherst County resident who claimed to be of White and American Indian only ancestry, won her suit against the county clerk who refused to give her a marriage license to marry a White man, Walter Plecker, Virginia's most ardent racial purity police, sprang into full action. He was convinced that Blacks would infiltrate the White race by claiming to be Indian, and as a result he began a fierce campaign to have all Virginia Indians reclassified as colored and barred from marrying Whites. This chapter will highlight Plecker's war against the Indians and argue that his efforts were more a reflection of his profound fear of Black contamination than of his prejudice against Indian peoples.

Chapter 4, "Denying Blackness: Anthropological Advocacy and the Remaking of the Virginia Indians," reexamines the role of twentieth-century anthropological advocacy on behalf of the Virginia Indians and highlights the ways in which such advocacy helped to codify anti-Black sentiment in tribal membership and state recognition policy in Virginia. In recent years anthropologists Frederic Gleach and Samuel Cook, responding to the criticisms advanced by American Indian and other indigenous scholars on the abuses of the anthropological enterprise, cite the case of the Virginia Indians as a model for the good that anthropological advocacy has done and can do. However, new evidence has revealed the sordid side of anthropological advocacy on behalf of the Virginia Indians. Therefore, Virginia's advocacy campaign should be cited as a cautionary tale rather than as a model for others to follow. Advocacy on behalf of the Virginia Indians did not eradicate racism, but rather reified the notion of racial purity furthering racial divisions. Consequently, the legacy of the advocacy campaign not only informs contemporary policies regarding tribal membership and state recognition, but also serves to maintain a conspiracy of silence regarding the historical relations between Black–Indian peoples and the reality of Afro-Indian people in the Commonwealth.

Part 2, "Black–Red Relations in the Present State of Virginia" consists of chapters 5–7 and an Epilogue which examines specific episodes regarding the social interactions of Black–Indian peoples and the ways in which Virginia Indians of African descent negotiate the complex terrain of race and identity.

Chapter 5, "Beyond Black and White: Afro-Indian Identity in the Case of *Loving v. Virginia*," re-examines the *Loving v. Virginia* Supreme Court case by focusing on the tri-racial community of Central Point, Virginia and Mildred Loving's self-identity as an Indian woman. Loving's self-identity was informed by the twentieth-century politics of racial purity, which resulted in a community-wide denial of African ancestry. I argue that Mildred Loving's marriage to a White man was not an affirmation of Black and White intermarriage, but rather adhered to the code of racial purity as was defined by Virginia's racial integrity law. Notwithstanding, I will also demonstrate the complexity of Mildred Loving's self-identity as she shifted during the course of her lifetime, conflicted by her own Blackness, which she embraced at times and denied at others. What can account for these identity shifts? This chapter will provide some clues to this question.

Chapter 6, "The Racial Integrity Fight: Confrontations of Race and Identity in Charles City County, Virginia," examines the effects of the RIA on this historic community in which the intermingling among Whites, Blacks, and Indians occurred to such an extent that despite how one may racially identify, almost everyone is somehow related to one another. Nevertheless, the legacy of the RIA continues to inform the everyday social relations of its residents, which are comprised of families who have remained in the area since prior to the American Revolution. At the center of this conflict is the Western Chickahominy Tribe, which received state recognition in 1983. African Americans, however, continue to challenge the Indian claim because of the tribe's historic and familial ties with the Black community. Some who refute the authenticity of the tribe are descendants of those instrumental in its reorganization in 1901, but were later disavowed due to their intermarriage with Blacks. Charles City County will serve as a case study to further highlight the ways in

which racial purity manipulated identities and relationships, even caus-
ing family members to turn against one another.

Chapter 7, "Nottoway Indians, Afro-Indian Identity, and the Contemporary Dilemma of State Recognition," provides an account of the
struggle of the Nottoway Indian Tribe of Virginia, Inc. against state
imposed racial reclassification. Although assumed to be extinct, the
Nottoway people have maintained their sense of Indian identity to the
present day. In 2006 Nottoway descendants petitioned the Virginia
Council on Indians (VCI) for a recommendation for state recognition.
While the VCI, which oversaw such matters, was hard pressed to resist
the impeccable historical evidence the tribe presented on its behalf for
recognition, the evidence regarding the historic relations between the
Nottoway people and African Americans, as well as current Afro-Indian
tribal members, who the tribe refused to disavow, became a point of
contention with the VCI. This chapter will investigate the saga of the
Nottoway Tribe's state recognition process with a particular focus on
the ways in which Blackness was used to determine the outcome of the
petition.

The epilogue, "Afro-Indian Peoples of Virginia: The Indelible Thread
of Black and Red," revisits Jasper and Lori Battle and provides an analysis of how they and others within the Afro-Indian community have
moved beyond racial integrity dogma to develop meaningful relations
based in mutual respect and trust.

The history of African American–American Indian encounters in
Virginia has been held hostage by "structural amnesia," a term used by
anthropologist Charles Hudson to describe the way societies organize
their historical realities by retaining only those stories relevant to the
"structure of their society" while those events deemed insignificant "were
relegated to historical oblivion."[29] This contemporary societal structure,
which Jack Forbes has dubbed the "white hub" promotes the master narrative of Europeans, namely Anglo-Saxons, as the central players which
make up our historical reality.[30] Notwithstanding, a White–Indian hub
has been the societal structure that has informed the discourse on the
effect of Virginia's RIA on Indians from the twentieth century to the
present. Consequently, what Walter Plecker, Virginia's first state registrar and the self-appointed guardian of the RIA, "did to the Indians"

as many have put it, has been central to the construction of the RIA's master narrative as well as to the struggle against Indian reclassification and the effort towards state, and now federal recognition. Yet, viewing the history and legacy of the RIA solely through a White–Indian lens gives credence to the myth of a White–Indian only historicity, while engaging in the erasure of Black–Indian intersections and the struggle of Afro-Indian peoples, who are no less significant to the Virginia story. Indeed, the history of the racial purity campaign is far broader and much more complicated than the master narrative which is now privileged, but must now be challenged.

A paradigm shift is overdue. The history of African American–American Indian encounters in Virginia must no longer be relegated to oblivion, but rather must move, in the words of Afro-Indian scholar bell hooks, "from margin to center."[31] The story of Black–Indian encounters and Afro-Indian peoples must no longer be the longest unwritten chapter in the history of Virginia. Hence, let this publication symbolize a new chapter in which Virginian history is embraced in all its controversy, contradiction, struggle, triumph and victory.

PART 1
HISTORICIZING BLACK–INDIAN
RELATIONS IN VIRGINIA

PROLOGUE

Lingering at the Crossroads: African–Native American History and Kinship Lineage in Armstrong Archer's *A Compendium on Slavery*

[Alexander] Chamberlain's call to explicate African–Native American folklore and mythology leaves the respondent at a crossroads. One might choose to proceed ignoring the well-worn paths of African and Native American traditions to either side. One might decide to turn back, returning to a road of familiarity. One might choose to follow only one path, either African or Native American, turning one's back on the tradition that lay across the way. Yet, one might instead choose to linger at the crossroads sitting down for a drink brimming with the salt water of the Middle Passage and the Trail of Tears, pouring a libation and offering tobacco, and listening carefully to the interwoven strands of storytelling from African and Native American literary traditions.

—JONATHAN BRENNAN, *WHEN BRER RABBIT MEETS COYOTE*

As the above epigraph suggests, an attempt to explicate Armstrong Archer's *A Compendium of Slavery as It Exists in the Present Day in the United States of America* has indeed left respondents at a crossroads. Its title places the text squarely within the anti-slavery literary tradition, but its subtitle, "To which is prefixed a brief view of the author's descent from an African King on the one side and from the celebrated Indian Chief Powhatan on the other," at once problematizes such a simplistic categorization.[1] A brief look into earlier attempts to explicate the work provides a case in point on what it means to be at the crossroads.

Abraham Chapman was the first to bring attention to Archer's *A Compendium*. In his edited work *Steal Away: Stories of the Run Away Slaves* (1971), Chapman chose to follow the African path. Prior to the firsthand accounts of slave escapes in this short work, Chapman provided truncated narratives from several published accounts of African captives that highlighted African life and the Middle Passage experience. The narrative of the capture of Archer's father in Africa, his voyage to the French West Indies, and his later relocation to Virginia appears in part 1 of the work, "Memories of Africa and the Slave Ships." Chapman identified the work in the table of contents by the author's name and the first part of the subtitle, which highlight Archer's Afro-Indian ancestry. Nevertheless, he provided little explication of the text. Chapman's only purpose was to highlight the journey of Archer's ancestors from Africa to the Americas.[2]

Frederic Gleach provided the first, and as of this writing, the only, in-depth analysis of *A Compendium*. At the crossroads, he too chose one path—that of the American Indian. In his essay "A Traditional Story of the Powhatan Indians Recorded in the Early 19th Century," Gleach provided a nuanced and sophisticated explication of the Archer narrative. He focused on Archer's father's account of his experience as a slave and later freed man. In addition, he placed Archer's African–Native American heritage within the context of the changing race relations between the two peoples during the period from the seventeenth century to the late-nineteenth century. Nevertheless, as his title suggests, Gleach's intent was not to linger at the crossroads. As in Chapman's volume, the African aspect of Archer's work became subordinate to the Native American aspect. Hence, Gleach's examination of the text focused on Archer's work as an example of the cultural continuity of the Powhatan Indians.[3]

While Chapman's and Gleach's approaches to the text are both useful, the time has come to provide a holistic analysis of Armstrong Archer and his work. Instead of viewing Archer through either an African or

American Indian lens, this chapter aims to linger at the crossroads, to borrow from Brennan, with a drink brimming with the salt water of the Middle Passage and dust from the sandy shores of Tsenacommacah (seen-a-coo-ma-ca)—homeland of the once mighty Powhatan Confederacy, where the histories and bloodlines of Black and Indian peoples converge. Archer's biographical narrative may appear totally unrelated to the subject of slavery, but like many abolitionists in the 1830s, Archer drew analogies between slavery and American Indian removal. According to Archer, removing Indians from their ancestral lands, and converting those lands into a "nursery of slaves" was antithetical to American ideals of freedom and liberty being denied to both groups.[4] Yet, Archer's claim to an African–Native American mixed race identity went beyond mere analogies to identify kinship relations between the two peoples. Archer's narrative is a significant historical document as it details his father's capture, slave voyage to the Americas, subsequent status as a free man, and later marriage to a Powhatan woman. In addition, it provides the only recorded seventeenth-century Powhatan tale to demonstrate the prevalence of Powhatan cultural continuity nearly two hundred years after contact with Europeans and Africans. Hence, taken together, Archer at once becomes the keeper of both African and American Indian oral traditions now preserved in print for all posterity. Archer's narrative also has historical significance as it may be the only surviving mid-nineteenth-century account written by a Powhatan Indian of African descent to provide clues about early contacts between African Americans and American Indians in Virginia. In fact, Archer serves as metaphor for the confluence of African American and American Indian history, the changing reality of Black–Indian relations in Virginia, as well as the manipulation of race and identity within America's racial hierarchy.

Armstrong Archer, a free "mulatto" from Norfolk County, Virginia, and later resident of Brooklyn, New York, published *A Compendium of Slavery* in 1844.[5] Archer joined a pantheon of African American pamphleteers such as Richard Allen, Henry Highland Garnett, Marie W. Stewart, David Walker, and Elizabeth Wick, whose appropriation of the pamphlet tradition, a genre which began in the 1790s, served as an avenue of protest against a host of social issues including slavery, racism, sexism, and repatriation. The pamphlet tradition began in the seventeenth century during the English Civil War and gained popularity among American revolutionaries such as Thomas Jefferson, James Otis, and Thomas Paine. In the hands of Black authors the pamphlet contributed to the growth of a burgeoning Black literary tradition that gave voice to Black political thought where there otherwise would not have been. Unlike slave narratives, the pamphlet allowed for flexibility and versatility, which granted authors much more editorial autonomy over content and form. Pamphlets were far less expensive to publish than books. In fact, they were most often self-published; direct contact with a local printer was all that was required to get one's work into print. They were sold on street corners, on the lecture circuit, and at conventions at nominal cost.[6]

Archer self-published *A Compendium* while on a business trip to London on which he embarked sometime during the spring of 1844. He may have spent as long as seven months overseas, as indicated by a character reference written on his behalf by Rev. Duncan Dunbar. It was signed and dated April 30, 1844. Dunbar was a prominent White Baptist minister with influential ties in the United States and Great Britain. It is probable that Archer left for London soon after he received his friend's endorsement. Archer's travel to London was not unique; numerous abolitionists, both White and colored, traveled to London seeking moral, political and financial support from British abolitionists. Britain became a sanctuary for numerous exiles throughout Europe and the Americas seeking freedom from oppression. Among this population were fugitive slaves from the United States., Frederick Douglass was perhaps the most famous. "To Black Americans who formed an important part of the community of exiles in the years after 1830," stated R. J. M. Blackett, "Britain's moral prestige was a direct consequence of her decision to abolish slavery in the West Indies . . . Black Americans visited Britain in significant numbers in the thirty years before the Civil War."[7] This included many free Blacks as well. No records survive regarding Archer's overseas activities. It is probable that he spent much of his time traveling the lecture circuit attempting to distribute his anti-slavery pamphlet. It is also likely that he meet with prominent clergy to discuss the evils of slavery and the inequities suffered by the free Black population in the

United States. What is certain is that Archer returned from London to
New York City aboard the Westminster on November 30, 1844, with
copies of his published pamphlet.[8]

Archer's sixty-eight-page pamphlet began with the usual certifica-
tions of good character, in this case proof of ordination and Dunbar's
character reference, which were standard in antebellum African American literature. The references were followed by an illustration depicting
Pocahontas's rescue of John Smith. The illustration was followed by a
brief introduction.[9] The body of Archer's work was divided into three
parts, titled "My Father's Narrative," "The Powhatan Indians—Pocahontas," and "Slavery."[10]

Archer began the introduction to A Compendium by dedicating his
work to "the people of Great Britain and Ireland," calling it "an illustrious and magnanimous empire." The British Empire paraded its moral
authority over its American counterpart due to its abolition of slavery in the British West Indies with the Emancipation Act of 1833.[11] The
abolition of British slavery notwithstanding, there remained a glaring
contradiction in Britain's claim to moral authority. At that time Ireland
was fighting for its independence from Britain, which a majority of Black
abolitionists linked with the anti-slavery and civil rights causes in the
United States supported. The United Kingdom of Great Britain and Ireland was formed by the Act of Union and ratified by the Irish and British
parliaments in 1801. Bigotry against Irish Roman Catholics and a failure
on Britain's part to support socio-political reform to benefit the Irish, left
many on the Emerald Isle disillusioned and calling for Home Rule—an
independent Ireland ruled by the Irish. Although Black abolitionists,
such as Frederick Douglass, spoke out against the anti-Black racism
prevalent among Irish immigrants, they nevertheless made a distinction
between the Irish in the United States and the Irish in Ireland and supported Ireland's advocacy for self-governance. On the one hand, Irish
immigrants were viewed as having "nothing but 'abuse' and unconquerable aversions . . . towards the colored race" and on the other hand, the
Irish in Ireland were believed to have "opposed human bondage and
sympathized with the abolitionists."[12] Due to Irish disenfranchisement,
deprivation of education, and blocked employment opportunities, Black
abolitionists, as with the American Indian, drew analogies between the

Irish struggle for independence and the Black freedom struggle in the United States. Yet, unlike his contemporaries, Archer remained silent on this issue no doubt to avoid offending British sensibilities.

Archer continued his introduction with a short discussion of slavery informing the reader of his long desire to provide a personal account on the subject, having witnessed its horrors firsthand during his first twenty-five years as a resident of Virginia. The Commonwealth according to Archer, "was the most bloodthirsty and slave breeding state in all the union" manifesting slavery "in its greatest lenity to its most atrocious severity."[13] Nevertheless, this was the extent of Archer's personal comments regarding slavery in the Commonwealth. The remainder of the introduction was spent lambasting the American Colonization Society (ACS), promoters of Black repatriation to Africa, whose purpose he viewed as not only counterproductive to the anti-slavery cause, but a rip-off scheme that coerced free Blacks into selling choice property in exchange for a romanticized life in Africa that was more myth than reality.[14]

In parts 1 and 2 of the body of the text, Archer provided genealogical and historical details that cast Africans and American Indians as unwilling victims in a colonial scheme that betrayed ideals of liberty and equality said to be the cornerstone of American society. Regarding his motivation for highlighting his African and American Indian royal ancestral roots, Archer assured the reader that his purpose was not to indulge in mere vanity by appropriating the heroic deeds of his forbears to inflate his own reputation; but, rather to demonstrate that knowledge of one's country and forbears is necessary in understanding one's self and the historical events that have come to shape one's own reality. Hence, Archer contended that his family history would serve to lay bare "the vile and impious stratagem" of the kidnappers who captured his royal ancestors off the coast of Africa during their attempt to abolish the slave trade, on the one hand, and the "sympathy and patronage" of his ancestor Pocahontas towards the English who first arrived in Jamestown in 1607, on the other. In other words, Archer's lineage served to shift American ideals from theory to practice as outlined by the personal responses of Africans and American Indians to the colonial agenda of their European counterparts. Archer began with his father's narrative as it was told to him in the first person voice:

At the age of fourteen, about the year 1784, when the slave trade was carried on with its usual fury in that part of Africa called Guinea, which comprises several thousand miles of the sea coast, and extends into the interior for the distance of four or five week's journey, thereby including within its boundaries innumerable kingdoms and principalities, I fell a victim to the intrigues of wily kidnappers. The place of my nativity, Kamao, which derived its name from a certain delicious fruit abounding most plentifully in that province, was indeed very fertile in all that might contribute to a comfortable and happy subsistence, and few were the cares of my youthful days . . .

. . . My father's name was Komasko, and he could repeat the names of many of his royal ancestors with great ease, and he appeared to delight in reiterating their exploits, and dwelling on their respective characteristics.

The royal life of the Archers in Guinea was soon interrupted, however, by the trickery of slave traders who coerced the men to come aboard one of the slave ships to make them a part of the human merchandise bound for western slave markets.

While one of the slave ships awaited the completion of her cargo of human chattels on the coast of Guinea, my father had just concluded a treaty with one of the neighboring kings for the suppression of the slave trade within their territories, which, as was now too evident, began to depopulate the countries around, and diminish the physical strength of their respective states. It was not until they saw themselves almost unable to defend their country against hostile invasions, that their eyes were opened to the fatal consequences of selling their own flesh and blood, their countrymen, and dearest friends, to strangers, for little or no value. In this state of affairs, particularly in that section of the coast of Guinea to which my father's country was contiguous, the slave trade received for a moment a merited check, which threatened its entire abolition in those districts . . .

. . . Some natives were at length sent up the country, loaded with presents for the two leagued chiefs, assuring them that the strangers were no other than a friendly power arrived on their coasts, for the sole purpose of exterminating the slave trade, which proved so destructive to their countrymen. The chiefs were particularly requested to appear on the sea coast without delay in order to ratify a treaty for the abolition of the slave trade, where they might also take along with them as many fighting men as would appear to them requisite for their personal safety, in case they suspected the friendly intentions of the foreigners.

. . . Their arrival was hailed as a fit occasion for feasting, dancing, and all other merriments, and of drinking the most intoxicating liquors that could be distilled or adulterated for the destruction of the simple Africans. My father and the allied chief were first received on board the fatal ship, Penelope, where they experienced the most signal marks of generosity and hospitality. Thus pleased, they, poor unwary creatures, without hesitation, and at the urgent request of their dissembling hosts, made signal to their attendants to join them in their festivities, with which their followers immediately complied.

Once the unsuspecting royals and their attendants were aboard the ship, they had stepped beyond the point of no return.

As each boarded the Penelope, for this was the name of the slaver, he was politely told to deliver up his arms until they were ready to land again, the ship being at this time about a mile from the shore. For some time everything promised fair for the ensnared Africans. But, alas! their doom was already sealed. Their liberties were now lost in a dream of pleasure, from which they were to awake only to witness the enormity of human atrocities, to behold their final captivity, to subsist on the bitter fruits of their own credulity, and to feel the iron shackles with which their friendly hosts had bound them hand and foot. No sooner did the poisonous draught lay them senseless on their back, then the blood-thirsty traitors pounced on their helpless prey, to embrue their hands in the innocent blood of their fellow-men.

Thus ended the memorable treaty of 1784 on board of the tragic Penelope, that ill-fated ship which, with all hands on board, was lost on the same coast two years afterwards.

With their fates sealed, the African royals were bound for the West Indies.

After five weeks' torture and stormy weather, we came at last in sight of the island of St. Domingo. Having landed, we soon perceived that our dark and lacerated bodies commanded a much higher value than the toys and gewgaws for which Africans had frequently sold each other in their own country . . . To make this sad story short, I have now only to say, that my father and I were sold to the same master, with whom we lived for ten years, when my father died, after having made a sincere and public profession of Christianity for several years before his death. Our master's name was Pierre Bouchereaux, a Frenchman, of considerable wealth, both in slaves and landed property. Peace be to his soul, for he was kind and a humane friend to his African slaves. A few days before my father died, he requested of Mr. Bouchereaux, as the last favour, to set me free, which would make his last hours easy, and comfort him in his journey to ever-

lasting life. As we were both favourites in the master's family, the prayers
of my dying father were at once granted.

Immediately on my release from the bonds of servitude, I betook myself to the state of Virginia, in the United States. In the course of four
or five years, being free, I accumulated some property. Finding myself
somewhat comfortable in my circumstances of life, I married an Indian
woman, one of the lineal descendants of king Powhattan, whose name
was Tee-can-opee.[15]

Archer's father's narrative provided rare details of his voyage from
Africa to the Americas, which are verifiable when compared with the
historical record. First, while enslaving African nobles who became captives of warring tribes was nothing new, what was rare was that Archer's
forbears were taken from the African coast rather than the interior from
which most captives were obtained. No doubt the truce bargain and
treaty ratified by the two neighboring chiefs toward the abolition of the
slave trade was threat enough for the British to take rare action against
these coastal nations with whom they had enjoyed profitable trade relations for decades. Second, the method of seduction used to lure the chiefs
and their fighting men onto the ship and the enticement of liquor to
secure their capture was certainly plausible. A similar incident occurred
as late as 1858 when famous drummers and several members of the royal
family of the Ewe Tribe were kidnapped off the coast of Ghana.[16] Third,
there were a number of British cargo ships with the name Penelope,
several of which indeed perished at sea.[17] Fourth, Saint Dominigue's
northern port, Cape Francois, was the most desired slave port in the
French West Indies and received a high volume of slaves from foreign
ports. Why Saint Dominigue? The market size, rapid sales, quick turn-
around, easy credit, and cash accessibility available at Saint Dominigue
proved profitable for those in the slave business. By 1783, the year prior
to Archer's ancestors' arrival, France temporarily opened up the southern port of the island to foreign ships due to commercial neglect on the
part of the French. Of the 90,000 African arrivals brought to the French
Caribbean by foreign ships, 86 percent came by way of British vessels. St.
Dominigue was the French West Indies' major importer of slave labor
(disproportionately male) and a major exporter of sugar, indigo, and
coffee. Arguably the most prosperous colony in the Americas, it became
known as the "Jewel of the Antilles."[18]

One can only speculate why Archer's forbears received favorable treatment, allowing his grandfather and father to be sold to the same slave master, Pierre Bouchereaux, upon their arrival in St. Dominigue. The *Code Noir* (Black Code), a decree outlining the laws governing slavery, forbade prepubescent children from being sold away from their parents; but Archer's father, who was fourteen at the time of his captivity, could hardly be included in this category. Perhaps the British trader who befriended the two men during the voyage, Mr. Johnson, made known to the buyers their noble status and was able to persuade Bouchereaux to purchase them both. As a result, Archer's ancestors avoided separation as well as the harsher realities of slave life in the French West Indies. Archer's grandfather's ability to secure the freedom of his son upon his deathbed may well demonstrate the men's favorable position with their slave owner. Under the *Code Noir,* Bouchereaux was free to manumit a slave "by any act toward the living or due to death, without their having to give just cause for the action."[19] Archer's father joined the population of free people of color known as *gens de couleur libres* which was comprised of freed Africans and mulattoes born of French masters and slave mistresses. Theirs was an ambiguous existence within the slave colony. The *Code Noir* granted full citizenship rights to its freed population, while at the same time enacted discriminatory codes which placed limitations on this group. Nevertheless, many became prosperous owning both land and slaves.

Yet, Archer's father, despite his attachment to Bouchereaux, wasted no time leaving the island and traveling to the mainland of the newly formed United States. Why would a newly freed man leave one slave state where he was familiar with the land, language, laws, and customs, only to head for another with which he was far less familiar? It appears that historical events of the day may not have left the elder Archer much choice. It also appears that Archer's father's account of his manumission may be based in romanticism rather than fact. The date given for Archer's forbears' capture was 1784. According to the narrative the men remained in captivity for ten years which places Bouchereaux's act of manumission in 1794, which was a pivotal year for Saint Dominigue; the island was reeling in chaos from what is known today as the Haitian Revolution. The threat of insurrection was always a source of anxiety on the island; but with the outbreak of the French Revolution in 1789, racial unrest in Saint Dominigue was heightened. The population of free people of color began fiercely agitating for political equality, while the slave population laid claim to the rhetoric of freedom trumpeted by revolutionaries. In March 1790 the National Assembly passed a decree which outlined stringent penalties for those who would start an uprising, but was silent on the political rights of the free colored population. By October of the same year, free people of color staged an uprising. Many were arrested and in February 1791 the leaders of the uprising were publicly executed. In an attempt to tamp down racial tensions and appease the free colored population, the National Assembly in the following month, to the chagrin of many White planters, granted political rights to those whose father and mother were born free. Of course, this decree did not address the issue of slavery; hence on August 22, 1791, a slave uprising, unlike anything ever witnessed in human history, ensued. Two years later as the threat of a British and Spanish takeover of the island aided by rebel slaves grew, governmental agents from France abolished slavery in Saint Dominigue during the fall of 1793. Although this initial act was rejected by the National Convention, the executive power that comprised the constitutional and legislative assembly in France from 1792–1795, the Convention abolished slavery in the entire French West Indies on February 4, 1794. With the political and economic systems of the once prosperous Saint Dominigue on the brink of collapse, hordes of refugees boarded boats headed for the mainland United States. Archer's father was no doubt a passenger on one of those boats. He became one of numerous refugees arriving at the port of Norfolk, Virginia in search of a new place to call home.[20]

The first boat load of Saint Dominigue's refugees, about 300 vessels that comprised primarily French masters and their slaves, arrived in Norfolk in early July 1793. Within days officials from Norfolk provided emergency funds and Richmond advanced "six hundred pounds ($2,000)" toward a relief effort.[21] Charitable contributions came pouring in from residents whose sympathies lay with the French colonists. The response was remarkable given that Norfolk had not yet fully recovered from the devastation of the Revolutionary War which ravished its once stable economy built by its extensive West Indian grain trade. Wherein

Norfolk was once the pride among cities of British North America, reputable for its geographic and economic expansion, by the 1790s it "had earned a reputation of altogether legendary portions for ugliness and nastiness."[22] By 1796 Norfolk began to see some recovery. It appears that Archer's father began to recover as well, though life for a free person of color, particularly an emigrant from the West Indies, was sure to be as challenging and ambiguous in Virginia as it was in Saint Dominique.

Prior to the Manumission Act of 1782, which allowed for the voluntary manumission of slaves, the population of free people of color living in Virginia was small due to legislative restrictions imposed on slave manumissions. After 1782, however, such restrictions were lifted. By the end of the American Revolution the free colored population in Virginia doubled from 3,000 to 6,000. Of the five regions of Virginia, the Appalachian Plateau, the Valley and Ridge, the Blue Ridge Mountains, the Piedmont, and the Tidewater, the latter had the highest concentration of free people of color. Norfolk County was among a number of counties in the Tidewater Region with a sizeable community of color. With the economy on the upswing by the late 1790s, Norfolk became a magnet for free people of color. In 1790 the free colored population in Norfolk was sixty-one. By 1800 it was 350, a growth of almost 500 percent.[23]

Unlike the Spanish and French colonies, where the free colored population served as a buffer class between the White and slave populations, British colonies never had use for such an arrangement. Within this two-tier hierarchy, free people of color had limited rights and were viewed as being only a half step away from their enslaved brethren. Many Whites believed there were only two types of colored people: slaves and slaves without masters. The latter was viewed as most dangerous due to the belief that the free colored population undermined slave society by contributing to the enslaved population's discontent and penchant for insurrection. With the arrival of free people of color from the West Indies, whom many believed were influenced by the sentiments of the French and Haitian Revolutions, Whites fear of insurrection in the Virginia Tidewater heightened. Norfolk politicians complained about the number of Blacks from the island. Other residents complained "that native Blacks were made more 'impertinent' by association with those from the West Indies."[24] Despite the artificial distinctions Whites may have made about Blacks, "Norfolk blacks of whatever circumstances were, at the opening of the nineteenth century, daily victims of racial prejudice and mistreatment."[25]

Despite his inauspicious arrival to Virginia with just the clothes on his back and a Creole language of French and African words that would surely turn the heads of any Norfolk resident, White or Black, Archer's father became a property owner. He also married a Powhatan woman, Teecanopee, a descendant of Powcanoe, Pocahontas's younger sister. Powcanoe's tribal affiliation was Pamunkey, by this time a remnant of their former selves tucked away on a remote reservation in King William County. Some Pamunkey, like other small bands of the former Powhatan Confederacy, which once comprised thirty tribes, were scattered in small bands throughout the Tidewater Region. Some of the Powhatan remnants became totally absorbed in the White or colored communities, some forsaking their affiliation with their former tribal communities. While Teecanopee no longer resided within the reservation community, the retention of her Powhatan name signified her continued association with Powhatan identity and culture. Her adherence to Powhatan tradition is moreover poignantly reflected in her marriage to Archer's father, an African. Traditionally, American Indians in general and Powhatan people in specific did not view intermarriage as strange or abhorrent. In fact, Powhatan viewed English disdain for intermarriage with Indians as an insult. While a marriage like the Archers' would have been frowned upon by the late nineteenth century, in early nineteenth century Virginia, the marriage of an American Indian and African would have been simply viewed as par for the course. Teecanopee embodied this and other Powhatan traditions that she passed on to her Powhatan son of African descent, Armstrong Archer, born sometime during the years 1800–1812.[26]

In part 2 of *A Compendium*, Archer demonstrated the strong sense of his Indian identity with a focus on the Powhatan Indians and Pocahontas. Before reminding the reader of the historical context which led to Pocahontas's alleged rescue of John Smith, Archer lamented the loss of the Powhatan Confederacy to which he refers as "the seat of freedom and liberty where the warriors scarcely knew the bounds of their hunting grounds; and little indeed did they dream that those vast and lofty forests would ever become the nursery of slaves, and the luxuriant domains of their ferocious masters."[27] In other words, to speak of freedom and liberty in a space once used for hunting but now transformed into plantation slavery, was the height of contradiction. Further using analogies to highlight the interconnectedness of slavery and American Indian removal, Archer lamented the use of blood hounds to hunt down runaway slaves and American Indians attempting to dodge Andrew Jackson's Indian removal order. He also chided President Van Buren for his use of blood hounds during the second Seminole War.[28] Archer depended on the written accounts of Virginia Indians by Thomas Jefferson, B. B. Thatcher, and William Stith to highlight the history of White–Indian relations from the 1607 landing at Jamestown to the John Smith/Pocahontas saga. However, he departed from recorded history and provided a personal historical account of a story he had heard numerous times while visiting with his Powhatan relatives. It is probable that while Archer resided with his parents in Norfolk, he would occasionally visit with relatives on the Pamunkey reservation where he would hear hero stories told by the male elders about Manotee, Powcanoe's eldest son.[29] Archer documented the following account in his narrative:

> From this same tribe, among whom Powcanoe was married, I am lineally descended, according to their osmago, or tradition. The Indians of Virginia at the present day relate some curious and interesting stories concerning Manotee, the eldest son of Powcanoe. The substance of one of them is as follows:—During a predatory excursion against the whites, Manotee, the grandson of Powhattan, conceived and executed a plan for taking a piece of cannon from the English colonists. In order to succeed in this attempt, he proposed to some twenty or thirty warriors that they should visit the white settlement and offer them presents of Indian corn, venison, fish, and deerskin; at the same time they were to give every assurance of friendship on their part. As the colonists were frequently destitute of provisions, especially in the spring of the year, the presents were highly appreciated. Koriasko in return merely requested that they would fire off one of their pieces of cannon. To this the English immediately agreed. During the firing of the big gun, the Indian chief watched and observed all their movements, so that he not only learned the manner of loading their guns, but marked particularly the place where they kept their ammunition, and likewise instructed his companions to make the same observation. Having fired four or five shots, which delighted rather than terrified the warriors, Manotee pretended to have some great secret

to disclose, and led aside the governor for the purpose of apprising him of an imminent danger. During this interval the Indian warriors performed many ceremonies which excited a great deal of interest on the part of the whites. They covered their faces and eyes with their hands, as a sign of mourning, which they accompanied with shouts of lamentation. Without any delay the governor called his council, and gave them to understand that Manotee came to the settlement for the purpose of saving them from utter destruction, as a hostile tribe was encamped about three miles from the colony, and intended to commit a general massacre. As soon as Manotee saw them apprehensive of danger, he presented himself immediately before the council, and suggested the propriety of arming themselves, and starting in quest of the enemy. He likewise proposed that the governor and himself should command the expedition, while ten of his warriors should remain as protection for their wives and families. To this proposal the English at once consented, and set off instantly in pursuit of the hostile tribe. The Indian chief shrewdly led the armed colonists to the place where he and his companions had encamped the night before. On their arrival here, Manotee and his warriors showed, or at least pretended to show, a great deal of surprise and vexation at not finding the enemy. The English returned to their settlement, no less gratified at their safety than the Indians were, by having succeeded in securing the piece of cannon through this deception. Those Indians who had remained as a guard for the settlement had no sooner seen the whites depart, than they started off with a piece of cannon, ammunition, and two of their boats. Having arrived at the appointed place, they were soon rejoined by Manotee and his warriors. Although the English felt indignant at this stratagem, which threw them into the greatest consternation, and deprived them of the cannon and a considerable quantity of ammunition, the fraud turned out at last to be the means of saving the lives of several of the colonists, who had been out on a hunting excursion, and had wandered in the woods for many days, exhausted with fatigue and hunger. In this state of privation, they found themselves one day in the vicinity of an Indian settlement, by means of the report of the gun which had been stolen some few days before. They soon found themselves in the presence of Manotee and three or four hundred warriors, who were summoned to witness the novelty and curiosity of gunpowder. The chief candidly acknowledged the artifice which he had used in taking off the cannon; and, as remuneration, he received the English with the most exemplary hospitality. After loading them with presents of provisions and other articles, he sent four Indians as guides, who should conduct them to the colony. This and many other stories about Manotee are still alive in the memories of the Indians of Virginia, the descendants of that noble chief.[30]

Archer's recollection of Manotee provided exceptional insights into seventeenth-century Indian–White relations from the perspective of the indigenous population. Despite the consensus of prominent citizens, such as Thomas Jefferson, that Powhatan culture and society were extinct by the turn of the eighteenth century, Archer's story provided evidence to the contrary. His story demonstrated the cultural viability of the Powhatan people well into the nineteenth century. It also demonstrated the maintenance of an historical consciousness grounded within an indigenous worldview that defied European standards of history. The timing of the story, for example, given the details regarding the extent of European settlement and the absence of the incident of the stolen canon from English accounts may raise questions of historical validity. Yet, as Sioux scholar Vine Deloria argued regarding the concept of history in American Indian societies, "'The way I heard it' or 'it was a long time ago' usually prefaces any Indian account of past tribal experience, indicating that the story itself is important, not the precise chronological location."[31] Therefore, the aim of such stories was not to establish absolute truth, but rather was used in "defining a people's identity."[32] Within this context, Manotee, the protagonist, plays the trickster—a trope figure found in both African American and Native American literary traditions. Animal and human trickster tales were used to demonstrate how the weak, through his or her wit, could outsmart the strong and mock the myth of the superiority of the oppressor. The difference between the two types of tricksters was that the animal trickster's victories were always more spectacular than its human counterpart, the latter being constrained by human limitations. Hence, in Archer's story, the human trickster Manotee could steal the ammunition, lead the Englishmen on a hunt for fake enemies, and make a fool of the English, who prided themselves on their superior weaponry but couldn't find their way back home from a hunting expedition. In the end Manotee reimbursed the English for the stolen ammunition and led them back to the fort loaded with presents, a finale representative of the human trickster trope.[33] Archer's contribution to American Indian cultural preservation cannot be overstated. Despite the present day denial of African American–American Indian kinship relations by many within Powhatan tribal communities, the modern-day Powhatan owe a great deal of gratitude to this nineteenth-century

Afro-Indian. His preservation of the Manotee tale provided indisputable evidence of the continued existence and cultural continuity of the Powhatan people long after they were believed to have disappeared.

Archer did not remain in Virginia among his African American and Native American relatives whose stories he had come to love while growing up in the Commonwealth. The harsh reality of living as a free person of color in a slave state may well have been the motivation for Archer's decision to leave Norfolk and relocate north. Due to the discrepancy of his date of birth and a lack of records, it is difficult to determine precisely when this relocation occurred. If, as his narrative stated, he resided in Virginia for the first twenty-five years of his life, then his departure occurred anytime from 1826 to 1836. What is certain is that life for the free colored population in Virginia grew more intense during this period as the abolitionist sentiments from the North and the threat of insurrection from the South set southern Whites' teeth on edge. Consequently, the free colored population was a constant target of White intimidation. First, Whites' land-grabbing efforts to dispossess Native Americans of their reservations by agitating for their reclassification as free Negroes placed an enormous strain on the once plutonic Black–Indian relations. Second, bands of vigilantes took to abusing the bodies and properties of their victims with no fear of legal reprisal. Free people of color could fall victim to trumped-up legal charges like insurrection conspiracy, forging travel passes for slaves, or failing to pay a debt, with little to no evidence. Third, from 1827 to 1830, there was much debate in the Virginia legislature regarding the repatriation of free Blacks to Africa. It seems that the American Colonization Society (ACS), which was active in Norfolk and Prince Anne counties at the time, was driving the debate, as well as the vigilantes. Regarding the ACS, Archer's acquaintance and Prince Anne County resident Willis Augustus Hodges contended that the organization:

> acted as if these lawless bands had been hired by them to commit these depredations on the people of color to induce them to go to Liberia. Instead of trying to bring these outlaws to justice, the Colonization [Society] would say that they were sorry for us, and would allow us if we ever wished to enjoy happiness and become men in every sense of the word, to leave the United States, our native land, and emigrate to the unknown and wild lands of Africa.[34]

Hodges's sentiments indeed provide a context for Archer's strong opposition to the ACS expressed in his introduction.

Fourth, Nat Turner's rebellion in Southampton County, Virginia, in the summer of 1831, sparked terror in the heart of the Commonwealth that reverberated throughout the nation. Turner's rebellion will be discussed in further detail in chapter 7. Suffice it for now to say that the ordeal in Southampton made life for people of color, both slave and free, Black and Indian, nearly intolerable. For Archer this period marked the end of the road for him in Virginia. In the words of Zora Neale Hurston, "The wind said north." So Archer left his childhood home for a new life in the "free" states north of the Mason and Dixon line.

Archer became a Baptist minister receiving his ordination at the North Beriah Baptist Church (later the North Baptist Church) in New York in 1837. He was immediately dispatched to Boston to pastor the historic First African Baptist Church on Belknap Street in Beacon Hill. However, the church was riven as warring factions engaged in a heated debate over the question of the role of the church in the antislavery movement. The growing tensions within the church body would prove difficult for any newly ordained minister. Archer remained at the church for a year. After his request for dismissal was granted, he returned to New York and moved to a village on Long Island in Kings County not far from Brooklyn ironically known as Williamsburgh.[35]

According to Hodges, who arrived in Kings County several years after Archer, Williamsburgh was a "growing village," and was preferable to urban living because it offered better economic opportunities for Blacks and less antagonism from Whites. Hodges's sentiments were later proven correct as, "Almost two decades later a writer in the *Weekly Anglo-African* described Williamsburgh as a thriving settlement . . . The colored people having bought and settled here when land was cheap . . . have grown up with the place and . . . have kept admirable pace with the whites."[36] Hence, from 1840 to 1860 Williamsburgh, which became home to a number of Archer's acquaintances from Prince Anne and Norfolk counties, served as a safe harbor for free people of color seeking upward mobility. Much about Williamsburgh had changed within those two decades and during the same period, much had also changed about Archer. By 1860, he not only changed his location, and his profession, but most importantly, he changed his racial identity.

Although Archer remained active in his clergy obligations after leaving the African Baptist Church of Boston, the discrimination faced by Blacks in the North and the continued enslavement of Blacks in the South, caused him to side with the sentiments of his former parishioners in Boston who believed that church membership did not exempt one from agitating for social justice on behalf of one's self and others. Therefore, he joined the ranks of numerous Black clergy who engaged in the dual responsibility of feeding the flock and advocating for social change. When the state of New York disenfranchised Black men by limiting the franchise to those whose property taxes were worth at least 250 dollars, Blacks organized a Convention for the Colored Inhabitants of the State of New York in Albany. On August 13, 1840, Archer chaired a meeting at the Colored Methodist Meetinghouse to draft a resolution in support of Black suffrage and to appoint a delegation to represent the colored citizens of Williamsburgh at the convention the following week. Archer was one among six appointed to the delegation. During the Albany convention, he was also appointed among nine others to serve on the business committee. Archer's northern experience was indicative of many American Indians or people of part American Indian descent who were absorbed into the African American community as a result of relocation. It seems that one of the aims of his 1844 pamphlet was to reclaim his American Indian identity.[37]

Throughout the 1840s Archer remained active in the religious and political spheres; but in 1849 he married and at this time his life began to undergo a major shift. Similar to his father, Archer did not marry a woman of African descent, but rather a Portuguese woman—an emigrant from Madeira. In 1850 the couple resided in the Fifth Ward—a community of color that appears to have been delineated by color. One segment of the community enumerated on the census was identified as Black, while the other segment, where Archer and his wife Frances resided, was identified as mulatto. The racial identity of those in communities of color as either Black or mulatto was not unusual. Color designations were left up to the discretion of the census enumerator. In this case, however, there appears to have been a deliberate demarcation along the color line.[38] Notwithstanding, it seems that the Archers resided in a boarding home with other adults with varying occupations.

Archer continued to list his occupation as Baptist minister. By 1860, however, his occupation was identified as farmer. Along with the change in occupation came a change in residence from New York to New Jersey, where he lived with his wife and their two sons, James, nine, and Joshua, three. The oldest child's birthplace was listed as New York while the second child's birthplace was listed as New Jersey. Hence, the period the Archers relocated to the Garden State occurred sometime between the years 1851–1856. The family took up residence in Acquacknouk Township, in Passaic County. Among its forty residents were a number of German immigrants. All residents, including Archer and his family, were racially identified as White.[39]

The 1860 Federal Census marks the end of the paper trail for Archer and his family who afterwards disappeared from the historical record without a trace. This was an inescapable fate for many people of color who made the tough decision to pass as White. One can only speculate about how and why Archer decided to leave the colored community and to live out the remainder of his days as a White man. He certainly had the opportunity to do so two decades prior when he first left the Commonwealth, so why now? Perhaps being older and less idealistic about the future for colored citizens in the North and the desire for better opportunities for his children was reason enough to divorce his former racial identity and become, in the words of James Weldon Johnson, "an ex-colored man."[40] The poet Langston Hughes aptly captured this dilemma in the first lines of his poem "Lament for Dark Peoples":

> I was a red man one time
> But the white man came
> I was a black man too
> But the white man came

Hughes's assertion may certainly appear hyperbolic at first glance. Identity based on a color hierarchy was foreign to both African and American Indian people prior to European contact. Nevertheless, the poem taken in its entirety, reflects not only the shifting nature of racial identity, but also the ways in which America's racial hierarchy imposed alternative identities on people of color whose own sense of identity became redefined as a result of America's racial dictatorship. Archer's later choice in life to deny his African and American Indian heritage serves as metaphor for the manipulation of race and identity—the result of the American racialized value system.

Whether coincidental or deliberate, Archer's choice of relocation may well have served as a constant reminder of who he truly was and the life he left behind. The township and county names of his new place of residence, Acquacknouk and Passaic, were derived from Lenape words meaning "a place in a rapid stream where fishing is done with a net" and "valley" respectively.[41] The Acquacknouk Indians, the original inhabitants of the township, though different in dialect and culture, bore some similarity to the Powhatan people. Their dialect was derived from the Algonquian language, and their totem, the turtle, was similarly revered by their southern counterparts. Certainly Archer's inquisitiveness would have led him to inquire about these "strange" words. Just as retaining the indigenous names and a few words from the language of his progenitors served to help him preserve the memory of his ancestral roots proudly expressed in his narrative, perhaps the Algonquian words associated with his new location served to preserve his sense of Indianness despite his change of identity.

No doubt Archer spent time fishing along the banks of the Passaic River, a tradition of importance to the coastal African and Tidewater American Indian cultures from which he was lineally descended. Perhaps it was during those times as he looked out on the pier that the memories of his African father whose voyage across many waters that had brought him to his Powhatan mother were keenly felt. Perhaps during these moments Archer lingered at the crossroads pouring libation and offering tobacco in homage of the confluence of the histories and kinship ties of the two peoples which he embodied.[42] And while the racial dictates at the time may have left him little choice but to outwardly live as a White man, on the inside he remained keenly aware of whom he was. To borrow from Langston Hughes, Archer was "a Red man—a Black man too," in a country where Whiteness reigns supreme.

ONE

Notes on the State of Virginia: Jeffersonian Thought and the Rise of Racial Purity Ideology in the Eighteenth Century

This belief is founded on what I have seen of man white, red, and black . . . they [American Indians] are formed in mind as well as in body on the same module with the "Homo sapiens Europaeus" . . . I advance it therefore, as a suspicion only, that the blacks . . . are inferior to the whites in endowments both of body and mind.

—THOMAS JEFFERSON, *NOTES ON THE STATE OF VIRGINIA*

In 1780, while the United States remained at war for its independence from Britain, Joseph Jones, a member of the Virginia congressional delegation, received a questionnaire from then secretary of the French legation to the United States, François Marbois. Marbois had compiled and distributed the questionnaire to delegates in order to obtain information concerning each of the thirteen states. Comprised of twenty-two questions, Marbois's questionnaire inquired of such things as the state's history (pre- and post-colonization), climate, waterways, natural resources, boundaries, inhabitants (particularly aborigines and Africans), militia, education, religious worship, commercial production, and currency.

Jones presented Marbois's inquiry to the one person he felt capable of handling such a myriad of questions concerning the Virginia colony: Thomas Jefferson. Jefferson enthusiastically worked on answering the questionnaire. He reorganized the questions and set out to answer them, in most cases, as "accurately" as possible.[1]

That Jefferson took this project seriously was expressed in a letter he wrote to Charles-François d'Anmours, the French vice consul residing in Philadelphia. Jefferson disclosed to d'Anmours that he was diligently at work on Marbois's questionnaire and that this work was "making me much better acquainted with my own country [Virginia] than I ever was before."[2] Certainly, Jefferson was already knowledgeable in many areas having been the privileged son of one of the largest planters (i.e. slave owners) in the colony. He received an impressive formal education in addition to being an independent learner. His thirst for knowledge seemed unquenchable and this was reflected in the meticulous way he went about answering the inquiry. Jefferson first began with the questions he could readily answer with little difficulty. Concerning the questions of which he knew the least, he spent hours researching the topics. Jefferson seemed quite proud of the work he had completed. This had been no simple question and answer exercise, but rather a scholarly endeavor replete with footnotes and appendices. Upon completion he not only sent a copy to Marbois, but to his closest friends as well. Initially, Jefferson opted for a limited readership. In a letter to Marquis de Chastellux in 1785, Jefferson stated, "The strictures on slavery and on the constitution of Virginia . . . are the parts which I do not wish to have made public, at least, til I know whether their publication would do most harm or good."[3] Yet, his strictures on slavery and the constitution proved of little consequence. It was his "strictures" on Black inferiority and repatriation that proved most detrimental to the African American population.

Jefferson's assertions concerning the so-called inherent inferiority of people of African descent "were more widely read, in all probability, than any others until the mid-nineteenth century."[4] Indeed, it appears Jefferson's response to Query XIV remains the most famous, or rather infamous passage in the book that was to be his only published work. Most often this passage is highlighted to demonstrate the contradictions of Jefferson's attitudes toward Blacks. How could a man who declared all men created equal make such disparaging remarks about people of African descent? Scholars have spent decades trying to reconcile these contrasting views. The answer to this question becomes more complex when viewing Jefferson's favorable remarks in Query VI regarding the aboriginal population of North America. Jefferson's persistence concerning American Indian equality with Whites is often cited to highlight his contrasting attitude towards African Americans and to demonstrate his philanthropy towards American Indians. As Winthrop Jordan asserted, "Confronted with three races in America he determinedly turned three into two by transforming the Indian into a degraded white man yet basically noble brand of white man."[5] Yet, this romantic view of American Indians was only reserved for frontier Indians as Jefferson viewed Indians living in his own state less favorably. In Query XI Virginia Indians were not transformed into noble Whites, but rather transformed into ignoble Blacks due to their intermixing with the African American population. Jefferson's assertion that Virginia Indians were "more Negro than Indian" informed the attitudes of twentieth-century Virginia eugenicists whose mission was to preserve White racial purity by any means necessary. This campaign to preserve White racial integrity threatened the existence of Indians within the Commonwealth by constructing an Indian identity bound for extinction due to Black "contamination" and presaged Virginia's twentieth-century eugenics campaign to redefine all Virginia Indians as Negro.

In Query VI of *Notes on the State of Virginia,* Jefferson refuted the assertion of leading French Naturalist George Buffon, who concluded that life forms in the "new world" were degenerate, as the climate was colder and wetter than that of Europe. According to Jefferson, not only did Buffon insinuate that the animals on the American continent were inferior, the Frenchman also believed humans native to the continent to be inferior as well. Of course Jefferson took offense to this as he was a native born American. However, in defending the equality of Europeans born in North America to those born in Europe, Jefferson did not turn to American-born Europeans as proof that Americans were in equal standing with their counterparts across the ocean; instead he turned to the indigenous population. Jefferson's seizure upon North American aborigines to construct American identity was typical of eighteenth-century colonists who had to navigate through their "liminal" status of non-identity during the revolutionary period. Thus American Indians became central to the colonists' "rites of passage" from British subjects to American patriots.[6]

Consequently, Jefferson refuted Buffon by constructing American identity based on the image of the noble savage. Jefferson described American Indians as "formed in mind as well as in body on the same module with the 'Homo sapiens Europaeus.'" He continued his discourse by commending the indigenous population for their bravery in battle, their innate affection displayed towards kinship, and their superior gift of oration. The latter he saw in some sense as superior to anything Europe had produced. Jefferson contended, "Of their eminence of oratory . . . Some, however, we have of very superior lustre. I may challenge the whole orations of Demosthenes and Cicero, and of any more eminent orator, if Europe has furnished more eminent, to produce a single passage, superior to the speech of Logan, a Mingo chief." "Logan's Lament," a speech delivered to Lord Dunmore on behalf of Mingo Chief John Logan during the peace treaty proceedings with the Shawnee Indians in 1774, was viewed by Jefferson as the standard bearer of American Indian rhetoric and intellectual prowess. While Europeans used the development of a written language as a yardstick for civilization, Jefferson defended its absence among American Indians: "Before we condemn the Indians of this continent as wanting genius, we must consider that letters have not yet been introduced to them."[7]

To further defend the equality of American Indians to Europeans, Jefferson contested the views of another European, Don Ulloa, for his unfair assessment regarding the so-called degeneracy of the aborigines. Ulloa based his assessment of the indigenous population on what he determined to be the inferiority of South American Indians to Europeans. Although Jefferson agreed with Ulloa's assessment, he opposed the European's conclusions because he believed the southern American Indian's degeneracy was not innate, but rather the result of slavery: Ulloa "saw the Indian of South America only and that after he had passed through ten generations of slavery," contended Jefferson. "It is very unfair, from this sample, to judge of the natural genius of this race of men."[8] Jefferson insisted that the indigenous population of North America far better reflected the genius of American Indians as they had not been so altered by the consequence of enslavement as those in South America.

Throughout his life Jefferson remained convinced of the natural genius of American Indians, although he also invoked the image of the deficient Indian to justify an Anglo expansionist agenda. Hence, Jefferson's campaign for what Robert Berkhofer termed "expansion with honor," advocated for the amalgamation of the two peoples.[9] Jefferson expressed this sentiment numerous times as in this statement from an 1803 letter to Benjamin Hawkins: "In truth the ultimate point of rest & happiness for them [American Indians] is to let our settlements and theirs meet and blend together, to intermix, and become one people. Incorporating themselves with us as citizens of the United States, this is what the natural progress of things will, of course, bring on, and it will be better to promote than to retard it."[10]

Jefferson's advocacy for White–Indian amalgamation may seem contradictory given his own as well as Virginia's obsession with racial purity and proscriptions against interracial sex and marriage as reflected in its early statutes. The first known Virginia statute recorded in 1630 called for Hugh Davis "to be soundly whipped for . . . defiling himself with a Negro." The year 1691 marked the first formal legal proscription against intermarriage between Whites and people of color which included Negroes, mulattoes, and Indians. The law was intended to control the increase of mixed race children whom legislators described as "that abominable mixture and spurious issue."[11] This disparaging statement referred to the offspring of White and non-White couples. There were no such proscriptions against non-White interracial couples; therefore, African and American Indian liaisons went unmolested. During the formative years of the Virginia legislature, it was customary to amend a law by reenacting it and including the amendment within the body of the legislation. In addition, all laws were repealed during each session and either reenacted using the same language of the old law or with further amendments included as necessary.[12] Such was the case regarding the regulation of race, sex, and marriage as the 1691 statute was reenacted and amended in 1705, 1723, 1765, and 1785. The amendments reflected a change in racial definition and/or an adjustment of the penalties for violators of the law. Penalties from the colonial era to the end of the Jim

Crow era were severe for those who violated racial purity laws. Jefferson's altered position regarding amalgamation with Indians, however, was in keeping with earlier sentiments expressed by other prominent Virginia citizens who promoted an assimilationist agenda as a means to further colonize the indigenous population and to acquire their lands.

By the mid eighteenth century some White Virginians began to rethink proscriptions against intermarriage with Indians. There was little intermarriage between Whites and Indians after the John Rolfe and Pocahontas union. Unlike the Spanish and French, who freely intermarried with the Indians, such practice was forbidden by the English. As Peter Fountaine stated in 1757, "but this our wise politicians put an effectual stop at the beginning of our settlement here, for when they heard that John Rolfe had married Pocahontas, it was deliberated in Council whether he had not committed high treason by doing so . . . and had not some trouble intervened which put a stop to the inquiry, the poor man might have been hanged."[13] Fountaine contended that intermarriage with the Indians would have insured better White–Indian relations in the Virginia settlement as it "would have incorporated them with us effectively, and made of them staunch friends."[14] Colonel William Byrd concurred asserting that the English's disdain towards intermarrying with the Indians, whom they viewed as reprobate heathens, cost them a lasting peace with their colonial subjects. While these gentlemen questioned the logic regarding proscriptions against White–Indian intermarriage, others attempted to repeal laws against such proscriptions. The first attempt to repeal proscriptions against White–Indian intermarriage was made in 1699 by Sir William Johnson who submitted a petition to the Virginia Burgesses. He had married an Indian woman and fathered children by her. It is said that through this marriage he gained influence over the Six Nations (Iroquois Confederacy), thus he believed other White men should follow his example. In 1784 Patrick Henry sponsored a bill in the Virginia Legislature proposing monetary incentives for Whites who married American Indians.[15] Neither bill became law. Overwhelmingly, Anglos did not view Indians or rather, as will be discussed later, Virginia Indians as suitable marriage partners.

While Jefferson proposed that Anglos and American Indians become one people, he proposed the opposite for Anglos and Africans as his image of the latter was less sanguine. In assessing the genius, or supposed lack thereof in people of African descent, Jefferson came to a far different conclusion than that he had ascribed to American Indians. Jefferson asserted, "in reason they [African Americans] are inferior . . . in imagination they are dull, tasteless, and anomalous . . . never yet could I find that a black had uttered a thought above the level of plain narration."[16] While Jefferson thought it unfair of Ulloa to draw conclusions concerning American Indians based on people who had passed through ten generations of slavery, people of African descent, who were victims of European slave markets since the fifteenth century, were not given the same consideration. Jefferson felt there was no need to look to Africa to ascertain the original character of African Americans. He concluded, "It would be unfair to follow them to Africa for this investigation. We will consider them here, on the same stage with the whites and where the facts are not apocryphal on which a judgment is to be formed."[17]

Why would Jefferson insist that American Indians be viewed in "their original character" prior to European contact, but insist that this would be unnecessary for people of African descent? First, Jefferson, like most Europeans, embraced the myth of Africa as "the dark continent," whose inhabitants were bestial in spite of their human form.[18] Second, Jefferson believed that despite their supposed savage beginnings, enslaved Africans had been well-exposed to the high culture of Europeans in America and Europe, an advantage he claimed American Indians did not have.

Nonetheless, Jefferson refuted any evidence that countered his suspicions of Black innate inferiority. He dismissed the works of African writers Phillis Wheatley and Ignatius Sancho. Of Wheatley's 1773 publication, *Poems on Various Subjects: Religious and Moral,* Jefferson stated, "Religion has indeed produced a Phylis Whately [*sic*] but it could not produce a poet. The compositions published under her name are below the dignity of criticism." While Jefferson felt Sancho's writings displayed more literary promise than Wheatley's, he did not believe the African's work was equal to his European contemporaries. Jefferson contended, "Upon the whole, though we admit him to the first place among those of his own colour who have presented themselves to the public judgment, yet when we compare him with the writers of the race among whom he lived, and particularly with the epistolary class, in which he has taken his own stand, we are compelled to enroll him at the bottom of the column." Jefferson believed that Sancho's work did not measure up to European standards because "his imagination is wild and extravagant, escapes incessantly from every restraint of reason and taste and in the course of its vagaries, leaves a tract of thought as incoherent and eccentric, as in the course of a meteor through the sky." As far as Jefferson was concerned, "The improvement of the blacks in body and mind, in the first instance of their mixture with the whites . . . proves that their inferiority is not merely of their condition of life."[19]

Jefferson's latter statement concerning African American "mixture with the whites" carries a dual meaning. First, as noted above, Jefferson did not believe that Blacks benefitted from exposure to European culture. For example, both Wheatley and Sancho were educated by White benefactors as part of an "experiment" to answer the question of whether people of African descent possessed the intelligence to master the arts and sciences. Their publishing accomplishments caused many to declare the experiment a success. These advocates believed that slavery interfered with the intellectual potential of Blacks. Once slavery was abolished, Blacks would be on par with Whites. Yet, Jefferson refuted this assertion and pronounced the experiment a failure. The Founding Father believed that Wheatley's and Sancho's achievements had been weighed in the balance and found wanting. Thus, instead of being a "credit to their race," the authors proved that Black inferiority was innate. Therefore, based on his assessment, Jefferson believed Black exposure to the so-called higher order of European society was futile.

The second meaning of Jefferson's statement regarding Blacks' admixture with Whites pertained to miscegenation and its affect upon Black intelligence. In 1791 Jefferson received, in the form of a letter and a present from Benjamin Banneker, further evidence that people of African descent were indeed on par intellectually with Whites. Banneker was a free, self-taught African American scientist and mathematician. While employed as a surveyor for the area that is now Washington, D.C., Banneker designed an almanac. At the time of his correspondence to Jefferson, Banneker's almanac was in the hands of a printer awaiting publication. Banneker's letter sought to dispel Jefferson's "suspicions" concerning Black inferiority. Banneker placed the culpability of Black underachievement squarely on the shoulders of American slavery. The scientist believed that his eloquent letter and almanac were undisputable proof that people of African descent were equal to Whites in mind, body, and reason. To further emphasize his point, Banneker gave Jefferson a copy of his original manuscript stating, "I chose to send it to you in manuscript previous [to publishing] thereto, that thereby you might also view it in my own handwriting."[20] In addition to submitting a handwritten manuscript, Banneker wanted to dispel all doubts concerning his racial identity. Banneker was well aware that there were Europeans and Americans who attributed Black achievement to a mixture of White ancestry. This was certainly true of Jefferson whenever he "heard of a colored person distinguishing himself or herself in the arts, sciences, or literature, his first question habitually was how much White 'blood' this particular individual possessed."[21] Lest Jefferson, or anyone else credit his achievement to his supposed mixed ancestry Banneker stated, "Sir I freely and Cheerfully [sic] acknowledge, that I am of the African race, and in color which is natural to them of the deepest hue."[22] It seemed that Banneker had covered all of his bases. Jefferson received the scientist's work with great enthusiasm. He soon sent Banneker a thank you letter and stated that his work was evidence that Blacks were not innately inferior and agreed that slavery was responsible for stifling their potential. He also forwarded Banneker's work to Monsieur Condorcet, Secretary of the Academy of Sciences in Paris stating, "I consider it as a document to which your whole colour had a right for their justification against the doubts which have been entertained of them."[23] Interestingly, when submitting Banneker's work to Monsieur Condorcet, Jefferson lied about how he came to obtain the almanac. Jefferson claimed that he had procured the surveyor job for Banneker and received the almanac as a token of appreciation. As Banneker's letter demonstrated, however, Jefferson had no prior knowledge of the scientist or his work. Nonetheless, Jefferson's enthusiasm concerning Banneker as well as people of his "colour" quickly vanished.

In a lengthy letter to James Monroe in 1801, Jefferson continued spouting his ideas of deporting people of African descent out of the United States. He repeated these same ideas in a letter he wrote to Joel

Barlow in 1809. Whereas he had beforehand extolled Banneker as proof that Blacks were not innately inferior, to Barlow Jefferson minimized "the respected mathematician's" accomplishment: "The whole [race] do not amount, in point, of evidence, to what we know ourselves of Banneker. We know he had spherical trigonometry enough to make almanacs, but not without the suspicion of aid from Ellicott, who was his neighbor and friend."[24] Ellicott, whom Jefferson referenced in the above quote, was Andrew Ellicott whom Banneker identified as the man who procured the surveyor job for him. Hence while Jefferson could not dismiss Banneker or his proof on the basis that he was of mixed racial origin, he could dismiss him on the grounds that his association with Whites proved that neither he nor others of his race could make it without White assistance. Jefferson reinforced this assertion in a lengthy letter to Edward Cole in the summer of 1814.[25] Although Jefferson did not think people of African descent could make it without Whites, he advocated their removal from Whites for fear of admixture. Jefferson stated, "Among the Romans emancipation required but one effort. The slave, when made free, might mix with, without staining the blood of his master. But with us a second is necessary, *unknown to history*. When freed, he is to be removed beyond the reach of mixture" [italics mine].[26]

Why was Jefferson, on the one hand, so adamant about American Indian equality, but on the other hand so adamant about Black inferiority? Wasn't it he who stated that "all men are created equal"? How can men be both equal and inferior? On first glance the statement indeed appears to be one of Jefferson's greatest contradictions; however, interpreted within the context of Enlightenment philosophy by which Jefferson and others of his day were greatly influenced, it becomes apparent that the statement was never intended to invoke an all-encompassing equal humanity. When Jefferson stated that all men are created equal he was speaking within a revolutionary context that involved the grievances between the American colonists and the British government. Jefferson believed the American colonists had reached the post-political phase in their relationship with the mother country, and that they were now ready to return to the pre-political where all men are free and created equal to choose a government which they believed would protect their natural rights: life, liberty and the pursuit of happiness. Hence, the statement that all men are created equal means that "by nature no man is 'subjected to the will or authority of any other man' . . . whatever the many inequalities among human beings may be, whether intelligence, virtue, beauty, or strength, none of them gives a rightful claim of authority over another."[27]

While inequalities of intelligence, virtue, beauty, or strength could not be the impetus for anyone's claim to rule or to establish authority over others, Jefferson used these "inequalities" in the most egregious passage in his *Notes* to establish two distinct policies regarding African American and American Indian peoples that persist to this day. The policy simply entailed the forced exclusion of the former and the forced inclusion of the latter. As a case in point, Jefferson drafted a marriage bill in 1786 titled *A Bill Annulling Marriages Prohibited by Levitical Law and Appointing the Mode of Solemnizing Lawful Marriage.* Jefferson sought to amend previous proscriptions on intermarriage by rendering such unions unrecognized within the Commonwealth: "A marriage between a person of free condition and a slave or between a white person and a negro or between a white person and a mulatto shall be null."[28] Although the language of the bill appears to be contextualized within a religious framework, by this time racial difference was substituted for religious difference. As acceptance of the Christian religion increased among the non-White population, it became impossible to maintain a politics of difference based in religion. Consequently, what W. E. B. Du Bois later dubbed "the grosser physical difference of hair, skin, and bone," came to dominate the discourse on interracial marriage as theories of scientific racism consumed the thoughts of European and American intellectuals.[29]

The foundation for Du Bois's "chilling threesome," to use the words of cultural critic Stuart Hall, can be located in Jefferson's articulation of what Elise Lemire identified as a sexualized idea of preference:

> Are not the fine mixtures of red and white, the expression of every passion by greater or less suffusions of colour in the one, preferable to that eternal monotony, which reigns in the countenance, that immoveable veil of black which covers all the emotions of the other race? And to these, flowing hair, a more elegant symmetry of form, their own judgment in favor of the whites, declared by preference of them, as uniformly as is

preference of the Oranootan for the black woman over those of his own species. The circumstance of superior beauty is thought worthy attention in the propagation of our horses, dogs, and other domestic animals, why not in that of man.[30]

Jefferson's sexualized idea of preference, drawn from early Western thought, was symbolic of the varying policies Anglo Americans advanced in their respective relations with Africans and American Indians. The English denotations and connotations of color particularly that of white, black, and red, proved a reflection of their most ingrained values. Prior to having any association with "Black" people, the English definitions of Black reflect its negative associations within the Anglo-Saxon imagination. Blackness was defined as: "Deeply stained with dirt; soiled, dirty, foul . . . malignant . . . iniquitous . . . disgrace . . . horrible, wicked."[31] Of course, Whiteness was envisioned as its polar opposite, thus the two were viewed as incompatible. Therefore, "white and black connoted purity and filthiness, virginity and sin, virtue and baseness, beauty and ugliness, beneficence and evil, God and the devil."[32] On the contrary, the mixing of white and red were viewed quite differently as they were seen as complementary, provided the white predominated. This combination symbolized beauty, nobility and desirability. Consequently, "whiteness, moreover, carried a special significance for Elizabethan Englishmen: it was, particularly when complemented by red, the color of perfect human beauty, especially female beauty."[33] While one drop of Black "blood" was enough to contaminate, one drop of Indian "blood" was enough to "enhance, ennoble, naturalize and legitimate."[34] The notion of the innate complement of white-red combination would later become metaphor for twentieth century Virginia Indians and advocates who articulated an authentic Indian identity within the confines of an exclusively White–Indian ancestral past.

In addition, to further his sexualized idea of preference, Jefferson exploited the time-worn myth of African women copulating with apes, to establish within the Chain of Being a hierarchy of sexual desire wherein "each race or species [desired] to couple with that race or species above it on the chain of 'preference' for its greater beauty."[35] Therefore, Jefferson invoked a "thoroughly racialized" definition of preference and desire in which "Preference for a person is imagined as desire for the race traits that supposedly distinguish them."[36] Yet, just as the Negro-ape association, always conceived in sexualized terms, invoked an image of "beastly copulation" and "unnatural mixture," it lent credence to the notion that interracial sex and marriage were perverse and deviant.[37]

Incidentally, Jefferson's opponents would use his own logic against him as they engaged in an unrelenting character assassination for his "alleged" affair with Sally Hemings. In poems written during the period called Port Folio poems, Jefferson's opponents asserted that his desire for Hemings "must be to desire her black race traits and thus to be a perverse man, whereas to desire white traits, by implication, proves one's good taste."[38] Not only did Jefferson's relationship with Hemings bring into question his honor, it also brought into question his race as many interpreted his attraction to mean a negation of his Whiteness. As a result, Jefferson underwent a metamorphosis and was transformed from White to Black. As Lemire contended, "linking Jefferson's lust for Sally with his own blackness . . . makes the point that the objects of people's sexual attraction are not only what make people honorable or not but also comprise their racial membership. Jefferson literally loses the Whiteness that made him 'THE PEOPLE'S MAN' because of his inter-racial lust."[39]

Jefferson's interracial relationship never had quite the literal consequences Lemire imagines. His supposed metamorphosis from White to Black never went beyond the imaginary creations of the Port Folio poems created by his opponents as a part of their political assassination campaign to thwart the President's bid for reelection. Despite their best efforts Jefferson won reelection and remains a favored son of Virginia to this day.[40] However, Jefferson's sexualized idea of preference which linked sexual desire to racial membership, as will be discussed further in chapter 2, was literally made policy during the early nineteenth century as American Indians faced the threat of detribalization and dispossession of their reservation lands because of their intermixture and association with people of African descent.

In addition to his paranoia of Black intermixture as a justification for Black repatriation, Jefferson justified his Black deportation policy on political grounds. On the political front Jefferson proposed that emancipated slaves be deported due to "Deep rooted prejudices entertained by the whites; ten thousand recollections, by the blacks, of the injuries they have sustained; new provocations; the real distinctions nature has made; many other circumstances, will divide us into parties, and produce convulsions which will probably never end but in the extermination of one or the other race."[41] But what about the indigenous population for which Jefferson so eagerly advocated amalgamation? Did not Whites entertain deep prejudices towards American Indians? Anglo-Americans had a long list of pejoratives for American Indians—"many of the same pejoratives that had been applied to Africans appear in descriptions for Indians."[42] The difference was that the disparaging attitudes towards American Indians were a result of cultural difference and not racial difference. The English thought American Indians to be "biologically admirable but socially abhorrent; nature had blessed them, but nurture had cursed them."[43] While Anglos viewed American Indians as possessing physical beauty, they "harbored a deep prejudice against almost all aspects of Indian culture."[44] Despite the fact that the American Indian could not, in the words of the old adage "change his skin," he could, however, change his culture and thus become a civilized Anglo-Saxon. At least this is what Jefferson and those who embraced an assimilationist policy had hoped. Nevertheless Jefferson's plan had two flaws. The first flaw was that the amalgamation policy was not endorsed by the majority of Anglo society. Indians were not viewed as potential equals, but "as a degraded savage and an encumbrance on coveted lands."[45]

The second flaw with Jefferson's plan was that American Indians opposed it because amalgamation would result in their extermination. Jefferson certainly was aware of this as he stated to Benjamin Hawkins that the natural progression of English–Indian relations was that the Indians become U.S. citizens and thus one people with the Whites. This clearly demonstrated Jefferson's deep prejudice toward American Indians. In essence, amalgamation entailed that the "Indians" would have to "adopt 'white' America's language, laws, and customs" and "cease being Indians."[46] By the close of the eighteenth century, after almost two centuries of European contact, American Indians were demonstrating their firm resistance to the annihilation of their cultures and tribal identity. The Powhatan remnants, as demonstrated by Armstrong Archer and many other Algonquian people, experienced slow cultural change, even those who had lost their lands. Did Jefferson really believe American Indians would simply roll over and become English? Certainly, the slow cultural change and the recent history of English–Indian relations, which led to the American gentry's declaration of independence, suggest otherwise.

That American Indians had not embraced the Anglo assimilationist agenda is evident when viewing the list of grievances Jefferson outlined in the Declaration of Independence. Among the grievances Jefferson listed against George III he stated, "He has endeavored to prevent the population of these States; for that purpose obstructing the laws of naturalization of Foreigners; refusing to pass others to encourage their migrations hither and raising the conditions of new Appropriations of Lands." During the years leading up to the American Revolution, Jefferson, along with his colleagues George Washington, Patrick Henry, and George Mason, became a land speculator. They were looking to profit from the annexation of Kentucky as well as westward expansion. Jefferson attempted to obtain patents during the winter of 1768–1769 for seven thousand acres of land to the west of the Appalachian Mountains. His plan was to sell them off as farmsteads of about two hundred acres a piece. Jefferson was confident that he would have no problem finding buyers.[47]

In addition, Jefferson, in an unprecedented move, became a partner in three land firms which would have resulted in his obtaining seventeen thousand acres of lands belonging to the Indians. However, between 1763 and 1774, the British Parliament passed several measures that prevented Jefferson and his colleagues from laying legal claim to their patents. Also, in an effort to thwart further Anglo encroachment, the Shawnees and Delawares began a crusade to build a pan-Indian alliance for the protection of their lands. If Jefferson was suffering from historical amnesia, these coalition building tribes were not. They were well aware that European advancement meant American Indian decimation. It was quite evident that the Virginia gentry's attempt to acquire more land would result in "new provocations" and further strain Anglo-Indian relations. Britain was not willing to break its alliance with the American Indian population. This was due more to the Old Country's effort to avoid a costly war than any moral obligation on Britain's part. Yet, inadvertently, Britain's American Indian alliance resulted in the war for American independence. It seems that American Indian "diplomats powerfully influenced the most important decision white Americans ever made."[48] Although the Patriots had some tribal allies, the large majority of American Indians fought alongside the British. They were quite aware that a Patriot victory would result in the demise of their homeland, culture and tribal identity. Subsequently, it did not take long after the War of Independence for the new found government to enact its plan. Once independence was declared, all legislation restricting land patents was repealed. Thus, Jefferson's post-independence policy towards the Indians seems to have been less of an attempt towards philanthropy and more an effort to recoup his earlier losses. As Vine Deloria contended, "There was never a time when the white man said he was trying to help the Indians get into the mainstream of American life that he did not also demand that the Indian give up land, water, minerals, timber, and other resources which would enrich the white man."[49] Jefferson told a group of American Indians visiting with him in 1808, "You will become one with us . . . Your blood will mix with ours, and will spread with ours across this great land."[50] In essence, the currency that Jefferson offered American Indians in exchange for their lands was Whiteness.

Jefferson's assimilationist agenda seems to have only included those tribes from which he sought to acquire new lands—but what about the Virginia Indians? Jefferson dealt with this question briefly in Query XI of the Notes. Ironically, Jefferson viewed this group within the rhetoric of the vanishing Indian. He began this query with an overview of the aboriginal population upon European contact. According to Jefferson, whose history was derived from the work of Captain John Smith, upon first English arrival in 1607, at least forty tribes inhabited the region. He divided these tribes among three confederacies: the Powhatans, the Mannahoacs, and Monacans. He next provided information regarding their languages, and social structure. Jefferson then discussed the approximate territorial boundaries of the Powhatans and the number of their inhabitants. He also briefly mentioned tribes such as the Meherrins and Tuteloes which bordered the Carolinas. Next, Jefferson arranged the tribes on a chart by tribe, country (county), city/town, and the number of warriors. This chart was outdated, however, as the information was based on 1607 and 1669 figures. Regarding the American Indian population in Virginia, Jefferson provided a matter-of-fact overview, void of the romantic language used to refute Buffon. Just as Jefferson's statements in the original draft of the Declaration of Independence absolved American colonists of any responsibility for the perpetuation of the peculiar institution, his statements in the *Notes* absolved the colonists of any responsibility regarding the decimation of Virginian tribes. Concerning their loss of land, Jefferson assured his readers that it was not the result of conquest, but of purchase. Their numbers were reduced due to "Spirituous liquors, the small pox, war, and an abridgement of territory." While Jefferson stated that the Massawomecs constantly harassed the other two confederacies, he failed to mention the 1622 and 1644 Powhatan uprisings, and Bacon's 1676 Rebellion which pitted Anglo invader against Virginia aborigine. Nevertheless, Jefferson continued his discourse by providing details of American Indian burial practices. He concluded the chapter by lamenting the loss of the aboriginal languages and provided a list of tribes that remained in a "respectable and independent form."[51] None of the tribes on Jefferson's list were those residing in Virginia. The exclusion of Virginian Indians from Jefferson's list of Indians who remained in "respectable and independent form" drew a line in the sand and separated those Indians who were fit for amalgamation with Whites and those who were not. It is clear that he had little regard for the Virginia Indians as opposed to those he had yet to conquer. Of the remnants he wrote:

> Very little can now be discovered of the subsequent history of these tribes severally. The *Chickahominies* removed, about the year 1661, to Mattapony river. Their chief, with one from each of the tribes of the Pamunkies and Mattaponies, attended the treaty of Albany in 1685. This seems to have been the last chapter in their history. They retained however their separate name so late as 1705, and were at length blended with the Pamunkies and Mattaponies, and exist at present only under their names. There remain of the *Mattaponies* three or four men only, and they have more negro than Indian blood in them. They have lost their language, have reduced themselves, by voluntary sales, to about fifty acres of land, which lie on the river of their own name, and have, from time to time, been joining the Pamunkies, from whom they are distant but 10 miles. The *Pamunkies* are reduced to about 10 or 12 men, tolerably pure from mixture with other colours. The older ones among them preserve their language in a small degree, which are the last vestiges on earth, as far as we know, of the Powhatan language. They have about 300 acres of very fertile land, on

Pamunkey river, so encompassed by water that a gate shuts in the whole. Of the *Nottoways,* not a male is left. A few women constitute the remains of that tribe. They are seated on Nottoway river, in Southampton county, on very fertile lands. At a very early period, certain lands were marked out and appropriated to these tribes, and were kept from encroachment by the authority of the laws. They have usually had trustees appointed, whose duty was to watch over their interests, and guard them from insult and injury. The *Monacans* and their friends, better known latterly by the name of *Tuscaroras,* were probably connected with the Massawomecs, or Five Nations.[52]

Jefferson envisioned the American Indians of Virginia as historical artifact, rather than present day reality. In Jefferson's estimation, the Virginia Indians were all but extinct. There were those who relocated to territories outside of the region. The remaining remnants sought allegiances amongst each other, but their numbers were so decimated, their survival would be no less than miraculous. Jefferson's population estimates for the Algonquian Powhatan remnants as well as their Iroquoian Nottoway neighbors, however, were grossly inaccurate. Regarding the Powhatan remnants, James Mooney, a late nineteenth century authority on southeastern Indians, estimated that their numbers during Jefferson's time would have been at approximately 1,000. The Nottoway, as will be discussed further in chapter 7, numbered at approximately seventeen with an even distribution of males and females according to an 1808 census. In a July 17, 1820, correspondence to Jefferson regarding the Nottoway language, Peter Stephen Du Ponceau, who succeeded him as President of the American Philosophical Society, estimated the number of Nottoway domiciled on the remainder of the reservation as twenty-seven men, women and children. Currently seven Powhatan remnants, two Nottoway remnants and a remnant of the Monacan Nation represent the state recognized tribes of Virginia. It is safe to say that Jefferson's memorializing of the Virginia Indians was indeed quite premature.[53]

In Jefferson's estimation, however, the Virginia tribe's diminished population was not the only thing that threatened their survival. Jefferson appeared to put a premium upon Indianness based on the amount of admixture of those tribes which, while on the peripheral of Virginian society, remained firm within the Commonwealth. Helen Rountree contended that Jefferson's assertion pertaining to the Pamunkey being "tolerably pure from mixture with other colours" meant that the tribe was free of any admixture, or that they had only mixed with Whites.[54] Yet, according to Jefferson's historicity of White–Indian relations, the only transactions which occurred between the two peoples were business transactions resulting in the purchase of lands. While a few prominent Virginians prided themselves on being descendants of Pocahontas and John Rolfe, in Jefferson's estimation the two peoples had hardly intermixed. Contrary to Jefferson's earlier construction of a national identity based on an Indian Other, he put great distance between the White and American Indian populations in Virginia. Jefferson's construction of the Virginia Indians was typical of the way in which eighteenth century colonists constructed Indian Others, which was along two axes. The first was "the noble savage—in terms of the positive and negative values that could be assigned to Indians and that could then be reflected back upon a Self, either as cultural critique or colonial legitimation. Equally important, they imagined a second axis focused not on Indian good or evil, but upon the relative distance that Indian Others were situated from this Self-in-the-making."[55]

Subsequently, in constructing a Virginian identity Jefferson "illuminated his conception of white Virginians as a distinct 'people'" which held American Indians aloof from the White population.[56] Jefferson was well aware that the cornerstone of Virginian identity hinged on the racial allegiance to safeguard the Anglo-Saxon gene pool, hence the stringent anti-miscegenation laws. Even if the anti-miscegenation laws were relaxed to include American Indians, Jefferson believed the Virginia aborigines' intermixture with Blacks placed them outside the possibility of intermixing with Whites. As a result, he sought to construct an identity detached from both aborigines and Blacks thereby propagating the myth of racial purity. In the final analysis, according to Jefferson, the American Indian population in Virginia only mixed among themselves and/ or with Blacks. With the Mattaponi's association with the Pamunkey, which could introduce the stain of Blackness among the remnant tribes, Virginia Indians were doomed as Jefferson quantified their Indianness based on their level of admixture with African Americans. This is salient in his comparison of the Pamunkey and Mattaponi tribes. In Jefferson's estimation the Pamunkey were more Indian than the Mattaponi whom he claimed had more "Negro blood" than Indian. As Jefferson asserted in the *Notes,* the blood of one race infused with that of the other will always result in the negation of one to the other.[57] Jefferson's rhetoric of blood presages the mid nineteenth-century use of the term "amalgamation" implying "that something biological and thus quantifiable is happening when two people 'mix' and that that biological act is of more substance than behavior."[58] Thus, long before it became codified in tribal, state and federal policy, Jefferson gave credence to the saying, "When is an Indian no longer an Indian? When he has Negro 'blood.'"

Jefferson's denial of Anglo amalgamation with the Virginia tribes and his assertion that they had interbred with Blacks, reflects nothing less than the sentiments that were espoused by twentieth century eugenicists in an effort to safe guard the so-called racial integrity of Virginia's White population. This campaign to "preserve the integrity of the white race" which sought to, as Michael Dorr suggested, "deny enslaved [and free] Africans their liberties which included . . . procreative freedom," presaged twentieth-century Virginian eugenicists who sought to "deprive the personal procreative liberties of blacks, poor whites, and the 'mentally defective' to prevent their destroying the lives and people of Virginia through genetic pollution."[59] Similarly in regards to Jeffersonian thought and its effect upon eugenicists, Peter Onuf wrote:

> The presence of two peoples in one country (Virginia), and their conspicuous tendency to mix, jeopardized the integrity of both. Sexual selection and family formation constitute the critical moment in the history of a people. But this was a moment of general vulnerability when sexual liaisons could transgress and compromise the "natural" boundaries that distinguished nations [peoples]. Jefferson's advocacy of scientifically managed breeding may have reduced "man" to the level of "domestic animals," pointing ominously towards the eugenics theories of later generations of scientific racists. But his primary intention was to secure the sexual frontier between two nations, translating his fantasy of a clear (impregnable?) boundary into a morally imperative law of nature.[60]

While both Dorr and Onuf aptly demonstrated Jefferson's influence on later eugenics and scientific racial theorists, their tendency to remove American Indians from the summation of their analysis demonstrates a continued problematic of conceptualizing race within a biracial paradigm. Although Dorr stated that the racial integrity campaign infringed upon the "procreative liberties" of Virginia's marginalized population, he failed to include American Indians on his list. Similarly, Onuf's assessment of Jefferson's negotiations of racial boundaries only mentions the existence of two races in Virginia when there were at minimum three. While Jefferson's goal may indeed have been "to secure the sexual frontier between the two nations" (Anglos and Africans), that frontier had been under British colonial occupation for almost two centuries. At the time of Jefferson's writing, Virginians were at war with Britain for their independence. If victorious, they would redefine their identity and region under new terms. As the renaming and redefining of indigenous people has always been fundamental to colonialism, Jefferson also intended to secure that frontier by "sexually colonizing" the Virginia Indian population through their reclassification as Black lest they use their Indian identity to pass into the White race and introduce that "spurious issue" into the White gene pool (a project Walter Plecker took up in the twentieth century). This would, in turn, redraw racial lines along a biracial instead of tri-racial axis.[61] Thus, the effort to preserve White racial integrity in Virginia not only infringed on the "procreative freedom" of Blacks, but also on those of American Indian ancestry in general and those of Afro-Indian ancestry in specific.

The seemingly overt contradictions in Jefferson's life have earned him "the sobriquet of American Sphinx."[62] Nonetheless, Jefferson's thoughts and actions in Queries VI, XI, and XIV of the *Notes* appear less paradoxical regarding his attitudes and policies towards Africans and American Indians. The "sage of Monticello" had spoken and provided his scholarly opinion regarding those things he had observed of men White, Red, and Black. This "tricolor metaphor" underscored the taxonomy which placed Whites at the top of a pseudo-racial hierarchy that mandated its preservation at all cost. As Jefferson once stated, "The law of self-preservation overrules the laws of obligation to others."[63] In the case of Virginia, his self-preservation effort required the deportation of Africans and the extermination of American Indian identity. Jefferson was not so much the creator of the moral, political and scientific theories espoused in the *Notes* which later informed the Virginia Racial Integrity Act of 1924 (and other eugenics efforts throughout the nation). He was merely chiming in with the harmonizing sentiments of his day. Nevertheless, as David Walker prophetically warned "the coloured citizens of the World" forty years after the publication of the *Notes,* sentiments espoused by such a revered and beloved son of Virginia (and America) would not pass into oblivion.[64] Indeed, it is a legacy with which we continue to struggle to overcome.

TWO

Redefining Race and Identity:
The Indian–Negro Confusion and the Changing State of Black–Indian Relations in the Nineteenth Century

And there was the Indian–Negro confusion. There were Negroes who were part Indian and who lived on reservations, and Indians who had children who lived in towns as Negroes, and Negroes who were Indians and traveled back and forth between the groups with no trouble.

—RALPH ELLISON

The reconfiguration of the identities of African and American Indian peoples and the confluence that ensued from their social intermingling had, by the nineteenth century, resulted in what Ellison aptly dubbed "the Indian–Negro confusion."[1] Despite White Virginians' obsession with racial purity and strict anti-miscegenation statutes, such restrictions did not apply to the non-White population, which comprised Negroes, Indians, and mulattoes among other groups. While the definitions of these categories would prove flexible over time and were not applied with any measurable consistency, the reality is that during the course of American and Virginian history, peoples of African, American Indian or Afro-Indian descent, were included in these categories throughout the colonial period. Africans and American Indians freely intermarried and cohabitated since many shared a common lot as chattel slaves or free disenfranchised citizens. They also shared racial labels during the antebellum period as Virginia identified its nonwhite population with terms largely associated in contemporary American society with people of African descent such as Negro, mulatto, colored, free Negro, free person of color, or Black. It was not until 1870 that the category "Indian" was recognized and included on the federal census; despite this, American Indians of whatever "degree" (i.e., full blood, half blood, or quarter blood) continued to be defined with the same racial labels as their African American counterparts. Incidentally, with racial mingling occurring between Africans and American Indians during a large portion of the colonial and antebellum periods, in addition to the cross sharing of racial labels, the line between who was American Indian and who was African American became blurred. Notwithstanding, the tendency to manipulate the racial identity of American Indians was a self-serving objective on the part of the White settler class turned American citizen to justify the involuntary appropriation of American Indian lands and to increase the slave population.

The imposition of racialized identities based on the hegemonic notions of a Western value system underscored by a racial hierarchy resulted from what Michael Omi and Howard Winant identified as racial formation, "the socio-historical process by which racial categories are created, inhabited, transformed, and destroyed . . . it is a process of historically situated projects in which human bodies and social structures are represented and organized."[2] Such representation was the result of the United States' centuries-long "racial dictatorship" resulting in:

> three very large consequences: first, they defined "American" identity as white, as the negation of racialized "otherness"—at first largely African and indigenous . . . Second, racial dictatorship organized (albeit in an incoherent and contradictory fashion) the "color line" rendering the fundamental division in U.S. society. The dictatorship elaborated, articulated, and drove racial divisions not only through institutions, but also through psyches, extending up to our own time the racial obsessions of the conquest and slavery periods. Third, racial dictatorship consolidated the oppositional racial consciousness and organization originally framed by marronage and slave revolts, by indigenous resistance, and

by nationalisms of various sorts. Just as conquest created the "native" where once there had been Pequot, Iroquois, or Tutelo, so too it created the "Black" where once there had been Asante or Ovimbunda, Yoruba or Bakong.[3]

Winant and Omi's list must be expanded to include a fourth consequence of racial dictatorship: that of blood politics, which unevenly defined the criteria for "Black" and "native" categories resituating human bodies and social structures which often resulted in the disruption of family units as described by Ellison. America's racial formation project has been widely based on the Anglo Saxon's fixation with "Blackness," resulting in "a tendency to define all part-African persons by their degree of 'blackness' rather than by their entire ancestry."[4] Throughout American history a person's legal status has been based on the percentage of perceived Blackness beginning at one-eighth, which later increased to one-fourth and by the twentieth century was defined by any ascertainable amount of Negro "blood." Hence, Black identity became largely defined by what sociologists call the law of hypo-descent, popularly known as the "one-drop rule." In other words, one drop of Negro "blood," makes a person a Negro, negating all other ancestry. On the contrary, American Indian identity not only required an absence of African ancestry, but it also comprised a blood quantum requirement—a substantial amount of Indian ancestry in order for an individual or tribe to be considered authentic. As Karen Blu aptly stated, "It may only take one drop of Black blood to make a person a Negro, but it takes a lot of Indian blood to make a person a 'real' Indian."[5] Consequently, the process of defining who was "Black" and who was "Indian" took on two opposite extremes.

The use of a double standard in defining Black and Indian racial categories has resulted in the over representation of Blacks on one hand and obscurity of Indians on the other. As Jack Forbes quipped, "whites . . . are always finding blacks, and they are always losing Indians."[6] In this same vein, Thomasina Jordan often admonished people to "look for the indelible thread of red in the tapestry of the American people."[7] One must also look for the indelible thread of Red and Black, which has woven peoples of African American, Native American, and Afro-Indian descent into a complex synthesis of cultural, political, and social relations. Examining the ways in which Virginia authorities manipulated race and identity by redefining racial terms and exploring the use of the notion of blood quantum to determine American Indian identity will effectively trace that thread and demonstrate the effects of the politics of blood and race on nineteenth-century Black–Indian interactions.

The year 1619 has been earmarked as the earliest date of arrival for "Negroes," to the English colony; yet they accompanied Spanish North American expeditions almost a century before the English arrived in Virginia. There is also evidence that they cohabited with the aborigines in the early seventeenth-century. In 1603, seven Negroes escaped from Saint Augustine with some maintaining their freedom and "marrying Indian women." Franciscans found Negroes and Indians cohabitating together in Florida and "repeatedly admonished the aborigines that it was an unclean thing to keep Negro mistresses."[8]

Yet, can one assume that the use of the term Negro as used in the sixteenth and seventeenth centuries referred to people of African descent? While the term "Negro" is often interpreted in our modern time to mean people of African descent, sixteenth-century Spanish definitions of the term are shrouded in ethnic and racial ambiguity as the word "negro" was not synonymous with African. The earliest use of the term can be traced to late medieval Italy and the Iberian Peninsula. People were classified in diverse categories among which were "nero, nigri, nigre, negro, negre, preto (black)."[9] Negro, or any of its associated terms, did not denote a particular race, ancestry, or ethnicity. It was usually a simple description for "perceived color or appearance."[10] Negro was used by various European nations as a broad term which was applied to numerous groups of non-white people. Hence what is meant by the term Negro as well as equivalent terms is "a range of color shades—for humans generally dark brown—always less extreme than true black but approaching the 'darkness' of black, and also including very often people of medium shades of brown whose color seems to contrast sharply with white or 'clear' shades."[11]

Regarding its use as a descriptor for American Indian people, Europeans often referred to the indigenous populations of their various colonies as Negroes. For example, in the Portuguese colony of Brazil, Indians were called "*negros da terra*" meaning "Negroes of the land" and Africans were called "*negroes da Guine*" meaning "Blacks of Guinea."

At times Portuguese authorities used the terms "indio" and "negro" interchangeably when referring to the native population of Brazil. This practice continued into the early eighteenth century. However, by the mid-eighteenth century, when slavery in the region became increasingly Africanized, the Portuguese authorities issued a decree that the term Negro would no longer be used for Indians, but for African slaves exclusively; by this time, many of the "*negros da terra*" were mixed-bloods.[12]

Due to the Europeans' broad use of the term Negro, it appears that the racial identity of the "Negars" brought ashore the James River in 1619 remains ambiguous as well. John Smith recorded in his *Generall Historie* of Virginia, "About the last of August came in a dutch man of warre that sold us twenty Negars."[13] These twenty were stolen from a Spanish vessel by Dutch pirates off the West Indian coast. The names of eleven of the twenty captives have been preserved which bear their Spanish affiliation. One captive was a Negro woman named Angelo. According to Helen Catterall this name is not common in England or found in Africa. Additional names were "Anthony and Isabella" and "there were also two other Anthonys, two Johns, and William, Frances, Edward, and Margarett, whose names may or may not have been anglicizations of Antonio, Juan, Guillen, Francisca, Eduardo, and Margarita."[14]

The use of the term "Negars" to describe the new arrivals is not without significance. The Dutch adopted the term from the Spanish as they had no such equivalent in their own language. Well into the eighteenth century the Dutch used "*Moor and Moriaan*" when referring to "Black Africans and not negro or neger"[15] Similar to the Spanish, it appears that the Dutch used the word Negro as a general term for slave. Yet, the early English definition for Negro remains ambiguous. It does not appear that the term was initially synonymous with slave due to a large portion of the free population in England and in Virginia having this classification.[16] In the Virginia colony the colonial legislation often used the categories Negroes, Indians and mulattoes to describe free and enslaved people. For example, Chapter XXIII of a 1705 statute which defined slaves as real estate referred to "All Negro, mulatto, and Indian slaves."[17] A 1723 statute that established a number of free people as tithables referred to "All free Negroes, mulattoes and Indians."[18] Was the term Negro, as used in the above statutes, synonymous with African?

The English in the sixteenth century "were referring to the people of Africa as Moors, and then later as Blackamoors, Ethiopians, and negroes."[19] While the above 1705 statute referred to Negroes, mulattoes and Indians, another 1705 statue asserted, "And for further Christian care and usage of all Christian servants it is enacted that no Negro, mulatto or Indian, although Christian, or Jew, *Moor,* Mohammedan, or other infidel, shall purchase any Christian servant, *except of their own complexion,* or such as we declared slaves by this act" (emphasis mine).[20]

What is of interest here is that the Virginia legislature identified "Negroes" and "Moors" separately. If the term Moor was used for people of African descent, then who were the Negroes in the above passage? The same question can be asked regarding the term "Moor." It was also translated with great flexibility and could include people of Arab descent.[21] In addition, Negro was not synonymous with "Black" because it also encompassed "brown." While a definite answer may not be attainable perhaps the reference in the above passage regarding the disallowance of these and others to purchase Christian (White) slaves, but only those of their own "complexion," demonstrates that the English use of the term also denoted color perception and not racial category.

The Oxford English Dictionary provides an 1827 example of the use of the terms "black" and "negro," which further demonstrates the broad use of these terms: "The great muffled drum, aye played on by a black man; in this case an African neeger, sax feet." If the term "Black" was used exclusively for African, there would have been no need for clarity in the latter part of the sentence. Also, the use of the term "African neeger" suggests that the term "Negro" was also broadly used in nineteenth-century Britain as well as in the United States. As the California Supreme Court declared in 1854, "The word 'Black' may include all negroes, but the term Negro does not include all black persons."[22]

Often, the term "Negro" included people of American Indian or part American Indian ancestry as well. This certainly was the case in colonial and antebellum Virginia. In 1670, 40,000 people, including "2,000 'black slaves,'" were reported as residents of the Virginia colony; however, the colony did not have that many Africans. There was, however, a large number of Indians in the area, which likely comprised part of the population of the reported "blacks."[23]

Many American Indians imported to or exported from the colonies were listed as Negroes. Approximately sixty-nine Indians were included among "a list of 'Negroes'" brought to Virginia from North Carolina from 1710 to 1718. A similar occurrence happened in New York from 1715 to 1736. A number of studies have shown that, "many slaves of probable (or stated)" American Indian ancestry imported into this colony "from Campeche, Jamaica, Honduras, the Carolinas, and Virginia" were listed as Negroes.[24] People of Indian or part-Indian ancestry were listed as Negroes well into the colonial and antebellum periods. A 1786 runaway slave advertisement for "an East Indian negro man called Jean, a slave born" demonstrates the broad use of the term "Negro" in Virginia.[25] The term Negro eventually became synonymous with slave in the Spanish, Dutch, and Portuguese colonies. It also became so in the English colonies as well. Nevertheless, although slave became virtually synonymous with Negro, Negro was not synonymous with African. Consequently, the term Negro was never legally defined by the Virginia legislature. Thus, from the outset it appears that the racial identity of people of color within the Virginia colony was ambiguous and remained so in years to come.[26]

Among the population residing in colonial and antebellum Virginia were people designated as mulattoes. In contemporary society people often assume that a mulatto was a person of mixed European–African heritage; however, similar to the term Negro, mulatto was also used broadly and included anyone of mixed ancestry. In 1705 Virginia defined a mulatto as "the child of an Indian, and the child, grandchild or great grandchild of a negro shall be deemed, accounted, held, and taken as a mulatto."[27] This definition included people of European-Indian ancestry and "all part-Africans to the one-eighth degree."[28] The definition, however, also reflected a double standard. A child with one Indian parent and one White parent was a mulatto, but a child with one Negro grandparent or one Negro great-grandparent was still considered a mulatto. Clearly, this presages the disparity in defining African American and American Indian peoples that would become standard U.S. policy. In 1785 the definition of mulatto was modified to state, "Every person of whose grandfathers or grandmothers anyone is and shall have been a Negro, although all of his progenitors, except that descending from the

Negro shall have been white persons, shall be deemed mulatto, and so every person who shall have one-fourth or more Negro blood shall in like manner be deemed a mulatto."[29] As late as the mid-nineteenth century, people of American Indian and Afro-Indian ancestry were listed as mulatto. Thus, during the antebellum years, American Indians were seldom designated as such even in King William, King and Queen, Caroline, Essex, Southampton, and Northampton counties where there was a concentration of Indians. Inhabitants of the Pamunkey and Mattaponi reservations, as well as the Nottoway and Gingaskin reservations, were listed as mulattoes. Even those of no apparent "Negro" admixture, like the Nansemond Indians of Norfolk County, Virginia, could be classified as mulatto. The latter case is quite significant as Jack Forbes noted:

> The Nansemond Indian group living near Portsmouth were classified as "M." This is especially significant since the Nansemonds were categorized as "I" (for Indian) on an 1860 local tax roll. At various dates, certificates were apparently issued to Nansemond Indian people, such as the following: William Bass, the bearer, tall, swarthy, dark eyes . . . is of English and Indian descent with no negro blood, numbered as a Nansemond by his own choosing. This was in 1742. But in the following century many Nansemonds were harassed as "mulattoes" and listed in the 1850 census with "M" after their names. Nonetheless, a local county court ruled in 1833 that they were "not free negroes or mulattoes, but are of Indian descent."[30]

As the case of the Nansemonds demonstrate, people of American Indian descent, as well as any person of color could be assigned multiple racial identities throughout their life time as designations of mulatto, free person of color, free Negro, or even Black (mostly used by the United States census) had no fixed definitions. In addition, because interracial mixing was more the rule than the exception, the precision of racial identity proved problematic. By the end of the eighteenth century, racial intermixture had become so widespread that many classed as mulattoes no longer retained the physical markers to indicate an African ancestral connection. Many would simply be regarded as Whites or Indians.[31] Yet many mulattoes of a combination of racial mixtures retained African features. As a result, the courts were filled with judicial cases that put a person's racial identity on trial. There were numerous cases all over the

South in which a plaintiff of ambiguous ancestry attempted to prove that they were of Indian rather than of Negro ancestry. Often these cases were decided by a jury—a difficult task given the imprecise criterion established by the law in deciding if the plaintiff was White, Negro, mulatto, or Indian. The jury was expected to render a verdict based on inspection. However, these verdicts proved inconsistent, as two people with the same reported racial composition or even the same ancestry could receive two entirely different verdicts. Hence, racial demarcations became so blurred that racial categories were impossible to maintain with any amount of precision.

American Indians are largely absent from the conventional discourse on American slavery. Much attention has been given to their role as slave holders and slave catchers; yet they were also the victims of chattel slavery. As numerous Virginia legislative statutes illustrate, Africans were not the only slaves in Virginia, or in the United States for that matter; nevertheless, "The association between Black people and the enslavement in American culture has become instinctive, natural."[32] As the late Sioux scholar Vine Deloria stated, "It is fortunate that we [Native Americans] were never slaves. We gave up land instead of life and labor."[33] However, nothing can be further from the truth. The peculiar institution comprised a multi-racial population that included American Indians. Land dispossession, disease, and war indeed contributed to the decline of the American Indian population; but the American Indian slave trade was also instrumental in the decimation of Native peoples as Charles Levasser reported in 1700, "the greatest traffic between the English and the savages is the trade of slaves which the natives take from their nations whom they war with continuously . . . this greatly destroys the nations which are our neighbors."[34] The slave population in the Americas underwent three stages: during the first stage the slave population was comprised of American Indians, during the second stage the population was comprised of American Indians and Africans, and during the third stage the population became more Africanized in regions like the Atlantic seaboard of North America. This in turn obscured slavery's American Indian origins as well as the origins of numerous people of American Indian or part-American Indian ancestry who remained entrapped in the peculiar institution.[35]

It is impossible to estimate the number of Indian slaves in any given English colony since, among other factors, "extant Indian slaves either receive no mention, or are classed with negro slaves without distinction."[36] Nevertheless, colonial records provide some clues regarding the impact of Indian slavery within the colonies. New England and the southern colonies had considerable concentrations of Indian slaves. Indeed, due to the economic structure of the South, it is not surprising to find that the highest concentrations of American Indian slaves were found in the southern colonies.

Much like the French, the Spanish, and Indians themselves, the English obtained the majority of their Indian slaves through war. As the result of the 1622 Opechancanough uprising, it was advocated that the captives be forced to work in mines or on Summer Islands. Thus, while some were retained within the Virginia colony (primarily women and children) others (primarily men) were exported out of the colony and traded. Again, Indian war captives were enslaved during the aftermath of the second Opechancanough uprising, which occurred in 1644. Evidence that the practice of Indian slavery occurred in the early Virginia colony as a customary law can be demonstrated by a 1655 statute regarding Indian hostages. This is the first time the word "slave" is used in Virginia legislation pertaining to Indians. Act I states, "Indian children brought in as hostages are not to be treated as slaves."[37] Apparently, adult hostages could be held as slaves. Sometimes Indians were sold to the English by their own countrymen as in the case of an Indian boy named Weetoppen who was sold by the "King of Waineoakes [Weyanokes] to an English woman Eliza Short on July 2, 1659."[38] The deed was later nullified by the House of Burgess on the grounds that the King had no right to sell the boy because he was a Powhatan and desired baptism. However in a letter to Robert Smith in 1668, Governor Berkeley, then Militia Commander in Rappahannock County, proposed to wage a war of extinction on the "Doagges" of Northern Virginia and to take their women and children as spoils of war to be sold into slavery. The Rappahannock court approved the measure.[39]

Although initially there were laws that forbade the enslavement of Indians, by the last quarter of the seventeenth century, Indian slavery was sanctioned by the courts. Act V of a 1670 statute forbade free Negroes or

Indians from purchasing Whites, but "they are not debarred from buying any of their own nation."[40] This act clearly demonstrates that Indians made up a portion of the slave (and slaveholding) population in Virginia. In the same year, a question arose regarding the status of Indian war captives sold to the English. The dispute involved whether these captives should be "servants for life or terms of years."[41] Act XII determined, "it is enacted that all servants not being Christian imported by shipping shall be slaves for their lives, but what shall come by land shall serve, if boys or girls, until thirty years of age; if men or women, twelve years and no longer."[42] American Indians certainly received an advantage over African slaves as the majority of them came by land. Nonetheless, Nathaniel Bacon during his 1676 coup declared all Indians taken as spoils to be slaves.[43] Although the act was repealed in February of 1677, the repeal did not serve as an emancipation proclamation for those already enslaved.[44]

Two years later, in an effort to boost military morale, Bacon's law, which provided legal sanction for the enslavement of Indian war captives, was reinstated. Act I of 1679 stated, "And for the better encouragement and more orderly government of the soldiers, that what Indian prisoners or other plunder shall be taken in warre, shall be free purchase to the soldier takeing the same."[45] The enslavement of Indians was legally sanctioned in Act I of 1682, which stated "all Indians, which shall be sold by our neighboring Indians, or any others trafficking with us for slaves, are hereby adjudged deemed and taken to be slaves to all intents and purposes any law, usage, or custom to the contrary notwithstanding."[46]

Act IX of 1691 and Act XII of 1705, which declared that "It is enacted that there be a free and open trade with all Indians and at all times," are often interpreted as the legislative acts that abolished Indian slavery. Yet once again these acts did not serve as an emancipation proclamation for those already enslaved as can be demonstrated by the acts of 1705, which deemed "all Negro, mulatto, and Indian slaves" as real estate, or 1723, which forbade the emancipation of "Negro or Indian" slaves "except for meritorious service."[47] The acts of 1691 and 1705 did nothing to put an end to Indian slavery in Virginia during the colonial period. A 1709 slave conspiracy provides indisputable evidence of the continued enslavement of American Indians in Virginia. Early in 1709 authorities discovered a slave plot organized by Negro and Indian slaves in the counties of James

City, Surry, and Isle of Wight. On March 24, 1709, an investigation led by the Governor in Council found that, "a Late Dangerous Conspiracy formed and carried on by greater numbers of ye said negroes and Indians slaves for making their Escape by force from ye Service of their masters, and for ye Destroying and cutting off Such of her Majesties Subjects as Should oppose their Design."[48] By the conclusion of the investigation, numerous slaves had been "punished and Discharged"; however, the three men believed to be the lead conspirators, Scipio, Salvadore, and Tom Shaw remained confined. A fourth conspirator, Peter, remained at large and eluded capture for at least a year. The final fate of the men remains unknown.

In addition, during the period of 1710 to 1718, which covers the years of the Tuscarora and Yamasee Wars, Indian slaves were imported into the Virginia colony by individual entrepreneurs from the Carolinas via small vessels to the Upper District of York. This region was far less frequented by African slave traders. As a result, the area became heavily dependent upon Indian slaves who comprised 28 percent of the labor force.[49] Hence, the slave population was not mono-racial, but multiracial and included peoples of American Indian or part-American Indian descent.

Colonial and early-nineteenth-century runaway slave notices confirm the diversity of the slave population. Runaway slaves were described in a variety of terms, such as "likely negro," "negro," "negro (but not black)," "black" (rarely used), "mulatto" (very bright to dark), "copper colored," and on several occasions "White." By the mid-nineteenth century White authorities had at least sixty-one terms for non-White people. Below is a list of late-eighteenth- and early-nineteenth-century runaway slave notices in Virginia that described Negro and mulatto slaves as Indian, having an "Indian" appearance, or having an affiliation with Indians:

> 1752 Ran away, a young Indian fellow named Ned . . .
>
> 1768 Isaac, an Indian slave . . . in Buckingham . . .
>
> 1772 A Run away woman named Molly . . . of Charles City County . . . by her complexion would pass for one of the Indian race . . .
>
> 1773 Run away . . . a Wench named Aminta . . . has much the Look of an Indian, and is so, her Mother having been brought from the Spanish Main to Rhode Island, has long black Hair . . .

1775   Ran away . . . Phebe . . . a remarkable white Indian woman . . . she has long black hair . . .

1775   Ran away . . . in Dunmore County . . . a Negro fellow name Sam . . . it was discovered that he was attempting to inveigle away a number of negroes to the new or Indian Country (where he had been most of the last summer) . . .

1776   Ran Away from Amherst County a "Negro Fellow named Ben." He . . . has an Indian Woman for his wife . . .

1776   Ran away . . . Harry, Virginia born . . . a dark mulatto, with long bushy hair . . . he is of the Indian breed . . .

1780   Run away . . . a negro man named Joe . . . he is of the Indian breed with long hair tied behind . . . [50]

1801   A bright Mulatto man named Jack . . . with very long pretty black hair . . . and has something of the appearance of an Indian . . .

1802   RUN AWAY from subscriber in Manchester, a dark brown mulatto man named Jim . . . the features of his face resembles those of the Indians . . .

1813   Run away . . . a negro man Michael . . . he had on him a new Indian blanket . . .

1816   Runaways—two negro men who were sent to Buckingham from Kanawha . . . One by the name of John, a tall Black Fellow . . . The other a very bright Mulatto named Rueben . . . long hair which he tied behind his back. . . . and had been living on the Tombigbie River in the Mississippi territory and were brought from them in the fall of 1814, where they had lived for some years previous and had learned to speak the Indian language very well.

1817   Runaway—sometimes calling herself Cecilia Green . . . a pale mulatto woman . . . with small sunken eyes and Indian hair . . .

1818   A Mulatto woman named Letitia . . . has the hair and complexion of an Indian . . . [51]

In addition to runaway slave notices, judicial cases involving slavery attest that Indians continued to be bought and sold within the Virginia colony subsequent to the act of 1682, as "indicated by the evidence of witnesses and the assertions of counsel in cases brought from *ninety to one hundred and fifty years later,* and by acts passed in the eighteenth century" [italics mine].[52] The most frequent suits brought by plaintiffs against their slave owners were based on the assertion that the plaintiff was descended from an unlawfully enslaved American Indian woman. If this could be proven, the slave most often won his or her freedom. The following examples will serve as cases in point. In 1772, Robin and other Indians in *Robin v. Hardaway* brought suit for their freedom. This case involved Indian women who were transported into the Virginia colony and sold as slaves during several intervals between 1682 and 1748. The statute of 1682 was used to sanction their enslavement. Mason, for the plaintiff, argued that the statutes of 1684, 1691, and 1705 repealed the statute of 1682; however Colonel Bland, for the defense, argued that the statute of 1684 only repealed the act of 1679, which reduced captives of war to slaves but did not repeal the act of 1682. He also insisted that the law of 1691 was not an act of emancipation. Nonetheless, the court disagreed and found for the plaintiff.[53]

In 1787 the case of Hannah and other Indians in *Hannah v. Davis*, the plaintiffs brought suit stating that their enslavement was illegal based on the 1705 statute regarding free and open trade with American Indians, and thus their descendants could not be held as slaves. The court agreed and found for the plaintiffs.[54]

In 1792 in the case of *Jenkins v. Tom*, the plaintiff Tom bought suit against his owner claiming that his ancestresses, Mary and Bess, were American Indians who had been wrongfully enslaved. Mary and Bess were brought into the colony sometime in the 1670s. A witness testified that he was told by a person, who at the time of the trial was deceased, that the women had been brought to the colony in a ship. While the ordinance of 1670 stated that non-Christians brought into the colony by sea would be slaves, the court decided in favor of the plaintiff.[55]

During the nineteenth century, however, it became increasingly difficult to sue for freedom using the American Indian ancestress defense due to a dispute regarding whether hearsay should be admissible in court. In the 1807 case of *Pegram v. Isabell,* Isabell "styling herself an Indian and a pauper," petitioned the court to grant her freedom from her owner, Elizabeth Pegram.[56] This case was peculiar in that Isabell filed her complaint based on evidence presented by the plaintiff's lawyer that her mother, Nanny, and others had successfully sued for their freedom. While the District Court ruled in favor of the plaintiff, the judge set aside the verdict and ordered a new trial as "the case . . . was too imperfect for this Court to determine the question of law arising upon it."[57] Isabell's new trial occurred the following year. Isabell provided additional evidence regarding her mother's suit, which she won in 1799. According to the suit Nanny was descended from an American Indian woman who was transported into the colony after the 1705 statute. However, Nanny's successful judgment was not enough. The court decided that both sides had to determine upon "what grounds the judgment in that suit was rendered." They also had to show "whether the plaintiff Isabell was born before or after the emanation of the writ in the suit"; however, Isabell's lawyer argued that if hearsay was admissible in court, then Nanny's judgment of freedom ought to be admissible. The case remained unsettled.[58]

Another case involving the question of hearsay being admissible in court occurred in the 1827 case of *Gregory v. Baugh,* identified as "a man of color," brought suit against Thomas Gregory "to recover his freedom." Baugh's grandmother was Sybil, an American Indian woman described by two witnesses as "a copper-coloured woman, with long, straight, black hair with the general appearance of an Indian."[59] The deposition stated that it was evident that Sybil was a mixture of Indian and Negro, but that all who knew her called her Indian Sybil. Fifty-five years earlier, Sybil was granted an order by the General Court allowing her to "sue her master in *forma pauperis.*" Thomas Jefferson was assigned as the prosecuting attorney and was fully persuaded that the case should be decided in Sybil's favor. Notwithstanding, Sybil died before the case could come to trial.

A little over half a century later, Baugh, with only hearsay as evidence, attempted to complete what his grandmother was unable to finish. However, while the jury decided the case in favor of the plaintiff, Judge Carr reversed the decision and remanded the case for a new trial. Among the questions he raised regarding the outcome was, "I think it would behove us well to consider whether hear-say [sic] of a title to freedom, resting on mere conjecture . . . would be at all admissible for any purpose? I think not."[60] In 1831 Baugh received a new trial, yet Judge Carr continued to voice his reluctance to admit hearsay as evidence. He stated that while hearsay was admissible in previous cases, he felt that the court had relaxed the standards of evidence too much. After all was said and done, it appears that the judge's decision was maintained. As the above judicial cases demonstrate, statutes enacted to protect American

Indians from further enslavement proved ineffective and unenforceable for nearly three-fourths of a century. While many resisted their enslavement by running away or suing through the courts, many were absorbed into the slave population where they remained for the rest of their lives.

Numerous slave narratives bear witness to American Indian slavery. The testimony provided by two Petersburg, Virginia residents serves as metaphor for the ambiguity of the legal status of American Indians within the Commonwealth. In 1937 Octavia Featherstone told a WPA interviewer, "No, none of us was ever slaves . . . I forgot to tell you how and why we was free. You see Gramma bein' a Indian, she came of de Indian Tribe which cause our freedom. You know Indians was never slaves, so dey chillum was always free, dat is cordin' to law."[61] However, Della Harris stated, "My muma was a genuine Indian. Some people say you can't own Indians. I don't know how come, but I do know she was owned by dese people, but she sholy was an Indian."[62] While Harris appeared to contradict Featherstone, taken together both woman illustrate the complexity and contradiction regarding the legality of American Indian slavery within the Commonwealth of Virginia.

After the American Revolution, the free "colored" population grew considerably. As demonstrated above, by the end of the British colonial period, the slave population not only consisted of Africans, but also of American Indians and part American Indian peoples from the Americas, among whom were descendants of Virginia's indigenous population. Due to the revolutionary spirit of the era, a number of people from this population were manumitted and greatly increased the free "colored" population within the Commonwealth. As a result, "a considerable element in the free colored population of the nineteenth century was of Indian extraction."[63] This is evident by the 1804 will of Thomas Nelson of Bleak Hill Plantation in King William County, Virginia that stated, "I give to my mulatto woman named Jenny and her children Billy, Harry, Jack, Bob, Edmund, Carter, Lucy and Lewis their freedom." Jenny, also known as Jane Spurlock, was both the slave and mistress of Nelson who fathered her eight children. Two of Spurlock's children, Carter and Edmund, came to represent those who "in the 19th century . . . are among the core Rappahannock [Indian] families from which the modern tribe traces its descent."[64]

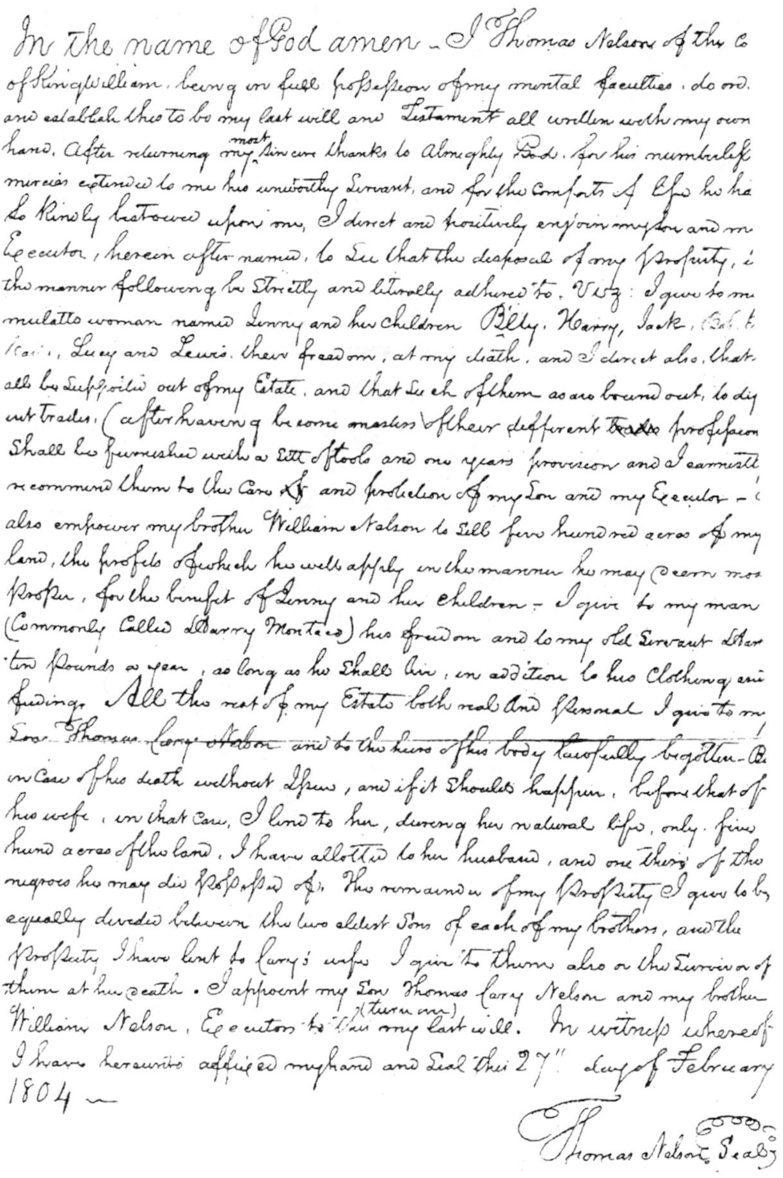

In the name of God amen — I Thomas Nelson of the Co
of King William, being in full possession of my mental faculties, do ord.
and establish this to be my last will and Testament all written with my own
hand. After returning my most sincere thanks to Almighty God, for his numberless
mercies extended to me his unworthy Servant, and for the Comforts of life he ha
so Kindly bestowed upon me, I direct and positively enjoin my son and m
Executor, hereinafter named, to see that the disposal of my property, i
the manner following be Strictly and literally adhered to. Viz: I give to m
mulatto woman named Jenny and her Children Billy, Harry, Jack, Robert
Caty, Lucy and Lewis, their freedom, at my death, and I direct also, that
all be supported out of my Estate, and that such of them as are bound out, to dif
ent trades, (after having become masters of their different ~~trades~~ profession
Shall be furnished with a sett of tools and one years provision and I earnestl
recommend them to the Care ~~of~~ and protection of my son and my Executor — I
also empower my brother William Nelson to sell five hundred acres of my
land, the profits of which he will apply in the manner he may deem mos
proper, for the benefit of Jenny and her children — I give to my man
(Commonly Called Harry Montaco) his freedom and to my old Servant Har
ten pounds a year, as long as he shall live, in addition to his Clothing and
feeding. All the rest of my Estate both real and personal I give to m
~~Son Thomas Cary Nelson and to the heirs of his body lawfully begotten~~ — Bu
in Case of his death without Issue, and if it should happen, before that of
his wife, in that Case, I lend to her, during her natural life, only, five
hund acres of the land, I have allotted to her husband, and one third of the
negroes he may die possessed of. The remainder of my property I give to be
equally divided between the two eldest Sons of each of my brothers, and the
property I have lent to Cary's wife I give to them also or the survivor of
them at her death. I appoint my Son Thomas Cary Nelson and my brother
(turn over)
William Nelson, Executors to this my last will. In witness whereof
I have hereunto affixed my hand and Seal this 27" day of February
1804 —

Thomas Nelson (Seal)

FIG. 2.1 The will of Thomas Nelson that freed progenitors of the modern-day Rappahannock Tribe. Courtesy Library of Virginia.

Regarding the free population, non-Whites were enumerated separately from Whites. In the 1790 census they were listed as "all other free persons." In subsequent years they were listed as "free persons of color." In the 1850 census, however, an overwhelming majority of Virginia Indians were classified as colored. For example, William Scott of Richmond, Virginia appeared as Indian on early tax records, yet, in the 1810 census he was listed as a free person of color. All of his descendants were listed as mulatto. John Dungie, in his petition to the Virginia legislature, was said to be a descendant "from the aborigines of the Dominion," yet referred to as a person of color. Littleton Scholar, a Nottoway, was identified as a full-blood Indian on an 1810 census; yet in 1830 his sons were listed as "free people of color." Incidentally, Edmund and Carter Nelson, whom the Rappahannock consider their ancestors, are listed as heads of household from 1820 to 1840, with everyone including themselves identified as "Free Colored Persons" (Carter in 1820 and 1830; Edmund in 1830 and 1840); however, in 1850, Edmund is listed as a mulatto. Local tax rolls seldom used the Indian designation. Prior to 1812 most Indians or people of Indian extraction were listed under the white-tithable column. By 1813, Indians were overwhelmingly listed as mulatto with some of darker complexion listed as Free Negro. The Essex County "Register of Free Negroes," one of the few surviving registers in Virginia, identified those with common Rappahannock surnames as mulatto. Identification of American Indians or part American Indian people as Indian by census takers and county authorities prior to the Civil War was the exception, not the rule. When the Indian designation was included on the 1870 census only 229 citizens were identified as Indian.

Despite its present denial, as demonstrated above, there is sufficient documentary evidence to suggest that there were longstanding interactions between people of American Indian and African descent in the Commonwealth. While there were no laws against miscegenation between African Americans and American Indians, there were certainly consequences. By the late eighteenth century, the rhetoric of "blood" and mixture imposed Eurocentric notions of American Indian identity that determined entitlements to land and property. This presaged the federal policy of blood quantum used during the late nineteenth century to determine the eligibility of land allotments that were based on one's so-called degree of admixture. The doctrine of blood quantum can be located in its European antecedent, which used "fractional amounts of blood to describe ancestry."[65] Among its long held English traditions, common law distinguished between "'whole blood' and 'half-blood' relatives for purposes of inheritance."[66] This concept was used to define one's legal status and to distinguish people with the same parents from those with a single parent in common. Applied within the context of Virginia, people of mixed-race ancestry came to be defined by degree of "blood" with the advent of the definition of mulatto in 1705. Within this context, ancestry based on the concept of degree of admixture was used as a means to exclude mixed-race people from the privileges of White-ness, of which the most salient pertained to land rights. White settlers, determined to wrestle every square inch of land away from American Indians, made numerous attempts to rob indigenous populations of their reservations by using the language of blood and admixture to reclassify American Indians from aborigines to free Negroes. The Gingaskin Tribe of Northampton County on the lower Eastern Shore provides a poignant example of this pervasive tactic.

When John Pory, Secretary of the Virginia Colony, arrived in 1621 on the peninsula that would later become known as Virginia's Eastern Shore, there were approximately 2,000 inhabitants, some of whom were known as the Accomack Indians. By 1640, as English planters began moving in and encroaching on Indian lands, the Accomack, noted for their diplomacy and friendliness, found themselves checkered in and virtually landless. In December of that year, the General Court and Council granted a patent for 1,500 acres to be reserved for the Accomack Indians; it turned out, however, that once the land was surveyed, the reservation was comprised of only 650 acres. Once the reservation was established, the tribe assumed the name Gingaskin. The Gingaskins ex-perienced constant harassment and encroachment on their land by local Whites. In 1773 they petitioned the General Assembly to appoint trustees to protect their lands. Thus, neighboring Whites decided that instead of trying to obtain the land via squatter's rights, they would obtain it legally by petitioning the legislature.

The first petition requesting the termination of the Gingaskin reser-vation was submitted to Northampton County authorities in 1784. White petitioners demanded that the almost seven-hundred acre reservation "be leased out and the rest be set aside for the Indians but made 'subject to taxation as other lands.'"[67] They justified their petition by claiming that only six genuine Indians remained within the tribe and that the "land is at present an asylum for free negroes and other disorderly persons, who build huts thereon and pillage and destroy the timber without restraint to the great inconvenience of the honest inhabitants of the vicinity, who have ever considered it a den of thieves and a nuisance to the neighborhood."[68] The Assembly agreed to dissolve the reservation, but the dissolution was not fully enforced. Therefore, in 1787, the Virginia General Assembly was petitioned a second time regarding the dissolution of the reservation. This time the petitioners surmised that only four genuine Indians remained, and that the inhabitants of the reservation "have become a very great nuisance to the public by affording an Harbour and convenient asylum to an idle set of free negroes who have of late years connected themselves with the Indians and occupy the greatest part of their Lands, from whom pilfering and disorderly conduct the public are materially injured."[69] The petition further stated that the reservation should be dissolved because "the Indians of the Gingas King Tribe" were "being at this time almost extinct, not more than two or three remaining, and the Land entirely occupied by Mulattoes and free Negroes from the adjacent parts who are every day settling on the Land and are become a nuisance and injury to the people of the County."[70] The petition was denied, yet Whites in Northampton persisted. In 1812, a third petition was submitted to the General Assembly and once again Black admixture was used as the justification for detribalization. George Parker, a Gingaskin trustee, noted an increase of the tribe which was comprised of sixty members. He stated regarding the reservation that it "is now inhabited by as many black men, I believe, as Indian men . . . the Indian women have, many of them, married black men, and a majority, probably, of the Inhabitants are Blacks or have *black blood* in them."[71] Not only did Parker question the authenticity of the tribe as a justification for dissolving the reservation, he also believed that such a move would rid Indian Town of the numerous Blacks who frequently visited the area. Dissolution, therefore, would mean that "the Lands will probably soon pass into the hands of white people, by contract, and that the neighbourhood may be rid, at least of the worst part of this population,"[72] whom he believed contributed to the increase in crime. Parker recommended that the lands be divided with the stipulation that, "no free negro or mulatto (either with or without the exception of the offspring of the female Indians) be permitted to acquire any right, title, or Interest, whatsoever in the said Land by marriage, purchase, or Descent; and that no free negro or mulatto occupy a house upon the Land, or be received or taken as an Inmate in any of the Families thereon, except the Husbands of the female Indian women."[73] This time the Virginia General Assembly granted the petition. In 1815, the land was divided among eligible tribal members with the surplus sold to Whites. Ironically, the trustees whom the tribe had sought from the Virginia General Assembly to protect their lands from White encroachment were the very people responsible for the dissolution of the reservation.

In contrast to the Gingaskin Tribe, the dissolution of what remained of the Nottoway Indian Reservation in Southampton County was instigated by a legislative petition submitted by William Bozeman, the son of a Nottoway woman and Englishman. Bozeman, also known as Billy Woodson, did not reside on the reservation. He had attended a Quaker school in North Carolina and identified as White. In 1823 Bozeman, through his lawyer, petitioned the General Assembly as "An Aboriginal of the Nottoway Tribe," to receive his portion of the land. Bozeman asserted that the dissolution of the reservation and providing allotments to remaining tribal members would financially benefit his Nottoway kin and would lead to "a life of sobriety, industry and order."[74] Yet Bozeman, it seems "acted more as an emissary for Euro-Virginians seeking valuable reservation lands than a well-intentioned spokesman for the Nottoway People."[75] Bozeman's was the lone "Nottoway" signature on the petition accompanied by eighty-two endorsement signatures of White citizens, who would later become the beneficiaries of the reservation's dissolution which the Virginia General Assembly approved on February 23, 1824. In addition, as will be discussed in chapter 7, the support of local Whites to break up the reservation was also a means "to deprive the slave and 'free colored' populations of a safe haven in Southampton, Sussex and surrounding communities during tumultuous times."[76] Subsequently, the Nottoway did not make a mad dash to the courthouse to apply for their allotments. In doing so, they would have to relinquish both their way of life and their status as Indians and be reclassified as free Blacks. Six years later, due to increasing financial pressure, the first of the applications for land allotments was submitted to the county court. Once the application for allotment was granted, some, such as Edith Turner (Queen of the Nottoway) and William Bozeman, sold their allotments immediately. The last of the land was parceled out in 1878. While most of the land allotments had been sold to Whites by the mid twentieth century, a number of modern-day Nottoway continue to reside on their ancestor's allotments or near the area of the old reservation. Contemporary Nottoway reject scholarly interpretations that assert that the reservation sale was initiated and accelerated by their ancestors. They contend that the sell-off was instigated by White landowners vying to take control of the last of Indian lands. It also resulted in some Nottoway becoming involuntary slaves and servants to Whites due to their inability to pay the "free tax"—a tax imposed on them that resulted from the loss of their status as Indians.

In 1843 the Pamunkey reservation became the next target of land-hungry Whites. Using a similar tactic as had been done to the Gingaskin, the White inhabitants of King William County attempted to have the Pamunkey detribalized and dispossessed of their reservation lands because they claimed, among other things, that "The claim of the Indians no longer exist . . . His blood has so largely mingled with that of the Negro race as to have obliterated all striking features of Indian extraction."[77] However, the Pamunkey learned of the ploy and entered a counter petition stating, "And we have been informed by some that the fourth on the Indian blood has expired in this place. But if anything we can prove, there are many here that are more than half-blooded Indian, tho we regret to say that there are some here that are not of our Tribe."[78] Many of the "non-tribal" members present on the Pamunkey reservation were no doubt people of African descent. Had they been of White or Indian descent only, the Pamunkey would have stated so and substantially minimized their risk of dispossession. The counter petition was signed by the chief men of the tribe with the seal of Tarawell H. and James Langston set upon the document. Fortunately, the petition was denied and the Pamunkey continue to occupy their reservation to this day. Nevertheless, the Pamunkey's counter petition demonstrated that American Indian identity had been hijacked and replaced by a pseudo-tribal identity based on blood quantum and Negrophobia. Jefferson, in the *Notes,* described the Pamunkey as "tolerably free from mixture with other colours"; however, almost seventy years later, in 1854, Father William, a Catholic priest, described them as being significantly mixed: "Few of them, however, deserve the name Indian, so mingled are they with other nations by intermarriage. Some are partly African, others partly European, or rather I should say Virginian . . . is inhabited by the most curious intermixture of every class and colour of people."[79] Father William's assertion that many of the Pamunkey no longer deserved to be called Indian due to Black admixture echoed Jefferson's sentiments regarding the Mattaponi and demonstrates that miscegenation, particularly with people of African descent, jeopardized aboriginal status.

While the Pamunkey were able to maintain their reservation, the antagonism by local Whites continued unabated. In 1857 the Pamunkeys' guns were confiscated by White men who contended that they were colored, which made it illegal for them to own firearms. Governor Henry Alexander Wise intervened on their behalf and the Pamunkey were able to retrieve their guns; but the governor warned that if any became mixed with one-fourth or more Negro "blood," they would be held to the same rules as free Negroes and mulattos.[80] In 1866, the governor's admonitions became codified with the Virginia General Assembly's first official definition of Indian: "every person having one-fourth or more Negro blood shall be deemed a colored person, and every person not a colored person having one-fourth or more of Indian blood shall be deemed an Indian."[81]

By the post-Civil War period, the Pamunkey stepped up efforts to sever ties with the African American community. Prior to the Civil War, the Pamunkey attended Colosse Baptist Church, which had been attended by Blacks, Whites, and Indians. Tribal members discontinued attending the church in 1865. In 1866 The Pamunkey Indian Baptist Church was built and became the oldest Indian church in Virginia. In 1887 the Pamunkey set up tribal bylaws that included an anti-Black-miscegenation clause. It was the first of the bylaws which stated, "No Member of the Pamunkey Indian Tribe shall intermarry with anny [*sic*]

Nation except White or Indian under penalty of forfeiting their rights in Town."[82] With the American racial value system now well entrenched within the psyche of the Powhatan population, the Pamunkey went to great lengths to openly demonstrate their disdain for people of African descent. They believed Indians were equal to Whites, but that "blacks were far beneath their social level."[83] They had no problem hiring Blacks to work their "little farms," but when the Superintendent of Schools sent a Black female teacher to the reservation, they promptly turned her away preferring a White one instead. Despite their greatest efforts to downplay their historical connection to people of African descent, by the close of the nineteenth century the evidence of their historical kinship connections to Blacks was well documented in their physiology, as noted by Smithsonian Institution's John Pollard who stated in 1894, "no member of the Pamunkey tribe is of full blood. While the copper colored skin and straight, coarse hair of the aboriginal American shows decided in some individuals, there are others whose Indian origin would not be detected by the ordinary observer. There has been considerable intermixture of the white blood in the tribe, and not a little of that of the Negro."[84] It was the latter that proved most bothersome for the Pamunkey and other Powhatan remnants, who spent the next century in an attempt to expunge themselves of any trace of Blackness even if it meant the disavowal of familial ties.

Intermarriage and cohabitation occurred among American Indians and non-American Indian people long before the establishment of Euro-colonization. Because membership in American Indian societies was based on kinship systems and cultural criteria, exogamy was a cultural tradition.[85] Not only had much intermingling among tribes occurred before European contact, but afterwards, American Indians freely incorporated non-Indians into their societies; thus intermarriage/miscegenation was not uncommon. It was a means of replenishing the tribal population as was demonstrated by the Gingaskin. As a result, over half the population of American Indian people living east of the Mississippi River by the time of removal were "intermixed not only with one another, but with Negroid and Caucasoid racial stocks . . . Hence by 1830 at the latest, the notion of defining American Indian identity in terms of race had been rendered patently absurd."[86]

The Virginia Tidewater was no exception. The Powhatan did not find miscegenation, even with people of African descent, unusual or disturbing. Well, at least not until the Virginia legislature began to impose a racial definition of American Indian identity that posed to threaten their existence as Indians. During the antebellum period, anti-miscegenation laws and racial definitions proved ineffective in maintaining racial integrity. What maintained racial integrity were "strong ties of friendship, relationship, affection and family tradition to the despised and persecuted groups, and in most cases they remained with those who loved them and they suffered with them."[87] But by the close of the nineteenth century, the racial dynamics had changed and the old adage "blood is thicker than water," proved untenable. By the dawn of the Jim Crow era, the colonial imposition of American Indian identity based on the absence of African ancestry would further exacerbate antagonism among Blacks, American Indians, and Afro-Indian peoples as Powhatan remnants fought to maintain their status as Indians, which afforded them marginal access to White privilege.

The racial integrity fight, egged on by the early twentieth century eugenics movement and a renewed campaign to maintain White racial purity, ushered in one of the most pernicious campaigns of divide and rule ever witnessed in American racial politics. At the center of Virginia's intensified effort to maintain racial purity was Virginia's 1924 Racial Integrity Act (RIA). This legislative effort established a two-tier racial hierarchy, White and colored, resulting in a fierce identity war between the state and Virginia Indians, who pushed back with dogged resolve against the state's effort to reclassify them as colored. However instead of challenging the premise of racial purity dogma, the Powhatan remnants embraced it and in turn waged a war against African Americans and Afro-Indian peoples, many of whom were their own relatives. Consequently, the premise of American Indian identity became defined not by whom or what one was, but rather by whom or what one was not: Black. The twin myths of the one-drop rule and Black genetic contamination were the cornerstones of Virginia's racial purity obsession and justified the state's renewed efforts to police Black and Indian identity to better manage White supremacy at the dawn of a new century.

THREE

Race Purity and the Law: The Racial Integrity Act and Policing Black-Indian Identity in the Twentieth Century

It's powerful . . . That one drop of Negro Blood—because just one drop of black blood makes a colored man. One drop—you are a Negro! Now why is that? Why is Negro blood so much more powerful than any other kind of blood in the world . . . Explain it to me. You're colleged.

—LANGSTON HUGHES, *SIMPLE TAKES A WIFE*

. . . for the problem of the Twentieth Century is the problem of the color line.

—W. E. B. DU BOIS, *SOULS OF BLACK FOLK*

A cursory view of Virginian newspapers at the turn of the century makes evident, as Du Bois's prophetic articulation demonstrates, that there was an intense preoccupation regarding the color line among the citizenry of the Commonwealth. As the mantra "emancipation equals amalgamation" was rearticulated within a post-slavery context, White southerners began to equate the push for social equality with Blacks as an endorsement of miscegenation. White Virginians, like most White southerners, viewed miscegenation as an affront to White womanhood and as an endangerment to the purity of the White race; they, therefore, swore their allegiance to the tenets of White supremacy by vowing strict adherence to remain pure from the taint of Negro "blood." Consequently, anti-miscegenation sentiment intensified within the Commonwealth. No other subject, it seemed, could arouse the imagination and cause a public sensation (or panic) as an accusation in support of or engagement in an interracial affair. "A Miscegenation Case in Hanover," an article printed in the Sunday edition of the *Richmond Times-Dispatch on* August 4, 1902, provides a glaring example of the sensationalism garnered by such a charge. According to the article, a mob of White citizens had gathered around the Hanover County Courthouse to get a glimpse of the couple being charged for the crime of miscegenation. The couple's names were withheld; however, they were nevertheless described as a "fair and young" White woman from Connecticut and an "ugly negro man" from Virginia. The crowd hooted and jeered as the offending couple was led away from the courthouse to the jailhouse. The article concluded by informing its readers that the citizens of Hanover County were more amused by the incident than anything. They found laughable what many viewed as the White woman's "unconscious attempt" to subvert Virginia's anti-miscegenation law.

While the paper chose to focus on the "amusing" aspects of the Hanover incident, the case also demonstrated the seriousness of the crime of miscegenation. The Hanover Case, in addition to others over the next two decades, provided justification to those among the Virginia gentry who believed that additional laws must be passed in order to better police and enforce anti-miscegenation statutes. By 1923 when the eugenics movement was gaining momentum, calls for more stringent anti-miscegenation legislation that included more severe penalties reached a fever pitch. Initially, racial purity advocates were concerned about "mulattoes" attempting to pass as White and in turn pollute the White gene pool by marrying unsuspecting Whites. The focus of the racial purity effort shifted, however, as racial purists were seized by an incessant paranoia of "negroid" Indians who they believed had taken advantage of the Pocahontas Exception by marrying Whites, posing a serious threat to the maintenance of Virginia's rigid racial order. The passage of the Racial Integrity Act (RIA) in early spring of 1924 unleashed the abusive power of the state's Vital Statistics Office under the direction of Walter A. Plecker.

Plecker's declaration of war on the Indians was the result of court cases involving Ray Winn of Charles City County and Atha Sorrells of Amherst County, who successfully challenged the RIA less than a year after the bill's passage. The plaintiffs were able to convince the courts that their nineteenth-century ancestors' racial designation as "colored" denoted Indian rather than African ancestry. Lawyers for the plaintiffs argued persuasively that their clients were only of White–Indian ancestry and in turn obtained legal sanction for Winn's and Sorrells's marriage to White people. Plecker forcefully pushed back against the courts' rulings with a fierce effort to define Virginia Indians out of existence. This effort led to the near obliteration of the American Indian population due to the registrar's campaign to have Indians in Virginia declared nonexistent and to disallow anyone to be identified as Indian on public documents (i.e. birth, death, and marriage certificates). The consequence of this pernicious campaign galvanized tribal communities and spawned a century-long struggle to maintain Indian identity. The success of this effort achieved mixed results and "served to poison African [American]–American [Indian] relations as well as to split communities, churches, and even families."[1] This chapter will focus on the RIA and its dogged overseer, Walter A. Plecker, Virginia's first State Registrar.

The Virginia General Assembly approved an "An Act to Preserve Racial Integrity," on March 8, 1924. The original bill, introduced by seven sponsors to the assembly as Senate Bill 219, bore the title "To preserve the integrity of the white race." The original title was the brainchild of John Powell, cofounder of the Anglo Saxon Clubs of America (ASCOA) in Richmond, Virginia in 1922, and it expressed his raw sentiments as an ardent White supremacist. Powell was also a celebrated composer. During his earlier writings Powell praised African Americans for their contributions to American music. He later rejected those sentiments and by 1923 his focus turned to issues of race and miscegenation. According to Powell, intermixing with Blacks would cause "contamination of the races [and] would lead to eventual degeneration of the whole Caucasian race and thereby the annihilation of white civilization."[2] In the face of such dire consequences, unprecedented legislation was necessary to insure the preservation of the White race. Walter Plecker concurred stating that the original title was "preferable as it is the protection of the white race that is aimed at and not the others."[3]

Powell advocated a two-phase plan to prevent what came to be known as "race suicide." First, Virginia had to pass stricter legislation which would make intermarriage and the intermingling of the races a felony. Among the other stipulations of the bill, Powell called for the state to implement a system of registration and birth certificates that would record the racial composition of every resident of the Commonwealth, require those seeking a marriage license to take an oath attesting to racial identity, and ensure that only Whites be allowed to marry Whites. Powell recognized that while the law might not decrease the number of "mixed bloods" in the Commonwealth, the collection of information would "enable us to know with approximate certainly who is or who is not tainted."[4] Powell lent credence to the myth of hypo-descent, or what is commonly referred to as the one-drop-rule, by further stating, "History, ethnology, and biology all bear out the Anglo-Saxon conviction that one drop of Negro blood makes the Negro."[5]

Yet, Powell believed that mere separation of the races was not enough as there was always the possibility of intermixture so long as Whites and Blacks shared the same continental space. The second phase of his plan, therefore, called for the repatriation of Blacks to Africa. Powell's rhetoric of anti-miscegenation and repatriation echoed the sentiments of his forebear Thomas Jefferson and his contemporary Earnest Sevier Cox. Cox was a fellow member of the ASCOA and the author of the book *White America: The American Racial Problem as Seen in a Worldwide Perspective,* published by the ASCOA in 1923. He argued that Whites were the only race of people to achieve civilization throughout human history. White superiority notwithstanding, each civilization perished due to contact and intermixture with the colored races. If the United States wished to avoid the fate of its predecessors, Cox admonished, intermixture must be avoided at all cost and repatriation must be embraced. Cox's work received rave reviews from many eugenicists around the nation including *The Eugenics News,* the official organ of the

American Eugenics Society, and Madison Grant, whose work *The Passing of the Great Race: Or the Racial Basis of European History,* published in 1916, became a classic in eugenics thought. While many expressed unbridled enthusiasm for Cox's contribution to the ideology of eugenics, the "science" of good breeding, Powell's sentiments regarding *White America* placed Virginia as the vanguard state for the implementation of eugenics ideals stating, "I commend 'White America' to all Virginians. If Virginia leads in making America a white nation such service will be infinitely greater than any the state has performed throughout its glorious history."[6]

Powell's and Cox's commitment to racial purity, however, paled in comparison to that of Walter Ashby Plecker. Plecker assumed his new post as state registrar in 1912, just as the eugenics movement was gaining momentum in the United States. Unapologetically sympathetic towards the eugenics cause, he concurred with Cox that the RIA was "the most perfect expression of the white ideal, and the most important eugenical effort that has been made in 4,000 years."[7] Plecker was aware that the law did nothing in terms of the "illegitimate mixture of the races." He was most concerned, however, with "legal mixture," which he believed the new law sufficiently addressed. Plecker supported the new law by publishing journal articles and a series of pamphlets on the subject including works aimed at school-age children to teach them the hazards of race mixing. He gave speeches at numerous medical conferences and often spoke of Virginia as a shining beacon of eugenics leadership. Plecker's obsession with racial purity, however, soon included a deep paranoia on the subject of White–Indian intermarriage. Plecker believed that Virginia Indians had long disappeared from the Commonwealth due to Black–Indian intermarriage and cohabitation, which began with the introduction of people of African descent in the Virginia colony. According to Plecker those now claiming to be Indian were nothing more than what some had dubbed, "Negroes in feathers," believed to be exploiting the Indian claim so that they could marry Whites. Plecker's deep-seated resentment toward Virginia Indians was reflected in his comments regarding the Pamunkey Tribe's 1887 ban on Black–Indian miscegenation proclaiming, "Of course this is all well enough but they began about two hundred years too late."[8]

FIG 3.1. Pamunkey Indian School Children, 1900. BAE GN 00896 06198000, National Anthropological Archives, Smithsonian Institution. Used by permission.

If the Pamunkey and other Virginia tribes were two hundred years too late in their efforts toward racial purity, certainly the same could be said of the Anglo population, whose racial interbreeding with Indians, Blacks, and others began very early in the history of the Virginia colony. Even Plecker recognized as much conceding that Virginia was home to a large mulatto population, which he viewed as the racial peril of the Whites. Although early Virginia legislators devised stringent laws to discourage miscegenation, the mulatto population nevertheless increased. When the law failed in preventing racial intermingling between Whites and non-Whites, Virginians responded by "drawing strict racial boundary lines, defining some mixtures as white and others as mulatto."[9] In other words, some mulattoes were declared legally White. Nonetheless, the criteria for becoming legally White varied in relation to one's non-White ancestry. In 1705 a mulatto was defined as the child of a White and an Indian or the child, grandchild, and great-grandchild of a White and a Negro. Consequently, as legal scholars have explained, "Someone with one Indian parent and three white grandparents was, by implication, legally white . . . For Negro-White mixtures, it took two additional generations to 'wash out the taint' of Negro blood to the point that it was legally insignificant."[10] Subsequently, the 1785 statute that redefined mulatto as a person with one-fourth or more Negro "blood" widened the opportunity for some within the colored population to become legally White. As a result, "the effect of statutes defining a mulatto as someone with a certain proportion of Negro or Indian blood was to make 'white' into a mixed race category."[11]

Thomas Jefferson demonstrated this in an 1815 letter to Francis C. Gray, in which he outlined a sophisticated algebraic formula detailing how a mulatto could become legally White. In his discourse Jefferson remarked, "Our canon considers two crosses with the pure white and a third with any degree of mixture, however small, as clearing the issue of negro blood." Jefferson also stated that if the person was an emancipated slave, "he becomes a free white man."[12] This was precisely the road his former slave mistress, Sally Hemings, and several of the couple's off-spring took in stepping over the racial line from mulatto to White. As Ira Berlin aptly stated:

> Virginia provided the most detailed procedure for legal passing. In 1832, after loading new weights on the free Negro's liberty, lawmakers allowed light-skinned freemen to escape the new disabilities by applying to the county courts with "satisfactory evidence" of a white person that they were not black. If the courts concurred, such mixed bloods escaped the Negro proscription status. Since the law did not provide for positive rights, only those light enough to pass could move into the superior caste; others remained attached to the free Negro population although legally distinct from it. No other state passed a similar law. . . .[13]

The courts seldom attempted to determine the exact proportion of White ancestry in defining who was legally White, however, as most cases were settled based on the appearance of the petitioners as well as their lifestyle and how they were perceived within their respective communities. While there was plenty of guess work involved in racial identity during court proceedings, the significant thing is that, "The white population was in fact racially mixed, but . . . white Virginians could maintain the myth that it was not there at all."[14] Nevertheless, Plecker knew that there was plenty of "untraced (and in some cases

untraceable) Negro 'blood,' in the white population"[15] and he was determined that no more of this spurious issue and abominable mixture
would contaminate the White gene pool. Plecker, therefore, chimed in
with his colleagues warning Virginians that one drop of Negro "blood"
could transform America into a negroid nation. With the passage of the
RIA in 1924, Plecker believed that his post as Vital Statistics Registrar
placed him under divine mandate to enforce the law for the preservation
of the White race.

Not all White Virginians bought into the trio's (Powell, Cox, and
Plecker) paranoia of a negroid state, let alone a negroid nation. Some
rejected the state's racial politics and even mocked the law of hypo-
descent, which contradicted the very premise of White supremacy. *The
Nation,* a White-owned weekly, published an editorial called "Fellow-
Caucasians!" satirizing this contradiction:

> Well fellow-Caucasians, how about it? Are you willing to admit that all
> the blood of your race cannot absorb, and dissolve and obliterate a single
> drop from another racial stock? Are you willing to believe on the contrary
> that that single drop will absorb, dissolve, and obliterate all the white
> blood that flows in your veins? Is Caucasian blood no thicker than water?
> Indignantly we turn to the legislators of the State of Virginia to inquire: Is
> one Negro or Chinese or Melanesian more potent than 16 or 32 or 4,096
> white men? Is one pure white man not equal to the smallest imaginable
> fraction of any other kind of man? We should be tempted, were we not
> law-abiding even under severe provocation, to organize a society for inter-
> racial marriage, to test the capacity of the white race to meet the hazards
> of existence on a planet like ours.[16]

Despite opposition from some White residents, the lack of a critical
mass did little to stem the tide of Virginia's racial integrity campaign.

The RIA underwent several revisions before it was approved by the
Virginia General Assembly and subsequently signed into law by Governor Elbert Lee Trinkle on March 20, 1924.[17] One of its major points of
contention was the mandatory registration requirement. Although the
vital statistics for Black people often were not recorded during the antebellum period, Virginia did not require the registration of births and
deaths for any of its citizens until 1853. The collection of vital statistics
continued uninterrupted until 1896. The Commonwealth took a hiatus

FIG 3.2. Governor Elbert Lee Trinkle signed the Racial Integrity Act
into law on March 20, 1924. Library of Congress Digital Archive.

from collecting such information until 1912 when the Virginia Bureau of Vital Statistics was formed. As a result, legislators reasoned that compulsory registration was necessary to insure accuracy of the racial composition of the Commonwealth. Local registrars were to be responsible for obtaining such information from each resident of the county and were deputized to make use of any law enforcement necessary to secure the information. Those refusing to supply such information would be charged with a misdemeanor and fined no less than ten dollars and no more than one-hundred dollars. Anyone convicted of providing false information pertaining to race or color would be sentenced to one year in the penitentiary.

While many White Virginians supported the measure toward racial integrity, they found compulsory registration "obnoxious." As reported in local newspapers such as the *Virginia Pilot* and *Norfolk Landmark*, mandatory registration would require residents, "to take out a sort of passport correctly setting forth his racial composition . . . without such a passport, though his racial identity be as clear as crystal, he will not be able to obtain a license to marry his own kind."[18] According to the editorial, such a requirement would be nothing less than "bureaucratic meddlesome[ness]" as the entire population would be compelled to comply to "a documentary check" as a result of "one or two per cent of the population so indefinitely blooded and pigmented as to need registration." Hence, the editorial suggested a "simple and direct approach" to updating the anti-miscegenation law which was to tighten it "in the necessary degree and fix appropriate penalties for its violation." Moreover, it suggested that those seeking marriage licenses be compelled to swear under oath that they are "racially eligible for marriage under the new law." Hence, racial integrity would be preserved with less cost and burden to the people of the Commonwealth.[19]

Thus, compulsory registration and all clauses associated with it were stricken from the final draft. Residents whose births were not on file in the registrar's office could voluntarily obtain forms from their local registrar and have them submitted and processed for a fee of twenty-five cents. Staunch supporters of the original bill believed the elimination of compulsory registration greatly compromised the state's ability to obtain "complete and perfect records" of the racial composition of Virginia residents and "to mark accurately the racial dividing line."[20] Nevertheless, the final bill did deem a false claim to color and race a felony punishable by a year imprisonment instead of a misdemeanor as proposed by the original bill. Moreover, the bill gave clerks the authority to refuse marriage licenses to any couple suspected of being racially incompatible: "No marriage license shall be granted until the clerk or deputy clerk has reasonable assurances that the statements as to color of both man and woman are correct." If the clerk did not believe the couple's racial claims were accurate, he or she should refuse to issue the license "until satisfactory proof" was obtained.[21]

Perhaps the most contentious aspect of the original bill was the sponsor's definition of a "White" person. Initially, the Virginia trio advocated that the definition of "White person" include those with Caucasian "blood" only. However, the drafters of the bill loosened the definition with what is now known as the Pocahontas Exception to include those with no more than one sixty-fourth of American Indian "blood." Nevertheless, the final draft extended the fractional exemption to one-sixteenth, as many prominent families who claimed to be descendants of Pocahontas and John Rolfe would have found themselves reclassified as non-White. According to Plecker, this exception was made to honor and protect prominent citizens of White and Indian admixture. In other words, the marriage of Pocahontas and John Rolfe, as well as other claims to American Indian heritage by prominent Whites, became a metaphor for what Renato Rosaldo calls "imperialist nostalgia," a yearning "for the very forms of life they [the colonizers] intentionally altered or destroyed."[22] Such nostalgia also served to "transform colonized subjects into images in some way useful to the colonizers . . . but also contribute to the invisibility (perhaps even disappearance) of Native peoples."[23] In the case of Virginia and its racial integrity legislation, one drop of Indian blood, so to speak, merely served as a means to legitimate the power structure of Virginia's aristocracy as well as to validate their claims as rightful heirs to the Commonwealth. Senate Bill 219 was amended, therefore, to define a White person as someone who "has no trace whatsoever of any blood other than Caucasian; but persons who have one-sixteenth or less of the blood of the American Indian and have no other non-Caucasian blood shall be deemed to be white persons."[24]

While the RIA did not address the issue of repatriation, the Virginia trio found plenty of support for it among White separatists; but, to their surprise they also found ready allies among Black Nationalists, namely Marcus Garvey and his Universal Negro Improvement Association (UNIA). Garvey, a transplant from Kingston, Jamaica, came to the United States in 1916. He settled in Harlem, New York and founded the UNIA, which was established upon the self-help principles of Booker T. Washington. Garvey believed that the only way to fight racism was for Blacks to become economically independent. The only avenue to Black economic independence, Garvey asserted, was repatriation to Africa. Garvey embraced Black Nationalism by preaching Black pride and Black self-reliance, but he also spoke disparagingly of mulattoes. His rhetoric echoed that of White Virginians as he cautioned his followers that mulattoes would prove the downfall of efforts toward Black liberation by creating a caste system whereby light-skinned Blacks would rule over dark-skinned Blacks. Garvey, therefore, admonished his followers to "insist in a campaign of race purity, that is doing everything moral and social within the race and close ranks against all other races. It is natural that it is a disgrace to mix your race with other races."[25]

While Black journalists were outraged by Garvey's rhetoric, the Richmond trio at the helm of Virginia's racial integrity movement found Garvey and his organization awe inspiring. In a speech Powell delivered before the UNIA in New York on October 28, 1925, he told the audience that Garvey and his organization came to the attention of Earnest Cox through a letter he received from a Garveyite in St. Louis who commended Cox for his book, *White America*. Although the writer disagreed with Cox on numerous points, "nevertheless," he asserted, "the feelings of racial purity coincided with Garveyism."[26] Garvey himself wrote a letter to Cox in August 1925 echoing the same sentiments and calling the book "a masterpiece in history, ethnology, and general race literature."[27]

Not only did Garvey advertise Cox's book in the *Negro World* (the official organ of the UNIA) and in his book *Philosophy and Opinion*, the UNIA also became book agents selling upwards of 17,000 copies of *White America* in Detroit, Michigan alone.[28] Garvey downplayed the book's virulent racism and reasoned that Cox could not be faulted for writing a book from a White perspective. He contended that the main issue was that irrespective of each man's viewpoint, they had found common ground in relation to the solution to America's race problem—repatriation.

Garvey's support of repatriation and racial purity was a breath of fresh air to the Virginia trio. Despite the fact that Garvey was serving a five-year sentence in a federal prison for mail fraud, the trio clung to their Black Nationalist friend with an unshakeable resolve. Garvey spoke their language, embraced their values for a White America, and served as Black validation for Virginia's racial integrity scheme. Garvey further demonstrated his support for the racial integrity cause by sending his wife, Amy Garvey, to Richmond, Virginia. On August 14, 1925, Mrs. Garvey spoke to a mixed audience on the importance of maintaining racial integrity.[29] She also visited Virginia's Office of Vital Statistics to assure Plecker of the UNIA's firm support of the cause. The favor was returned in October 1925, when Powell paid Garvey a personal visit at his Atlanta prison while in the city to promote racial integrity legislation for the state of Georgia. Also, Cox, Powell, and Plecker wrote individual letters to President Calvin Coolidge requesting that Garvey receive an immediate pardon. They believed that the case against their Black comrade was a conspiracy conjured up by mulattoes to thwart Garvey's Back-to-Africa efforts. The mulattoes the trio spoke of no doubt referred to what Garvey identified as "The race enemy—The National Association for the Advancement of Colored People (NAACP)— ... They are seeking to build up a mongrel America."[30]

The NAACP despised Garveyism and believed that Garvey's movement was counterproductive to Black progress. W. E. B. Du Bois, editor of *Crisis Magazine,* the official publication of the NAACP, saw Garvey as a traitor to his race. Regarding his embrace of the Virginia trio and their racial integrity campaign, Du Bois contended, "Marcus Garvey ... is not attacking white prejudice, he is groveling before it and applauding it; his attack is on men of his own race who are striving for freedom."[31] Du Bois, a man of African, French, and Dutch descent, was under no illusion regarding racial purity. He believed that the entire doctrine was, as he had stated in a *Crisis* editorial regarding Cox's *White America,* "lies agreed upon." He summed up the entire race problem within one element—women, or rather the ownership of women. As Du Bois saw it, "To the ordinary American and Englishmen, the race question at bottom is simply a matter of ownership of women; white men want the right to use all women, colored or white, and they resent the intrusion of colored men in this domain."[32] While Madison Grant believed that the fight against intermixture was the fight to preserve White womanhood, stating, "it will prevent white women from marrying men of mixed racial origin," the NAACP believed such legislation was responsible for the degradation of Black women.[33] On January 12, 1915, the civil rights organization circulated an official statement regarding its position on intermarriage which read in part:

> The National Association for the Advancement of Colored People earnestly protests against the bill forbidding intermarriage between the races, not because the Association advocates intermarriage, which it does not, but, primarily, because whenever such laws have been enacted they become a menace to the whole institution of matrimony, leading directly to concubinage, bastardy, and the degradation of the Negro woman. No man-made law can stop the union of the races. If inter-marriage be wrong, its prevention is best left to public opinion and to Nature which wreaks its own fearful punishments on those who transgress its laws and sin against it.[34]

Founded in 1909, the NAACP began opposing anti-miscegenation laws early in its history, first with a bill submitted to the Nebraska legislature in 1914. Often, with the cooperation of local citizens, the organization conducted quiet campaigns against such measures. Most of their efforts were successful. One success included a campaign to eliminate wording in the 1923 Federal Marriage Bill, sponsored by Senator Arthur Capper of Kansas, that unambiguously supported eugenics. The provision forbade "the marriage of the feeble-minded, epileptics, those of communicable diseases and a prohibition of intermarriage of blacks and whites."[35] The bill was defeated. The organization, which was barely in its second decade, gathered all of its muscle to wage a similar campaign in opposition to Virginia's RIA. Despite its best efforts, however, the NAACP was unable to prevent passage of the bill. The organization immediately turned its attention to the enforcement of the law. Of particular concern to the NAACP were Plecker and the unsavory tactics he used in implementing the new law. Plecker intimidated local midwives who

FIG 3.3. Dr. Walter A. Plecker served as the Virginia State Registrar from 1912 to 1945. He was the state's most ardent racial purity policeman; his legacy remains a stain on the Commonwealth of Virginia. *Richmond Times-Dispatch*. Used by permission.

dared to disagree with him regarding the racial designation of a newborn on a birth certificate. He would return the certificate demanding that the designation be changed. His demands were always coupled with a threat to have the midwife imprisoned for providing false information about race as outlined in the RIA. In addition, he compelled school superintendents to remove children from White schools on suspicion that they were colored. A staunch Presbyterian, he even attempted to have a set of "illegitimate" twins ousted from the church's orphanage on the basis that they were most likely colored due to their illegitimacy. Even the dead were not safe from Plecker's abuse. In a letter entitled "To Undertakers and Coffin Dealers of Virginia," dated May 1924, Plecker admonished, "In reporting deaths we expect you to use care to see that color is correctly stated . . . Call attention to the penitentiary penalty for willfully making a false statement as to color."[36] If he suspected that a deceased person buried in a White cemetery was colored, he would demand that the body be exhumed and reburied in a colored cemetery. Plecker's abuse of power was nothing short of terrorism.[37] The NAACP viewed Plecker's extremism as dangerous; they knew he had to be stopped, but how?

When members of the NAACP learned that Plecker had used, or rather misused, his franking privilege with the Children's Bureau by sending out two pro-eugenics Virginia Health Bulletin pamphlets, *Eugenics in Relation to the New Family* and *The New Virginia Law to Preserve Racial Integrity,* under the auspices of the federal government, they pounced.[38] James Weldon Johnson immediately submitted a letter of complaint to John Davis, then Secretary of Labor. In his letter to the secretary, Johnson outlined his complaint regarding Plecker's misuse of his franking privilege to distribute anti-Negro propaganda, which included quotes from Plecker's publications. Johnson demanded the registrar's immediate removal. He sent copies of the letter to local and national papers, to representatives of Congress, and to President Coolidge. Davis knew he could not ignore Plecker's indiscretion. Hence, the state registrar lost his federal appointment with the Children's Bureau. An article in the *St. Luke Herald,* a newspaper founded by Black female entrepreneur Maggie Walker, celebrated the NAACP's victory by stating regarding Plecker, "the scalp of the chief of the John Powelian of Richmond, Dr. W. A. Plecker . . . off came his official head as if a mule had kicked it. There was no ceremony about it."[39] Despite the victory, the NAACP thought the swiftness of Plecker's dismissal from the Children's Bureau was almost too good to be true. Some wondered whether he would later challenge the dismissal and wanted to garner as much evidence against him in case he later tried to become reinstated. Florence Kelley, General Secretary for the National Consumer League and National Board member for the NAACP, wrote to James Weldon Johnson requesting copies of any correspondence received from Plecker that would solidify the case against him. Kelley sent a second letter to further inquire if any steps had been taken in Virginia to remove Plecker as Vital Statistics Registrar.[40] Walter White, responding to Kelley in lieu of Johnson who was on vacation, stated that "It is going to be a pretty hard job for the NAACP to get any action in Virginia against Plecker. It is probable that our demand that he be dismissed would make many friends for him in that State."[41] Lucy Mason, General Secretary of the YWCA in Richmond, concurred, stating that the newspapers ran stories regarding Plecker's dismissal from the Children's Bureau that inflamed many White Virginians. They wrote editorials "defending him and stating . . . that the action taken by the federal government in no way affected Dr. Plecker's status in Virginia."[42] Mason, who was seen as one of the few progressively minded Whites in Virginia, was not in sympathy with Plecker's agenda. But she warned that continued attacks on the state registrar would galvanize support for him, as "most people in this community will be in sympathy with his opinion."[43] However, Walter White wasn't quite ready to give up the fight. He wrote Maggie Walker inquiring, "Could you not get some of the white people who would be receptive to go after Plecker's scalp?"[44] White believed that agitation from within the state rather than from without could prove effective in reaching the organization's ultimate goal, which was to oust Plecker. Unfortunately Mason's assessment proved all too correct, as Plecker's influence shielded him from further assault.

The Children's Bureau scandal and the NAACP were the least of Plecker's worries. During that time he was faced with a more pressing issue as individual Virginians began to use the claim to Indian ancestry as a means to challenge the two-tier racial structure imposed by the RIA. As stated in Article four of the RIA, local clerks had the right to refuse a marriage license to anyone he or she suspected had provided inaccurate or false information pertaining to race. The first legal challenge to the RIA occurred six months after the bill's passage, when the local registrar of Rockbridge County, A. T. Shields, refused to grant a marriage license to James Conner, a White man, and Dorothy Johns, described as a woman of mixed ancestry. Johns's lawyer filed a *writ of mandamus* to compel the clerk to issue the license. Johns's uncle testified that the family was a mixture of White and Indian ancestry. However another witness claimed that he had been acquainted with the Johns family for years, and that one of Johns's relatives was "a black man, while others of the family were yellow."[45]

Plecker attended the hearing armed with the birth records of the county from 1853 to 1896 that demonstrated that some of Johns's relatives had been listed as "colored." The inconsistency of the racial designation of some families in the mountain region was the registrar's salient concern as expressed in a letter to Senator Marshall Burnskill Booker of Halifax County a month before the RIA was signed into law. Plecker urged the senator to support the racial integrity bill due to an overwhelming number of cases in which a couple was designated colored on the marriage license, yet their children were designated White on birth certificates. Plecker interpreted the racial designation colored to signify the presence of African ancestry and expressed his concern that this resulted in a high percentage of "mixed breeds" who were "prolific and multiply with alarming rapidity." Plecker feared that the fecundity of these families would result in the genetic contamination of the entire region. He concluded that the RIA was the only remedy to the problem. John's lawyer, however, disagreed that colored as indicated in the records meant Black; he argued that the term "colored" meant Indian. Judge Henry S. Holt rendered his decision in favor of the state, but added a caveat. He stated that while it was not his intention to criticize the legislature, he believed the law would impose unintentional consequences on mixed communities "in that families would be arrayed against families."[46] The judge's statement was indeed well on point.

Judge Holt found a similar case before him not long after his ruling on the Johns case. This time Shields had refused a marriage license to Robert Painter, a White man, and Atha Sorrells, a woman of mixed ancestry and a distant relative of Dorothy Johns. Much like Johns, Sorrells's lawyer submitted a *writ of mandamus* on her behalf to compel Shields to issue the license. Many believed, however, that the Johns case set a precedent, and that Sorrells would suffer the same fate as her distant cousin. The Sorrells case followed the same pattern as the previous case. Sorrells and her witnesses testified that she was solely of White and Indian admixture. There were no witnesses at the trial to refute this. Nonetheless, after the decision, a Richmond paper identified her as "a white girl of negro extraction."[47] Plecker, once again armed with the county vital records, stated that Sorrells's grandmother was listed in the records as a "free colored." As in the Johns case, it was again argued that the racial designation "colored" alluded to Indian ancestry and not to African ancestry. To the chagrin of Plecker and his likeminded associates, Judge Holt decided in favor of Sorrells and compelled Shields to issue the marriage license.[48]

Holt arrived at his decision based on several reasons which he outlined in a lengthy opinion handed down on November 17, 1924. First, while Holt was sympathetic to the racial integrity cause, he found the portion of the law that granted power to the clerk questionable because "The Clerk in refusing license is not required to take evidence and cannot without a hearing." Thus, the law did not provide for due process. Second, the law required that the burden of proof be placed upon the applicant. Yet, how could one be absolutely sure that he or she did not possess a "foreign" strain. As Holt purported, "In twenty-five generations one has thirty- two millions of grandfathers, not to speak of grandmothers, assuming there is no intermarriage. Half the men who fought at Hastings are my grandfathers . . . Certainly, in some instances there was an alien strain. Beyond peradventure I cannot prove there was not." Holt reasoned that since there was no law to prevent the intermarriage of those who were unable to prove there was no foreign strain, both the clerk and the applicant were put in a no-win situation. As Holt asserted, "Alice herself [meaning the character in the children's book *Alice in Wonderland*] never got into a deeper tangle." Third, the definition of White person as defined by the RIA was contested by the judge as he listed several authoritative sources of which no two sources agreed. Holt further contended that many would be surprised to learn that under Virginia's definition, a Hungarian would be excluded from marrying a White person, but "an Arab, North African, a Tordas of India, an Ainus of Japan, or the Wild Man of Borneo," would not. Hence, Holt concluded that "common sense" must underpin statutes. As such, "The negro alone in Virginia presents a racial problem and it is only necessary to prescribe that there shall be no intermarriage with them within degrees of consanguinity ascertainable and sufficiently remote to provide as a practical proposition against reversion to type." Holt determined that in the case of Atha Sorrells, "the evidence in this case which covers a period of 130 years, certainly the weight of it, to the effect that there is no strain present in the applicant of any blood other than white, except Indian, and there is not enough of that to come within the statute. The license should issue."[49]

Holt's decision stunned Plecker and his colleagues. As the trio saw it, not only would the decision allow for the intermarriage of Whites with the very people they deemed least desirable, it also brought into question the validity of Plecker's and Powell's most prized possession: the birth records from the previous century. As Powell saw it, the nineteenth-century vital records were, "our greatest protection against the infusion of negro blood. Under this precedent any negroid in the state could go before a court and say, "My ancestors are recorded as coloured, but that does not mean negro; they were Indians."[50] Powell went on to state that this declaration of being Indian and not Negro would be the ticket to Blacks ability to marry Whites and thus pollute the White gene pool. Hence, Powell vehemently defended the accuracy of the "race" records.[51] Nonetheless, as has been demonstrated, the term "colored" was loosely applied in the nineteenth century and thus one could not assume the racial composition of those considered non-White, or White for that matter, with unquestionable precision. Yet Powell was hardly interested in taking an honest look at Virginia's racial politics. His immediate aim was to repair the "breach in the dike" before the flood waters of miscege-nation overflowed their racial banks. Initially he proposed appealing the Sorrells' decision, however after seeking the advice of the State Attorney General John Richardson Saunders, he thought better of it. On appeal the RIA could have been declared unconstitutional. Hence, Powell con-vinced Plecker that the better course of action would be to amend the law so as "to clarify the terminology of the law and amend the section permitting individuals of one-sixteenth Indian blood to intermarry with whites so that the possibility of whites marrying negroid Indians would be precluded."[52] Yet, as the two men moved forward with plans to pursue a legislative amendment, they were plagued with still another setback.

On December 11, 1925, a little more than a year after the Sorrells decision, Ray Winn, a Chickahominy Indian, was found innocent of the felony of miscegenation. Winn had been indicted due to his marriage to his second wife, Mary Wilson, a White woman whom he married after the death of his first wife. Winn's first marriage, which occurred in 1911, was to a Chickahominy woman whom he married in New Kent County. They were both racially identified on the marriage license as Indian. On October 31, 1925, two months prior to Winn's indictment, the

Richmond school board had upheld the decision of the superintendent to have his children removed from the White school on suspicion that they were Black. By this time Winn had remarried. His failure, however, to persuade the school board that his children were unmixed with Negro "blood" brought about the subsequent charge of miscegenation. At the school board hearing, Plecker, armed with a genealogical chart compiled from nineteenth-century vital records, described Winn as a "Negroid 'near white,'"[53] and testified that he and his first wife's common ancestor (they were first cousins) was a colored woman of Afro-Indian heritage. The elderly chief of the Chickahominy Tribe, however, refuted Plecker's testimony stating that the woman in question was a full-blooded Indian. He also testified that Winn "had only Indian and white blood in his veins and had never known any of his family to have associated with colored people but had either kept to themselves or had white friends and companions."[54] While the children's removal from the White school was upheld, the Hastings court determined that the state had not provided sufficient evidence to sustain the charge of miscegenation. Not only was Winn's marriage declared legal, but the court also determined that Winn "was entitled to be considered upon equality with all white men."[55] While Plecker was both stunned and humiliated by this subsequent defeat, it only served to reinforce his resolve to lobby for a legislative amendment to the RIA that would rid Virginia of its Indian menace once and for all.

If pursuing the route to a legislative amendment was the most practical means to diverting a constitutional challenge to the RIA, it certainly proved daunting as it took three attempts over a period of four years to amend the original legislation. The first attempt occurred in 1926 when two bills, House Bill No. 224 and Senate Bill No. 68, were introduced to amend the definition of "colored" to include "all persons with any known, demonstrable, or ascertainable admixture of Indian or Negro blood."[56] The only exemptions would be those descendants of Indian–White marriages prior to 1619 and those descendants of Indian tribes of Oklahoma and Texas residing in Virginia. Once again many Virginia citizens geared up for a fight, as the proposed definition would class numerous prominent citizens as non-White, including descendants from two historical marriages, which they claimed occurred "about 1644 and in 1684."[57] Since these events were enshrined in Virginian history, it would stand to reason that all of those who claimed such ancestry would fall under the category of "known" admixture. The amendments underwent several revisions to appease the prominent citizenry nonetheless on March 12, 1926, "the bills died in the Senate" because the senators "voted to postpone the action indefinitely."[58]

The second attempt to amend the RIA occurred in 1928. This time the legislature tried to close a loophole as it was discovered that "the definition of 'white person' in the 1924 Act and the definition of 'colored' and 'Indian' in the 1910 statute" did not take into account all racial possibilities.[59] According to the 1910 statute, a colored person was anyone with one-sixteenth or more Negro blood. An Indian was anyone not deemed a colored person possessing one-fourth or more Indian blood. Thus, people of tri-racial ancestry possessing, "one-thirty second or less Negro blood, less than one-eighth Indian blood and the rest white, had no defined racial status in law "[60] House Bill No. 2, known as the Price Bill, was introduced to close this loophole. James Price of Richmond, the sponsor of the bill, proposed that, "every person having an ascertainable degree of Negro blood descended on the part of the father or mother from Negro ancestors without reference to limit of time or number of generations removed, shall be deemed a colored person."[61] The blood requirement for Indian classification would remain at one-fourth. This bill also died due to opposition from the public.

While the Indian population had been silent during the passage of the 1924 RIA, they vehemently expressed their opposition to the Price Bill. The Pamunkey, Chickahominy, and Mattaponi leaders argued that the new legislation would "destroy the identity of their tribes and subject them to the same treatment as Negroes."[62] The Chickahominy tribe decided to draft its own racial integrity bill. Much like Price, they proposed that the blood requirement for the Indian classification be one-fourth; however, they also included a clause that would render all marriages between Negroes and Indians null and void. The Price Bill passed in the House of Delegates on January 27, 1928. A week later when the Senate Court and Justice Committee met for its consideration, tribal resistance resumed. Chief Tecumseh Cook of the Pamunkey Tribe declared, "I will tie a stone around my neck and jump in the James River rather than be classed as a Negro."[63] Although an editorial in the *Richmond Planet*, a Black-owned newspaper, was sympathetic to the Indians, it voiced resentment toward the Chief's slur. Nonetheless, the *Planet,* too, was opposed to the amendment. It claimed that the Price Bill would threaten the racial integrity of the Negro in that "50,000 white-Indian-Negro mixed breeds," would be classified as "colored."[64] It seems that every segment of the Commonwealth, White, Black, Indian, and whatever mixture thereof, had become obsessed with racial integrity.

Although legislators reasoned that the 1924 RIA was sufficient, a third attempt to amend the racial terminology of the law occurred in 1930. This effort was the result of a decision handed down by Judge J. W. Chinn of Essex County who determined that children with less than one-sixteenth Negro "blood" could attend White schools. Because the law did nothing to prevent this, many deemed it necessary to amend the law, "not as a campaign against the Negro, but to keep the white schools white."[65] Of course there was much opposition to Senate Bill No. 49, as many saw this as an affront to the Indian population as well. In keeping the White schools White, the law would not only bar Negroes, it would also bar Indians. Despite much activism from the White community on behalf of the Indian population, the racial integrity legislation was amended to enact "a definition of 'colored person' which complemented the definition of 'white person' in the 1924 Act."[66] The definition of Indian was also restricted to include only those on the reservations. Thus Senate Bill No 49 entitled "An Act to amend and re-enact section 67 of the Code of Virginia defining colored persons, American Indians and tribal Indians," was approved on March 4, 1930, stating "Every person in whom there is ascertainable any negro blood shall be deemed and taken to be a colored person, and every person not a colored person having one-fourth or more of American Indian blood shall be deemed an American Indian, except that members of the Indian tribes living on reservations allotted them by the Commonwealth of Virginia having one-fourth or more Indian blood and less than one-sixteenth of negro blood shall be deemed tribal Indians so long as they are domicile on said reservation."[67]

Of course there was much commentary regarding the above amendment to the 1924 RIA. W. E. B. Du Bois, who closely followed the proceedings via the *Richmond Times-Dispatch,* simply could not restrain his sarcasm toward Virginia's obsession with racial purity. In an editorial entitled "Virginia" published in the *Crisis,* Du Bois stated:

> It is with difficulty that one keeps from laughing over the plight of Virginia and its "race purity" legislation. For something like 311 years whites, Negroes, and Indians have been inter-marrying and inter-mingling in this state. Recently the Legislature has been trying to unscramble the races, and some papers, like the *Times-Dispatch,* are getting quite hysterical about it. Essex County, for instance, has a number of "colored" children in the white schools—that is, children in whom experts may seem to see blood that is not pure "white." "Mixed schools!" yells the *Times-Dispatch* in its frantic desire to keep these poor babies out of the best schools of the community. But some of the Indians object. It is a little hard to distinguish between Negro and Indian blood, and these folks want the benefit of the doubt. But the *Times-Dispatch* gnashes its teeth and orders the Legislature to pass a law defining a colored person as one having "any ascertainable amount of Negro blood." But this surely is not enough. Does the *Times-Dispatch* want its sister to marry a man who has an unascertainable amount of Negro blood? My God! What a loophole![68]

Although Du Bois aptly captured the lunacy of Virginia's racial purity obsession, the racial integrity campaign was no laughing matter. Plecker's fanaticism for racial purity during the years leading up to the amendment of the RIA intensified and he pursued his war against the Indians with a terroristic vengeance. During this time Plecker focused much of his disdain on the Pamunkey and Mattaponi tribes, the only reservation Indians in the Commonwealth. He believed the tribes were unquestionably Negro and that their long awaited detribalization and dispossession of tribal lands were well overdue. He garnered support among his colleagues and attempted to revive the nineteenth-century movement to detribalize and dispossess the reservation occupants. Plecker received unexpected encouragement from Charles Davenport, Director of the Eugenics Records Office (ERO) in Cold Springs, New York. Davenport informed the registrar by way of correspondence that the Shinnecock Tribe of Long Island, New York had recently lost their reservation because the state had declared them no longer Indian due to Negro admixture.[69] Plecker was ecstatic in his response to Davenport stating, "I am pleased to have your statement as to the closing of the 'Indian' reservation on Long Island. I believe that should be done in

the case of our 'Indian' reservations in Virginia."[70] Davenport promised to forward more information regarding the dispossession of the
Shinnecocks; however, Plecker, through his own inquiry, soon learned
that Davenport's information was incorrect. The Shinnecocks had not
lost their reservation which they (as well as the Pamunkey and Mattaponi) continue to maintain to this day.[71] Despite his inability to garner
sufficient support for dispossession, Plecker's hatred continued toward
the reservation tribes whom he stated were most troublesome; he also
expressed equal disdain toward anyone supporting the notion that the
Rappahannock, Chickahominy, and Nansemond existed as tribes in
the present state of Virginia.[72] His attacks against Virginia Indians were
so relentless and intense that a year after the RIA was signed into law
Governor Trinkle asked the registrar to "ease up on the Indians and
not embarrass them any more than possible."[73] Plecker responded with
vitriol to the governor arguing "I am unable to see how it is working any
injustice upon them or humiliation for our office to take a firm stand
against their intermarriage with white people, or to the preliminary
steps of recognition as Indians with permission to attend white schools
and to ride in white coaches."[74] Governor Trinkle backed down.

Plecker's war against the Indians was twofold. His first line of attack
was to use the Bureau of Vital Statistics as a bully pulpit to promote his
anti-Indian views, which began with the notion that Virginia Indians
were nonexistent. The Virginia press provided an open-ended platform
that Plecker used to espouse his racist views. Plecker's anti-Indian media
campaign began with an editorial in the *Richmond News Leader* on July
2, 1925, in which he "took the position that the 3,000 Indians of Eastern Virginia—the Pamunkeys, Mattaponis and others—are negroid."
As proof, Plecker cited Henry Howes's *History of Virginia* (1845), John
Pollard's *Pamunkey Indians of Virginia* (1894), and Alexander Francis Chamberlain's *Encyclopedia Britannica* article on "North American Indians" (1919), all of which stated that the Virginia Indians were
mixed with White and Negro "blood." The latter was all that mattered as
Plecker contended, "My only duty and zeal in this matter is to establish
the truth as to whether these people have any negro 'blood.' It is not a
question of the amount or of the proportion of negro, Indian and white."
Hence, any ascertainable amount of Negro "blood" rendered one a Ne-

gro through and through and served as justification for advocating that the use of the Indian label be discontinued.

Prior to the Sorrells victory, however, Plecker had no problem signing off on vital documents that contained the racial designation "Indian." In fact he had done so for residents in Charles City, Amherst, and Halifax counties both prior to and immediately following the passage of the RIA. He later agreed to a compromise with the various sects of non-reservation Indians and allowed them to be identified on government documents as "Mixed Indian." He also compiled a list of Mixed Indian families. Despite the fact that the "mixed" in Mixed Indian denoted the presence of African ancestry, which prevented those with the designation from riding in the White section of the train or marrying White people, the benefit of the mixed Indian category allowed families so identified to enroll their children in local Indian schools so as to prevent them from having to attend colored schools with Black children. In this manner, they were able to maintain a distinct identity separate from their African American counterparts. The Sorrells and Winn victories, however, were reason enough for Plecker to renege on the compromise and insist that the use of the term "Indian" be discontinued altogether.[75]

On May 3, 1938 Plecker responded to A. P. Bohannon, a resident of Halifax County, who reminded the registrar that at one time county officials were allowed to use the "Mixed Indian" designation. Plecker stated that he initially agreed to the compromise in order to prevent those residents identifying as Indian from "being registered as white." Now that the vital statistics office had determined "after more study" that all Virginia Indians were of Negro extraction, "the word Indian should not be used at all. . . . Therefore, they should receive their legal classification as colored."[76] Plecker noted that there were exceptions, but none applied to any of the residents in Halifax County. With respect to exceptions, the registrar highlighted one man of White–Indian only ancestry in Lexington, Virginia, a migrant from the west, who had married into a "good [read: White] family in Rockbridge [Virginia]." Plecker also acknowledged that there were several other cases in the Southwest region of Virginia "where Indians of white admixture, the white probably predominating, have married white women and their children are passing as white. These cases, however, are Indians mixed with white and not with negro."[77] In other words, the Pocahontas Exception proved the only acceptable rule to White–Indian social intimacy, while social intimacy with Blacks was strictly forbidden. No exceptions.

Plecker's second line of attack against the Indians was to gather additional evidence that would shore up the validity of Virginia's "race" records, further lending credence to the registrar's ethnocidal campaign against those he insisted were merely pseudo-Indians. The Sorrells and Winn victories had not only challenged the RIA, but they also undermined the validity of the previous century's vital records. But Plecker's faith in his precious records remained unshakeable. He was determined to find further evidence to support his conviction. Hence, he turned to the Eugenics Records Office (ERO) for help.

The ERO was established in New York in 1910 by leading eugenicist Charles Davenport and was privately funded by some of the wealthiest citizens in the nation. Davenport employed numerous field workers who collected pedigrees on people whom he thought had interesting traits. One such field worker was Arthur Estabrook. A sociologist by training, Estabrook traveled all over the country to remote areas compiling pedigrees and submitting ethnographic reports to the ERO. In 1923 Estabrook discovered a group of people living near Amherst County "known as 'Ishes.' They were given this name because during the Civil War they were in a territory neither designated Black nor White and they themselves were not classed as either."[78] However, Estabrook renamed them the "WIN Tribe," because they were known to be tri-racial people of White-Indian-Negro ancestry. He gathered his pedigrees with the help of Dr. Ivan E. McDougle of Goucher College and a number of senior sociology majors from Sweet Briar College, a White women's school located in Amherst County.

Estabrook published his findings in a book he titled *Mongrel Virginians* (1926). On the advertising brochure above the title of the book in brackets were the words, "What Happens When White, Indian, and Negro Blood Intermingles?"[79] Estabrook claimed his work was scientifically sound in demonstrating "the effects of racial miscegenation."[80] The book, according to Estabrook, provided "the biological reasons why" miscegenation was detrimental to society.[81] In the final analysis the sociologist determined that intermixture had caused the WINs to suffer retrogression. Estabrook claimed that the White racial stock that was infused into the tribe reverted to the lower type, thus making the entire population "below the average socially and mentally."[82] The book concluded with a copy of the 1924 RIA.

In his review of *Mongrel Virginians,* written for the National Academy of Mental Health and the Annals of American Academy, Dr. Abraham Myerson of Tufts College Medical School called Estabrooks's publication "so unstimulating one does not feel like criticizing it or even making fun of it though the latter is about all that it deserves . . . absolutely unscientific in method . . . a really absurd and useless book."[83] By contrast, Plecker deemed Estabrook's work as his saving grace. He believed the pedigrees provided in the work could be used in conjunction with the early Virginia records to establish once and for all the racial identity of the Amherst citizens as Negro. At least that was what Plecker hoped. The registrar learned of Estabrook's research and wrote to the ethnographer as early as August 1924. Plecker inquired if he would provide any information possible to assist in the Dorothy Johns case. In addition, he also asked Estabrook if he would be a state witness. Plecker received a response from Estabrook on the day of the trial. He later thanked him for his "readiness to assist," although he did not disclose exactly what that entailed. Nevertheless, Estabrook provided a synopsis of his work, which Plecker read into evidence. As indicated in a later correspondence with Davenport, this was not Estabrook's desire. Nonetheless, Plecker was overjoyed with the outcome of the trial and voiced his confidence that the Johns case forever settled the racial identity of the citizens of Amherst County.[84] Plecker had not anticipated the Sorrells case as well as others that followed. Thus, the registrar wrote Estabrook several additional times requesting that he provide a list of the families he had interviewed for use as evidence in the impending cases. However, Estabrook had no intention of getting involved in Virginia's legal matters. To hold off Plecker, Estabrook simply told him that he could not release any of the information on the "Ishes" until all of the research was completed.

Plecker was desperate, however, due to the Sorrells win, and he grew extremely impatient. Soon after receiving Estabrook's response, the registrar wrote to Davenport, who was also Estabrook's immediate supervisor and volunteered to assist with the publishing of the information, provided the report contained the names of specific family pedigrees collected by Estabrook and his team. Davenport reported this to Estabrook asking, "Now what do you think of our doing this?" Estabrook replied to Davenport and informed the director of Plecker's intentions to use the information in conjunction with his records as evidence in several upcoming court cases involving citizens of Amherst County. Estabrook cautioned Davenport that making this information available to Plecker "would involve us in a great deal of trouble and I fear publicity that would come back to haunt us."[85] The only way the data could come back to haunt Estabrook and his colleagues was if it became a matter of public record in the Vital Statistics Office and thus challenged in a court of law. Hence, Davenport responded to Plecker with the same answer he received from Estabrook. *Mongrel Virginians: The WIN Tribe* was published in March 1926; however, instead of using actual names, Estabrook used fictitious names. Plecker once again tried to persuade Davenport to give him the list of actual names along with their pedigrees. Davenport responded that he could not because the information had been obtained with a pledge to confidentiality.[86]

The loss of the Sorrells case and his failure to persuade his northern colleagues to make available the pedigrees of the Amherst–Rockbridge communities motivated Plecker to embark on the task of creating his own pedigrees. Styling themselves as ethnologist and genealogist, Plecker along with his assistant Eva Kelley gathered information from tax rolls, census records, and birth, marriage, and death certificates to compile often inaccurate pedigrees of the Amherst-Rockbridge citizenry. With such pedigrees as his arsenal, Plecker challenged anyone from the region who submitted birth certificates with the racial classification of Indian or White. He not only refused to certify their claims, he also wrote notations on the backs of the certificates based on the pedigrees he constructed as proof that the submitter had filed a false claim. He also wrote letters of reprimand threatening the parties with legal action if they did not comply with his demands. Many shrank before Plecker's overbearing intimidation and for almost two decades following the Sorrells decision, Plecker's harassment of the Amherst citizens went unchallenged by many of his government superiors.

Yet, like Sorrells, many Amherst-Rockbridge citizens did not take Plecker's abuse lying down as they continued to submit certificates classifying themselves as White or Indian. Finally, in 1942 Plecker's hand was exposed and his methods were called into question. A battle ensued when William Kinkle Allen, an Amherst attorney representing several of its residents, wrote Plecker requesting that he submit copies of his clients' birth certificates without the notations on the backs of the certificates. Plecker replied with the usual time-worn rhetoric regarding the authority of his records, and his duty as registrar to make certain that his records remain accurate. Thus, in the case of the parties in question, his records demonstrated unequivocally that the classification of "colored" was indeed accurate. Plecker assumed his response was sufficient in rendering the situation moot, but he misjudged the attorney. Allen called on the assistance of a Richmond lawyer, Attorney J. R. Tucker. Tucker wrote Plecker and demanded that he provide photostat copies of the birth certificates as Allen had requested. Tucker ripped into Plecker for his abuse of power as state registrar and also challenged the accuracy of Plecker's pedigrees, stating "not only have you gone beyond your duties as prescribed by law, but that the notation which you have placed on the back of these birth certificates is contrary to the facts."[87]

Plecker's confidence that he could prevail in this newly declared war was unshakeable. He wrote to William Sandbridge, clerk of the Amherst Circuit Court, asking for his assistance in the matter. Sandbridge followed through and looked into the matter as Plecker requested, but the clerk's report did not help Plecker's case. Sandbridge informed Plecker that no evidence existed to support his claim that Tucker's clients had provided false racial information. State Attorney General Abram Penn Staples, whom Plecker had also consulted, came to the same conclusion. Plecker found that he had no choice but to issue the birth certificates to Tucker minus the notations as he had requested. In a letter to Powell, Plecker admitted that he was "somewhat indignant over the charge that Mr. Tucker made that we were falsifying our records." Yet, Plecker also admitted, "In reality I have been doing a good deal of bluffing knowing all the while that it could not be legally sustained. This is the first time my hand has absolutely been called."[88] In fact, as early as 1925 Plecker admitted that his assertions on Black–Indian intermixture were based on conjecture and he expressed his uncertainty about the validity of the nineteenth century scholarship that had served as the basis for his views. He inquired of Davenport stating, "I desire to know whether you consider these statements as authoritative and the result of investigation on the ground or whether the statements are simply passed down from writer to writer."[89]

Tucker may have won the battle, but Plecker won the war, as he had no fear of reprisal for his extralegal activities. In 1943 John Collier, commissioner of Indian affairs in Washington, D.C., wrote to the Virginia health commissioner on behalf of a family whose racial classification as Indian had been challenged by Plecker. The registrar was notified of the complaint and sent a letter to Collier. In his response, Plecker unabashedly boasted of the validity of his compiled pedigrees and insisted to Collier that his clients were Negroes because "practically all of the families of our so-called 'Indian' groups" had been traced "to the 1830 U.S. Census."[90] Plecker's reference to the 1830 census referred to Carter G. Woodson's 1925 publication *Free Negro Heads of Families in the United States in 1830*.[91] The exploitation of Woodson's work to further Plecker's racist cause clearly demonstrates the extent of his desperation and hysteria regarding racial integrity. In another case, in 1944, Plecker was having difficulty establishing the pedigree of a man by the name of Commodore Collins. Plecker requested that Collins provide genealogical information to validate his claim that he was White. Collins listed his grandfather as Solomon Collins. Plecker found that there was a listing for a person in Hancock County (now in West Virginia), by the same name in Woodson's book. As a result, in his letter to Senator Lloyd Robinette, Plecker surmised "there is but little doubt as to his being the grandfather of Commodore and upon that belief it becomes my duty to decline to register any of his descendants as white."[92] No doubt Plecker wrote a notation on the back of Collins's documents referring to the information found in Woodson's book.

Plecker had nothing to worry about in the way of reprisal from the senator. First, the Collins surname appeared on what many now refer to as "Plecker's hit list." In January 1943, Plecker distributed a letter with a list entitled "Surnames By Counties and Cities of Mixed Negroid Virginia Families Striving to Pass as 'Indian or White'," to local registrars as well as health, school and court officials. Plecker warned that such families were attempting to falsify racial information in order to pass into the White race stating, "One-hundred and fifty thousand other mulattoes in Virginia are watching eagerly the attempt of their pseudo-Indian brethren ready to follow in a rush when the first have made a break in the dike." Many of the names on the list no doubt came from Woodson's work. Second, a month prior to Plecker's response to Senator Robinette, on February 22, 1944, the Virginia General Assembly lent legal sanction to Plecker's extralegal activities by enacting a measure which gave the Vital Statistics Office the power, "to enter upon the backs of the original certificate and certified copy an abstract of such other certificates or records, showing their contents so far as they are material in determining the true race of a person or persons named in the original certificate or certified copy."[93] Plecker had finally prevailed.

Plecker retired as vital statistics registrar on June 29, 1946. He was eighty-five years old. Nonetheless, he had no plans of living out the remainder of his years in a rocking chair or on a fishing pier. In his resignation letter to Health Commissioner Dr. I. C. Riggin, Plecker stated that age and his desire to pursue further the field of ethnology was his motivation for retirement. He volunteered to be on hand for Eva Kelley, his faithful assistant who succeeded him. He even requested that the commissioner appoint him as "'Ethnologist,'—without salary or at a nominal one of one dollar a year."[94] In a letter to Powell, Plecker also expressed plans to resume his earlier publishing efforts. He proposed publishing a work titled "The Vanishing Race and Other Studies in Virginia Demography," which would include a history of the state marriage laws beginning in 1632. He concluded his letter stating, "I do not know, however, whether I will carry the plan to completion or not."[95]

Plecker published a brochure titled *Virginia's Vanished Race* in July of 1947. The work invoked old southern American and Nazi Germany rhetoric and pondered the question, "Is the integrity of the master race, with our Indians as a demonstration, also to pass by the mongrelizations [sic] route?" On August 2, 1947, the former registrar, who had a habit of stepping into traffic without looking, was struck and killed by a bus (some say a car) while crossing the street. Many have poked mean fun at Plecker's demise stating that the bus was driven by a Melungeon or some other mixed-race citizen. The driver was later identified as "Kenneth R. Berrell, whose racial origins have fallen into oblivion"[96] Regardless of the racial composition of the driver, Plecker's death was considered a gift by many. It marked the end of one of the most virulent, bureaucratic, and racist regimes in the history of the state and the nation.

Although Plecker was dead, the racial integrity fight was far from over. As Judge Holt stated in his opinion on the Sorrells case, "The negro alone in Virginia presents a racial problem." Thus, Plecker's attack on Virginia Indians in general and on what Powell called more specifically "negroid Indians," demonstrates their profound prejudice against the African strain rather than the American Indian strain. Plecker's onslaught against the American Indian population was relentless, but his actions were more a testament of Virginia's incessant and unyielding obsession with Negrophobia—a cancer now fully metastasized among a majority of present-day, state-recognized Virginia tribes.

However to place the causation of this tragedy solely on the shoulders of Walter Plecker, as much scholarship does, is misleading. Absent from the discourse on the contemporary dilemma of African American–American Indian relations in Virginia is the role that anthropological advocacy on behalf of the Virginia Indians served to widen the wedge between the two peoples, as well as those of noticeable African admixture within tribal communities. The uncritical construct of anthropological advocates as the heroic cavalry that rode in and saved the day fails to interrogate the sordid side of their activism: a racial integrity campaign built upon the very foundation of racial purity enforced by Plecker. The next chapter details the advocacy undertaken by anthropologists on behalf of Indian communities that ensued between 1920 and 1990. It consisted of a twofold campaign to deny Blackness and to reinvent Virginia Indians in the image of racial purity fit for state recognition.

FOUR

Denying Blackness: Anthropological Advocacy and the Remaking of the Virginia Indians

Of course working among Powhatan-Renape people and with other eastern Indians brought home to me the full impact of colonialism and also the difficulty of being Indian if one is also part African . . . Being a mixed-blood myself and also a mixture of many tribes, I had long been aware of the significance of being a "half-breed." Back on the east coast, however, I became increasingly aware that those of us who looked European and Indian had a hell of an advantage over people who looked Indian and African. I thought that the deferential treatment was so much white racist bullshit and still do. I really resent white people trying to dissect us and tell us what it is that makes a person a Native American.

—JACK D. FORBES, "SHOUTING BACK TO THE GEESE"

I write then in a field devastated by passion and belief . . . But armed and warned by all of this, and fortified by long study of the facts, I stand at the end of this writing, literally aghast at what [ethno] historians have done to this field.

—W. E. B. DU BOIS, "THE PROPAGANDA OF HISTORY"

Sioux scholar Vine Deloria, Jr., in his classic work *Custer Died for Your Sins: An Indian Manifesto* (1969), was perhaps the first American Indian academic to offer a critical analysis of the field of anthropology and its long-overlooked detrimental impact on the lives of indigenous peoples. Numerous indigenous scholars including Jack D. Forbes (Powhatan-Renape), Devon Mihesuah (Choctaw), and Linda Tuhiwai Smith (Maori), have followed Deloria and published incisive critiques of the improprieties committed by scholars in the name of scholarship and academic freedom. Frederic W. Gleach responded to these criticisms with a brief acknowledgment of "past" anthropological indiscretions, but asserted that anthropologists, particularly those working with eastern tribes, have done more good than harm. In "Anthropological Professionalization and the Virginia Indians at the Turn of the Century" (2002), Gleach stated, "I offer here neither an apologia for the improprieties of the past nor encouragement for continuing abuse of trust. But it is worth noting that anthropology also has sometimes benefited the people we work with."[1]

Gleach focused on the eight Virginia tribes that received state recognition during the 1980s and who were beneficiaries of anthropological advocacy—after their near relegation to historical oblivion as a result of "northern hegemony." Northern hegemony, according to Gleach, eclipsed the Virginia story of American history for that of New England. Gleach also provided a historical overview of the work of anthropologists James Mooney and Frank Speck in the late nineteenth and early twentieth centuries. Mooney and Speck revitalized interest and brought scholarly attention to the Virginia Indians, particularly those who had been a part of what was once the Powhatan Confederacy. Gleach, however, was more interested in exploring anthropological work conducted among the Virginia tribes as a broader critique of the hierarchy within the discipline, which often marginalized research conducted in the United States while defining research conducted abroad as true anthropology. Gleach contended that it was this lack of "exotic difference" that caused many, with the exception of a few local anthropologists, to overlook Virginia Indians.[2]

In "Anthropological Advocacy in Historical Perspective: The Case of Anthropologists and Virginia Indians" (2003), Samuel R. Cook concurred with Gleach's ideas on issues of hierarchy and exotic difference within the anthropological profession. However, Cook also believed that such advocacy on behalf of Virginia Indians could be understood within the framework of the professionalization of the field, but also "in terms of demographic feasibility, as well as the political climate of the twentieth century."[3] Cook further contended that due to the Virginia Indians' marginal condition, misrepresentation in public discourse, and pervasive racial persecution, anthropologists working with Virginia Indians "always found it necessary to assume an activist role."[4] Cook's intent was to propose a broader historical context in which such advocacy arose and also to offer a long overdue tribute to anthropologists whose advocacy should be highlighted as a shining example of "their commitment to the development of collaborative models of collecting data and representing indigenous people."[5]

Cook's articulation of anthropological advocacy on behalf of Virginia Indians as a collaborative model substituted his idealized views for the historical record and obscured the configurations of power involved in representation. Regarding representation, Edward Said, drawing on Michel Foucault's theories on discourse, noted in his classic book *Orientalism* that representations are not "natural" depictions of what is true, but are premised upon "exteriority of representation," which calls for the outsider to represent the other because the other cannot represent itself. Therefore, exteriority hinges "on the fact that the . . . scholar [anthropologist], makes the Orient [American Indians] speak, describes the Orient [American Indian], renders its mysteries plain for and to the West [White America]."[6]

In the case of American Indians, the process of representation called for a redefinition of Indian identity acceptable to the White imagination. As Vine Deloria contended, "Indians must be redefined in terms that white men [or women] will accept, even if that means re-Indianizing them according to a white man's [or woman's] idea of what they were like in the past and should logically become in the future."[7] Contrary to the claims of collaboration purported by Cook, the process of re-Indianizing, much like Said's *orientalizing*, involved the anthropologists and the Indians "in a relationship of power, of dominance, and varying degrees of hegemony."[8]

Through their effort(s) via "salvage anthropology," a mode of ethnography concerned with saving and preserving the history of Indian cultures on the brink of extinction, anthropological advocates attempting to rescue the Indian population from Virginia's ethnocidal practices, redefined Indian identity that hinged on the absence of African American ancestry.[9] As a result, Indian identity defined against an African American "other" proved instrumental in codifying the criteria for state recognition of Indians. Social anthropologist Georg Henriksen warned, "even with the best of intentions we may, in the role of advocate, easily further the colonial process still at work."[10] Thus, it is easy to understand why some critics who castigated the state of Virginia for its racist policies against Virginia Indians subsequently reinforced those policies by denying the past relations of African and American Indian peoples, a practice that continues into the contemporary era. To understand the complex relationship between the Virginia Indians, the state of Virginia, and anthropological advocates, we must first turn to the salvage campaign of Frank Speck.

Frank Gouldsmith Speck, considered the pioneer of salvage anthropology and known for his work among Algonquian Eastern Woodland Tribes, received his Master of Arts degree in anthropology from Columbia University in 1905 under the supervision of renowned scholar Franz Boas. Speck was among a generation of Boas protégés who would promote the Boasian approach to anthropology. Boas distinguished himself among his colleagues by departing from the American School of Anthropology pioneered by Josiah Nott, Samuel Morton, and Louis Agassiz, whose scientific racist theories, known as "Niggerology," the science of the inherent inferiority of African people, aimed to support pro-slavery ideology and were prevalent in the field from the mid- to late nineteenth century. As the focus of anthropology shifted by the late nineteenth to early twentieth centuries, anthropologists began to focus almost exclusively on American Indians. William T. Adams dubbed this practice "Indianology," the study of the languages and cultures of North American Indians. Boas embraced a cultural approach to anthropology made popular by the Americanist School of Anthropology pioneered by Albert Galatin and Peter S. Du Ponceau during the 1890s.[11] Instead of the racialist theories that attempted to explain human difference by lumping the world's population into racial categories and ascribing to these categories such characteristics as morality and intelligence, cultural theorists advocated that "human difference and human history were best explained by culture . . . they interpreted character, morality, and social organization as cultural."[12] To culturalists, racial categories "made no biological sense."[13] According to Boas, "it is not possible to assign with certainty any one individual to a definite group."[14]

Yet there was another side of the culturalist theory that was contradictory but, furthered the culturalist argument. While Boas and his protégés argued that race made no biological sense, they also said that race was all biology. In other words, "real racial differences only occurred in 'nonessentials' such as texture of head hair, amount of body hair, shape of the nose, or head, or color of the eyes and the skin."[15] Race was not "language, customs, intelligence, character, and civilization."[16] Notwithstanding, in his representation of North American Indians Boaz and other culturalists engaged in what Lee D. Baker has termed "red minstrelsy," which constructed "a very narrow image of an authentic Indian by staging, fabricating, authenticating and editing what was and was not Indian." To "fabricate the authentic," to once again borrow from Baker, means that by:

> salvaging lost languages, religious and spiritual practices, kinship and tribal organizations, or phenotypic diacritics, anthropologists weighed in with science to help ratify the idea that a genuine Indian identity could be constituted only through the race, language, and culture of specific tribal populations, and anyone who fell out of bounds of these demarcations was simply not a real Indian.[17]

Blackness became the salient marker to determine who was or was not a real Indian. Consequently, denying Blackness became the centerpiece of Speck's salvage campaign when working with the Virginia tribes who were contending with eugenics ideology, which promoted "the dogma that the hope of civilization depends upon eliminating some races and keeping others pure."[18]

Speck began his work among the Virginia tribes in 1919, five years prior to the passage of the Racial Integrity Act (RIA). By this time he had received his PhD in anthropology from the University of Pennsylvania and was acting chair for the school's new Department of Anthropology. Anthropologist Helen Rountree has argued that while Speck's work had a lasting impact on the Powhatan Tribes, his work among them was much

FIG 4.1. Dr. Frank G. Speck was a renowned anthropologist whose salvage work among the Virginia Indians included a campaign to "expunge the black blood" that served to counter Plecker's claim that Virginia Indians were Negroes. University of Pennsylvania Special Collections. Used by permission.

less impressive than his work with other tribes. According to Rountree, Speck "came to Virginia with the already formed intention of organizing into tribes any 'Indian' groups he found rather than observing them at length and collecting data about them before acting."[19] Rountree also realized that perhaps Speck's actions were dictated by the expediency of the moment. During the 1920s Speck published several articles in *American Anthropologist* and two monographs regarding the Powhatan groups. In these works Speck emphasized the technology and cultural continuity of the Virginia Indians. Rountree correctly suggested that Speck focused mostly on this aspect of Powhatan life because it was less controversial than others, including the racial identity of the Virginia tribes.[20]

However, in a racialized environment like that of Virginia, Speck could not totally ignore race. Similar to his predecessor James Mooney, Speck was under no illusions regarding the racial purity of Virginia's

Indian population and did not believe their admixture depleted their Indianness. Yet, unlike Mooney, Speck was initially noncommittal in rendering a judgment regarding the racial composition of the Powhatan Indians. In a 1907 article, published in time for the Jamestown tercentennial, Mooney stated:

> In all of these bands the blood of three races is commingled, with the Indian blood sufficiently preponderating to give stamp to the physiognomy and hair characteristics. It is probable that from intermarriage nearly the same mixture is in all alike, although it does not show equally in the features. Thus many would pass among strangers as ordinary negroes, a few show no trace of any but white blood; while a few families and individuals might pass as full-blood Indians in any western tribe.[21]

Almost a decade later in a letter to Speck, Mooney compared the Powhatan remnants to the Nanticoke Indians of Delaware whom he referred to as "a mongrel remnant," stating, "The Pamunkey, Chickahominy, Nansemond and 'Croatan' with all of whom I have been, are much the same in admixture."[22] Despite their racial mixture, Mooney believed the Virginia Indians could be "salvaged" if they maintained strict regulations regarding intermarriage and association with Blacks. Speck proposed the same course of action in an article "The Ethnic Position of the Southeastern Algonkian" (1924). Speck, however, remained noncommittal in his assessment of the racial classification of the Virginia Indians, stating, "As to racial classification at present we know practically nothing."[23] He thought the information would only be useful in determining whether the Powhatan remnants were culturally closer to "Algonkians" of the North or tribes of the Gulf area. Speck did not believe their mixed racial composition quantified their Indian identity. He did, however, note that while none of the tribes had retained myths or folklore that would be classed as "ethnically distinct," what they did possess contained extracts from both European and African traditions, suggesting that cultural intermingling among the three populations had occurred.[24] Speck still endorsed the tribes' segregation campaign stating, "The idea of racial segregation and reconstruction is growing among them and will probably develop into an advantageous local social movement."[25] Segregating the Indians, particularly from African Americans, would become the central focus of the salvage campaign.

As much as Speck tried to avoid the issue of race by subordinating Indian racial identity to a cultural identity, he knew he could not simply ignore the issue regarding the racial composition of the Virginia Indians. In *The Rappahannock Indians of Virginia* (1925) he stated:

> It appears that at least 10 mixed groups exist in the same general localities where their ancestors lived . . . Probably none of the numerous persons of Powhatan classification in the state could now boast of absolutely pure Indian blood—by which is meant an absolutely unmixed raciality of the potential two thousand ancestors that each would have had in the eleven generations elapsed since their first contacts with the Old World. They have nevertheless neither indulged in nor permitted intermarriage with representatives of the other peoples surrounding them for almost a century—drastic homogamy to compensate for earlier laxity. Only within the present younger generations have some marriages taken place with whites. They have developed an in-bred mixed physical type. This accounts for the high variability which they now exhibit in general. Most observers, however, agree in remarking on their Americanoid characteristics, which would seem to mean in bulk, the predominance of Indian blood. These racial characteristics are entirely aside from determination of their social traditions. This latter is emphatic and consistent.[26]

Speck as an ethnographer was engaged in what James Clifford called "culture collecting," in which "diverse experiences and facts are selected, gathered, detached from their original temporal occasions, and given enduring value in a new arrangement."[27] In this new arrangement, Speck had to detach the Virginia Indians from their past relationships with African Americans. Because collecting in the American sense is often viewed as a rescue effort, the collection contains "what 'deserves' to be kept, remembered, and treasured."[28] What is often collected is whatever is viewed by the ethnographer as being "traditional . . . they select what gives form, structure, and continuity to a world. What is hybrid or historical in an emergent sense has been less collected and presented as a system of authenticity."[29] However, salvage ethnography demands that what is now deemed traditional and authentic be redefined within a European racialized value system. Speck, in reconstructing the Powhatan Indians, located a usable past within the last century that invoked images of homogeneity disrupted only by an occasional interbreeding with Whites. Speck's construction of Virginia Indian historicity, which on the surface was based on a cultural approach to American Indian identity, was underscored by the racialized politics of culture which called for expunging the Black "blood."

Their present racial composition notwithstanding, Speck's attempt at damage control reinvented Indian social traditions based on ethnocentrism and xenophobia. Nevertheless, three years later Speck found his assertion that the Virginia Indian population exhibited "Americanoid" characteristics (a racial category not accepted among anthropologists) still had not brought him any closer to successfully defining Virginian Indian identity in terms of race. In *Chapters on Ethnology of the Powhatan Tribes of Virginia* (1928), Speck attempted once again to deflect attention away from the issue of racial composition stating, "Some have even presumed to deny their existence under implications of there being no longer pure-blood Indians among them. Elimination, however on this ground would involve great controversy, for it would mean that many existing Indian groups all over North, Central, and South America, maintaining active tribal traditions, even government, would be consigned to the anomaly of classification as 'whites or colored people.'"[30]

Speck's assertion invoked a traditional Indian sensibility that subordinated a racialist identity to that of a culturalist identity which, as asserted by numerous Indian scholars, traditionally had been the basis of American Indian identity. In addition, as Speck noted, in the case of Central and South America, in which Indian identity is still largely formulated based on cultural rather than racial composition, the Powhatan Indian identity would not have been challenged if members of the tribe remained true to their traditional culture. However, external factors pushed the leaders of the various Powhatan factions to impose strict regulations regarding intermarriage with Blacks. Intermarriage with Whites was not forbidden. As Rountree explained:

> The Powhatans, being people of their time, believed in not one but two 'one drop' rules. They like the whites believed that one drop of Negro "blood" made one black, and they emphatically denied that they had any Negro ancestry at all. But they also believed that if an Indian married a white, the children were Indian. They did not expect miscegenation with whites to produce white children; the children were to remain within the Indian community and be brought up as Indian, a cultural definition of "Indians" that social scientists agree with to this day.[31]

But were the Powhatan simply "being people of their time," as Rountree suggested? And with whom were social scientists agreeing regarding the "cultural" definition of Indian identity as described by Rountree? Such choice of language appears misleading. Definitions of Indian identity were European inventions borne out of an imperialist agenda to subjugate and exclude. Certainly Powhatan acceptance of a racialized definition of Indianness to exclude those of African ancestry on the one hand and a cultural definition to include those of European ancestry on the other, demonstrates that a Eurocentric imposition of Indian identity had taken hold. It demonstrates the extent to which the Powhatan had internalized the racism of mainstream White society. Social scientists of that era played an important role in constructing this approach to Indian identity. Similar to Said's articulation of orientalism, the hegemony of White American ideas about the Indian reiterated White superiority. Hence, what social scientists asserted was a cultural definition of American Indian identity was not cultural at all, but rather racialist and racist.[32]

Not everyone in the Powhatan Tribes agreed to abandon relations with the African American community. There were those who married outside of the tribe and moved away, refusing to submit to Virginia's sexual colonization scheme. Some left the state altogether assimilating into the general population while privately remaining Indian. Some of those who remained in Virginia chose to forfeit tribal citizenship rather than abide by the rules of racial purity now imposed by tribal leaders. Rountree interprets this exodus as "the ultimate effect of trimming away the less stalwart fringe people and leaving a much tougher and more determined core of Indians in the Powhatan Tribes."[33] Yet observed from a different perspective, what remained were those who became complicit and allowed themselves to be reinvented, or as Deloria says "re-Indianized" according to the White idea of Indianness.

Speck's advocacy on behalf of the Virginia tribes inflamed Vital Statistics Registrar Walter Plecker and his colleagues, who began corresponding about the matter in 1925. Plecker wrote to Davenport about a letter he received from a representative of the Valentine Museum in Richmond who was organizing an exhibit on Virginia Indians and had secured a list of contemporary Indian tribes living in the Commonwealth. Plecker dismissed the project on the grounds that the museum's population estimates, which he assumed were from Speck, were greatly exaggerated: "This may be the result of the work of our friend, Speck, of the University of Pennsylvania, who created the Rappahannock 'Tribe' and threatened to do the same for about a half dozen other groups of negroes."[34] Plecker met Speck's advocacy with stern opposition. He sought to have the scholar's work banned from the state. He knew full well the political risk that a challenge from a respected scholar could bring. Field supervisor and coauthor of *Mongrel Virginians* Ivan McDougle, also fearing Speck's political impact, put Estabrook on alert regarding the forthcoming publication of Speck's monographs. McDougle contended, "He has entirely disregarded all vital statistics since 1853 and all county records on these people. He has contented himself with living among these people and taking their own word for their history."[35] In other words, "these people," as McDougle called them, had no right to self-definition or self-determination. That was to remain in the hands of Whites, particularly those who placed American Indians on the Negro side of the color line. Although McDougle dismissed Speck referring to him as "this so-called scientist," he knew better than to underestimate the University of Pennsylvania professor's impact. McDougle urged Estabrook to visit Speck to ascertain just what he knew about "these people," but that Estabrook not reveal his own knowledge of them. Moreover, McDougle further warned Estabrook, "Whatever you do don't let him know about the 'Isshies.'"[36]

Speck was well aware of the political potential of his work having waged a successful campaign on behalf of the Nanticoke Indians in Millsboro, Delaware. Speck began work among the Nanticoke in 1912; he soon became an advocate working with its first modern chief, William Russell Clark, who was "rabid in his denunciation of any intimacy with Negroes through marriage or otherwise."[37] In 1922 Speck assisted the Nanticoke in becoming an incorporated Indian entity. The charter required "separate educational and religious instruction" and that tribal members "alienate themselves from any alliances with negroes or with descendants from the red-headed [Nanticoke] widow and her Black slave Requa."[38] Speck's Nanticoke campaign was the prototype for his Virginia campaign. He advised the Powhatan groups "to collect affidavits from their white friends, testifying to their status as Indians in the community."[39] He believed that the affidavits buttressed by his scholarly reputation would make a strong case for the Virginia Indians. Much like his predecessor James Mooney, he also advised tribal leaders to organize base tribal rolls similar to those of the western tribes. He also encouraged them to attend the 1924 Eastern Indian Tribes Conference at Nanticoke in Millsboro, Delaware.[40] As a practical matter, Speck adhered to a cultural definition of Indian identity; but, he nevertheless advised tribal leaders "to adopt some definite policy on the status of the race question."[41] Speck, in adherence to his training under Boas, was well aware that race and culture were not mutually exclusive.

Plecker's campaign to have all Virginia Indians classified as Negro on the 1930 U.S. census precipitated a battle with Speck and the Census Bureau. Speck lent his support to the tribes by writing to the Census Bureau confirming the Powhatans' Indian identity. His advocacy, however, was only partially successful as the Census Bureau agreed to list the groups as Indian with an asterisk, which meant that their racial classification was questionable. Hence, "Plecker and the Indians had both won—or lost—that round."[42] Despite this setback, Speck continued in his role as anthropological advocate, but the 1930s and the early 1940s proved daunting. For example, Speck's effort to revitalize "Indian" arts and crafts among the Virginia tribes by employing Indian teachers from the West, proved to be quite a disappointment. The attempt at artistic revitalization within the indigenous communities was a function of the culture concept known as the "art-culture system" in which "modern culture ideas and art ideas function together."[43] In this inclusive twentieth-century cultural category, there is no such thing as high or low culture, but instead it "privileges the coherent, balanced, and 'authentic' aspects of shared life."[44] No doubt Speck believed that such an enterprise would also serve as an objective witness to the phenomenon of cultural continuity as earlier discussed. But, Speck found it impossible to employ American Indian teachers. B. H. Van Oot, the state supervisor of trade and industrial education, informed Speck in 1932 that he had inquired with the U.S. Office of Indian Affairs and the U.S. Office of Education and that "At first a few applicants were interested, but later their interest seemed to lag, and I am reliably informed that they hesitate to live with the Pamunkey Indians whom they feared to be partly negroid."[45] Speck remained undaunted. He once again lent his support as Plecker fought to have his way on the 1940 census, but he and the Indians were not as successful as they had been a decade earlier. The number of Indians acknowledged in the state's population decreased from 779 in 1930 to a mere 198 in 1940.[46] This also was no doubt a consequence of the 1930 amendment to the RIA that redefined the term "Indian" only to include those domiciled on the King William County reservations.

Although he advocated unwaveringly on behalf of the Virginia Indian tribes, Speck's assessment of the racial composition of the Virginia Indians, much like Plecker's, was based on conjecture. By the 1940s, as Speck aimed to gain federal support for the Powhatan remnants, he found himself wedged between state-imposed and federally imposed definitions of Indian identity. Regarding the latter, federal definitions of Indian identity based on blood quantum, first used as a means to determine allotment eligibility during the latter part of the nineteenth century, had by this time become entrenched in U.S. Indian policy and dictated one's eligibility to receive healthcare, annuity payments, education and other services. In an official statement entitled "Testimonial for Indians of Virginia Approving Their Claim for Indian Classification" (1944), Speck maintained the same position he held in his 1928 monograph on the Powhatan Indians, which certified Indian authenticity based not on blood quantum but on the precedents set in other regions of North America:

> My testimony in regard to the authenticity of the direct descent of the tribal groups surviving in the tidewater area of Virginia is given without hesitation. Were these groups situated in Oklahoma, in New York State or in Canada there would be no reason to distinguish them as ethnically Indian. The physical types presented by these people would not be differentiated from those of the States and Provinces where Indian classification is never denied to those who are historically entitled to it ... The estimate is made upon grounds as valid as those which guarantee the classification of Indian groups in other parts of the United States and Canada.[47]

In a 1945 letter to Willard Beatty of the Department of the Interior, however, Speck conceded:

It is positively correct as you state that there are no official records that would establish blood quantums for any of the bands or individual families even. Accordingly the question of proportion could only be settled by guess methods, plus observation, plus tradition of intermarriage as recalled and stated by the family patriarchs themselves . . . I have been inclined to venture the estimate of from three-eighths to five-eighths Indians genic lineage as approximately true for practicability all the groups concerned in our correspondence. There are undoubtedly some families of more than this degree of Indian average-average as say two-thirds as a compromise for the bands which have been extremely strict about miscegenation for over a century; especially where it might involve negroid mixture. All of the bands concerned have disowned individuals who have crossed over to associate, social, or marital with the latter for some generations.[48]

Speck's uncertainty regarding the racial composition of the Virginia Indians can be further demonstrated by another 1945 letter, this one to James Coates of Norfolk, Virginia. Coates was an amateur ethnologist, collector, and longtime friend of the Pamunkey Indians. It appears that Coates initiated correspondence with Speck in 1940 to request his assistance in challenging the local draft board's racial classification of the Pamunkey as "colored." Coates and Speck became fast comrades in championing the Indian cause, and Coates joined Speck in advocating that the tribes create a Pan-Indian alliance. Yet when confronted with the question of the racial identity of the Virginia Indians, Speck was so uncertain that he asked Coates his opinion on the matter. But Coates's response provided no assistance to the anthropologist: "You flatter me considerably in asking my opinion as to the ratio of Indian blood among the native Indians of our fair State. Coming from you, this is indeed a compliment and I feel the figures you have quoted are as accurate as anyone could conclude from any amount of exhaustive study on the subject."[49]

While Speck was successful in securing enrollment for Virginia Indian high school students in Indian schools in North Carolina, Kansas, and Oklahoma, he never certified the Powhatan groups identity based on blood quantum. The only thing that he seemed to be certain of was the groups' supposed century-long segregation from people of African descent. John Garland Pollard reported in his 1894 pamphlet on the Pamunkey Indians: "they . . . *frequently* hire negroes to come in and work their little farms" [italics mine]. [50] This shows that the Pamunkey and no doubt other tribal remnants indeed had a connection with the African American community which continued into the late nineteenth century. This challenges Speck's claim that such relationships were nonexistent or ceased by the end of the colonial period. Consequently, Speck as Boasian protégé and leading ethnologist of the Virginia Indians, found himself trapped within the racial politics of culture.

White definitions of American Indian identity not only influenced how Indians were perceived by the larger community, but also how they were perceived by each other. Ironically, the Pamunkey turned down opportunities to build alliances with the non-reservation tribes for the same reason that the western Indians refused to come to Virginia during the 1930s to teach Indian art to the Pamunkey. During their initial correspondence, Speck requested Coates's assistance in encouraging the tribes to create a Pan-Indian alliance, an effort Speck had tried almost twenty years before without success; however, Coates's efforts proved equally unsuccessful. Coates often complained to Speck concerning the factions that existed among and within the tribes. In addition, Tecumseh Cook, chief of the Pamunkey, explained in a letter to Coates that the Pamunkey approached the problem of the Virginia Indians quite differently than Speck. Cook wrote, "We too are also interested in the Indians of Va., but not to the extent that we will *ever agree* with Dr. Speck in formulating a Confederacy of all Indians of Va. . . . Some of these people whom Dr. Speck wants us to unite with are not recognized as Indians by the State of Virginia."[51] The Pamunkey took an every-Indian-tribe-for-itself approach to race politics as their non-reservation comrades had everything to gain, but the Pamunkey had everything to lose. They possessed both their reservation and nominal state recognition, which they did not wish to jeopardize by associating with people whom the state, for the most part, viewed as Negroes. In fact, the Pamunkey did not agree to a Pan-Indian alliance until forty years later when the other tribes finally received state recognition. In other words, without White validation, American Indian identity was untenable.

In the meantime Coates began his own salvage campaign by extending his advocacy efforts to the other Virginia tribes. He wrote Speck concerning a petition he was putting together that would be signed by reputable Whites certifying that the Indians were "unmixed with negro elements whatsoever."[52] The petition stated in part, "We the undersigned being white citizens . . . certify . . . that in no case do these persons claiming to be members of the Pamunkey tribe, contain less than 25% Indian blood, no more than 75% white blood . . . and resent the claim of certain prejudiced individuals that these Indians contain Negro blood."[53] Other tribes submitted similar petitions. Amazingly, Coates was able to find ordinary White citizens to verify the blood quantum of Virginia Indians, something Speck, in his twenty years of research among the Virginia tribes, was unable to do.

While Coates continued his efforts towards certifying that the Virginia Indians possessed no Black ancestry, he complained to Speck that he was having less success persuading some of the Indians to sever their ties with the Black community. He recounted his recent visits to the Custalow's [Mattaponi], Jab Adam's [possibly Upper Mattaponi], and Otho Nelson's [Rappahannock] homes and complained, "I can see no hope of eventual salvation for all of the Indians in the State as some undoubtedly have given up the fight to earn their place in society and have become, a few of them, lax in the company they keep . . . some will have to be forgotten while others will be even more difficult to assist due to the thoughtless actions of a few." His greatest concern was for the Rappahannock Indians of Caroline County. Coates stated that upon his arrival to Otho Nelson's house, he had found the Rappahannock chief keeping company with a group of Blacks, which he described as a "heartbreaking situation." Coates feared that they would suffer undue consequences at the hands of "one of our 'small time' politicians" who would seize upon such acquaintances in order to discredit the Indian claim.[54]

Notwithstanding, Coates refused to give up the fight. He sent letters to tribal leaders requesting that the tribes update their base tribal rolls with the purpose of only including members of good standing, meaning only those of Indian or Indian–White ancestry:

> Your assistance is requested in providing me with a complete list of all persons who are members of your tribe in good standing. Do not include any one who is not entitled to the strict classification of Indians. *The purpose of this list is to separate all persons who are members of your tribe*

in good standing from any and all persons who may claim to be members
of your tribe and who are not entitled to that distinction . . . I urge you to
prepare this list without delay and with the greatest of care to see that no
one rightfully entitled to the distinction of being on the list is omitted,
and to be sure that no one, under any circumstances, be permitted to ap-
pear on the list whose good standing and blood relation is other than pure
Indian or Indian and white [italics mine].[55]

Yet, many of the tribal leaders were slow to respond to Coates's
request. Perhaps they dismissed the supposed importance of the tribal
rolls; or perhaps some were reluctant to agree to follow Coates's advice,
which would lead to further purging of the tribe thus resulting in an intense bitter tribal debate. Notwithstanding, denying Blackness provided
the avenue by which "anthropologists and other friends," to borrow the
words of Deloria, could remake the Virginia Indians into an image acceptable for state recognition.

Before his death in 1950, Speck was able to accomplish what some
have viewed as the pinnacle of success on behalf of the Virginia Indians—acquiring out-of-state enrollment for those Virginia Indians desiring a high school education. Five of the tribes operated their own
schools. Rappahannock educational opportunities, however, were almost non-existent. None of the tribal schools was sufficient to offer
high school classes to its students. Consequently, many Virginia Indians did not attend high school because "they couldn't go to the White
schools and wouldn't go to the Black schools."[56] As a result, Speck lent
his support in securing placement in Indian schools out of the region
for those desiring a high school education. Some students were sent
as far away as Bacone College, a post-secondary school for Indians in
Muskogee, Oklahoma that had a high school division. Some attended
Haskell Indian School in Lawrence, Kansas, while still others attended
the Cherokee Indian School in Cherokee, North Carolina. Regarding the
distance the children were sent, Willard Beatty wrote to Speck in 1946
stating, "This is quite a distance for the children to go, but it does offer
them a high school education without the necessity to attend a negro
school."[57] Samuel Cook identified Speck's success in securing the enrollment of Virginia Indians into western tribal schools as "a crowning
achievement."[58] Viewed from a different perspective, this demonstrates

the extreme lengths some American Indians and their advocates were willing to go to promote racial purity. Consequently, to the chagrin of the American Indian community, the primary Indian schools in Virginia were discontinued after desegregation; those attending secondary schools were no longer sent out-of-state but had to attend the local high school if they wished to further their education. Lou Ethel Trinchett, a Rappahannock student, dropped out of high school because "she didn't like going to the black school down the road, which was her only option at the time."[59] She stated that the Black students would call her and the other Indians names such as "half breed" and "savage." "They hated us."[60] There were certainly feelings of animosity on both sides, which serves as a poignant example of the poisoned relations between African Americans and American Indians wrought by the salvage campaign.

By the 1970s, anti-Black sentiment among the Powhatan remnants was well entrenched. Tribal leaders, influenced by the salvage campaign, continued in their efforts to exclude from the tribe African Americans and people of visible Afro-Indian ancestry. The continued practice of eliminating people of African or mixed African and American Indian descent from the tribes is evident from articles appearing in the Powhatan newsletter *Attan-ak-amik*, which means "our fertile country" when loosely translated from Algonquian. The newsletter was the official organ of a Pan-Indian organization, which was the second effort to revive the Powhatan Confederacy. This late twentieth-century effort was led by the late American Indian scholar and activist Jack D. Forbes, Professor Emeritus of Anthropology at the University of California Davis, and his longtime friend and comrade the late Chief Roy "Crazy Horse" Johnson who was leader of the Powhatan-Renape Nation located in Burlington County, New Jersey. These men came to Virginia in the late 1960s with the purpose of stirring up tribal remnants to reorganize the Confederacy. During the 1970s, Powhatan political activism increased and some of the tribes were able to obtain certain state grants to use toward education projects. They were also striving to acquire federal monies for public health services from the Bureau of Indian Affairs (BIA). Forbes urged the tribes to update their membership list, warning that "If they [the tribes] do not, the BIA will try to tell the tribes who their members are." Forbes also urged tribal leaders to update their policy statements

FIG 4.2. Dr. Jack D. Forbes (Powhatan-Renape) was professor emeritus of
Native American Studies at University of California, Davis. He spent much
of his fifty-year career as an academic investigating African–Native American
relations in the Americas. Courtesy of University of California, Davis.

regarding membership criteria. In urging the tribes to update their rolls and criteria for membership, Forbes encouraged the tribes to adopt an anti-racist stance stating:

> Also, we must be sure that our membership rules are fair to all who are of Powhatan blood. For example, some tribes now have rules that an Indian loses his or her membership if they marry a Negro, but they can keep their membership if they marry a white. This rule must be carefully thought about, because the white is as non-Indian as the negro. . . . Is it right for us to be mixed but to say to the current generation that they cannot intermarry? Perhaps what we need to stress in our rules is not "blood" so much as loyalty to the tribes and the Indian culture. Most eastern Indians have been intermarrying with whites, negroes, moors, Turks, and other groups for over 300 years. Our Indianness is not based upon a fictitious purity of blood (an idea of the racist white society anyway). Our identity is based upon being loyal to our tribes and our heritage.[61]

Forbes, well aware of Virginia's racial politics, believed the 1970s, a decade of the American Indian and Red Power Movements, was the perfect time for the tribes to reject the state imposed definition of Indian identity and assert their own, stating:

> The racist laws of the commonwealth of Virginia have tried to tell us that an Indian can have lots of white blood and still be an Indian, but if he has a "drop" of African Ancestry he cannot be an Indian unless he lives on a reservation. If a person has a little bit of African blood and lives on a reservation he is an Indian, but if he is so bold as to move off of the reservation he is no longer an Indian but a "colored" person. Of course, it is hard to imagine where the Virginia legislature got the right to decide who an Indian is, since that is a matter belonging solely to the Native American people to decide. A person of mixed racial background, whether part-white or part-African, is an Indian because of membership in a tribe, and because of culture, not because of the decision of a state legislature.[62]

Forbes further asserted that not only were prominent citizens, such as Crispus Attucks and Senator Hiram Revels, of Afro-Indian ancestry, but that they, as well as any other persons of Afro-Indian ancestry, were descended from two tribal peoples who shared many cultural similarities. Therefore, Forbes concluded, "If we have African blood we should be proud of it. It is good, honest, tribal ancestry."[63]

Forbes's views were a radical departure from the almost two-centuries old indoctrination of the White American mythology that Negro ancestry equaled Indian depletion and genetic contamination. Unlike previous scholar-activists whose advocacy endorsed racial purity dogma, Forbes urged the tribes toward decolonization, an act that begins with asserting one's right to self-definition. Nonetheless, while his associates endorsed the radical activism of the American Indian Movement through actions like the occupation of Wounded Knee and Alcatraz, Forbes's anti-racist rhetoric proved much too radical for the Powhatan remnants. In other words, the myth of African–Indian social and genetic incompatibility was far too entrenched in their psyche. With a new generation of anthropological advocates willing to corroborate a White–Indian only historicity coupled with the near reality of state recognition, those vying to become state-recognized Indians thought it better to stay the course.[64]

The re-Indianizing efforts of the anthropological advocates finally paid off in the 1980s as eight remnant groups obtained official state recognition: Western Chickahominy, Eastern Chickahominy, Mattaponi, Upper Mattaponi, Pamunkey, and Rappahannock in 1983; Nansemond in 1985; and Monacan in 1989. The Virginia Council on Indians (VCI), which oversaw Indian affairs and the recognition process, was organized in 1983.

Frederick Douglass once stated that "fashion is not confined to dress, but extends to philosophy as well—and it is *fashionable* now, in our land, to exaggerate the differences between the Negro and the European."[65] Certainly the trend begun by Frank Speck in the early 1900s to exaggerate the differences between Africans and Indians in order to promote the myth of their historical incompatibility remained philosophically fashionable throughout the remainder of the twentieth century. The 1990 publication of Helen Rountree's *Pocahontas's People: The Powhatan Indians of Virginia Through Four Centuries,* considered by most to be the definitive volume on the Powhatan Tribes, codified the Indian–White historicity as unquestionable truth.

While Rountree had no problem establishing interracial and marital ties between Whites and the Powhatan, she concluded that establishing such ties between Africans and Indians, with the exception of the Gingaskin, who were detribalized in the early nineteenth century, proved more difficult because there was not enough documentary evidence to prove that such relations had existed. However, in every place where documentary evidence exists, Rountree dismissed, distorted, or downplayed it.

For example, John Dungee, identified by the Virginia legislature as an aborigine of King William County, and his Negro wife, Lucy Ann, are often cited as proof that the Pamunkey intermarried with people of African descent. Rountree, while acknowledging that those with the surname Dungee had intermarried with Indians and Blacks, also stated that they were on the fringe of Indian society with no real standing in the Indian community. Therefore, according to Rountree, John Dungee "had no connection with the Pamunkey, and since he merely claimed some Indian ancestry rather than an Indian identity, there is no evidence to indicate that he 'fully' belonged to the lesser known ancestral Upper Mattaponi."[66] In other words Dungee was not a "real" Indian as defined by Whites. However, this is clearly ethnocentric presentism as Rountree applied a twentieth-century definition of Indianness, as defined by Whites to establish the tribal status, or lack thereof to a nineteenth-century subject. In further reducing Dungee to a mere Indian descendant with no tribal affiliation, Rountree stated in a footnote that, "an exhaustive search of federal, state, and county records has shown me no Dungees among them [Pamunkey] at any time."[67] Perhaps so, however, Speck found the name Dungee (spelled Dundjie) in the late 1920s among the Adamstown Indians, later known as the Upper Mattaponi. Allan K. Tupperance, who provided brief testimony on behalf of the Upper Mattaponi during a joint subcommittee exploratory meeting on the subject of state recognition in 1982, stated that his tribe was comprised of "descendants of the Mattaponi and Pamunkey."[68] In addition, the name Dungee appeared on the Upper Mattaponi tribal rolls submitted to James Coates in the mid-1940s.[69] Hence, Rountree's dismissal of Dungee as having no Powhatan affiliation appears premature. Moreover, the methodology of *Pocahontas's People* in which Rountree defines Indianness based on a construct which divides "core" Indians from "fringe" Indians is essentialist and holds Indian identity hostage to imperialist notions of tribal status.

Rountree, while maintaining that the Pamunkey only permitted Indian–White marriages, also acknowledged that there are three documented instances that demonstrate some social intimacy with non-whites, "one a marriage with an Indian and the other two a marriage and a liaison with Negroes."[70] She cited the often mentioned Negro slave Frank who ran away on several occasions and found refuge among the Pamunkey. Several run away advertisements for Frank appeared in the *Virginia Gazette* between the years 1769–1772. One advertisement claimed that Frank had a wife among the tribe. Rountree dismissed the evidence on the grounds that "the identity of the wife and the likelihood of her having children is impossible to ascertain."[71] Rountree further reasoned that since Frank was the only slave known to have fled to the Pamunkey reservation instead of to the Indian country farther west, his presence did not establish a pattern of the Pamunkey taking in Negro refugees. Neither did it establish a pattern for African–Indian intermarriage. As Rountree put it, "One marriage does not make a pattern."[72]

Ironically, Rountree never reconciled the Pamunkey's policy to remain aloof from Negroes with Frank's continual acceptance by the tribe as a refugee. If the reservation was not a place of refuge for escaped slaves, why didn't Frank seek refuge elsewhere? Also, how does one ascertain the likelihood of an African–Indian couple to have children? Is there some empirical evidence to demonstrate that African–Indian couples were less likely to produce children? Did Indian women suddenly become barren as a result of marrying or copulating with Black men? Rountree's explanations do not follow clear logic and do little to disprove an African–Indian connection. In fact, other records indicate that Frank was not the only runaway refugee among the Pamunkey. Also in 1772 a runaway by the name of Dick described as a thirty-year-old mulatto with "grey eyes, his hair is short, and curls close to his head, has a large black beard," and had been "brought several times from among the Indians on Pamunkey river," was believed to be headed back to the reservation with his brother with whom he had been on the run for "one to two years." Dick's brother was identified as the slave of David Scott from Prince George County and is very likely to have been the aforementioned Frank.[73] Also, in 1782 a runaway "negro man named George" who escaped from Williamsburg was believed that "he would make for the northward or the Pamunkey Indian town."[74] It indeed appears that the Pamunkey reservation was a safe haven for runaway slaves.

Rountree also cited a liaison which involved the ancestors of John Mercer Langston, an Afro-Indian of extraordinary accomplishments, whose slave grandmother, Lucy Langston, was "Of Indian extraction, she was possessed of slight proportion of negro blood."[75] Lucy's mother was probably the daughter of her Pamunkey Indian slave owner, John Langston, who in 1787 paid taxes on an adult slave and three slave children. The sex of the slave is unidentified, yet it is highly likely that the slave was female. Although Rountree acknowledged a probable liaison between Langston and his female slave, she quickly dismissed the notion that he was the father of her children because the family was sold away. Rountree concluded, "Father's often loved their slave children, and freed them rather than selling them away."[76] She also expressed doubts about the likelihood of Pamunkey slave owners fathering children with female slaves, but reasoned that if children resulted from such liaisons they "may have been allowed to remain on the reservation for a time, until such toleration became too dangerous."[77]

Rountree's contradictory statements about the probable liaisons between the Indian slave owning class and their Black subjects, coupled with her dismissal of the Langston liaison on the unfounded basis that fathers of slave children liberated rather than sold away their offspring, demonstrates a willful refusal to acknowledge the historical reality of Black–Indian relations in Virginia and the complexity of familial relations within the slave system. Regarding the latter, some slave owners, such as Thomas Cary Nelson and Ralph Quarles, the father of Lucy Langston's children, manumitted their children and made financial provisions for them. Overwhelmingly, however, slave owners demonstrated a blatant disregard for their slave children; they did not acknowledge, manumit, or provide for them any more than they did other slaves. In addition, a slave woman and her children fathered by her owner could be sold away for numerous reasons including debt, disloyalty, or tensions among the slave owner's White family members. Hence, Rountree's conclusions serve only to further the salvage campaign, perpetuating a White–Indian only historicity that denies of historic liaisons between African American and American Indian peoples in Virginia.

Moreover, Rountree exaggerated the documentary evidence regarding White–Indian marriages. She merely traced the Anglo surnames through the tribes to establish contact. Although she stated that one marriage does not establish a pattern, this is certainly all she used to establish a pattern of White–Indian intermarriage. To the contrary, the evidence clearly shows that when it came to White–Indian intermarriage, Pocahontas (and a few others) was indeed an exception. Similar to the attempts in the eighteenth century to legalize White–Indian intermarriage in Virginia, in 1824 William H. Crawford advocated for such a measure before the U.S. Congress. It was handily rejected. Whites found intermarriage with Indians just as disagreeable as they did intermarriage with Blacks. In reality interracial marriage was the exception; interracial sex was the rule.[78]

In another attempt to prove an unlikely historic alliance between Powhatan people and Africans, Rountree claimed that cultural and physical differences caused tension between the two groups. To assess the attitude the Indians held towards Africans, Rountree quoted Hugh Jones who in 1724 stated, "Indians hate and despise the very sight of a Negro." Rountree surmises that "the 'despising' of Negroes," stemmed from, among other things, "the revulsion that many people feel against those whose physiognomy and cultural background [are] different from their own."[79] The ethnocentricism of this statement cannot be overstated. Africans and Indians shared numerous cultural similarities such as a respect for nature, matrilineal heritage, familial relations based on extended kinship ties, and the importance of ancestors. Once communication barriers were overcome, Indians would have found themselves more culturally compatible with Africans than with Whites.

In addition, not only were there cultural similarities, there were also some physical similarities. Despite, the insistence of some Euro-American scholars that North American Indians were merely White people painted red, Powhatan people had dark complexions and, as Strachey stated, dyed their skin and let it dry in the sun in order to make themselves darker.[80] In other words, prior to European contact, Indians were not afraid of the dark. In fact, within the color symbolism of the Powhatan people, black bore spiritual significance. More to the point, "In the Powhatan context, black and red were commonly used as body paint for warriors and in ritual contexts, certain participants in the *huskanaw* (initiation ritual) were painted black . . . a black bird was worn by shamans and the body was frequently painted with red dyes."[81] In further documenting the physical appearance of Virginia Indians, Strachey said they had noses that were "broad flatt and full at the end, great bigge Lippes, and wide mouthes (yet nothing so vnsightly as the Moores)."[82] Strachey's ethnocentricism notwithstanding, it appears that Africans and Indians also shared more in common physically with each other than with Whites. In 1750, Peter Kalm, who asserted that the Virginia Indians thought the Negroes were devils, further stated that, "since that time, they have entertained less disagreeable notions of the Negroes, for at present many live among them, and they even sometimes intermarry, as I myself have seen."[83] Again, Kalm's assertion that the Virginia Indians initially viewed Africans as devils demonstrates a Eurocentric cosmology as the devil does not figure anywhere in traditional Algonquian religion. Nevertheless, although it was no secret that many Anglos found African physiognomy repulsive, it never stopped them from engaging in sex with Blacks, consensual or otherwise. Therefore, Rountree's assertion of an African–Indian incompatibility based on cultural and physical difference is unfounded.

Another example that demonstrates the great lengths to which Rountree resorted in corroborating the modern claim to an Indian–White historicity involved the Gregory Petition of 1843. The Gregory Petition was submitted to the Virginia legislature by White citizens of King William County in an attempt to dispossess the Pamunkey of their tribal lands. Rountree contended that Plecker misrepresented the document stating, "that they beg for pity and *admit the truth of the claims made by the white petitioners.*"[84] However, this was a deliberate maneuver to deflect attention away from the counter petition and onto Plecker as the demonized racial bigot out to get the Indians. Racial bigotry notwithstanding, Plecker did not lie about everything. The counter petition, as many scholars have acknowledged, and I concur, does suggest an admission on the part of the Pamunkey of allowing African or part-African people to reside on the reservation.[85]

Rountree's conscious manipulation of any evidence regarding contacts between Africans and Indians is further evident in an aside she wrote regarding Mooney's assessment of the racial composition of the Powhatan. Rountree quoted a statement from an 1899 letter in which Mooney allegedly wrote, "I was surprised to find them so Indian, the Indian blood being probably nearly ¾, the rest white, with a strain of negro." Rountree added a parenthetical note beside the quote stating, "Whoever was meant by that 'strain of negro' is gone today."[86] At least that is what she apparently hoped.

The erasure of African American–American Indian relations in general, and of Afro-Indian peoples in particular, from the historical consciousness of Virginia by anthropological advocates made them partners in the colonial process and ethnocidal scheme against Indian peoples of the Commonwealth. Both the enemies and the friends of the Indians believed that Negro "blood" depleted Indianness and contaminated the gene pool. While opponents believed the Virginia Indians to be beyond regeneration and moved to obliterate their presence entirely from the state, proponents believed they could be salvaged by constructing a usable past void of an African American presence that has become symbolic of Virginia Indian identity both now and in the future.[87]

Over two-hundred years ago Jefferson declared that the Virginia Indians could not be respected because of their intermixture with Blacks. By the late twentieth century, as a result of the salvage efforts of their advocates, eight remnant tribes gained the "respectability" of state recognition. Yet, in light of the numerous casualties along the way and the deep wounds that remain among their "Black" kin and former allies, a clear victory can never be claimed. Thus, anthropological advocacy on behalf of the Powhatan remnants should not be viewed as exemplary, but rather as a cautionary tale where advocacy can be at once beneficial and detrimental. This has certainly been the case of the Virginia Indians who have indeed won—and lost.

PART 2
BLACK–INDIAN RELATIONS IN THE PRESENT STATE OF VIRGINIA

FIVE

Beyond Black and White: Afro-Indian Identity in the Case of *Loving v. Virginia*

... writers are always finding blacks, and they are always losing Indians.

—JACK D. FORBES, *THE MANIPULATION OF RACE*

The 1967 case of *Loving v. Virginia,* in which the Supreme Court declared anti-miscegenation laws unconstitutional, has garnered far less scholarly attention than its 1954 predecessor, *Brown v. the Board of Education,* which overturned legalized segregation. What little has appeared in the way of scholarship has focused on the history of anti-miscegenation legislation, the events that led up to the presentation of the case to the Supreme Court, the case's legal precedents, and the unanimous decision delivered by Chief Justice Earl Warren. Until recently, with the exception of an article that appeared in *Ebony* magazine several months after the Supreme Court decision, writers have also given little attention to the personal lives of the actual plaintiffs now enshrined in American history as "the couple that rocked courts."[1] In particular, the racial designation of the Lovings has been taken for granted. An assertion in a *Life* magazine article reflected this assumption when it stated, "She is Negro, he is white, and they are married."[2] And although historian Peter Wallenstein asserted that the nine justices overcame their reluctance to rule on the question of miscegenation because interest in the question went beyond Black–White marriage, Lawyers Bernard Cohen and Philip J. Hirschkop's representation of the case as overturning the last of the odious laws of slavery and segregation once again reified the racial dichotomy of White and Black within American racial discourse. Consequently, the arguments presented before the court and later the majority opinion obscured racial issues beyond the Black–White boundary, namely the Afro-Indian identity of Mildred Loving. As Wallenstein asserted, "There was no doubt in anybody's mind as to the racial identities, white and black, of the people who claimed to be Mr. and Mrs. Loving."[3]

The uncritical assumption of the Lovings' racial identity, particularly that of Mildred Loving, can be further demonstrated in the ways writers have characterized the couple. In an article published by *Emerge* magazine to commemorate the thirtieth anniversary of the Loving decision, staff writer Victoria Valentine quoted Hirshkop as stating of Richard Loving, "You would think he was a real redneck. He looked like a real redneck. He talked with that accent. He was into things rednecks are into . . . The flaw in the redneck personality was he was just delighted with Mrs. Loving. They were very much in love."[4] Hence, Phyl Newbeck, though identifying Mildred Loving as a woman of mixed African and American Indian ancestry in her 2004 book on the Lovings, summarized Hirshkop's statements by concluding, "By many accounts, Richard Loving looked like the last guy in the world to risk going to jail to defend the honor of a *black* woman" [italics mine].[5] Collapsing Mildred Loving's racial identity into a singular Black identity was repeated by the assertion of Professor Robert Pratt who summed up his personal and historical narrative on the Lovings by stating that Mrs. Loving "still sees herself as an ordinary *black* woman who fell in love with an ordinary white man" [italics mine].[6] Newbeck, in turn, makes the same claim by taking Pratt's words and misrepresenting them as a direct quote from Mildred Loving. Hence, even those who acknowledge her mixed race identity eventually see her "Blackness" as a negation of American Indian identity. As Pratt acknowledged, those in the community knew Mildred claimed to be part Indian, but they primarily saw her as Black; however, the famed Supreme Court plaintiff did not see it that way.

During a July 2004 interview Mildred Loving declared, "I am not Black. I have no Black ancestry. I am Indian-Rappahannock. I told the people so when they came to arrest me." During that time Mildred Loving only identified as an American Indian with White ancestry, an assertion prevalent among Central Point residents. The framed District-of-Columbia marriage license that the Lovings proudly displayed in their bedroom on the day they returned to Virginia confirmed Mildred Loving's self-identity. It read: "Richard Perry Loving-White; Mildred Delores Jeter-Indian."[7] Therefore, it appeared that Richard Loving was not defending the honor of a Black woman, for in his mind he had not married a Black woman, but an Indian woman.

Yet, the issue of racial identity as it pertains to Mildred Loving proves far more complex. On her original Social Security application completed in 1957, a year prior to her marriage to Richard, Mildred identified herself as "Negro." Five years after her marriage however, in a letter to the American Civil Liberties Union dated June 20, 1963, she stated, "My husband is white, I am part negro and part indian."[8] Her identity as an Afro-Indian woman held firm, so it seems, until the late 1990s when she once again embraced an exclusively Indian identity. How does one account for the shifts in Mildred Loving's self-identity? Viewing the Lovings' case only in terms of Black and White and viewing Mildred Loving as an ordinary Black woman has obscured some of the far more complex issues, namely Black–Indian relations, Afro-Indian identity, self-definition, and the hegemony of racial politics that influenced these shifts in identity. A look at the rural community that nurtured Mildred Loving's identity and an examination of her representation in popular media will help explain some of the complex issues surrounding her intriguing story.

In 1792, Mary Hemings, the half-sister of Sally Hemings, approached her slave owner, Thomas Jefferson, with a request that she and her two children be sold to a local businessman by the name of Thomas Bell. Several years prior to that, Hemings had been leased to Bell and during the course of this time the two became lovers. Bell, as Jefferson was well aware, was the father of Mary Hemings's children. Jefferson granted Hemings's request. As Annette Gordon-Reed noted, "Bell and Hemings, who adopted the last name of her master/lover, lived as husband and wife for the rest of Bell's life in a relationship whose continuance Thomas

Jefferson made possible."[9] Of course, the "marriage" had no legal sanction. Nevertheless, as Joshua Rothman observed, Jefferson went beyond simply assisting one interracial family:

> The sale of Hemings to Bell was the first important moment in the evolution of what soon became a burgeoning multiracial community in downtown Charlottesville. The boundaries of this community extended beyond the town's borders and held together free and enslaved Virginians of European, African, and Native American descent through marriage, extended family ties, and mutual economic support networks.[10]

Almost one hundred and fifty years later, Richard and Mildred Loving would be nurtured in a multiracial community such as the one Jefferson helped spawn in Charlottesville.

Caroline County became the twenty-ninth county of the Commonwealth in 1728—the first year of the reign of King George II—and was named for his queen Wilhemina Charlotte Caroline, commonly known as Caroline of Ansbach. The county, which was formed from King and Queen, Essex and King William counties, is thirty miles long, twenty miles wide, and lies about thirty miles northeast of Richmond. It has two incorporated towns including the county seat, Bowling Green. Bowling Green is divided into a number of smaller communities, one of which is the town of Milford. Within Milford is a tiny speck known as Central Point, the small rural community that Richard and Mildred Loving called home. Central Point was Plecker, Cox, and Powell's worst nightmare. The extent of racial mixing made racial lines barely distinguishable. For this reason Central Point earned the nickname, "the passing capitol of America."[11] The Lovings' marriage license even identified their place of residence as "Passing, Virginia." The couple later built their home on Passing Road.

What is known of the early history of Caroline County and its surrounding communities has been written by local historians and provides a bare sketch of the multiracial character of its towns. The Rappahannock were the dominant Indian tribe in the area, having been forced south across the Rappahannock River from the Northern Neck due to White encroachment. As the English advanced across the Rappahannock River and continued southward, the tribe would be scattered over three counties (Caroline, Essex, and King and Queen). Although the

Rappahannock are predominantly located in King and Queen County, which lies south of Caroline, descendants of the tribe remain in Caroline County to this day.

The Rappahannock were not the only tribe in the area. The Dogue Indians, who lived originally in King George County (north of Caroline County across the Rappahannock River), split three ways as a result of a civil war. One of the splinter groups found its way to the area of Milford and set up a community later dubbed Doguetown. The Dogue have been long declared extinct; however, they may have been absorbed into another tribe and/or absorbed by non-Indians in the area. In addition to American Indians and Whites, people of African or part-African descent were also in the area very early in its history. From 1757 to 1764 "a licensed tavern was operated at Doguetown as an early slave-trading center."[12] There were other such taverns all over the county. Thus from colonial times a multiracial presence was evident in Caroline County.

Regarding Central Point, the area was recognized as having an American Indian presence during the period that the Lovings married. Ralph Fall, quoting a local historian, stated, "It is said that some of the descendants of the Indian villages located in the present Camp A. P. Hill area in colonial times and earlier have settled in and around Central Point, and here they can be found even to this day."[13] Hence, there were at minimum three racial groups which populated the area. Yet, with the high level of commingling that occurred in Central Point, accuracy in determining racial designation involved guess work. Famed African American journalist Simeon Booker, in his 1967 article on the Lovings, characterized the Supreme Court decision as "the high point of a great love story" and "the unpublicized smash-up of an illicit system of white-Negro relations in Caroline County."[14] This system involved sex across the color line, which produced a multiracial community minus the sanction of marriage. Cross-racial alliances, interracial intimacy, and mixed children, "the product of non-marital sexual relations" were prevalent.[15] As demonstrated earlier, this was a long-standing practice throughout the South as marriage across the color line was avoided so as not to legitimate bloodlines.

It is within this atmosphere that the love relationship of Mildred Delores Jeter and Richard Perry Loving blossomed. Like many in their community, Richard and Mildred's relationship began as a typical inter-racial moonlighting romance, yet Richard was not Mildred's first love as many have assumed. When they began dating, Mildred had already given birth to her oldest son Sidney, the product of a previous relation-ship. Sidney C. Jeter was born on January 27, 1957 (a year and a half prior to his mother's arrest) and was given his mother's maiden name, which he retained throughout his life. Richard Loving was identified as "step-father" on Sidney's original Social Security application. Sidney was raised primarily by his maternal grandmother. When Mildred became pregnant with her second son, Donald, who was fathered by Richard, the couple decided to do what no interracial couple in Central Point had dared attempt—get married. Donald was born October 8, 1958, five months after the couple married.[16] Of Richard Loving one local farmer said, "A lot of folks down here just don't have the guts Richard had. There has been plenty of mingling among races for years and nobody griped or tried to legalize it . . . Rich just wasn't the type. What he wanted, he wanted on paper and legal."[17]

Mildred, who claimed to have had no knowledge that marrying Richard was against the law, accompanied her fiancé to Washington, D.C. Not only was the couple attempting to circumvent the law regard-ing interracial marriage, but also regarding racial identification. Mildred had to have been aware that the state of Virginia would not allow her to identify herself as an Indian on her marriage license, as only reservation Indians were allowed to do so on public records. There was no such re-striction in the nation's capital, however. Mildred was among a number of people of color who traveled from Virginia to the District of Columbia in order to obtain a marriage license with an Indian racial designation. Her willingness to go to such lengths to obtain the Indian designation clearly demonstrates her resolve to take ownership of her racial identity. She and Richard married on June 2, 1958.

Immediately after they eloped, the Lovings returned to Central Point to reside with Mildred's parents while Richard made plans to build a house for his new family. The newlyweds slept in a downstairs bedroom where they proudly displayed their framed marriage license. On July 11, 1958, as the Lovings lay asleep in their bed, Sheriff R. Garnett Brooks, accompanied by two additional law enforcement officers, burst

No. 420276

Application for License

DISTRICT OF COLUMBIA, ss:

I, ... Richard Perry Loving ....
applicant for the issuance of a Marriage License to the persons named herein, do solemnly swear (affirm) that the answers to the following interrogatories are true, to the best of my knowledge and belief: So HELP ME GOD.

	MALE	FEMALE
Names	Richard Perry Loving	Mildred Delores Jeter
Ages	24 years	18 July 22, 1957 years
Color	White	Indian
Relationship	None	
Former marriages	None	None
Residence	Passing, Va.	Passing, Va.

WITNESS:

x *Richard Perry Loving*

Subscribed and sworn to before me this ___24th___ day of ___May___, 19 58

Officiating Clergyman:

HARRY M. HULL, *Clerk.*

By _____ Deputy Clerk.

No. 420276

Marriage License

To Reverend ___John L. Henry___
authorized to celebrate marriages in the District of Columbia, GREETING:

You are hereby authorized to celebrate the rites of marriage between

Richard Perry Loving, of Passing, Virginia

AND

Mildred Delores Jeter, of Passing, Virginia

and having done so, you are commanded to make return of the same to the Clerk's Office of the United States District Court of Columbia within TEN days, under a penalty of $50 for default therein.

A TRUE COPY

TEST: AUG 2 4 2012

FAMILY COURT

Clerk, Superior Court of
the District of Columbia

By ___Camelle J. Gorum___

Deputy Clerk

WITNESS my hand and seal of said Court, this ___2nd___

day of ___June___, anno Domini 19 58

HARRY M. HULL, *Clerk.*

By _____ Deputy Clerk

No. 420276

Return

I, Reverend ___John L. Henry___
who have been duly authorized to celebrate the rites of marriage in the District of Columbia, do hereby certify that, by authority of license of corresponding number herewith, I solemnized the marriage of ___Richard Perry Loving___ and ___Mildred Delores Jeter___

named therein, on the ___2nd___ day of ___June___, 19 58, at ___748 Princeton Place, N. W.___
(Name of church, or street address, etc.)

in said District.

6/4/58   ewg

Rev. John L. Henry

FIG 5.1. Copy of Richard and Mildred Loving's marriage license. Obtained from the Superior Court of the District of Columbia. Author's collection.

into the couple's bedroom and arrested them for committing the felony of miscegenation. Not only was the marriage license deemed invalid in the state of Virginia, but Mildred Loving's American Indian identity was also rendered invalid. In the eyes of the state of Virginia, she was a

Negro, which made her unqualified to marry a White person. With the marriage declared illegal, on July 17, 1958, two separate warrants were issued for Richard Perry Loving and Mildred Delores Jeter under criminal dockets 928 and 929 respectively, along with an indictment, which repeated the same charge.

The Lovings were in violation of Virginia code 20–54 which declared marriages between "white and colored persons" unlawful and 20–58 which deemed it unlawful to go out-of-state to marry with the intention to return and cohabit as husband and wife. Each entered a plea of not guilty, but on January 6, 1959, at their arraignment they changed their plea to guilty. The punishment for their crime was for each to spend a year in the county jail. However, Judge Leon M. Bazile suspended the sentence provided that the couple leave the state "at once and do not return together or at the same time to said county and state for a period of twenty-five years."[18] The Lovings moved to Washington, D.C., but they never adjusted to urban living. Mildred Loving later told legal historian Philip Nash of the *Washington Post,* "I missed my friends and family and walking on grass instead of concrete. . . . I missed the open spaces for the children and just walking down a country lane to pick up my mail."[19]

Mildred's cousin, with whom she and her family resided in D.C., suggested that she write to then Attorney General Robert Kennedy about her family's dilemma. If indeed she wrote to Kennedy and he responded with the advice that she write to the American Civil Liberties Union (ACLU), there is no surviving record of correspondence between the Attorney General and Mildred Loving. On June 20, 1963, two months prior to the historic March on Washington, Mildred wrote to the ACLU for legal assistance. At the time Bernard Cohen was doing pro bono work for the ACLU and decided to take the case. Cohen filed a motion in the Caroline County Circuit Court on November 6, 1963, requesting that the Loving's 1959 judgment be vacated and the sentences set aside. Unfortunately, Cohen would have to argue his case before the same judge who had handed down the original decision. Judge Bazile delayed hearing the case for more than a year. In the meantime Philip J. Hirschkop signed on as co-counsel when he joined the Cohen firm in mid-1964. In January 1965, Bazile heard the arguments on behalf of the Lovings but denied the motion stating, "Almighty God created the races white, black, yellow, malay, and red, and he placed them on separate continents. And but for the interference with his arrangement, there would be no cause for such marriages. The fact that he separated the races showed that he did not intend for the races to mix."[20] Yet, Judge Bazile went one step further. No doubt irritated that the Lovings had hired a northern attorney who challenged his previous decision, Cohen was a native New Yorker, Bazile took a personal jab at the couple in the conclusion of his opinion. He reminded them of their felony status stating, "Conviction of a felony is a serious matter. . . . And as long as you live you will be known as a felon." He concluded his opinion by quoting in part the words of Persian poet Omar Khayyam stating, "The moving finger writes and moves on and having writ—Nor all your piety nor your wit can change one bit of it."

Cohen next appealed to the Virginia Supreme Court, which on March 7, 1966, unanimously agreed to uphold the Lovings' conviction, leaving Cohen and Hirshkop only one other option: The United States Supreme Court. This was not surprising as the two lawyers predicted early on that the case would eventually reach the doorstep of the high court. However, whether the nine justices would hear the case was questionable, as they had previously refused to hear the case of *Naim v. Naim* in 1955.

The Naim case involved Ham Say Naim, a Chinese sailor, and his White wife, Ruby Elaine Naim of Virginia, whom he married in North Carolina. While Virginia held that Whites could only marry Whites, North Carolina restricted White–Black marriages only. Therefore, the Naim's White–Chinese marriage was legal in North Carolina. The couple returned to Virginia and lived for a time in Norfolk but later separated. Ruby Naim petitioned the Virginia court to grant her an annulment on the basis that her husband had committed adultery; however, if the court refused to grant her petition based on adultery, she requested that the petition be granted based on Virginia's anti-miscegenation law. The judge saw this as an open-and-shut case and granted Ruby Naim's petition based on the latter claim. However, Ham Say Naim, who was seeking American citizenship, which depended on his marriage to an American citizen, challenged the verdict stating that it violated his rights under the Fourteenth Amendment. Nevertheless, much like the Lovings who would use the same argument ten years later, the Virginia Supreme Court unanimously ruled against Ham Say Naim. Yet, unlike the Lovings, the

U.S. Supreme Court refused to hear the case. Subsequently, in the 1964 Supreme Court case *McLaughlin v. Florida,* in which a White woman and Black man were arrested for unlawful cohabitation, the justices, though not overturning anti-miscegenation laws, unanimously voted to overturn the couple's conviction, stating that "a state could not use the law that specifies race to keep people from living together."[21] At the time the Loving case reached the high court, seventeen states remained steadfast in their position against mixed race marriages. Realizing that they could no longer hold off ruling on the question of marriage across the color line, on December 12, 1966, the Supreme Court agreed to hear the Loving case.

Both sides presented their arguments before the court on April 10, 1967. Cohen and Hirschkop argued that Virginia's anti-miscegenation laws violated the Lovings' Fourteenth Amendment rights, which guaranteed due process and equal protection under the law. The argument climaxed with a poignant quote from Richard Loving who stated, "Tell the court I love my wife and it is just unfair that I cannot live with her in Virginia." However, R. D. McIlwaine, III, assistant attorney general for Virginia, argued on behalf of the Commonwealth, that the Fourteenth Amendment was beyond the reach of anti-miscegenation statutes and that its framers had not intended for it to subvert the power of the state to forbid interracial marriage. Therefore, McIlwaine argued, Virginia's anti-miscegenation statutes could not be overturned. The justices unanimously disagreed. On June 12, 1967, the high court overturned the Lovings' conviction and declared anti-miscegenation laws unconstitutional making it unlawful to deny citizens the right to marry solely on the basis of race.[22] One Caroline County leader didn't mince words when citing the impact of the Supreme Court's verdict, "The power boys in the county despised Richard because he ended the white man's moonlighting in romance. Now they got to cut out this jive of dating Negro women at night and these high yaller Negroes got to face up to the facts of life. They don't have to pass anymore."[23]

Although Caroline County has been described as "an area known for relatively benign race relations" and Central Point as "a place of surprising racial harmony" due to much commingling of the races, such characterizations obscure the complex ways the county residence negotiated race in their daily lives, as well as the deep racial feelings exhibited within the community. From an outside perspective it indeed appeared that Central Point was racially harmonious. Richard Loving's father, Twillie Loving, was an employee of P. E. Boyd Byrd, one of the wealthiest Black men in Caroline County. Twillie worked for Byrd for twenty-five years until a saw mill accident forced him to retire. Byrd, incidentally, was related to Mildred on her mother's side. Richard was good friends with Mildred's brothers and was also a partner in one of the most successful integrated drag racing teams in the country. Richard's drag racing partners were two Black mechanics: Raymond Greene, who, as of this writing, continues to own and operate Green's Garage and Towing on a part time basis (the only remaining business in Central Point) and Percy Fortune, Central Point's former grocery store owner. Of his two partners Richard stated, "These are my friends . . . for the sport has interwoven wives and children into a 'motor clan.'"[24] Although many residents in Central Point claimed Indian or part-Indian ancestry, both Green and Fortune identified solely as Black.

However, the question remains how did Richard Loving perceive his friends and his wife? Richard Loving has been characterized as a man who possessed a "raceless attitude."[25] According to Booker, Loving stated, "Everybody looked alike to me. I just never figured out all of this would happen. I just did not know about all of this stuff."[26] If these are indeed the words of Richard Loving, it is hard to imagine that he was being forthright. How is it that he could live in Virginia all of his life and not know about "all of this stuff"? Although he claimed that he had never ventured beyond the county line, he was well aware that Caroline County was segregated. In fact, he and his "colored" friends had gone to separate schools. Richard caught the "White" bus and attended "White" schools while his friends caught the "colored" bus and attended "colored" schools. The couple never attempted to obtain a marriage license in the state because they were well aware that Richard Loving could not marry Mildred Jeter in Virginia. It seems that Richard "did not figure all of this would happen," because he never thought that anybody from his "racially harmonious" community would reveal the couple's secret.[27]

To the contrary, Central Point was not as "raceless" as has been purported. Caroline County residents in general and Central Point residents in particular were indeed cognizant of the racial hierarchy that granted social privilege to Whites, an honorary White privilege to Indians (i.e. access to White hospitals and the White only section of rail and street cars), and no social privilege to Blacks. Observations made by Marshall Wingfield in his 1924 history of Caroline County inadvertently demonstrated that the residents of Central Point were well aware of Virginia's racial mores and, by the time the state had passed the Racial Integrity Act of 1924, an identity void of Negro ancestry was well entrenched. Wingfield, in describing the members of Saint Stephen's Baptist Church, the social haven of the Central Point community, stated:

> There are few members of this congregation who have as much as one-half negro blood. The people of the church and the community as a whole are very nearly white and out of their community could not be recognized or distinguished as colored people. *It is said that the predominating blood in them is that of the Indian and white races* [italics mine].[28]

It appears that despite a known Black presence, the residents of Central Point chimed in with those of the American Indian community in articulating an Indian–White only identity. Consequently, once out of their community, many simply passed for White. As Booker stated, Central Point "is the source from which hundreds of young men and women have migrated to cross racial lines, later marrying and working as whites in cities throughout the country." Many of the youngsters even attended "White only" establishments within the county without anyone suspecting that they were in violation of segregation laws. School officials at Union High School, where Mildred Loving attended before dropping out in the eleventh grade, were well aware that Central Point students frequently passed when they ventured beyond the boundaries of their community. One official stated, "These people have infiltrated the white race more than any group of Negroes. When a student plays hookey from school for a week and says an in-law is visiting the family, we understand. The kids just can't afford to catch the Negro school bus without giving away the racial identity." A teacher stated, "The light skinned students always come from Central Point . . . We hardly hear about them after they finish. They are clannish and proud."[29]

The integration of the armed forces put "passing Negroes" in a precarious position, as one resident recalled that he had to drive one of his

GIs to Central Point so that his White army buddies wouldn't know where he lived and betray his racial identity.[30] However, not everyone in Caroline County or Central Point was light enough to pass for White, thus those of darker hue attributed their pigmentation to American Indian ancestry. As Pratt noted:

> Some of the blacks in the area who were light enough to pass as white often did so, and some of those whose complexion was a little darker often claimed to be Native American, even though most of them were known to have black relatives. While there is undoubtedly a Native American presence in Caroline County, not everyone who claimed to be an "Indian" really was, but given the racial climate of the 1950s, some blacks thought it more socially acceptable to emphasize their Native American rather than their African ancestry.[31]

Choosing one racial identity over the other clearly demonstrates that contrary to the idyllic representation of a harmonious and racially benign society, Central Point was a microcosm of Virginia's established racial norms. Race indeed mattered in Central Point as it did all over the state as well as the nation. So strong was the resistance to being classed as a Negro that Oliver Fortune, a resident of Central Point, refused to report for military duty during World War II because he did not want to be enlisted as a Negro. Chief Otho Nelson, of the Rappahannock Tribe, writing to Frank Speck regarding Fortune's case stated, "The boy say he will go to the pen before he will take the negro status to go down in history as negro."[32] Although Fortune steadfastly denied that he was Negro, the Selective Service determined that his racial designation was correct because his parents had purchased a house as colored people and he had attended colored schools.[33] Incidentally, Fortune and two others were incarcerated for refusing to cooperate with the draft, but were later released and allowed to participate in a program for conscientious objectors.[34] In addition, Fortune's name appeared among the organizers of the Powhatan Confederacy during the 1970s as assistant chief of the Rappahannock Tribe.[35]

Much like Oliver Fortune, Mildred Loving's racial identification was established as a result of her birth certificate, which identified her parents, Theoliver Jeter and Musie Byrd, as colored. On his 1884 birth certificate Theoliver and his parents, Samuel and Susan Jeter, were also identified as colored. There is no data on Musie Byrd prior to her appearance as Theoliver's wife on the 1940 census in which she is identified as Black. The census data on both family surnames follows a similar pattern as noted in chapter 2. On census records from 1870 to 1930, the Jeters were identified as mulatto in the nineteenth century, but by 1930 were identified as Negro. On the other hand, the Byrds were overwhelmingly identified as Black until the 1910 census, in which they were identified as either colored or mulatto. The same occurred on the 1920 census, but by 1930 they were solely classified as Negro. Nevertheless, as has been demonstrated, racial designations on various government documents, including the U.S. census, have been problematic from the beginning. Notwithstanding, the Byrd surname is prominent among the Rappahannock Indians. The Jeter surname is also listed in the Rappahannock Tribe's corporate charter (1974) as a tribal affiliate. Many claim, however, that the Jeters are descended from the Cherokee who allegedly began to intermarry with the Rappahannock during the late eighteenth century. According to one anonymous informant, "The situation regarding Indian identity in Caroline County is very complex. There was a time when many in the Rappahannock community believed that they were Cherokee because that was all they knew."[36] Neither Mildred nor her brother, Lewis Jeter, supported the claim that their father was Cherokee.

Yet how does one explain Mildred Loving's early twenty-first-century self-identity as an Indian woman with no African American ancestry? During my interview with her she identified her mother as a full-blooded Rappahannock and her father as Rappahannock and White. When asked about her African American ancestry, she stated that to her knowledge she had no African American people in her family. "I know my grandmother was from Portugal [both of her grandmothers were born in Virginia], but as far as I know, no one in my family was Black." Yet, this statement differed from her assertion during a 1997 interview with Kim Douglass, a reporter for the *Free Lance-Star,* in which Loving identified herself as an Indian of mixed Portuguese and Black ancestry. In 2004, however, when I asked about the Rappahannock's historic association with Blacks in response to her denial of Black ancestry, Mildred flatly denied such associations stating, "No, the Rappahannock never had anything to do with Blacks."[37] While such a statement of denial from one who is hailed an icon of the Civil Rights Movement was indeed astonishing, it was also in keeping with the deeply entrenched notions of race and identity in Central Point. As one longtime Caroline County resident, who claimed familial ties with Mildred, quipped, "That's not true. That's why I hate to fool with them people down there in Central Point. They always trying to be something they ain't. Everybody either Indian or White. Nobody a nigger."[38] Another longtime resident stated:

> The we-only-White-and-Indian thing was what the old folks said and some people still like to believe that, but it's not true. There was a lot of mingling down here between the Blacks, the Whites, and the Indians. Not just in Central Point, but all over Caroline County. As far as the Rappahannocks go, they are mostly light skin, but they got Black relatives right here in this area. I know some of them. Honestly, people are so mixed down here you can't say what you are or what you are not. Sometimes, it is really hard to tell.[39]

Yet, for over thirty years Mildred had maintained an identity that acknowledged her Afro-Indian heritage. So why the sudden shift of identity during her later years? At the time of her marriage to Richard, she indeed identified as an Indian woman of mixed White ancestry. This self-identity in her early years was certainly in line with the racial feelings of Central Point, where denying Blackness was prevalent in the community. There was no such denial of Blackness, however, in her 1963 plea for help to the ACLU, where she identified herself as part Negro, part Indian. Perhaps residing with her cousin in Washington, D.C., who may not have identified as Indian, tempered this denial. While Mildred maintained a preference to self-identify as Indian, a preference she maintained throughout the remainder of her life, it may have become much more difficult to deny Blackness within a community of the nation's capital inundated with the Civil Rights Movement and Black pride. In addition, whether intentional or not, Mildred's request to the ACLU for assistance regarding her anti-miscegenation case positioned her as a civil rights activist within a movement viewed as the vanguard of the modern-day Black freedom struggle. Certainly, denying Blackness would have been counterproductive to her cause. Thirty-five years later when she sat down with the newspaper reporter and asserted that she was an Indian of mixed Portuguese and Black ancestry, her preference to identify as Indian did not include a denial of Blackness. As historian Robert Pratt noted during our February 12, 2012, conversation, "I've interviewed Mildred on numerous occasions, and she never denied being Black." What then can account for her denial of Blackness seven years after the 1997 Douglass interview? The answer may well lay in a related article on the Rappahannock Indians that appeared on the same page as Douglass's article.

While *Free Lance-Star* reporter Kim Douglass was working on the Loving story to commemorate the thirtieth anniversary of the Supreme Court decision, she was simultaneously working on a highly controversial story regarding political contentions within the Rappahannock community. It was an extensive story that was published as a two-part series entitled, "Trouble in the Tribe." The first part, "From a Rich Past to a Divided Future," focused on the tribe's 250-year struggle and its resilience in the face of colonialism and modern-day attempts of ethnocide. But recent tribal in-fighting had left the community vulnerable. While Douglass asserted that the root of the tribal contention was hard to pinpoint, one controversy seemed to have risen above all the rest. The most salient contention involved the policy enforced by some within the tribal leadership to exclude those of African American ancestry as was adopted in the 1995 amendment to the articles of incorporation (AOI), which stated, "Applicants possessing any Negro blood will not be admitted to membership. Any member marrying into the Negro race will automatically be admonished from membership in the Tribe."

Part two of the series focused exclusively on the tribe's anti-Black policy. For certain, airing the community's racial dirty laundry deepened tensions rather than alleviated them. Perhaps the cause of much of the chagrin, however, was due to the decision of the paper to juxtapose Douglass's article on Mildred Loving, which featured the headline "Is Mildred Loving Considered Black or Indian? Both She Says" with her article on the Rappahannock, which featured the headline "The Color Line: Rappahannock Indians Split Over Black Blood Lines." The intentions of *the Free Lance-Star's* editorial board regarding this matter must be left to conjecture. Perhaps the juxtaposition was merely coincidental or perhaps the paper saw the two articles as similar and decided to group them together. Or the juxtaposition may have served as an unintended reminder of the consequences of racism and the sacrifices made to overcome them. Whatever the intent, the Loving article, featuring an open acknowledgement by Mildred Loving, a Rappahannock, that affirmed an Indian identity and also acknowledged her Black ancestry, may have proven far more troublesome to the Rappahannock leadership. Given the unabashed anti-Black sentiments expressed by the group, it would not be a stretch to imagine that Mildred may have received a stern warning from tribal leadership to refrain from acknowledging her own Black ancestry as well as that of the tribe's or risk being ostracized by the Rappahannock tribal community. Both articles, so it seemed, had inadvertently raised questions regarding the racial purity of the tribal community. The tribe planned to move forward with a petition for federal recognition and could ill afford to have anyone, even a famed civil rights icon, jeopardize its chances. It seems highly probable that they sternly pressed Mildred who acquiesced to the tribe's demands to refrain from acknowledging Black ancestry. Tribal pressure notwithstanding, as demonstrated by another long time Central Point resident, some refused to buy into the Indian claim: "A lot of us feel that these folks claiming to be Indian are only getting away with it because they got that skin color and that hair. Regardless, we know who and what they are."[40]

It appears that many of Mildred Loving's close acquaintances assumed they knew who and what she was. Bernard Cohen, who had been Mildred Loving's lawyer since taking her case in 1963, was surprised to learn that his client self-identified as Indian. "That's news to me," he replied. When asked if at any time during the 1960s ordeal she had ever insisted that she was Indian only, Cohen replied, "No, she has always insisted that she was part Black and part American Indian."[41] According to Philip Hirschkop, Mildred's racial identity whether Black, Indian, mixed, or otherwise did not matter. It only mattered in that according to Virginia law she was non-white and therefore could not marry a White person. Nonetheless, it appears that Mildred's racial identity indeed mattered during the court ordeal. It seems improbable that she would have to insist that she was Black. Perhaps while everyone else insisted that she was Black, Mildred Loving fought against the erasure

The color issue

Rappahannock Indians split over black blood lines

Stories by KIM DOUGLASS

Last year, a movie was made about Mildred Loving (left), whose marriage to Richard Loving (seen in the photo she's holding) received national attention. Loving is a product of mixed races; she has black, Indian and Portuguese blood.

ROBERT A. MARTIN
Staff photographer

RACE HAS BEEN a painfully sensitive issue among Indians, including Rappahannock Indians, for generations.

For some, preserving their identity has become a matter of preserving "blood lines" and discouraging marriage with people of other races.

A dramatic example of this is the United Rappahannock Tribe, which excludes anyone "possessing any Negro blood" from membership.

That raises questions about whether the tribe should have received a $95,000 federal grant last year.

The tribe is registered as a nonprofit organization with the State Corporation Commission. On file are its articles of incorporation, which list membership rules and meeting schedules. The articles state that no one "possessing any Negro blood" may be a member of the tribe.

They also state: "Any member marrying into the Negro race will automatically be admonished from membership in the tribe." These rules were added in 1995.

The U.S. Department of Health and Human Services handled the federal grant. Based on questions from a Free Lance-Star reporter, it will look into whether the tribe violated the grant's terms by discriminating against Indians with black family members, spokesman Michael Kharfen said.

"When we issue a grant [it is understood] that the grantee will abide by applicable federal statutes, which includes . . . the civil rights statutes," he said.

It's unlikely that the government would ask for the money back, even if it decides the tribe violated civil rights law, Kharfen

Please see Indians, page A12

Is Mildred Loving considered black or Indian? Both, she says

MILDRED LOVING may be Caroline County's most famous example of how complicated the race issue has been in places like Central Point.

Loving is known as the black woman who was a plaintiff in the lawsuit that led to a 1967 U.S. Supreme Court ruling allowing whites to marry blacks.

A movie about her marriage to a white man, Richard Loving, was released last year.

But Loving also thinks of herself as an Indian. Her mother was part Rappahannock Indian, and her father was part Cherokee, she said recently at her Central Point home. The Indian community there thinks of her as one of its own.

She's a product of a number of races and ethnic backgrounds, including Portuguese and black.

But in the 1950s, her dark skin and her "mixed" background made her black. For years, historians say, there were only two

> 66
>
> **If I'm blue, green, red, it doesn't matter. I'm here.**
>
> —Mildred Loving
>
> 99

recognized races in Virginia—white and non-white.

Mildred and Richard Loving were childhood friends. They both grew up around Central Point. Six weeks after they married in 1958, Caroline Sheriff Garnett Brooks

Please see Loving, page A12

TODAY: The practice of excluding those with "Negro blood" raises a legal issue: Should the tribe have received federal grant money? | YESTERDAY: For generations, Rappahannock Indians have withstood challenges from outside the tribe. Now, the battles are within.

FIG 5.2. Front page of the *Free Lance-Star* (June 12, 1997) featuring articles on the Rappahannock Indian Tribe and commemoration of the 30th anniversary of the *Loving v. Virginia* decision. Used by permission.

of the Indian half of her identity. Yet, the Indian aspect, so it seemed, would further complicate the case, throwing a monkey wrench into Cohen's and Hirschkop's arguments. How were they to present a case about the interracial marriage of a White–Indian couple that called for the dismantling of the last odious laws of slavery and segregation to a Supreme Court that saw these issues only in terms of Black and White? The two lawyers no doubt saw their victory quickly slipping away and decided they couldn't afford to risk losing the case. But they indeed took a huge risk in presenting their case within a Black/White dichotomy as was clearly demonstrated during their oral arguments before the court.

Cohen and Hirschkop adopted a tag team approach for their Supreme Court strategy. Hirschkop began by arguing that Virginia's anti-miscegenation laws were grounded in slavery and the pathology of White supremacy while Cohen immediately followed with the Fourteenth Amendment. In his leading argument, Hirschkop asserted that the aim of the Racial Integrity Act (RIA), as the intent of the legislation suggested, was to preserve the purity of the White race. In providing the court the state's definition of a White person, however, Hirschkop ignored the definition within the legal statute and put forward the definition outlined in the original bill, which defined a white person as someone having only Caucasian "blood." Yet, that definition was rejected early during the bill's debate and was replaced with the Pocahontas Exception, which allowed Whites to possess no more than one-sixteenth of the "blood" of the American Indian. It appears that the Loving team adopted this strategy to avoid a discussion of the Virginia Indians, a clear indication of their possessive investment in a Black and White only racial discourse. Each of the lawyers, in fact, went out of his way to avoid the mention of American Indians altogether. An exception to this was Hirschkop's attempt to drive home the point that the definition of a White person was fluid because in South Carolina, Native Americans were classified as White and therefore White–Indian intermarriage was not forbidden there. The manipulation of the definition in Virginia as it pertained to the Pocahontas Exception was avoided altogether during the course of Cohen's and Hirschkop's argument before the court. According to the lawyers the plain and simple truth of the case was that Richard Loving, a "White" man, and Mildred Jeter, a "Negro" woman, were forbidden the right to marry under Virginia's anti-miscegenation statute.

Virginia's Assistant Attorney General McIlwaine concurred that the issue was simply a matter of Black and White. In an exchange with Chief Justice Earl Warren, who challenged the constitutionality of the Virginia statute on the basis that the proscription against intermarriage only pertained to White–Black couples, McIlwaine justified the statute by constructing a two tier racial reality which at once provided the state's ideological justification for the Racial Integrity Act and rendered the presence of Native American peoples irrelevant.

> Chief Justice Earl Warren: But you do put a restrictions on North American-Indians if they have more than one-sixteenth of Indian blood in them, do you not?
>
> Mr. R. D. McIlwaine, III: Yes, sir. But this is because in Virginia, we have only two races of people which are within the territorial boundaries of the State of Virginia in sufficient numbers to constitute a classification with which the legislature must deal. That is why I say the white and the colored prohibition here completely controls the racial picture with which Virginia is faced.
>
> Chief Justice Earl Warren: You have no Indians in Virginia?
>
> Mr. R. D. McIlwaine: Well, we have Indians Your Honor, but this is the point that we make with respect to them. Under the census figures of 1960, 79 and some odds hundreds percent of the Virginia population was made up of white people, 20 and some odd hundred percent of the Virginia population was made up of colored people, whites and Negroes by definition of the United States Department of Commerce Bureau of the Census. Thus, 99 percent and 44 percent, 100 percent of the Virginia population falls into these two racial categories. All other racial classes in Virginia combined do not constitute as much as one-fourth of 1 percent of the Virginia population. . . . Now, so far as the particular appellants in this case are concerned, there is no question of constitutional vagueness or doubtful definition. It is a matter of record, agreed to by all counsel during the course of this litigation and in the brief that one of the appellants here is a white person within the definition of the Virginia law, the other appellant is a colored person within the definition of Virginia law.[42]

Despite each lawyer's propensity to dismiss the relevance of Mildred's mixed race identity, the mass media periodically gave it an honorable mention. As the above epigraph demonstrates, however, writers always found Mildred Loving's Black identity, but often lost her Indian identity.

The Loving case garnered little to no attention outside of their Central Point community until the mid-1960s. The *Richmond News Leader* reported on the case more than any other paper in the state. Identifying her mixed race identity proved to be hit and miss. An October 28, 1964, article identified the plaintiffs of the suit as "Richard Perry Loving who says he is white and Mildred Jeter Loving who says she is a negro." However, the following day, the *Richmond News Leader* quoted Mildred Loving as saying that she "was half Negro and half Indian." Almost two months later on December 28, 1964, the *Richmond News Leader* lost her Indian half stating of Mildred that "she is Negro." On February 12, 1965, the paper rediscovered her Indian half and identified Mildred as "part Negro and part Indian." Nevertheless, two years later when reporting on the Supreme Court Decision, the *News Leader* once again lost the Indian half of Mildred's identity and simply identified her as Negro.[43] The *Richmond Times-Dispatch* reported her identity in a similar pattern.

The same occurred in national newspapers. The *Washington Post* on October 28, 1964, identified Mildred as Richard's "negro wife." Two days later she was identified as "part negro and part Indian." Two months later on December 29, 1964, the *Post* identified her as "negro." The *Post* continued to solely identify Mildred Loving as Negro in two subsequent articles, December 9, 1965, and June 12, 1965, however, on January 8, 1966, Mildred was once again identified as "part negro, part Indian." Nevertheless, the article dated July 30, 1966, and all other articles that follow, solely identified Mildred Loving as Negro. The same pattern is repeated in the *New York Times*. On December 13, 1966, the *Times* identified Mildred Loving as "part-Negro, part-Indian"; yet once again, when reporting the Supreme Court ruling on June 13, 1967, she was identified as "a negro woman."[44]

Although Mildred Loving's mixed race ancestry was increasingly acknowledged by the final decade of the twentieth century, her American Indian ancestry continued to be both lost and found. In a *New York Times* article published on June 12, 1992, commemorating the twenty-fifth anniversary of the Loving decision, author David Margolick identified Mildred Loving as Black.[45] Two months later an article in the *Free Lance-Star* of Fredericksburg, Virginia published on Saturday, August 1, 1992, also identified Mildred Loving as Black.[46] In addition, two commemorative articles appeared in the *Washington Post*. The June 12, 1992, article identified Mildred Loving as Black, however, two days later another article appeared in the *Post* identifying her as "Cherokee and African American."[47] The author, Philip T. Nash, also identified Richard Loving as "English and Irish." Yet, he acknowledged that, "Under Virginia law he was 'white' and she was 'colored.'"[48] In addition, Nash took a rare opportunity not only to analyze the meaning of the Loving legacy, but to critique the politics of race and to grapple with issues of race left unanswered by the court, namely that of the racial classification of mixed-race children. Nash contended:

> But the Loving decision was more than the victory of one couple. It was a landmark instance of using the law to achieve justice. It drew attention to the absurdity of "race" terms that are biologically meaningless and arbitrarily concocted to promote segregation and hierarchy . . . It freed children of mixed-race parentage from being considered bastards—although under our system of terminology they still must define themselves by the race of one parent and not the other.[49]

Although the Federal government refused to allot a separate mixed-race category on the 2000 census, it did, however, allow citizens, for the first time, to check off more than one racial category. The same was repeated for the 2010 census. While many people saw this as an end to the one-drop rule, incidentally, the Clinton administration ruled that any person who checked multiple boxes that included a Black identification, would still be counted as Black. In 2010, those who self-identified as White were more likely to check one racial designation while those who self-identified as Black came in a close second. Among those residing within African American communities who checked more than one racial category, 3 percent included American Indian as an additional racial designation. American Indians and Alaskan Natives were more likely than any other group to check more than one racial category. Among this group 5.2 percent checked African American as an additional racial category. In total only 2.9 percent of the American population chose a multi-racial identity on the 2010 census up from 2.4 percent in 2000, a clear indication that single race identity remains deeply entrenched within the American psyche. In comparison, although contemporary writers are more likely to acknowledge Mildred Loving as Afro-Indian, as did Congress in its 2007 resolution to acknowledge the 40th anniversary of the Supreme Court decision, it appears to be an honorable mention. In the final analysis writers do not view her as an Afro-Indian or an Indian woman, but simply as an "ordinary Black woman."[50]

Despite this representation, it seems that the story Mildred Jeter began to write on the day she became Mildred Loving, which is enshrined on her marriage license, is the story she vowed to take to her grave. The American Indian identity is strong within the Loving family as demonstrated by Mildred's grandson, Marc Fortune, the son of her daughter Peggy Loving Fortune. When Mildred Loving's son, Donald, died unexpectedly on August 31, 2000, Marc, according to one attendee, arrived at his uncle's funeral dressed in native regalia and performed a "traditional Rappahannock" ritual in honor of his deceased uncle.[51] In fact, all of the Loving children are identified as Indian on their marriage licenses. During an interview on April 10, 2011, Peggy Loving stated that she is "full Indian." This was also the testimony of her uncle, Lewis Jeter, Mildred's brother who stated during an interview on July, 20, 2011, that the family was Indian and not Black. Echoing his sister's words he stated, "We have no Black ancestry that I know of."[52]

On May 2, 2008, Mildred Loving died of cancer at her Central Point home. A little less than a year before her death, a *USA Today* article, written by Associated Press staff writer Dionne Walker, identified Mildred as "a black woman living in Virginia." A memorial article, written the following year by the same staff writer, identified her as "a Black woman." Memorials from three prominent Virginia Tidewater papers the *Richmond Times Dispatch,* the *Free Lance-Star* (Fredericksburg) and the *Virginian-Pilot* (Norfolk), all identified Mildred as Black in the opening lines. The latter paper, however, mentioned within the body of the story that she was also of Native American ancestry. National papers mirrored the local papers. Both the *Washington Post* and the *New York Times* identified Mildred as Black. International papers such as the *Times of London* identified Mildred Loving as being of "Native American and African-American descent," yet the headline identified her as a "Black

American who won a landmark Supreme Court Battle to have Its Laws Against Intermarriage Overturned." The *Independent* (London) also identified her as Black while the *Guardian* (United Kingdom) article, which was authored by Phyl Newbeck, identified her as African and Cherokee. The *Daily Post* (Liverpool) also identified Mildred as "half Cherokee with native American blood."[53]

Newspapers were not the only source of print media reporting on Mildred's death. On May 17, 2008, an article on Mildred Loving appeared in the obituary section of *The Economist,* an international, weekly magazine that covers a wide range of topics. Noteworthy is the author's focus on Mildred's Indian identity, which inadvertently reinforced the myth of an inherent White–Indian compatibility:

> All the law enforcement of Caroline County stood around the bed . . . All the men saw was her black head on the pillow, next to his . . . She didn't even think of it as a Negro head, especially. Her hair could easily set straight or wavy. That was because she had Indian blood . . . All colors of people lived in Central Point, blacks with milky skin and whites with tight brown curls . . . and who all had to use different counters from pure whites when they ate lunch in Bowling Green . . . *If there was any race Mrs. Loving considered herself it was Indian, like Princess Pocahontas. And Pocahontas had married a white man* [emphasis mine].[54]

In other words, Mildred, having followed in the footsteps of her royal American Indian female forbear, would have had no other alternative in a marriage partner. Her preference in claiming an Indian identity made it inevitable that she would marry a White man, who just so happened to be Richard Perry Loving. The premise of such a comparison, however, is highly flawed. Prior to her marriage to John Rolfe, Pocahontas was married to a Powhatan man by the name of Kocoum. Her marriage to Kocoum was dissolved, however, according to Powhatan tradition, once she was captured by the English. Pocahontas married Rolfe while she was under English captivity. While there certainly could have been a mutual attraction between the two, the marriage seemed more of a political arrangement to halt hostilities and ensure diplomatic relations between the English colonists and the Powhatan people, which lasted from 1614 until the 1622 uprising. Hence, the Pocahontas/Rolfe marriage was not the result of inevitability or a natural, racialized compatibility. Much like Pocahontas, Mildred's marriage to a White man was neither inevitable nor guaranteed. Her first love, according to Central Point informants, was a Black man who fathered her oldest son Sidney Jeter. The relationship did not last for reasons that remain unknown, but given the racial politics of the day, marriage to a man of color would have been far more plausible for Mildred than her marriage to a White man. Certainly, the social phenomenon of race relations in Central Point provided a higher probability for cross racial romantic liaisons, but given Virginia's proscription against interracial marriage in 1958 when Mildred became pregnant with Richard's son Donald, such a marriage was not inevitable, but rather untenable.

Mildred Loving has been hailed for over forty years as a champion of civil rights; however, she continued to be "as reluctant to acknowledge her contribution to it as she once was to participate in it."[55] Mildred's reluctance to be identified with the civil rights movement seems to have stemmed from the same attitude displayed by Oliver Fortune, who refused to be enlisted in the armed services as a Black man because he did not want to be remembered in history as a Negro, a person identified as having African ancestry. Of course, Mildred had a right to self-identify as she wished and to have that right respected by others. Nevertheless, viewed within the historical context of Virginia in general and Central Point in particular, ironically, "the couple that rocked courts" may have inadvertently had more in common with their opponents than they realized. Mildred's Indian identity as inscribed on her marriage certificate and her marriage to Richard, a White man, appears to have been more of an endorsement of the tenets of racial purity rather than a validation of White/Black intermarriage as many have supposed. Although in the 1990s Mildred Loving acknowledged that the Supreme Court decision helped to change a great deal in race relations; she also acknowledged that there were still some who held on to the old attitudes. According to Margolick's 1992 New York Times article, R. Garnett Brooks, the sheriff who arrested Richard and Mildred Loving in 1958 stated, "I was acting according to the law at the time and I think it should be still on the books . . . I don't think a white person should marry a black person. I'm from the old school. The Lord made sparrows and robins not to mix with one another."[56]

As the incident at the Rappahannock Indian Baptist Church showed, the former sheriff is not alone, as many in the American Indian community continue as steadfast in their racist attitude toward people of African descent, just as if *Loving v. Virginia* never happened. The 1967 Supreme Court decision has had little impact on African American–American Indian relations, as many cling to the old myth of racial purity—a myth that entrapped even Mildred Loving. Both in word and action, Blacks and Indians must maintain the protocols of segregation, as has been and continues to be dictated by the dominant culture, in order to preserve the racial integrity of the Virginia Indians. Despite this, Mildred Loving believed that "attitudes towards people have really changed. The old south is going away."[57] If the old South is indeed going away, as Mildred Loving suggested, it is doing so at a snail's pace.

SIX

The Racial Integrity Fight: Confrontations of Race and Identity in Charles City County, Virginia

If I thought I had one drop of nigger blood in me, I'd slit my throat open and would let myself bleed to death.

—THE LATE JOSEPH BOWMAN, FORMER CHARLES CITY COUNTY RESIDENT

Joseph Bowman turned himself abruptly about and walked toward his farmhouse with a cool wind gently touching his back. Once inside, he made sure the front door of the house was securely shut. Bowman then threw back his head and howled with laughter as he peaked through his window at the visibly astonished census taker still standing in the middle of the field not knowing what to make of his response. The White census taker had asked him whether he was an Indian or a Negro. Bowman, whose features marked an African and Indian duality, thought he'd have a bit of fun at the stranger's expense, asserting that he'd rather be dead than a Negro.[1] Bowman, in fact, considered himself a Negro. Yet, other members of the Bowman family in Charles City County with the same ancestry considered themselves Indian. That was indeed no laughing matter.

Charles City County was featured in Harvard Professor Henry Louis Gates's PBS documentary *African American Lives,* in which he traced the ancestry of eight prominent African Americans including his colleague Dr. Sara Lawrence Lightfoot. Lightfoot's family roots appear early in Charles City history, dating before the American Revolution. She, however, grew up in the Boston area and therefore knew very little about the county except for what she had learned from relatives. In *Balm in Gilead: Journey of a Healer,* a biography of her mother, Lightfoot recounted what she had learned about Charles City County from family lore. She described the county as "a close-knit community [that] became a haven for 'free people of color,' former slaves, and American Indians who had settled in the region."[2] Lightfoot also recalled that the Elam Baptist Church, the oldest African American church in the county, "grew and flourished" as a result of the growth of the community comprised of "mixtures of Indians and 'Coloreds.'"[3] During the documentary she sat across from Gates, eager to learn more about what he had discovered about her Virginia roots. Gates described Charles City County as an idyllic community centered on civic and religious activities. Gates's description of the county coupled with Lightfoot's memories of family stories moved her to respond, "This was such a harmonious community." His description and her interpretation, however, are indeed misleading.

While there has been and remains much cooperation and community-building in Charles City County, there is also deep-seated resentment surrounding questions of race and identity regarding who is Black and who is Indian. This has been a sore point of contention within the county since the late nineteenth century. The answer, however, is not simple. For over 300 years peoples of African, Indian, and European descent have intermingled and intermarried in Charles City County. An attempt to unravel the deep roots and tangled branches of a community in which everyone is somehow related despite seemingly varied racial identities could only be accomplished by severing familial ties. Such was the case when the Chickahominy Tribe embarked on its journey to formally reorganize in 1901 in an effort to gained state recognition.[4] While the modern day Chickahominy Tribe, for example, maintains an Indian identity by denying its historic ties to the African American community, members of the Black community, including disavowed relatives, maintain that they are pseudo-Indians whose forbears decided to assume an Indian identity to subvert Jim Crow laws. Questions regarding the authenticity of the modern day Chickahominy people will not be addressed here. Rather, the focus of attention will be to examine the ways in which confrontations of race and identity, underscored by the politics of racial purity, continue to dictate relations in the small community of Charles City County, Virginia.

The name Charles City County may evoke visions of a region with a mixture of suburban and urban enclaves. The county, however, is entirely rural. Its 2007 slogan, "Four Centuries, Three Cultures, Two Rivers, and One County," adopted for the 400th anniversary of Jamestown, aptly captures the depth and richness of the human experience within a scenic environment untouched by modern development. Charles City County became one of four boroughs established by the Virginia Company in 1619. The boundaries of the county were expansive, but it was divided in 1634 along with seven other original shires. Over time seventeen additional counties were carved from the county's original landscape. Today Charles City County is small comprised of approximately "204 square miles bounded by the James River on the south, the Chickahominy River on the east and north and by Turkey Island Creek to the west."[5]

The arrival of the English to the Tidewater Region in 1607 set in motion the development of plantation culture, which would come to define the county and indeed much of the South. The founding of Shirley Plantation in 1613 and the establishment of the tobacco culture that soon followed gave rise to a White gentry, whose genteel status owed much to the indentured and later slave labor forces that proved central to the economic growth of the county. Charles City County was home to a number of prominent White citizens who gained national fame such as "William Byrd, William Byrd II, Governor Benjamin Harrison, President William Henry Harrison, Governor John Tyler and his son, President John Tyler. It is also the home of [Ann Hill Carter] the mother of Robert E. Lee and [Martha Eppes Wayles], the wife of Thomas Jefferson."[6] Today visitors to Charles City County can relish in the romanticism of English gentry and plantation life by touring the grand houses, exquisite gardens, and walking trails of a bygone era; but there is little to remind them of the indigenous population that first occupied the territory. There is also little reminder of the slave labor that built and maintained the property and its owners, who enjoyed a life of privilege at the expense of those trapped by the peculiar institution. As James P. Whittenberg asserted about the preserved plantation estates:

> They are also monuments to an era when most blacks were slaves and Indians were outcast. Indeed, almost every structure directly associated with the pre-twentieth century black and Indian world in the county has disappeared. A few years ago, supposed slave quarters at Sandy Point collapsed from neglect leaving the birthplace of Lott Cary, ex-slave, Baptist Minister, and Missionary to Liberia, as the sole Black architectural survival from the plantation era.[7]

Despite this erasure, African Americans and American Indians were integral to the development and sustainability of Charles City County.

As previously discussed, the race and ethnicity of the "twenty and odd Negars" purchased by the English from the Dutch in 1619 remains ambiguous, but their presence in the Virginia colony marked the first immigrants of color to settle in British North America. At least ten of the arrivals settled within the "Borough of Charles City County across the James River at Flowerdew Hundred, a European settlement on Weyanoke [Indian] lands."[8] Hence, Charles City County became the birthplace of the first multicultural community in British North America, an interwoven tapestry of peoples of mixed African, Indian, and European ancestry. This small community of color that spawned during the early years of colonial expansion grew into a populous community comprised of slave and free residents. By the nineteenth century people of color represented 60 percent of the Charles City County population. Today at 85 percent, this proportion is the largest of any county in Virginia. Much like nineteenth-century Norfolk County, Charles City County was home to a thriving population of free people of color during the slavery era. According to Carter G. Woodson's *Free Negro Heads of Families in 1830*, there were at least 112 families of free people of color in Charles City County. Many of these families owned land during the antebellum period, giving Charles City County the highest percentage of non-White landowners in any Virginia county. Ruthville was the most prominent community of color in Charles City County and was comprised of a thriving mulatto class. The historic Elam Baptist

Church (also known as Old Elam) has anchored this small community since 1810.[9]

When Europeans arrived in the Tidewater Region, the area now known as Charles City County was inhabited by three Indian tribes. The smallest of the three was the Paspahegh Tribe, which numbered approximately 200 people. Its territory included three villages east of the Chickahominy River, but, the majority of the tribe was domiciled along the western side of the river in an area now known as Sandy Point. The Jamestown settlement was planted within Paspaheghian territory and from there expanded like an uncontrollable weed overtaking the indigenous peoples of the region. The Paspahegh clashed with English colonists within a week of their arrival. Continued warfare over the next three years took its toll on the small group. After 1610 what remained of the Paspahegh band had disappeared from the region. They most likely obtained refuge within another indigenous group.[10]

The Weanoc Indians occupied the north and south banks of the James River "from the mouth of the Appomattox River to the area of present day Weyanoke."[11] The tribe, which was comprised of two bands, the Tanx Weanoc to the north and the Great Weanoc to the south, totaled about 500 people. The Weanoc initially welcomed the English and entertained them with lavish parties and dancing; but repeated demands for food and White expansion within Weanoc controlled territory from 1613–1622 resulted in ongoing hostilities between the two groups. The Weanoc's participation in the 1622 and 1644 uprisings to drive the English off of the peninsula further exacerbated relations and rendered the Weanoc vulnerable. By 1646, the Weanoc were forced off their lands along the river. For the next fifty years, the band wandered between Jamestown, Virginia and Hertford County, North Carolina, seeking refuge away from the English and enemy tribes—namely the Tuscarora. By the 1690s, they took refuge among the Nottoway in what is now Southampton County, Virginia.[12]

The Chickahominy Tribe, the largest and most resilient of the three, numbered over 1,000 members with sixteen villages stretched between the James and Pamunkey Rivers. They were a "populous and stable people" known for their prosperity and military strength.[13] Powhatan, who had inherited six nations from his father, had by the early seventeenth century conquered all of the tribes within the territories "along the upper and middle course" of the James, Pamunkey, and Mattaponi Rivers.[14] His reach later extended into the northern and southern coastal regions as well as the Eastern Shore, which lay across the Chesapeake Bay. Yet, with all of Powhatan's expansion, the Chickahominy remained unconquerable. They were able to maintain their independence by paying Powhatan occasional tributes. The Chickahominy Tribe was not governed by a chieftain, but rather by a council of priests and assistant elders. Although there was a single spokesperson for the tribe, this was an informal position with no other power vested in it.[15]

The Chickahominy may have remained independent of the Powhatan Confederacy, but in times of Powhatan–English conflict, the tribe cast its lot with its Algonquian neighbors, thus jeopardizing its independence. The Chickahominy were accomplices in the capture of John Smith in 1608, which led to his captivity for two months. Yet, when the Powhatan Confederacy reached a peace agreement with the English in 1614 with the marriage of John Rolfe and Pocahontas, the Chickahominy, wedged between two powers, chose to submit to English rule rather than Powhatan's. They signed a treaty with the English agreeing to become a tributary to the Crown. They also agreed to forfeit the Chickahominy name for the title "Tassautessus," meaning Englishmen. They were not allowed into English territory and were forbidden from vandalizing English property. The eight elders of the tribe were charged with enforcing sanctions against those who violated the treaty. The tribe was also obliged to contribute 300 fighting men to English forces in the event of a Spanish assault. For these concessions, the Chickahominy received "a red coat, a chaine, and a picture of King James."[16]

Peace hovered over the region during the next eight years, but tensions simmered beneath the surface as the English encroached on tribal lands through their expansion along the coastal region and inland. On March 22, 1622, Opechancanough, Powhatan's successor, staged a surprised attack on the English in an effort to rid the region of the English nuisance once and for all. In all, 350 colonists were killed. English reprisal was swift, fierce, and extensive, lasting almost a decade. William Piece was placed in charge of the campaign against the Chickahominy. His instructions were to "pursue the Salvages with fire and sword."[17]

The economic warfare commenced by the colonists, which included setting up ambushes along Indian hunting routes and setting ablaze the Indians' corn fields, took a devastating toll on the native people. In 1631, the Chickahominy and Pamunkey signed another peace treaty with the English, but an uneasy peace ensued for the next thirteen years as there was mistrust on both sides. As a last ditch effort to rid the Tidewater Region of the colonists, Opechancanough, joined by the Chickahominy and other allies, made his final attack in 1644. Fatalities among the colonists totaled 500. Losses notwithstanding, by this time the colony was expansive. There was hardly a dent in the now expansive colonial population. Once again, English reprisals were swift, fierce, and extensive.

In 1646, the Powhatan, now under Necotowance, Opechancanough's successor, entered into a third peace treaty with the English. For their part in the insurrection, the Chickahominy were forced to cede their lands on the "Lower Penninsula."[18] The tribe left Charles City County and relocated to an area "between the Pamunkey River and branches of the Mattaponi."[19] In addition, article nine of the treaty held Necotowance responsible for the return of "guns, English prisoners, Negro and Indian servants to the English," illustrating the development of a cross-cultural alliance in early Virginia. In 1661 Chickahominy elders petitioned the Virginia General Assembly for a new land grant due to repeated White encroachment. The petition was granted for "all the lands from Mr. Mallory's bounds to the head of Mattaponi River & into the woods of the Pamunkies."[20] In 1691 the Chickahominy were urged to trade their lands in King William County for an area in King and Queen County. By 1694 the poor state of the land sent the Chickahominy back to Pamunkey Neck where they were granted reservation lands totaling a little over 6,000 aces. By 1750, however, through trickery, deceit, and White encroachment, the tribe had lost its reservation lands.

With the loss of its independence, land holdings, tribal structure, and much of its population, it looked as though the last days of the Chickahominy were fast approaching. The community dispersed; some remained with the Pamunkey and others domiciled along the Mattaponi River. The latter are believed to be the progenitors of the present day Upper Mattaponi Tribe. A large portion, however, returned to Charles City County. Of this latter group, some believe the modern day Chickahominy emerged. Yet, the emergence of the modern day Chickahominy Tribe has not been without controversy. While many White residents in Charles City have hailed Chickahominy renewal as a testament of survival and a triumph of the human spirit, African American residents, view the entire ordeal as a fraud. As David Lazarus Jones asserted, "they are not authentic, but indeed self made."[21]

Two competing theories have emerged regarding the origin of the modern day Chickahominy Tribe. According to tribal lore the motivation to reorganize grew out of resentment regarding a land struggle between the colored and Indian populations over the central ridge area of the county. The latter had returned to the area in 1850 in hopes of reclaiming their ancestral lands ceded in the 1646 treaty. Upon their return, however, instead of having to contend with White encroachment, they found themselves contending with free Blacks for land that was once theirs in a bygone era. This, coupled with tensions that arose from disputes about the tribe's racial identity, led to a deeper cohesiveness among the Indians. This cohesion motivated them to formalize as a separate entity that would protect Indian identity by maintaining segregation of the two groups.

This traditional origin story, however, has been vehemently contested by those in the African American community who contend that there was no separate Indian community or Indian identity among the citizens in Charles City County prior to 1898 and that the motivation to separate from the Black community was based in colorism—a desire of light-skinned Blacks to maintain separateness from the Black community. Hence both theories promote a denial of racial mixing of peoples of African and Indian descent in Charles City County. On one hand present day Chickahominy tribal members deny familial relations with those in the African American community, while on the other most Blacks, who acknowledge such familial ties, also deny the Indian ancestry of the modern day Chickahominy Tribe; in addition, they deny the reality of Indian ancestry within the Black community. Both theories are, of course, problematic.

Despite present day denials, the indelible thread of Black and Red within the Charles City County community comes into focus at the intersection of surnames and genealogies of residents in both communities. The Bradby surname is dominant among tribal members within the Pamunkey, Mattaponi, and Chickahominy groups and demonstrates the interconnectedness of these tribal entities. The Chickahominy trace the Bradby name in their tribe to a White Baptist minister, James Bradby, who came to live among them in 1793. Bradby married a Chickahominy woman and converted the tribe to the Baptist faith. Other surnames such as Jones, Winn, Holmes, Stewart, and Miles are also traced to White progenitors (instead of Indian progenitors). "Proud acknowledge-ment of a White progenitor," as aptly noted by anthropologist Theodore Stern, "reveals how thoroughly the Chickahominy have come to accept the racial ranking of Virginia society."[22] While such surnames are also associated with families in the African American community, for the Western Chickahominy the dominant surname Adkins raises questions regarding the validity of its modern day origin story.

The tribe traces the Adkins surname to six siblings, three brothers and three sisters, whose parents were John Adkins, Sr., and Elizabeth Bradby. In 1850, Eli Adkins became the first to acquire land, seventy-five acres in central ridge now known as Bradby's Run. In 1852 Edward Adkins acquired twenty-nine acres on the ridge in an area called Stony's Run, and William H. Adkins, Eli's brother, acquired fifty-nine acres on East Run. In 1853, Daniel Adkins, brother of William and Eli, acquired seventy acres on North Run, and Allen and John Adkins, sons of the original three Adkins, jointly purchased ninety acres on East Run. The Adkins family continued to move into the area and acquire land. These are the esteemed progenitors of the Adkins line, the dominant family of the modern-day Chickahominy Tribe. Nevertheless, "The presence of the same [sur] name . . . among the adjacent Negroes may reflect an unacknowledged and discountenanced union in bygone days."[23]

Indeed. The Adkins name appeared in Charles City County and in central ridge far earlier than 1850. The first Adkins to appear in Charles City was a woman, Mary Adkins, born 1704. In addition to Mary, at least fifteen others with this surname were born in Charles City before 1820. Eli and William H. Adkins were both born in 1818 and both died in 1868 at the age of fifty. In fact, by the mid-nineteenth century central ridge was considered a community of free Blacks. The names of the progeni-tors of the Chickahominy Tribe are listed on the Charles City County

Register of Free Negroes and Mulattoes. Yet, is this enough evidence to prove that the origin of the modern-day Chickahominy Tribe is Black rather than Indian? And if the verdict is yes, how does one reconcile this conclusion with assertions that a number of mid nineteenth-century Adkins and Bradby residents were described as having a "bright complexion, straight hair and high cheek bones?"[24] Doesn't this argue for an Indian origin? Neither assertion provides enough evidence to settle the question one way or the other. As previously discussed, for much of the nineteenth century Blacks and Indians were lumped into the non-White racial category known as colored. In addition, phenotype has had little to do with one's racial category, as numerous people, despite phenotype, have been labeled and identified as Black. Additionally, due to admixture, phenotype often varies in communities of color even among those within the same family and of the same parentage. The Free Registry describes Eli Adkins, for example, as "a bright mulatto man with prominent features" while his brother Daniel is described as "a man of brown complexion."[25] Culture more often than phenotype determines how one racially identifies. Further complicating the matter are the deep roots and tangled branches of the Charles City County community, whose familial ties are interwoven to the point that they are difficult to unravel as Michael Puglisi aptly demonstrates:

> . . . in 1862 a William Adkins married Martha A. Jones. Possibly, William was among those Adkins who bore Indian characteristics. Certainly, his children were in the vanguard of those who chose to join the newly reorganized tribe after the turn of the century. Martha's sister Mary had married John Adkins in 1852. John Adkins was the uncle of the William Adkins who married Martha Jones in 1852 [should read 1862]. John and Mary Adkins produced six children. Two sons, Henry and Allen Adkins, joined the tribe. Another son, John Adkins, and three daughters, Nancy Wyatt Adkins, Deborah Adkins, and Robinette Adkins, did not. Nancy Adkins married Lebius Bowman, a black man. Their descendants still reside in the county. Herein lies a clear case of siblings who chose different paths in self-identification. Since both John and William Adkins may have possessed Indian characteristics—or at least identified themselves with those who did—it is perhaps understandable that their male children would eventually affiliate with the tribe. Conversely, female offspring who, like Nancy, married black men with no Indian ancestry, might have been more likely to follow their husbands' affiliations with the

black community than either their male siblings or women who married men claiming kinship with the tribe.[26]

Then there is the Jones family, who further demonstrates the complexity of familial ties in the region.

One branch of the family traces itself back to Riley Jones, a mulatto, and his wife Deborah. They had five children, of whom John Henry Jones married Nancy Adkins and Nancy Jones married Tom Allen Adkins. Since Nancy Adkins and Tom Allen Adkins were sister and brother, two sets of siblings had in fact married each other. It is worth noting also that Nancy and Tom Allen Adkins were sister and brother to the William H. Adkins who later led the reorganization movement. Tom Allen identified himself as an Indian, and therefore, the descendants of that union automatically became members of the tribe. Their descendants compose a large percentage of the current tribal membership. The union between John Henry Jones and Nancy Adkins, however, produced five children, four of whom never affiliated with the native group. Of the remaining children born to Riley and Deborah Jones, Sarah married another Tom Adkins (who also claimed Indian ancestry) and identified with the Chickahominy, while brothers Jarad and Seth followed their father's lead and identified with the black community. The Jones family, then, provides another clear example of a female who elected to follow the cultural identity of her husband, regardless of the actions of her biological male siblings. The same self-selection process, but with the opposite result, occurred in the case of the one child of John Henry and Nancy Jones who became a member of the tribe. Their daughter Martha Jones married Paul Jones, a distant cousin who identified himself as an Indian. The children of this union were born into the tribe despite the fact that their cousins from Martha's four siblings identified themselves as black. On another branch of the Jones family tree, Francis Jones, the daughter of Wyatt Jones and the niece of Riley Jones, married Porterfield Bradby. Along with three of their children, Francis and Porterfield Bradby appeared on the initial roll of the reorganized tribe. But the couple is known to have produced seven children, four of whom never joined the tribe.[27]

While the above scenarios provide excellent examples to demonstrate the entanglement of kinship ties and bloodlines between African American and Indian peoples, and the role phenotype came to play in one's decision to embrace an Indian rather than a Black identity, Puglisi's tendency to view the issue as merely a decision of race obscures the larger issue of kinship realities within Charles City County.

First, his assertion that Lebius (also spelled Lebeus) Bowman and other Adkins spouses were Black with no Indian ancestry is based in conjecture. Lebius and the Bowman family's racial identity as mulatto on the census from 1860 to 1920 is a clear indication that the family was consistently viewed as people of mixed race origin. Is this evidence of Indian ancestry? Not necessarily. Yet, given the history of Charles City County, it is highly likely. Hence, any attempt to sort out who does or does not have Indian, African, and/or European ancestry in Charles City is akin to attempting to find a needle in a hay stack. Second, Puglisi's own preoccupation with phenotype, which he displays on several occasions, signifies a definition of Indian identity based on mainstream assumptions regarding physical features of American Indians. Nevertheless, phenotype is a poor indicator for determining a person's ancestral background.

Third, and most important, the Adkinses, Joneses, and Bradbys, among others, were more than the sum of their racial parts. They were families with bonds of kinship that spanned generations. The decision to "go Indian," as some put it, transcended the question of race. It became a question of race vs. family. To understand this, one must understand the importance of kinship ties in Charles City County. Community members overwhelmingly reference their neighbors by family name association. For example, when responding to a question regarding a mutual acquaintance, an informant stated, "Oh yes, I know her. She's actually a Charity, but she's married to a Bradby." Another resident stated, "When I meet an older person who doesn't know me they ask 'What's your name?' When I tell them they reply, 'Aw, you a Adkins.' Then they ask me about my grandparents. Once they have that information they reply, 'Oh yes, I know who you are.' From there they start to name my parents and other relatives of mine."[28] In other words, familial knowledge can transform a total stranger into an intimate acquaintance in an instant.

Consequently, those forty-eight members who left the Cedar Grove Baptist Church on April 13, 1901, to form the Samaria Indian Baptist Church and subsequently reorganized the tribe in 1908 are viewed by disavowed relatives as having chosen race over family. As Richard Bowman poignantly asserted, "It split families, sister against brother, brother against sister." Mr. Bowman, a descendant of the Adkins clan outlined above, recalled the words his grandmother Nancy Wyatt Adkins told him when her oldest brother Henry Elridge Adkins came to recruit her to join the tribe. "No brother," she stated, "Mama born us into this world colored; I'm going to leave out of here colored." Adkins's assertion illustrates that she was not merely choosing to follow the race of her husband or simply making a choice based on race as Puglisi suggested. By invoking their mother, Mary Jones Adkins, and referring to Henry as "brother," she may well have intended to remind him that it was not race, but kinship ties that bind. Incidentally, Mr. Bowman, who solely identifies as Black, is the second cousin of the current Chickahominy chief Stephen Adkins by way of John L. Adkins, Jr., who was Bowman's great-grandfather and Adkins's great-great-grandfather. The complexity regarding the entanglement of kinship relations and the racial division within the family unit was poignantly captured by Mrs. Bowman who stated, "They are the same as we are, but we are not Indians."[29]

According to family lore passed down by Nancy Wyatt Adkins, the motivation to identify as Indian began in 1890 when census enumerators identified Charles City County residents as Indian because some in the community "looked" Indian. Hence, members of the same family with the same parentage were identified as Black or Indian based on the perception of the enumerator. Anthropologist James Mooney's visit to the county in 1898 further exacerbated the issue. Mooney, seeing people in the region whose features displayed varying degrees of stereotypical American Indian characteristics, encouraged them to formally organize as an Indian tribe. In 1899 he compiled an Indian census that listed forty families he considered to be Indian. Prior to this time, according to Adkins, no one talked about being Indian.

Some have challenged Adkins's assertion by pointing out the oral tradition within the tribe, which contends that a small group of Chickahominy migrated to Canada to avoid conscription in the Confederate Army during the Civil War. During their time in Canada they lived among and intermarried with the Ojibway (Chippewa Indians) there. They returned after the war bringing at least one Ojibway wife with them. Yet, this story is problematic for several reasons. First, while the 1861 Canadian census indeed showed that residents from Charles City resided in Canada West in an area known as Chatham Gore Township in Kent County, the census, taken on January 13, indicated that they were there prior to the outbreak of the war on April 9. In fact, one resident, Porterfield Bradby, was born in Canada in 1859. Hence, the Charles City group was in Canada at least two years prior to the war. Second, at the time of the 1861 census it does not appear that those from Charles City were living in an Indian community at this time. With Wapole Island, an Ojibway settlement nearby Chatham-Kent, they certainly had the opportunity to live in an Indian community. Wapole Island notwithstanding, they at least lived in a multicultural community comprised of Canadians as well as English and Irish expatriates, all of whom were identified as mulatto, despite there being an Indian category on the census. Mary Ann Shadd Cary, who emigrated to Canada West in 1850, stated, "ten, twenty or more families are often settled near one another, or interspersed among the French, Dutch, Scottish, Irish and Indians in the woodland district."[30] Third, the Charles City group did not establish deep roots within the Canadian border. Most returned to Charles City after the war. According to Mooney, at least one Ojibway wife returned with them. It was likely the wife of Henry T. Bradby, since according to Mooney's 1899 Indian census Bradby had married "a real Canadian Indian." A number of residents who returned to Charles City appear on Mooney's 1899 list including Porterfield Bradby and his family. However, not one from the Canadian group joined the tribe when it formally organized in 1908. Nor were they listed on the 1910 Indian census; by 1910 Porterfield Bradby and his family were residing in the Charles City County Tyler District and were identified as mulatto.[31]

One person may have been identified as Indian in Charles City County prior to 1890. On September 20, 1872, Spotswood Adkins filed a claim for reimbursement of property loss during the Civil War with the Southern Claims Commission. At this time Spotswood was identified as colored. In 1877, however, when the claim finally made its way before the commission, Spotswood was identified as Indian. When the claim was settled the following year in 1878, he was identified as Pamunkey Indian. He later identified as Chickahominy and became a member of the modern-day band.[32]

Spotswood appears to be the exception rather than the rule. If indeed there were others who identified as Indian prior to Mooney's 1898

FIG. 6.1. Chickahominy Indian men paying tribute to Governor Westmoreland Davis (absent) on the front steps of the executive mansion in Richmond, Virginia, on December 19, 1919. From left to right, front row: Mr. Throckmorton, H. A. Adkins, Chief O. W. Adkins, First Lady of Virginia Marguerite Davis, Rev. P. E. Throckmorton, Tazewell Adkins, Elias N. Adkins, and Harvey N. Adkins; from left to right, second row: C. Mulford Crutchfield, Mrs. Hunter, and E. Victor Williams. SPC Se Powhatan Confederacy Chickahominy BAE 1–9 01787700, National Anthropological Archives, Smithsonian Institution.

visit, it is clear that there was no separate Indian community in Charles City County until the dawn of the twentieth century. This split began on April 13, 1901, with a mass exodus from Cedar Grove Baptist Church. Prior to the walkout, life for those in what would later become known as the Chickahominy Indian community was centered on the community church. According to traditional tribal lore Cedar Grove was a White church that opened its doors to Indians and Blacks. But as Black membership increased, Whites abandoned the church. Indians would soon follow to form Samaria Indian Baptist Church.[33] Despite the story's long-standing tradition in the tribe, it is grossly inaccurate.

Cedar Grove Baptist Church was formed by members of the historic Elam Baptist Church on October 9, 1875. Elam was not only the first church organized by free people of color in the county; its unique history lay in the fact that it had not been formed out of a White church. Elam became the mother church of a number of churches in the area including Cedar Grove. For a time the pastor was a White man—his daughter is buried in the cemetery—although Cedar Grove has never had a White membership. The majority of the members who left Elam to form Cedar Grove were from the Adkins and Jones families; but there is no indication that they intended to organize an Indian Church at that time. Two of the five original trustees were William H. Adkins and James E. Adkins, a cousin and brother of Spotswood Adkins respectively. These men served as witnesses to Spotswood's 1872 Commissioner's claim. Both men were identified as colored on the claim and neither referenced an Indian identity during his testimony before the Commission officers. Regarding Spotswood Adkins, William stated, "They were Union people just as we were. They were born free and they thought the Rebels wanted to make them slaves and that the Northern army would give them all their rights." Interestingly, Adkins does not connect Spotswood's status as a free man with his status as Indian. Free people of color of Indian ancestry often noted their Indian status as the reason for their free status. Nevertheless, much like Spotswood, both William and James may have adopted an Indian identity and sensibility by the close of the 1870s. The three men helped organize Cedar Grove. Now they, along with some of the others who had left Elam to organize Cedar Grove in 1875, felt compelled to leave Cedar Grove to form a new church, the Samaria Indian Baptist Church. The same day as the Cedar Grove exodus, members from Little Elam Baptist Church, another descendant of the original Elam organized in 1886, left their church to join Samaria as well. Hence, Samaria Indian Baptist Church grew out of not one, but two churches built by and for people of color many of whom were of mixed African and American Indian ancestry. In 1908 the Chickahominy Tribe was formally formed. William H. Adkins (great uncle of Mr. Richard Bowman), who served in leadership roles at both Elam and Cedar Grove, was installed as the tribe's first modern day chief.[34]

The inability to fully unravel the African American and American Indian threads of the modern-day African American and Chickahominy communities led Puglisi to conclude, "The central unresolved question—and one that, given the vagueness of the documentary record, is likely to remain unresolved—is whether the true racial composition of that early nineteenth-century community on the central ridge of the county was the seed from which both the modern Black and the modern Indian groups grew."[35] But that question only remains unresolved to those who wish to stay within the confines of an either/or binary or the safe haven of political correctness. Taking into consideration the long, tangled threads of African American and American Indian histories, kinship ties, and bloodlines in Charles City County, the evidence is clear. Not only was the racial composition of the central ridge community Red–Black (or Black–Red), but the indelible thread of Red and Black is woven into the fabric of both communities. What indeed remains unresolved is whether these two communities can come to terms with that reality.

Notions of Virginia Indian identity among prominent Whites were not fixed, but rather fluctuated over time as can be seen in three instances which span the time period prior to and immediately following the Racial Integrity Act (RIA). First, in 1910 the Census Bureau included a separate Indian census that required enumerators to include information on American Indians such as tribal affiliation and percentage of White, Indian, and Negro ancestry. No percentage of Negro ancestry was recorded for the two reservation Indian groups that reside in King William County, Virginia—the Pamunkey and the Mattaponi. Nevertheless, the Indian census for the Chickahominy tribal members residing in the Chickahominy and Harrison districts of Charles City County showed a number of tribal members as possessing from one-sixth to one-eighth Negro "blood." Of course this was total speculation on the part of the census taker, Walter M. Nance. What is of interest here, however, is that Nance was the son of Littleberry M. Nance, a prominent White citizen who served on the tribe's six-member Board of Trustees. Hence, prior to the RIA, White allies, at least in this case, were less compelled to deny the presence of some Black ancestry among tribal members.

Second, Walter Plecker, arch nemesis of the Indian community, had little problem acknowledging the Indian presence in Virginia prior to and during a short period after the RIA was signed into law. During the period 1919–1924, Plecker signed off on a number of birth certificates for members of the Chickahominy Tribe with the designation "Indian." Opechancanough Adkins, for example, was born in Charles City County on February 11, 1924, and received an Indian designation on his birth certificate, which Plecker signed on July 8, 1924, four months after the RIA became law.

Third, when William Archer Thaddeus Jones attempted to have his race reclassified from "colored" to "Mixed Indian" in January of 1925 so that his children could be enrolled in the Indian school, Plecker sent a list the bureau had compiled of "Mixed Indians" in Charles City County to authorities to assist the school board in making a decision on Jones's behalf. Jones, whose father, William Archer Jones had been rejected by the Chickahominy Tribe some years prior because he did not possess a sufficient amount of Indian "blood," based his "Mixed Indian" identity claim on the fact that his mother Emma Langston was a "full blooded" Pamunkey Indian. Jones's sister Mattie, who was married to Curtis Wynne, whose father was Pamunkey and whose mother was "white and colored," had several children who attended the Indian school. Although Plecker complied with Jones's request by providing the board with the list of "Mixed Indians," the board in turn left the final decision to the bureau. By that time, however, Plecker's disdain for Virginians who claimed an Indian racial identity was beginning to crystalize. The bureau refused Jones's request and his children were unable to join their cousins in attending the Indian school.[36]

Immediately following Plecker's refusal to grant Jones's racial reclassification request, the registrar dismissed the legitimacy of the Chickahominy Tribe as a "political trick to enable the white people to maintain control of the county government, Indians not being voters."[37] This assertion was not without merit. Consequently, because American Indians were not granted U.S. citizenship until 1924, the decision to break away from the African American community and claim an American Indian identity greatly diminished the political influence of the Charles City County colored population. Yet, the irony of Plecker's statement cannot be overstated. Why would an ardent White supremacist concern himself about White county officials rigging the system to maintain power and control? For certain, Plecker's concern had nothing to do with a rigged political system, but rather with the fear of interracial marriage. The Chickahominy Tribe was of particular interest to Plecker because of an impending trial against Ray Winn, who was indicted for the crime of miscegenation for marrying a White woman. To gear up for the trial, Plecker persuaded a number of people to come to his office to give depositions identifying the Chickahominy as Negro. Recounting what he was told some years later, Plecker wrote, "The title 'Chickahominy Indians' was assumed by a group of negroes about 1902 at the time when the Jim Crow law for the separation of the races in public conveyances was passed."[38] Plecker argued that those whom he considered pseudo-Chickahominy only wanted to become Indian after the Pamunkey were granted special passes in 1900 to ride in the White only section of the train. Plecker stated, "They gave a big 'fish fry' which is now a historical event in Charles City County, and invited a number of white people, including two or three lawyers whom they served bountifully."[39] As a result of the sumptuous fish fry, they won the favor of the local Whites. The lawyers, in turn, provided them with cards designating them as Indian so that they would not be subjected to Jim Crow.

It took Plecker awhile to manipulate the system in order to prevent the Chickahominy from receiving special cards to ride in the White section of the train; in the meantime, he used his position as registrar of Vital Statistics to prevent non-reservation Indians from receiving an Indian designation on birth certificates and marriage licenses. Tribal members, however, found a way to circumvent these efforts. Like Mildred Loving, Charles City County residents traveled to Washington, D.C. to obtain marriage licenses with an Indian designation.[40]

As Plecker's war against the Indians intensified, so too did the denial of African American ancestry and proscriptions against African American intermarriage and alliance within the tribal community. The Chickahominy were emphatic that the two communities were to remain separate at all cost. The Samaria Indian School, established the same year of the church, ended at the eighth grade. The only high school available to Indian students was the "colored" high school. To prevent tribal children from having to attend the colored school, anthropologist Frank Speck, with the assistance of Willard Beatty from the Department of the Interior, arranged for students to attend the High School Department at Bacone College in Oklahoma in the latter half of the 1940s. Those who did not wish to travel out west simply discontinued their education. Proscriptions against Indian–Black intermarriage were also strictly enforced. Failure to comply resulted in the forfeiture of tribal membership as "those party to intermarriage with Negroes . . . have been dropped from the genealogies and some lines have been 'forgotten' for a similar reason."[41]

Such was the case of the family of Spotswood Adkins whose children became estranged due to the spouses they chose to marry. For example, Spotswood's daughter Ida married a man by the name of Burl Charity who was also her first cousin. Marriage to first cousins was not uncommon in Charles City, but the Charities were African American, hence Spotswood Adkin's disapproval. Ironically, Spotswood's wife Mary Eliza, whom he married on October 1, 1873, was also a Charity, however, this marriage occurred some twenty years prior to the organization of the modern day Chickahominy Tribe. After Burl Charity's death, Spotswood refused to provide assistance to Ida and her four children. Ida remained on her own until her second marriage to Levy Bradby. Despite the Bradby name, which was common among the Chickahominy, Levy was not recognized by the tribe. After Ida gave birth to twins, Levy abandoned her; Spotswood refused once again to come to his daughter's aid. As a result, Ida and her children left Charles City County, relocated to Richmond, Virginia, and lived the remainder of their lives as colored people.

All of Spotswood Adkins's children married non-tribal members and it seems that none of them retained an Indian identity. Spotswood, however, remained closely affiliated with the tribe. When he died in 1922 his funeral and burial were held at the Samaria Indian Baptist Church. His wife, Mary Eliza Charity Adkins, died in 1939, but she was buried in the cemetery at the historically Black Gilfield Baptist Church. Family members speculate that she may have been turned out of the tribe once Spotswood, "the 'real Indian' was dead."[42]

While some people were dropped from the tribal rolls, others voluntarily left the tribe and returned to the African American community.

Such was the case of Andrew Warren Adkins. Adkins's family joined the group that left Cedar Grove Baptist Church to form Samaria Indian Baptist Church in 1901. On the 1900 census Adkins, his parents, and his siblings were identified as Black. The family appeared on the 1910 Indian census, however, as Chickahominy Indian. Yet, Adkins could never fully commit to severing familial and friendship ties with the Cedar Grove and African American communities. He therefore chose to relinquish his ties with Samaria and the tribal community and returned to the Black church and community where he had been born and nurtured. By 1917, according to his World War I draft record, Adkins identified himself as Black. Adkins earned a Bachelor of Arts and a Bachelor of Divinity degree from Virginia Union University, a historically Black university in Richmond. He became pastor of the Grafton Baptist Church in Middlesex County on Virginia's eastern shore. He also taught at the Middlesex Training School. On June 15, 1918, Adkins married Mattie Hamlet who had been his teacher some years prior while he was attending night school. Hamlet was quite ambitious herself. She was a graduate of Thyne Institute, a residential school in Mecklenburg County, Virginia located some 140 miles from her native home of Newport News. She also pursued advance study at Virginia Union University and Virginia State College. Moreover, she continued teaching for a time even while raising a family. In 1920 the couple moved to Alexandria, Virginia, where Adkins became pastor of the historic Alfred Street Baptist Church, the first Black Baptist Church north of Richmond, Virginia established in 1803. He continued as pastor until his untimely death in 1963. In 1921 Adkins, beginning with one classroom, founded the high school division of the Parker-Gray Elementary School, which prior to that time only offered courses through eighth grade. It became the first Black secondary school for African Americans in Alexandria. Adkins served as principal and taught math classes at Parker-Gray until his retirement in 1954. The Adkins children inherited their parents' knack for high achievement, earning advanced degrees in medicine, law, science, and social work. Most notably, Andretta Adkins Alexander, who held a master's degree in mathematics, worked as a cryptanalyst for the U.S. National Security Service. Her brother, Rutherford Adkins, a physicist, became a Tuskegee Airman and served as president of Knoxville College and Fisk University. The cases of Spotswood Adkins and Andrew W. Adkins, whose fathers were first cousins, provide additional examples of the confluence and disruption of Black–Indian kinship relations in Charles City County.[43]

In 1994 Anita and Hugh Harrell, founders of the Weyanoke Association of Red–Black History and Culture, organized a six-month symposium series titled *Red & Black: The Legacy of Native and African Peoples in Charles City County.* The series aimed to provide a forum for residents to discuss openly what many had long discussed in private: that is, the historical intersection of the African American and American Indian experience and the animosity wrought by the severance of family ties. The Harrells wanted to discuss ways to heal the contemporary rift between the two communities. Initially they received little support for the idea as both sides displayed stubborn resistance. The Harrells were successful in bringing together both communities for the symposium, which featured African American and American Indian keynote speakers and panelists in an attempt to bridge the gap between the two groups. Yet, as the symposium progressed, it was clear that there were two separate agendas. While on the one hand those representing the African American community demonstrated a willingness to discuss past wrongs and ways to move beyond them, on the other hand those representing the Chickahominy preferred to gloss over the issues and downplay the anti-Black policies long held by the tribe. This became most evident during the question and answer period of the fifth session of the symposium. After a few questions were fielded from the audience, a young Chickahominy woman, Charlotte Allen, approached the microphone and began reading a prepared statement. As she fought back tears she told of her experience of being ostracized by the tribe because she had married a Black man. The man she married is William Allen. Although Allen identifies as African American, he is the great-grandson of Allen Adkins the cofounder of the modern-day Chickahominy Tribe. Nevertheless, according to local residents, Charlotte's relationship with Allen evoked the wrath of her parents, who upon learning of the relationship put her out of the house. When tribal members learned that she had been taken in by Allen's family, they further antagonized her and her host family by circling the house during the night in a pick-up truck while yelling, "nigger lover." As Mrs. Allen read her statement regarding tribal rejection, she became so overcome with tears that a member of the audience had to read much of the statement for her. Another symposium attendee, Lloyd Jones, a nephew of the Bowmans, also recalled being victimized by the tribe's anti-Black policy while in elementary school. Jones was among a bus load of African American school children who were stranded one winter afternoon when the bus broke down across the road from the Samaria Indian Baptist Church. The bus driver crossed the road and inquired of those present in the church if the children could wait inside until another bus arrived to take them to their destination. He was told they could not.[44]

Dr. Edna Greene Medford, Professor of History at Howard University, grew up in Charles City County and served as a symposium panelist. She confirmed that divisions existed between the African American and Native American communities and that such divisions resulted in rifts between family members.[45] Judge Holt, during his rendering of the Dorothy Johns decision in 1924, predicted accurately that the enforcement of the RIA would split families and cause many to disassociate from those family members whose African features predominated. This indeed was the case in Charles City County; some have argued that Chickahominy membership criteria ignore kinship and are based arbitrarily on phenotype: a light skin and fine hair texture.

Chickahominy leadership denied the accusations. Leonard Adkins, who was at that time Chief of the Chickahominy Tribe, dismissed the accusation that membership was based on anything other than being Chickahominy and having one's ancestor "listed on the tribal roll when the tribe reorganized."[46] But this certainly cannot refer to the 1908 reorganization; William Allen would certainly qualify for tribal membership since his great-grandfather helped reorganize the tribe. In addition, there are present day descendants whose grandparents appear on the 1910 Indian census and yet are denied tribal membership.[47]

Stephen Adkins, the current tribal Chief, who during the mid-1990s was assistant chief of the Chickahominy, responded as most people on the privileged side of racism would. Displaying a severe case of historical amnesia, he was oblivious to the tensions between Blacks and Indians. While Adkins was aware that there had been barriers concerning people marrying outside of the tribe, he stated that he was not sure why. He surmised that perhaps such views were influenced by "the social system of the time" or that people left the tribe because they were ashamed to be Indian. Yet, he was emphatic that no one was banned from the tribe for marrying an African American; he also believed relations between African Americans and Indians had improved. "I don't feel like there is tension. I think we have come a long way. To a large extent, the kids are colorblind."[48] In response to Jones's assertions regarding the school bus incident, Adkins stated that he would have allowed the children into the church if he were there on the day the bus broke down.

Lenora Adkins, Leonard Adkins's daughter, in an attempt to downplay the role of blood politics in tribal membership, stated in a separate article, "Indian is more than a racial category. It is also about practicing the culture and beliefs. Having the blood is one thing . . . having the culture and practicing the traditions is another."[49] Nevertheless, while the contemporary Indian residents of Charles City deny that skin color and hair texture were ever used in determining tribal membership, the evidence supports the perceptions of members of the African American community who contend that a lighter complexion and straight hair were viewed more favorably when applying for tribal enrollment.

Choctaw scholar, Devon Abbott Mihesuah, in writing about the identity of indigenous women, concurs that appearance has played a central role in deciding tribal membership. Mihesuah contends:

> For the most part scholars [and others] have ignored the role appearance played and still does play in Native women's lives. Appearance is the most visible aspect of one's race, and it determines how Native women defined themselves and how others defined and treated them. Their appearance, whether Caucasian, Indian, African, or mixed, either limited or broadened Native women's choices of ethnic identity and their ability to interact with non-Natives and other Natives. Appearance played a crucial role in determining status and ease of mingling within different cultural groups or societies. Consequently, many mixed heritage white and Native women had numerous "worlds" open to them, while most full-blood Native women and those of mixed black and Indian heritage did not.[50]

Charles City County, much like any other community of color which internalized the values White society attached to color as Mihesuah

FIG. 6.2. Two unidentified Chickahominy women, circa 1900. Photo lot 74.
National Anthropological Archives, Smithsonian Institution. Used by permission.

outlines above, suffered from what writer Alice Walker dubbed colorism.
Walker defined colorism as "the prejudicial or preferential treatment of
same-race people based solely on their color."[51] This color-based, White-
imposed value system has its roots in slavery, wherein people of color
possessing Europeanized features came to be viewed and treated more
favorably by Whites. In other words, the level of discrimination one
faced was directly proportional to one's skin shade and hair texture.
Mulattoes, though viewed as an anomaly, were seen as more intelligent
than their darker counterparts. They were often trained as skilled la-
borers and artisans. Consequently, such color consciousness and the
value system associated with it became deeply rooted in the African
American community. Not surprisingly church politics were also often
underscored by colorism and illustrate the depth of this mentality within
communities of color.[52]

Although Charles City's historic Elam Baptist Church did not spring from a White congregation, its protocols maintained the racial and gender mores of White Christian indoctrination. White visitor Eben N. Horsford noted in 1852 that there were four entrances to the church: two for the men of the church, one for women, and one for Whites.[53] In comparison to its White counterparts, slaves occupied the balcony of the church while the free colored portion, comprised mostly of mulattoes, occupied the pews on the main floor. After slavery, it seems the church continued separate settings based on color as dark-skinned Blacks were relegated to the back or balcony of the church while light-skinned Blacks occupied the front. Even leadership positions appear to have been based on color as one churchgoer asserted, "Only light skinned members could be leaders in the church."[54]

Some churches took extreme measures to maintain a strict color line. In such cases church membership criteria was based on one of three tests: the paper bag test, the door test, or the comb test. To pass the paper bag test potential members were required to place their arm into a brown paper bag to insure the skin was lighter than the bag. Sometimes the door of the church was painted a light brown color. One had to be the color of the door or lighter to be welcomed to join the church. The hair test required that potential members be able to have a fine tooth comb run through their hair before being extended the right hand of fellowship. While such assertions may seem quite fantastic, these practices were widespread throughout Virginia and Louisiana.[55]

Given the tribe's close association with the African American community and the church, it is not at all unreasonable to assume that skin color and hair texture were among the criteria for tribal membership as "the racial color caste systems which became a norm in black communities also were established in many Native communities and darker-skinned groups were seen as inferior, ugly, etc."[56] As previously discussed, those with features betraying any African ancestry were purged from the tribes. As a result "tribal rules crystallized into laws prohibiting marriage with blacks. Appearance of Indian ancestry became even more important and desirable: 'typical Indian' traits of copper skin, dark eyes, hawk nose, and straight black hair."[57] Much like Indian men during the slavery era, Indian men in the twentieth century wore their hair long to distinguish themselves from Negroes and mulattoes. The purpose of this was to demonstrate that "the hair was straight, not kinky."[58] Also, in a deposition given during the Winn trial, Charles City County resident George Marston asserted that the Chickahominy used the comb test to deny an acquaintance tribal membership. Marston recounted the story of William Archer Jones, father of William Archer Thaddeus Jones, who was refused tribal membership during the tribe's reorganization because he did not pass the comb test. "Old William Archer Jones at the time he applied for membership with the 'Indians,'" recounted Marston, "had to take a comb test before he could get into the 'tribe.' If the comb would go through his hair without hanging it showed he was of sufficient Indian blood to be admitted. If the comb hung, it showed he had negro blood and could not come in." According to Marston, those performing the comb test pulled Jones's hair so hard that he cried out, "Great God Almighty! Take it out before you pull all my hair out."[59] Consequently, Jones was not admitted to the tribe. Certainly such extreme measures are no longer used to determine tribal membership. The tribe has adopted the use of blood quantum, one-fourth Indian "blood" is required to be considered for tribal membership. Nevertheless, phenotype appears to remain an unwritten criterion. It not only determines tribal membership, but it also determines if one can dance at the annual Chickahominy powwow.

If indeed membership into the Indian community was based on culture rather than blood as Lenora Adkins asserted in 1995, than those practicing the culture should be welcomed to dance at the Chickahominy public powwow held every fourth weekend in September. In 2009 two Afro-Indian male dancers were singled out for violating tribal rules as "only Native American dancers" are allowed in the dance circle. One of the men questioned regarding his Native American "credentials" was Harold Caldwell. Caldwell has a deep, smooth, chocolate-brown complexion, and features associated with the characteristics of African Americans. He informed the men that he was in fact a Muskogee Creek Indian. He stated that he had been dancing for fifteen years and that this was the first time anyone had questioned his American Indian identity. The response of a Chickahominy representative was "How do we know you are who you say you are? For all we know, you could be a hobbyist."[60] Caldwell was not expelled from the circle that day. He was warned, however, that he would not be allowed to dance at any future powwows hosted by the tribe.

Although Caldwell was not expelled from the dance circle in 2009, the following year his wife Shonda Buchanan found herself flanked by three male representatives of the Chickahominy Tribe and accosted for entering into the tribal circle without a tribal card. Ms. Buchanan has a light-caramel complexion and has Nubian locks, which hang below the small her back. She entered the dance circle during an Intertribal dance dressed in full tribal regalia. She was accompanied by three female companions who were not dressed in powwow regalia but were draped in Indian shawls. Nevertheless, as Buchanan asserts, "They 'look' Indian; I do not."[61] Some would argue that Buchanan was ejected from the pow-wow circle not because of her phenotype but, rather because she did not have a tribal card. Yet, neither did her three companions who were allowed to remain in the circle. It would stand to reason than that all four women should have been ejected from the circle. Herein lies the double standard, as Pamunkey Indian Lester Stewart aptly acknowledged, "But you know Indians are funny. Ida Miles would say Indians were like flowers—all different colors. Now the good colors, 'the whites only,' didn't bother you. But if I look dark, they might put a foot in my ass."[62] Indians who are White in appearance face fewer challenges regarding their claims to Indian identity.[63]

Per my own observation of the dancers at the 2010 powwow, it appeared that indeed phenotype played a role regarding who was allowed in the powwow circle. The diversity of the American Indian community is undeniable, as Julienne Coleman observed while watching the powwow dancers at the 2010 Nottoway Indian powwow, "marveling at how different they looked—different shades of skin."[64] The community of dancers at the Chickahominy powwow, however, appeared contrived and was reflective of a deliberate effort to keep out any one of noticeable African American ancestry. The color range of the dancers was from light brown to pale white. The hair range was from straight to slightly curly. But there were no dancers of visible African American ancestry, a clear misrepresentation of Native America.

Charles City County has shown a few glimmers of hope regarding cooperative efforts between the African American and American Indian communities. As a result of the Red–Black symposium, relations for a time between the two communities seemed more congenial. According to one resident who attended the local high school in the mid-1990s, although she did not socialize with her Indian schoolmates outside of school, Black and Indian students got along well. She has a sibling four years younger than she, who did, however, socialize with her Indian schoolmates outside of school. "She and a number of other Black kids would hang out at the tribal center. I don't know if that happens much anymore though." Also, Charlotte Allen, the young woman who was ostracized from the tribe for her marriage to William Allen, reconciled with the tribe, and her two sons are now tribal members.[65] Moreover, it appears that the Samaria Baptist Church (the word "Indian" was dropped in 1987) atoned for its earlier misdeed by opening its doors to members of the St. John Baptist Church, an African American church that suffered a major fire in 2004. The St. John's congregation was allowed to use the Samaria facility to hold its own services until the completion of their new facility in 2009. Despite these efforts, however, as recent events have demonstrated, old habits die hard. With current efforts underway to achieve federal recognition, it appears that the Chickahominy have once again stepped up efforts to keep the African American community at arm's length. The tribe's federal recognition effort has also reignited the debate within the African American community regarding the authenticity of the Chickahominy Indian claim.

In 1999, the Harrells began a yearly tradition known as Coming Together, an annual festival held the second Saturday in August in Charles City County to commemorate the confluence of the history and culture of peoples of African and American Indian descent by marking the arrival of the "twenty and odd Negars" to Virginia in 1619. The festival is now in its fourteenth year. It is supported by residents of surrounding counties as well as participants from out-of-state. Yet, the Harrells receive little support from Charles City County residents. For certain, the wounds within both the African American and American Indian communities wrought by the racial integrity struggle are deeply rooted.

It will take more than a symposium and an annual festival to repair the damage done in the name of maintaining racial purity.

Decades after the formation of Samaria Indian Baptist Church and the subsequent reorganization of the Chickahominy Tribe, the confrontations of race and identity regarding who is Black and who is Indian continue to be a point of contention in this small community. It does not appear that the issue will be settled anytime in the near future. For the time being, Charles City County, a rural community that proudly characterizes itself as "three cultures, two rivers, and one county," remains ruptured in half by a racial integrity fight that has now entered into its second century.

SEVEN

Nottoway Indians, Afro-Indian Identity, and the Contemporary Dilemma of State Recognition

In 2006, it is tragically ironic that some Virginia Indians and Anglo-Virginians still have little reticence in accepting light-skinned descendants of Indian tribes, who readily admit and celebrate their European duality as recognized Indians, yet anguish over the dark-skinned duality of Indian–African ancestry as somehow being of less legitimate descendancy.

—CHIEF LYNETTE ALLSTON, NOTTOWAY INDIAN TRIBE OF VIRGINIA, STATE RECOGNITION PETITION COVER LETTER, 2006

The Recognition Committee appointed by the Virginia Council on Indians has completed the review of the petition submitted by the Nottoway Indian Tribe of Virginia for State Recognition. After careful review and debate on the information submitted by the petitioners, it is the recommendation by majority vote that the Nottoway Tribe of Virginia be Disapproved for State Recognition in the Commonwealth of Virginia.

—VIRGINIA COUNCIL ON INDIANS RECOGNITION COMMITTEE REPORT TO THE NOTTOWAY TRIBE OF VIRGINIA PETITION FOR STATE RECOGNITION, 2009

In the spring of 2009, the Nottoway Indian Tribe of Virginia (NITOV) received a long-awaited response from the Virginia Council on Indians

(VCI) to its petition requesting a recommendation for state recognition. The answer was a resounding no.[1] Few were surprised by the outcome. Over the past two decades several tribes attempted to gain formal acknowledgement, but no petitioner had been granted state recognition since 1989. House Joint Resolution 54, which granted six tribes state recognition in 1983, concluded with the following statement: "That the General Assembly of Virginia by virtue of the United States Census and other evidence acknowledges the fact that members of other Indian tribes reside within the Commonwealth." The six tribes recognized by HJR54 were the Pamunkey, the Mattaponi, the Upper Mattaponi, Chickahominy, Eastern Chickahominy and Rappahannock. The Virginia General Assembly's statement echoed the sentiments reflected in the 1982 Report of the Joint Subcommittee, which recommended that a Commission on Indians, later renamed the VCI, be appointed as an advisory body. Its purpose would be to "advise the Governor as to how programs affect Indians, direct research on Indian history, provide liaison with the Indian tribes, and recommend through the Governor any needs for legislation in the future."[2] The need for future legislation could include resolutions to grant state recognition to petitioning groups based on recommendations from the VCI. Subsequently, two additional tribes, The Nansemond Tribe (1985) and the Monacan Nation (1989) received state recognition via House Joint Resolutions 205 and 390 respectively. Those two resolutions notwithstanding, the VCI had not at that time adopted a formal recognition process.

On September 18, 1989, the VCI formalized six criteria that must be met by tribes petitioning for state recognition: 1) Petitioners must demonstrate that the tribe was indigenous to Virginia at first contact with Europeans; 2) that they reside at a specified location within the current boundaries of the state; 3) that the tribe is not recognized in another state; 4) that tribal members are directly descended from the indigenous group for which they seek recognition; 5) that they demonstrate tribal governance and have adopted clear criteria for membership; and 6) that the petitioner is not the splinter group of another currently recognized tribe. Some embraced the newly adopted criteria believing that it brought much needed professionalization and standardization to the process of state recognition. But others criticized it believing the criteria only served as a stumbling block to specific tribes the council anticipated would seek recognition. Still others believed that the criteria were designed to permanently close the door to state recognition altogether. It seemed, however, that instead of six criteria, there were seven. The seventh criterion was an unwritten rule requiring that petitioning tribes be racially pure by demonstrating an absence of African American ancestry and affiliation. The written criteria were updated in the spring of 2006, the same year the NITOV moved forward with its formal petition. But racial purity remained as an unwritten criterion. It would prove to be the salient issue that informed the VCI's decision to deny the Nottoway a recommendation for state recognition.

The unwritten criterion of racial purity can be seen very early in the VCI's newly adopted state recognition process. The United Cherokee Indian Tribe of Virginia, Inc. (UCITOVA) of Amherst County, also known as the Buffalo Ridge Cherokee, were the first petitioners to go through the state recognition process under the newly adopted criteria. In 1992, according to procedural guidelines, the Virginia General Assembly responded to a petition requesting formal recognition submitted on behalf of the UCITOVA by passing Senate Joint Resolution 15. The study resolution, sponsored by Senator Elliot Schewel, charged the Secretary of Health and Human Services in cooperation with the VCI to determine if the documentation submitted by the tribe met the criteria for state recognition. According to the Secretary's final report, the tribe submitted:

> a voluminous amount of data and historical documents, including *The Buffalo Ridge Cherokee: The Colors and Culture of a Virginia Indian Community,* Rice (Appendix B); *Some Common Cherokee Surnames in Amherst County,* Rice (Appendix C); *The Buffalo Ridge Cherokee, A Report on the History of the Buffalo Ridge People of Amherst County, Virginia,* dated August 12, 1992, with an accompanying document binder (Appendix D); and "Supplemental to the Buffalo Ridge Cherokee Report," dated November 23, 1992, with accompanying documents (Appendix E).[3]

On June 12, 1992, the UCITOVA's documented petition was received by the VCI subcommittee appointed by Stephen Adkins (Chickahominy), the council's acting chair. The first meeting of the subcommittee convened on August 8, 1992. Less than five months later, on December

21, 1992, the subcommittee presented its findings and recommendation to the council. By late January 1993, Howard M. Cullum, secretary of health and human resources, issued a report to Governor L. Douglas Wilder et al. concurring with the council's recommendation to deny the UCITOVA state recognition. Cullum's fourteen-page report stated on several occasions that the Virginia Cherokee "did not meet the council's criteria for state recognition" but, it failed to disclose which criteria the petitioners failed to meet.[4] Publicly stated reasons notwithstanding, the section of the report labeled "Findings," demonstrated that the issue of racial purity was the salient influence in the VCI's recommendation to deny the UCITOVA state recognition.

The report's "findings" provided no discussion of the documentary evidence the tribe submitted to the council in support of its petition for state recognition, but only a passing mention as outlined in the above quote. Instead, the section began with a discussion of the reduction of the Indian population, which the author attributed largely to the intermarriage of Indians with Black slaves, whose appearance became negroid over time. The report stated further that a considerable number of these negroid Indians of Amherst County not only maintained a Cherokee identity and tradition that had been passed down from one generation to the next, but they also retained documented Cherokee surnames. Nevertheless, cultural continuity took a back seat to the discussion of racial mixture with a primary focus on the shared racial designation of mulatto. The report acknowledged that the term could also refer to an Indian–White admixture, but the Indian–Black admixture was heavily emphasized.

The findings as presented to the Virginia General Assembly were nothing new. First, the UCITOVA and the people of Amherst County were known for their tri-racial mixture of African, European, and Indian ancestry. Arthur Estabrook wrote about them in his now infamous book *Mongrel Virginians*. They were the first to challenge the legality of Virginia's Racial Integrity Act. Their surnames were on Plecker's "hit list," as he tried with mixed results to prevent county clerks from issuing marriage licenses to those attempting to marry White people. Second, their phenotype was no different than that of their Powhatan counterparts, whose physiognomy James Mooney described in the early twentieth century as displaying a variation of such intermixture. Mooney asserted, "Thus many [Powhatan] would pass among strangers as ordinary negroes, a few show no trace of any but white blood; while a few families and individuals might pass as full-blood Indians in any western tribe."[5] A perusal of the pictorial representations of tribal members in Horace Rice's history of the UCITOVA attests to the same fact that they shared the same variation in physiognomy as their Powhatan counterparts. The difference, however, was that the UCITOVA was not a part of the salvage campaign that insisted upon expunging members whose features betrayed African admixture or that members refrain from interaction with Blacks. To the contrary, they openly admitted that some of their members were Cherokees of African descent:

> They present themselves in all colors. Some have black eyes while others have blue eyes. Some have blonde and black hair while others are redheads. Some are dark skinned, some are light skinned, but they are all related. . . . They are German-Native-African Americans. They are Anglo (English)-Native-African Americans, German-Native Americans, Anglo-Native Americans, Irish-Native Americans. The common thread that runs through these people is the Native American, Cherokee thread. This thread, this heritage that has not broken and will not be broken, has been the force that has united this band of people, individuals mixed with a variety of ethnic and racial backgrounds.[6]

It was evident from Cullum's report that intermarriage with people of African descent carried an opposite meaning in the minds of the VCI, of which many members were steeped in racial purity dogma. Despite the tribe's adherence to a Cherokee identity and tradition, African American kinship ties raised questions of legitimacy regarding their Indian identity claim. By the UCITOVA's own admission the unwritten criteria of racial purity had been violated; therefore, there could be only one response: petition denied.[7]

In 1996, the Patawomeck Tribe of Stafford County submitted a petition to the VCI seeking a recommendation for state recognition. From the outset the challenge for the Patawomeck was its scarce documentation in support of its case. Three years later the tribe, unable to meet the subcommittee's continued demands for more documentation, withdrew its petition. The Occaneechi Band of the Saponi Nation, who occupied the Piedmont Region of Virginia and North Carolina, and the Tri-County Rappahannock Indian Tribe of Essex County sought state recognition in 1998 and 1999 respectively. The Occaneechi case was exceptional due to its borderland location. In addition, the tribe had sought to gain recognition in North Carolina, but later decided to withdraw its petition from the Tar Heel State and seek recognition in Virginia. Despite support from Nansemond and Monacan tribal representatives, the Occaneechi were denied state recognition in Virginia. The Recognition Committee outlined five reasons for the tribe's rejection, the last being "Not enough intermarrying of the tribal people or intermarrying with other Indian tribes."[8]

Sometime in early 1999, The Tri-County Rappahannock Indian Tribe under the leadership of Nokomis Lemons submitted a documented petition to the VCI for the tribe to be considered for state recognition. It appears, however, that an unsuccessful attempt was made in 1997. The two salient issues that arose during the 1999 process involved questions regarding the timing of the submission of the petition and whether or not the Tri-County group was a splinter of the United Rappahannock, now led by Anne Richardson. Regarding the timing of the petition, Lemons was asked if indeed the Tri-County group had intended to be a separate entity from the United Rappahannock, why hadn't they, similar to the Eastern Chickahominy and Upper Mattaponi, sister groups of the Chickahominy and Mattaponi Tribes respectively, sought state recognition in 1983 or before 1989 when there was no set criteria? Lemons responded that the timing was irrelevant. What was relevant was that her group met all of the criteria and should be granted recognition. She also refuted arguments that the two groups shared bloodlines and that her group had been previously enrolled as United Rappahannock tribal members. Yet, the issue regarding the Tri-County people as a splinter group remained a point of contention throughout the recognition process. Lemons argued that the 1981 incorporation of the Tri-County Rappahannock Indian Tribe, which occurred two years prior to the United Rappahannock Tribe receiving state recognition, demonstrated without question that there were two Rappahannock groups.[9]

But was it so clear? During the 1997 tribal fall out, a major controversy surrounded the question regarding the late Chief Otho Nelson's successor. Some favored Lemons due to her depth of experience as an Indian activist while others favored Richardson as the heir of the now deceased chief. If there were indeed two groups why was Lemons vying to be chief of the United Rappahannock? To add to the confusion, Kim Douglass's 1997 article on the Rappahannock fallout referred to Lemons as "chief of the new Rappahannock Tribe."[10] Yet, how could the tribe be new when it was incorporated in 1981? It appears that the Tri-County organization may have experienced a period of inactivity and for a time became so intertwined with the United Rappahannock that there was a temporary merging of the two groups sometime during the 1980s.

Take for example Chief Nelson's (affectionately known as Captain Nelson) 1982 testimony before the Joint Subcommittee Studying the Relationship Between the State and Indian Tribes in which he stated, "In 1974, the Rappahannock Indian Association was reincorporated under the name of the United Rappahannock Tribe, Inc. in a successful effort to unite all Rappahannock descendants in the tri-county area, namely King & Queen, Essex and Caroline."[11] Yet according to the 1974 Articles of Incorporation (AOI), the purpose of the tribe was to meet the needs of the local Rappahannock community, which comprised those living in "Central Point-Sparta-Alp-Passing area [Caroline County]" and "Beazley and Indian Neck [King and Queen County]." The Essex County Rappahannock community, also known as the Portabago Rappahannock, was excluded from the United Rappahannock membership in 1974 and in 1981 when the AOI was amended that July. During his testimony, Nelson made no mention of the Tri-County Rappahannock Indian Tribe which was incorporated on September 22, 1981, with amendments receiving approval on January 27, 1983. It appears that the intention of the Tri-County group was to include those who were excluded from the United Rappahannock Tribe. Nevertheless, according to Douglass, Steve Morton, whose signature as chairperson appeared on the Tri-County's AOI and its amendments, was criticized by his wife for depriving his younger children of their Indian culture because although he remained active in the church, he refused to allow them to participate in tribal activities such as dance and beadwork sponsored by the United Rappahannock. In addition, Morton's oldest daughter, Marie Fortune, was still an active member of the United Rappahannock Tribe. There is no mention of any Tri-County Rappahannock-sponsored activities. In fact, there is no mention of the Tri-County Rappahannock Indian Tribe. This may be the clearest indication that for a time there was an informal merging of the two groups. By 1987, relations between the two groups began to decay. At issue was the decision to oust Lemons from the tribe because of her involvement with a traditional Indian dance troupe that taught Native American dance to the non-Indian spouses of tribal members, a violation of the United Rappahannock code of conduct as outlined in the 1974 AOI. Lemons, it was said, "believes her participation with this 'mixed' group is one reason she was excluded from the tribe."[12] Things came to a head when Lemons along with her immediate family articulated opposition to the anti-Black statements included in the United Rappahannock's 1995 amendments to the AOI. Lemons, whose husband is White, did not mince words when expressing her opposition to what she and others identified as racism: "I married a non-Indian . . . That did not change me at all. I am still an Indian. I am still Rappahannock."[13] On April 20, 1997, with Haywood Hedgeman, brother of Lori Battle, as chief, the Tri-County Rappahannock amended its AOI to change its name to the Rappahannock Indian Tribe, Inc.[14] By June 1997 Lemons had taken over as chief and submitted a petition to the VCI requesting a recommendation for state recognition with a follow up in early 1999.

As of November 1999, the VCI remained fixated on the splinter group issue. A question arose regarding who was included in the definition of Rappahannock when HJR54 granted the Rappahannock state recognition in 1983 as the bill did not specify which group had been granted recognition. While the bill specifically named two Chickahominy groups and two Mattaponi groups, it simply referred to the Rappahannock Indian Tribe as "Rappahannock." Despite the fact that the question had been addressed during the 1997 recognition process by Ronald Forehand, a representative of the attorney general's office, the Recognition Committee suggested that an inquiry be sent to the attorney general's office requesting clarification of the term "Rappahannock" because neither the United Rappahannock or the Tri-County Rappahannock were specifically named in the bill. The question put forward to the attorney general's office was whether the term "Rappahannock" referred to the group that had testified before the Joint Subcommittee or to all Rappahannocks? According to Lemons, Forehand's 1997 response to that question was that the term stood for "all Rappahannocks, whether they be United Rappahannock or Rappahannock, that all should be included, not excluded."[15] If indeed Forehand's s response was as Lemons stated, then it would stand to reason that those now seeking state recognition were already members of a recognized group and would by definition be a splinter group. Yet without the 1997 minutes to provide a context for Forehand's alleged response, the only solution was to once again submit an inquiry to the attorney general's office. In addition, the Recognition Committee requested a more specific definition of splinter group, since it was not clearly defined in the criteria.

According to Rountree, in response to her inquiry about the original intent of the splinter group clause, Oliver Perry (Nansemond), who was responsible for writing most of the criteria, explained that it was "to keep tribes from defecting and going off and forming other tribes from the same people. He wasn't talking about anyone that had organized prior to 1983."[16] Nevertheless the confusion persisted. The VCI voted at that time to define a splinter group as a group that was both related by blood and had been on the rolls of a recognized group. At the close of the November 1999 meeting, it was clear that Lemons's petition on behalf of her tribe would be rejected. Anne Richardson's non-compliance with the VCI's request for a genealogy of the United Rappahannock's members, though she did submit the tribe's Charter Rolls, made it difficult for the Recognition Committee to ascertain the validity of Lemons's claim that hers was not a splinter group.[17] Certainly, the Tri-County group was punished for allowing its faction to fall into inactivity in the name of tribal unity. Lemons and her family, in particular, were paying a high price for their outspokenness against the racially slanted policies of the United Rappahannock Tribe. Racial politics aside, the VCI comprised members who had never undergone the rigors of a recognition process and lacked the necessary experience to take on such a daunting responsibility.[18]

By the new millennium, the atmosphere among communities of unrecognized tribes regarding state recognition was one of cynicism. Consensus was that the VCI had abandoned its original intent of assisting tribal communities and had become an exclusive club dominated by representatives of the eight state-recognized tribes under the influence of Dr. Helen Rountree, the eminent scholar of the Virginia Indians, for the purpose of keeping all others out. As Bill Wright, NITOV Councilman, later quipped, "The gate has been closed and Rountree holds the key."[19] Unfortunately, this may not have been an overstatement.

From 2000–2005, the recognition process remained at a standstill. There were no petitions filed for state recognition. In fact, the VCI refused to respond to requests for information regarding the state recognition process, a blatant violation of the Freedom of Information Act (FOIA).[20] It seems the focus for recognition had shifted from the state level to the federal level as six of the eight state-recognized tribes began petitioning Congress for federal recognition in hopes of achieving their goal by 2007, in time for the 400th anniversary of Jamestown.[21] Yet, the process in Virginia was not totally dead, but rather undergoing a complete overhaul. Virginia Code 2.2–2629 was originally enacted in 2002 to update the duties and powers of the VCI and was amended and reenacted in 2005. The VCI was granted total control over updating the recognition process; members were charged with establishing criteria and recommending to the governor and the general assembly those tribes that meet the criteria for state recognition. While there may not have appeared to be much of a departure from the initial process, there was a major departure indeed. Virginia's state-recognition procedure and criteria were now modeled after the federal process. According to the new criteria, ratified on May 16, 2006, Virginia tribes seeking state recognition must:

> 1) Show that the group's members have retained a specifically Indian identity through time; 2) Demonstrate descent from an historical Indian group(s) that lived within Virginia's current boundaries at the time of that group's first contact with Europeans; 3) Trace the group's continued existence within Virginia from first contact to the present; 4) Provide a complete genealogy of current group members, traced as far back as possible; 5) Show that the group has been socially distinct from other cultural groups, at least for the twentieth century and further back if possible, by organizing separate churches, schools, political organizations or the like; 6) Provide evidence of contemporary formal organization, with full membership restricted to people genealogically descended from the historic tribe(s).[22]

In their 2007 nationwide survey of the state recognition process, Koenig and Stein identified Virginia's process as "the most structured and detailed state law recognition processes in the United States."[23] Yet the implicit contradiction appears to have been lost in the article. Koenig and Stein's thesis was to examine the process of state recognition as an alternative to federal recognition for tribes, specifically those in Virginia, who found the Bureau of Indian Affairs (BIA) criteria and process too onerous. But Virginia's newly ratified criteria borrowed heavily from that of the BIA. According to Rountree, such requirements as outlined by Virginia's tribal recognition process were tenable because the tribes that had gained recognition during the 1980s could meet all six criteria.[24] Chief Stephen Adkins supported Rountree's assertion stating that the revised criteria were "an outgrowth of the 1983 studies which relied on the federal criteria for recognition."[25] Such claims, however, are not supported by the historical record. For example, Rountree asserted in 1999 "that the recognition process [adopted in 1989] was not as stringent" during the period the original eight gained recognition. As noted earlier, however, there was no formal process. The legislation that granted recognition to the eight tribes did not address the question of continuous existence as a formally organized tribal unit. Also, tribes were not required to submit genealogical information attesting to their descent from an historic tribe as "there was no genealogy presented on paper." Rountree testified at a hearing on behalf of the tribes "regarding their genealogy," from information she claimed she compiled from public records.[26] Moreover, a review of over 700 pages of VCI documents demonstrated that "there is not a single pre-recognition document on file with the Virginia Council on Indians for any of the currently recognized Tribes related to their genealogy, their tribal rolls, their organizational structure, their continuous existence, etc. contrary to Chief Adkins's carefully crafted statement."[27] During his talk on Virginia Indians at the Virginia Museum of Science on January 27, 2012, Chief Adkins publically admitted his contention with the BIA criteria, particularly criterion B., which requires tribes to demonstrate continuous existence as an Indian entity from historic times to the present.

The debate over the newly adopted criteria may easily be dismissed as irrelevant. Why does it matter that the eight tribes did not undergo a formal process? Why complain about something that happened years ago? Does not the VCI, like other organizations, have the right to update its procedures and processes? Certainly the answer to the latter question is yes. And yes, the controversy surrounding the newly adopted criteria would be irrelevant, except that at the time that the VCI upped the ante on the criteria for state recognition, six of the eight tribes seeking federal recognition attempted to do so by circumventing the BIA and its mandatory criteria to obtain recognition through an act of Congress. While the VCI required petitioners to adhere to stringent criteria based on BIA regulations, no such information was forthcoming from those seated on the VCI seeking federal recognition. According to a BIA official, the Virginia Six "have not provided the basic documentation going beyond the current members."[28] According to the Virginia Six, however, the Commonwealth's Racial Integrity Act (RIA) and Plecker's war on the Indians obscured documentary evidence supporting their claim to Indian identity and made it impossible to meet the BIA's strict guidelines. They had gained state recognition based solely on testimony and were determined to gain federal recognition in a similar manner. This was all justifiable, of course, as theirs was a special situation and required that Congress grant them special consideration. Ironically, however, the VCI process granted no such special consideration to tribes seeking recognition within its own state.

Prior to ratifying the new VCI criteria four tribes, leading with the NITOV, filed letters of intent to petition the VCI for state recognition.[29] On February 21, 2006, the NITOV's letter of intent was read into the VCI minutes and on October 17, 2006, a documented petition on behalf of the tribe was hand delivered by Chairperson Lynette Allston to the VCI office. They were the first, and to date the only tribe, to file a petition under the newly ratified guidelines. The NITOV petition contained a detailed cover letter accompanied by hundreds of pages of supporting documents, including but not limited to: primary and secondary sources charting the Nottoway Tribe's existence from the mid-seventeenth century to the present; genealogical data tracing ten family lines back to nineteenth century Nottoway ancestors; and affidavits from local residents, one as old as eighty, attesting to their continued existence and identity as Indians in southeastern Virginia. The seriousness with which the tribe engaged the recognition process was reflected in its presentation. As Mitchell Bush, a retired BIA official and Recognition Committee member stated, "It is as good as and perhaps better than many petitions I've seen come through the BIA."[30]

The Recognition Subcommittee first convened on January 16, 2007, to discuss the recognition process and how best to proceed.[31] The council also determined that proof of the evidence that the tribe had met the criteria would be based on two standards: "a) a preponderance of evidence and b) greater weight of the evidence."[32] The NITOV were confident that at the end of what was supposed to be a one year process, the proof of evidence would show that the tribe had indeed met the criteria for state recognition. Despite this confidence, tribal members were not naïve. They were well aware of the VCI's unwritten criteria of racial purity. While the evidence presented by the tribe would easily demonstrate that they were Indian people, it would also demonstrate the tribe's historical and contemporary ties with the African American community. Rather than engage in denial or remain silent, the tribe decided instead to be proactive and confront the elephant in the room head on.

In her October 17, 2006, cover letter to the VCI, which accompanied the tribe's documented petition for recognition, NITOV Chairperson Lynette Allston took an uncompromising stance regarding the issue of intermarriage asserting, "The most obvious and sensitive issue is disparate consideration of racial intermarriage and tribal identification."[33] In other words, because one's presumed admixture was based on pigmentation, a dark skin color served as a marker for the presence of African American ancestry whether real or imagined. The presence of dark-skinned tribal members raised questions about the legitimacy of a tribe's identity claim. Nevertheless, skin pigmentation as the basis to measure a group's Indianness would prove problematic as the Nottoway were described by eighteenth-century surveyor William Byrd as possessing "Mehogony Skins" or "the Copper Colored ones of Nottoway towne."[34] Hence, the Nottoway, as Allston aptly asserted, "were a dark-skinned people long before any extensive intermarriage with either Europeans or African Americans." Hence, pigmentation should not serve as the barometer by which to measure Nottoway Indian identity. Notwithstanding, Allston, whose husband and children are of Afro-Indian lineage, embraces the mixed race reality of the NITOV unabashedly and un-apologetically.[35] She asserted that the historical significance of African American–Native American intersections had been subjected to erasure due to European hegemony, which privileges Euro-Indian realities at the expense of all others. Allston poignantly stated the heart of the matter asserting, "It is further obscured by a prevailing sentiment that it is acceptable to trumpet Indian–European ancestry, but taboo to celebrate Indian-Afro ancestry. Leaving out the Indian-Afro or non-Anglo, side of the story destroys context, balance, and invalidates conclusions. The resulting hazy, partial portrayal of Indians, particularly, the Nottoway, is an unjust one of a people . . . making them appear passive, victimized and lacking in will . . . making them disappear."

The historical record, as Allston was well aware, told a different story. The Nottoway, like other Indian nations that became tributaries to the British Crown during the colonial era, had a long history in the upper-Tidewater Region prior to European and African contact. They were identified in the unexplored region of John Smith's now famous 1612 map as Mangoags. The term could mean "anything from enemy to outsider to other."[36] By the seventeenth century this group was known as the Nottoway—derived from Nadawa. It is said that they inherited the name from Powhatan who viewed his Iroquoian neighbors as "stealthy and snake like."[37] The NITOV interpret the label as a compliment, rather than a negative connotation, as many others tend to do. As diplomatic emissaries between the colonial government and their more radical southern and western Iroquoian brethren, these modern day Nottoway view the term as pointing to methods of diplomacy that served to stave off the assaults of those whose more powerful weaponry posed a threat to their ancestors' survival.

That survival was certainly put to the test after Edward Bland's expedition in the spring of 1650, which exposed the lands south of the James River to land-hungry Anglos eager to expand into new territory. At that time the Nottoway occupied three villages in the area today known as Sussex County. Despite their location along a main trading path between the Powhatan and Tuscarora nations, the Nottoway had remained untouched by colonial powers until the last quarter of the seventeenth century. They were hunters and gatherers. They were governed by tribal societies that distributed power among several principal authorities rather than concentrating it within a singular chiefdom. Due to White encroachment and harassment from enemy tribes such as the Seneca, Tuscarora, and Sapony, the King of the Nottoway joined four other tribal nations in signing the 1677 Treaty of Middle Plantation.[38] Treaties were often one-sided arrangements that benefited the English far more than the Indians. Unsurprisingly, the 1677 treaty failed to bring the promised protection of the colonial government to the Nottoway. The tribe, therefore, remained vulnerable to White encroachment and to enemy tribes. In 1681, the Nottoway relocated to Assamoosick Swamp in Surry County. Plagued again by the same vulnerabilities, the tribe relocated once more in 1694 to the mouth of the Assamoosick Swamp in what is now Southampton County.[39]

In 1705 the land grabbing intensified as the House of Burgesses lifted its settlement restrictions along the Blackwater frontier placing great restriction on Indian hunting grounds. That same year on April 28, the Nottoway Tribe was forced to adhere to the restrictions of the colonial government, which marked out two tracts of land within the area the tribe had occupied since its relocation in 1694. The tracts known as the Circle and the Square became the Nottoway Reservation. The first tract, the Circle, comprised three miles and was located east of the Nottoway River along the Assamoosick Swamp. In the center of the Circle tract was the "Nottoway great towne."[40] On the west side of the Nottoway River near Buckhorn Swamp was the Square tract comprised of six square miles. These two reservations equaling about 40,000 acres of land would serve as a safe haven for Nottoway allies, including Indians as well as Blacks.[41]

Prior to the Nottoway's relegation to the Circle and Square Reservation, a remnant of the Weyanoke Indians who once occupied the region within the area now known as Charles City County found sanctuary among the Nottoway in the 1690s. A group of Nansemond found sanctuary within the Nottoway community from 1746 until approximately 1786, and by 1792 other Nansemond would seek refuge among the Nottoway as most of their women had already deserted the tribe and were living within the confines of the Nottoway reservation. Also among those finding a safe haven within the boundaries of the reservation were some Meherrin who found welcome among their Iroquois cousins.[42]

The Nottoway not only extended their hospitality to their Indian allies, they also welcomed Blacks both slave and free into their community. As people of color, Blacks and Indians alike were targets of White hostility on a daily basis. The potential for insurrection escalated fears of Black on White violence and the free Black population bore the brunt of White retaliations during periods of racial unrest. In 1793, the year Norfolk received an influx of refugees escaping the St. Dominigue Revolution, the threat of insurrection kept Virginians on heightened alert as plots had been reported in various places including Richmond, Petersburg, Norfolk, and Portsmouth. Reports the following year of poison murders committed by slaves in nearby Hertford County, North Carolina, increased White anxiety. By the turn of the century, Black unrest and insurrection conspiracies were reported in Richmond, Petersburg, Nottoway, York, Accomack, and Powhatan counties. The fear of Black violence continued to preoccupy the thoughts of White Virginians in the succeeding decades of the early nineteenth century. Free Blacks in Southampton, a number of whom had commingled and intermarried with the Nottoway, readily escaped to the reservation to avoid White retaliation. In the fall of 1799, the Nottoway provided cover for a number of free Blacks during the unrest resulting from the deaths of two slave traders who were left dead on a Southampton road when a group of slaves being forced to march to Georgia staged a mutiny. Once again, free Blacks escaped to the reservation during the aftermath of the murder of William Summerell, a White overseer who was killed on his Southampton farm in 1802. Yet, these incidences were only a prelude for what was to come. The Nottoway reservation would become central to the survival of many free Blacks in the aftermath of the Nat Turner rebellion.[43]

On the early morning of August 22, 1831, in Southampton County, Nat Turner and six others, in an attempt to start an armed rebellion to overthrow slavery, went house to house killing every White person in their path including men, women and children. Turner picked up at least forty additional recruits along the way and had built a small army by midday. But before the day was over, as the county caught wind of the insurrection, Turner's small army scattered. Some, including Turner, escaped while others were captured by state and federal troops. The number of White casualties was fifty five. The state executed fifty five Blacks, acquitted a few, and banished others. Turner hid out in a number of locations until his capture in a cave on the Musgrave property in Capron on October 30, 1831. He was tried on November 5. On November 11, 1831, Nat Turner was hanged and afterwards he was skinned.[44]

Prior to his capture and execution, Turner received help from the Nottoway. Whether he was of Black–Nottoway ancestry is still cause for speculation. The Turner name is prevalent within the Nottoway Tribe, African American, and White communities. Intermingling and commingling across racial lines was the rule, not the exception; therefore, it may be that Turner was indeed Black Nottoway. What is certain is that Turner had friends among the Nottoway. According to oral tradition, the reservation served as Turner's sanctuary during periods prior to the rebellion when he would temporarily run away only to later return to his owner. It is probable that he avoided the reservation on the occasion of the insurrection so as not to implicate his Indian allies. Nevertheless, his friendship with the Nottoway helped him survive during the two-month period that he hid out from authorities. Slaves and free Blacks were watched closely in the hope that they would betray Turner's location. But the Indian women who occasionally slipped him food went undetected by Whites.[45]

The Nottoway reservation did prove, nonetheless, to be a sanctuary during this time to many other free Blacks including Turner's relatives. White vigilantes, determined to claim revenge for those Whites whose lives had been lost in the wake of the rebellion, targeted Turner's family and other Blacks whether slave or free. Approximately 200 Blacks with no ties to the insurrection were murdered by White mobs overcome by a fit of hysteria. While numerous free Blacks headed for ships supplied by the American Colonization Society to transport Blacks from Norfolk to Liberia, others scrambled for cover any place they could. Some free Blacks found sanctuary on the farms of sympathetic Whites. Others headed straight for the reservation. Incidentally, Turner's daughter Charlotte was taken to the reservation for safe keeping when she was just three years old. The reservation became her permanent home. She later married John Turner, a Nottoway, and gave birth to a daughter Fannie. Vivian Lucas, a contemporary member of the NITOV and great-great-great-granddaughter of Nat Turner, serves as testament to the Black–Indian alliance that was instrumental to the survival of her forbears.[46]

It is this history of Black–Indian cooperation and intermarriage that Allston refused to deny, stating a month prior to the first meeting of the Recognition Committee, "We are Indian people. We have always been Indian people. As such we intermarried with Blacks, Whites and other Indians and I won't deny any of it." The effect on the recognition process of such a bold proactive stance regarding the issue of intermarriage, particularly Indian–Black intermarriage, remained to be seen.[47]

The recognition process got off to a rocky start. After the initial meeting of the Recognition Committee, the NITOV raised questions of impropriety with Rountree at the center of the controversy. Although Rountree was not yet a member of the Recognition Committee, she served as a consultant to the committee. She nevertheless attempted to further assert herself in the process by appointing herself as recording secretary. There were no initial objections to this; however, once the minutes were made public, the NITOV immediately drafted a letter of rebuttal citing a number of omissions to the January 16, 2007, minutes. The committee never addressed those concerns or any others the NITOV submitted in writing throughout the process. The matter was settled by turning over recording duties to another VCI member. Also, from February 2007 to May 2007 the process was stalled resulting from meeting cancellations due to lack of a quorum and the resignation of committee members.[48] The process resumed on June 19, 2007, with a second group of committee members chaired by Paige Archer (Meherrin). By the fall of 2007 the NITOV cleared two of the six hurdles when the committee voted unanimously that the tribe demonstrated that they were a historic tribe in Virginia comprised of ten verifiable genealogical lines, thereby fulfilling the second and fourth criteria respectively.[49]

Much had been accomplished during the fall of 2007, but winter was nigh in more ways than one. First, in November 2007, Rountree became the center of controversy once again when it was learned that she had circulated unsolicited advice to committee members privately via a November 2, 2007, email that she submitted to the Recognition

Committee. Desiring a greater role, Rountree complained that her duties as consultant marginalized her and granted her little opportunity to be directly involved in the recognition process. She further complained of what she perceived as intimidation on the part of the petitioners, who she believed were using "persuasive arguments" to influence the committee's interpretation of the documents. As a remedy she proposed that the entire procedure should be restructured immediately. This would include redefining the role of the consultant to reflect an increased input into the process and closing off the process to the public asserting, "Committee meetings should not be public meetings anymore." The latter, which would also result in closing off meetings to the petitioners, could be accomplished by requesting an exception to the FOIA from the Virginia General Assembly. If such an exception could not be obtained immediately, the process should be put on hold until such a time that an exception could be granted.

Second, the committee underwent another shake up with the resignation of Committee Chairperson Paige Archer. By January 2008, then VCI chairperson Chief William Miles (Pamunkey) appointed a new committee. To the chagrin of the NITOV, Rountree was promoted from consultant to a voting member of the committee. Not only did the NITOV protest her committee appointment on the grounds that her presence on the committee reflected a conflict of interest, but they also protested her reappointment as recording secretary. Their protest was met with mixed results. Newly appointed Recognition Committee Chairman Earl Bass assumed the duty of recording secretary; however, Rountree remained on the committee.[50] Three of the now five committee members as representatives of Virginia's recognized tribes threatened to shut down the process if the retired professor was removed. The consensus among the three, Chief Anne Richardson (Rappahannock), Chief Earl Bass (Nansemond), and Arlene Milner (Upper Mattiponi), was that Rountree knew "more about Virginia Indians than anyone in this room."[51] Such a statement was astonishing coming from three Virginia Indians, two of whom were tribal chiefs. Sharon Bryant, newly appointed VCI representative from the Monacan Tribe, dissented. She voiced her concern regarding the over reliance of the tribal leadership on Rountree and sided with the Nottoway, stating that had Rountree written that the Monacan people were extinct as she had written about the Nottoway, she would not want the anthropologist as a voting member on the Recognition Committee. Bryant's dissent notwithstanding, the depth of Rountree's influence was summed up by Chief Earl Bass's assertion, "I simply cannot function without her."[52]

On April 15, 2008, the NITOV received a major blow to their recognition effort when the committee voted 4–1 that the tribe had failed to meet the first criterion: "Show that the group's members have retained a specifically Indian identity through time." At the core of the committee's argument, as highlighted by both Milner's letter and Rountree's position paper submitted to the Recognition Committee, the petitioners failed to provide any evidence that they identified and lived as Indians through time because they showed no proof of separate Indian schools and churches and because their surnames did not appear on Walter Plecker's 1943 "hit list." As Milner contended regarding an Indian identity, "Other Indian groups were presented with the option of going to the schools built for Black children or not going to school at all. Many Virginia Indian children *did not go to school at all.* But many Virginia Indian groups had the vision to build their own schools and even provided their own teachers, even though there was very little money at the time. In this way, the Virginia Indians retained their Indian identity."[53]

With respect to Rountree's comments, she dismissed any post 1880 scholarly references that made mention of the survival of the Nottoway because such references did not name specific people and therefore one could not assure that those referenced were ancestrally linked to the current petitioners. But more to the point, petitioners had been racially designated as something other than Indian and demonstrated no discontent with such designations throughout the twentieth century. As evidence that the petitioners were satisfied being something other than Indian, Rountree pointed to the absence of Nottoway surnames on Plecker's list. According to Rountree it showed:

> plainly that the ancestors of all of the recognized tribes were standing up to that racism by saying that they were not 'colored'. All of the surnames in the recognized tribes' enclaves are listed in the appropriate counties. Meanwhile, the circular shows equally plainly that the Petitioners' ancestors and relatives were not doing anything of a sort, for there is no listing

at all for Southampton County and the Petitioners' surnames do not appear in other places (Portsmouth, Nansemond County) where some of them were living at the time.[54]

Milner's and Rountree's assertions demonstrated a full-throated endorsement of the twentieth-century salvage campaign politics, which proved to be nothing more than the other side of the racial purity coin. In addition, their assertions further demonstrated a troublesome aspect of the recognition process—the notion of a monolithic historical reality in which a tribe's Indianness is judged by a one size fits all historical construct. The NITOV does not fit within the master narrative constructed by those who embrace salvage politics. To insist that one's surname on Plecker's list, segregated Indian schools and churches, and open declarations of one's Indian identity are the only measures to validate tribal identity claims reduces the complexity of Virginia Indian history to a one-dimensional reality that fails to capture the nuance and multiplicity of experiences of Indian peoples throughout the Commonwealth. Those whom Rountree stated publicly asserted their Indian identity did so under the direction of anthropological advocates who used their academic positions to influence the political process on their behalf. The Nottoway, who lived quietly for much of the twentieth century, resided within a historical landscape very different from the lower Tidewater Region in which open assertions of Indian identity would have proven detrimental rather than beneficial. Certainly, theirs was a much-needed retreat from the constant battles for cultural survival they had endured since their first encounter with the English in the 1650s. By the early twentieth century, they were battle weary and needed time and space to heal from their wounds. If the Powhatan remnants that gained recognition in the late twentieth century can disappear for some 300 years and later reemerge to stake their Indian claim, certainly the Nottoway deserved this much-needed hiatus. During this period, however, they thought it would be best to remain quiet. As Vivian Lucas asserted, "During that time it was unwise to trumpet any connection to Nat Turner's ancestry ... Just as it was to any Nottoway/Indian ancestry. On the one hand you were viewed as issue of a killer of white people, and on the other you were an offspring of a 'drunken' and disgraced Tribe of Indians. Add to that mix some White ancestors, and you had best keep a very low profile in a local community where Whites controlled the economy and the law."[55] The Nottoway had no anthropological advocates egging them on. In fact, anthropologists, including Rountree declared the tribe extinct; they experienced the opposite.[56]

While anthropologists and other scholars were writing the Powhatan remnants into existence during the twentieth century, the Nottoway were simultaneously being erased. James Mooney's "The Powhatan Confederacy Past and Present" (1907), Thomas Parramore's, "The Passing of the Nottoway" (1978) and Briggs and Pittman's "The Mets and Bounds of a Circle and a Square (1997) have contributed significantly to the myth of the vanished Nottoway. Yet, no publication has influenced the interpretation of Nottoway history more than Rountree's often-quoted article "The Termination and Dispersal of the Nottoway Indians," (1987).

This article by Rountree alleged that the Nottoway voluntarily sought tribal termination by the Commonwealth and was extinct because members had intermarried with Blacks—clearly a distortion of history. The Nottoway were no different than members of any other tribe in the Commonwealth—all of whom had intermarried with Blacks, Whites, and other tribal peoples. Rountree's emphasis on Black intermarriage, as previously observed, aimed to discredit and invalidate the Nottoway as an Indian people. Yet, most bothersome about her 1987 article is that she resorted to a method historians refer to as reading history backwards, in which past events are judged according to a current context. In this case, Rountree relied on the Allotment Act of 1887 and the Termination and Relocation Acts of 1953 and 1956 respectively as a basis for her assertions that Virginia terminated its relationship with the Nottoway in 1824.[57] Not only are her conclusions incorrect, but the entire premise of utilizing late nineteenth century and mid-twentieth century federal policy to explain early nineteenth century, Virginia–Nottoway relations is, in a word, faulty. This is the danger of reading history backward— those who do so often get the story backward. To her credit, Rountree in 2002 conceded that "No Virginia government agency has ever used the term [termination] about the Nottoway reservation, much less about Nottoway descended individuals."[58] Unfortunately, by the time of her retraction, the damage had already been done.

It was clear that Rountree privileged eurocentric notions of Indian identity grounded in a false sense of authenticity. To the contrary, the NITOV's view of themselves is based on an indigenous worldview. They did not, nor do they today, quantify their Indianness by degree of admixture or with whom they associate. They are an inclusive people who, while remaining distinctly Indian in identity and culture, see no need to disavow Black familial ties or live antagonistically with those in the Black community. As Attorney Allard Allston asserted in a letter to the VCI:

> During the Plecker era, many of your tribal members found safety, welcome and sanctuary in the predominant White community, and you have not turned your backs on that community and blood linkages that resulted. Some Nottoways found safety, welcome and sanctuary in both the White and the African-American communities. They have not turned their backs on either. Each maintained their Indian identity in ways societal conditions regimented. Neither has a richer or truer history than the other. To be primarily Indian in genealogy & culture should not require that you deny some of your own relatives.[59]

Rountree and others insists that such antagonisms toward Blacks are warranted if a tribe is to maintain an Indian status, as she asserted in the final pages of the Recognition Committee report. Rountree provided several reasons why the NITOV failed to remain socially distinct as Indians, including the fact that during the era of segregation the Nottoway did not "set up their own for-Indians-only school or else keep their children home in order to preserve an 'Indian' reputation; that, in turn, resulted in a negligible in-marriage rate."[60] Such a statement should give one pause. Are we to assume that Rountree's sympathies rest with those who adhered to segregation rather than those who opposed it? Are we to assume that because the Nottoway refused to embrace the assertion that "We couldn't go to school with whites and we wouldn't go to school with blacks," that they are somehow not Indian enough?[61] And what evidence does Rountree have that "a negligible in-marriage rate" with Blacks occurred as a result of the Nottoway attending public schools? This is mere conjecture that advances the archaic notion that integration equals miscegenation. If we are to accept such logic, should not Rountree concede that such negligible in-marriage rates occurred among even those who built separate Indian schools, since such schools were discontinued as a result of the 1954 *Brown v. Board of Education* decision? The problem with Rountree's work stems not from a simple matter of a difference of interpretation, but rather a matter of a deliberate distortion of facts. Her assertions regarding the Nottoway are grounded in classic salvage doctrine, which lends credence to the notion that the only Indians suitable for state recognition are those who participated in the salvage campaign.

Because the VCI required that petitioners meet all six criteria, the NITOV's failure to meet the first criterion appeared to have sounded the death knell of the tribe's quest for recognition. The committee debated whether it made sense to move forward, but Jane Hickey, a representative of the attorney general's office, advised the committee to review and vote on the remaining criteria. Yet, the process was already in its second year. The petitioners seemed exhausted and were ready to pack it all in. But the process was being closely watched by a number of concerned citizens many, of whom expressed disappointment at what they perceived as bias on the part of the Recognition Committee. Citizens sent expressions of support to the tribe, which helped carry the petitioners through the remainder of the process. As the process moved forward, however, the situation remained bleak. On May 20, 2008, the third, fifth, and sixth criteria received split votes: Bush and Bass voted yes on all three and Milner and Rountree voted no. Despite not having submitted a formal letter of resignation, Chief Anne Richardson had ceased to fulfill her obligation as a committee member.

The debate and subsequent vote for the first criterion set in motion the votes on criteria three and five, which required petitioners to demonstrate continuous existence and cultural distinction, respectively.[62] Few were surprised that the tribe did not receive the required votes to clear those two hurdles. What was surprising, however, was that the tribe did not receive a unanimous vote in favor of criterion six, which required that petitioners demonstrate contemporary formal governance and criteria for tribal membership. As per the recognition requirements the tribe demonstrated its "current" and "formally organized government," by providing a certificate of incorporation, tribal bylaws, and a current tribal roll comprised of members whose genealogies attest to their descent from the historic Nottoway. Despite meeting this requirement, the votes in opposition to the sixth criterion were based on a perceived structural deficiency of tribal governance rather than on what the criterion required, which was a demonstration of governance. Mitchell Bush, who voted affirmatively, conceded that the structure could be improved; but he also believed structural preferences should be negotiated, not given an automatic no vote.[63]

On June 17, 2008, Chairman Earl Bass declared the recognition process concluded. The split votes on criteria three, five, and six would remain as Ms. Richardson had expressed to him a desire to abstain from voting on those issues. Nevertheless, the process was far from over. On June 9, 2008, prior to the final meeting of the Recognition Committee, Senator Louise Lucas of the 18th Senatorial District sent a carefully scripted letter to then Attorney General Robert McDonnell requesting that his office investigate the VCI's recognition criteria, which "may have inadvertently raised the bar for Virginia recognition in an inequitable and possibly discriminatory manner." Lucas not only wanted an investigation into the language of the criteria to determine whether or not the VCI as an advisory body had created de facto regulations, but also to determine if the council had violated the FOIA as it appeared from the October 23, 2003, minutes that the criteria were developed in executive session away from the scrutiny of the public. Although Rountree went un-named, Lucas also requested that the retired professor be investigated to determine if indeed her tenure on the Recognition Committee was a conflict of interest. She concluded the letter by expressing her confidence that the attorney general's office would provide a thorough investigation into these issues. The Senator's confidence, however, appeared to have been betrayed. In his response to Ms. Lucas on August 27, 2008, Robert McDonnell stated that the attorney general's office was confident that the VCI was in full compliance of the FOIA. Nevertheless, on February 24, 2009, the attorney general's office admitted that there was no evidence to support the earlier assertion that the VCI had indeed complied with the FOIA.[64]

By this time, the NITOV and the VCI were engaged in a tug-of-war over the language and factual information inserted in the VCI's final Recognition Committee Report (RCR). The RCR underwent three revisions. The third time wasn't necessarily the "charm" in this case. Although the April 17, 2009, RCR claimed the decision to not recommend the NITOV for state recognition was reached by a majority vote, it only provided individual committee member's comments regarding one's "aye" or "nay" vote on each individual criteria. The report did not provide a summary of its findings, and it failed to provide a majority opinion pinpointing exactly which criterion the Nottoway failed to meet. Most egregious, however, was that the RCR violated the code of privacy by publishing extensive genealogical information on individual tribal members. Such information should not have been included in a public document as it does not fall under the FOIA. Despite its assigned mission to provide an in-depth analysis of findings and recommendation regarding the recognition process, the RCR revealed more about the VCI than it did about the NITOV. The report was shockingly deficient and unprofessional, which may well serve as an indication of the VCI's unpreparedness to properly oversee the state recognition process.[65]

On May 19, 2009, the council voted 6–3 to concur with the recommendation of the Recognition Committee not to recommend the NITOV for state recognition. It appeared to be the final nail in the petitioner's recognition coffin. Yet, the NITOV remained undeterred. They knew the VCI process did not carry the force of law as some VCI members had claimed. They quickly moved forward believing that the dream of state recognition was not dead, but only deferred. The next course of action was to appeal directly to the Virginia General Assembly (VGA).

On January 13, 2010, Senate Joint Resolution 12 sponsored by Senator Louise Lucas and House Joint Resolution 32 sponsored by Delegate Roslyn Tyler, "Extending State Recognition to the Nottoway Indian Tribe of Virginia," were offered to the VGA on behalf of the petitioners. Although Rountree submitted correspondence opposing the resolution, the VCI remained indifferent.[66] They believed that the resolution would not make it out of committee in the Republican-controlled House. The VCI representatives voiced no opposition to the HJR 32 when it was presented before the House Rules Committee on February 2, 2010.[67] But when the resolution was passed out of committee by unanimous vote, the VCI sprang into action. On February 12, 2010, representatives from the VCI appeared before the Senate Rules Committee to voice their opposition

FIG 7.1 Nottoway Indian Tribe of Virginia (NITOVA) Recognition Presentation. Pictured from left to right are Tribal Councilman Leroy Hardy, War-Chief Bill Wright, Assistant Chief Archie Elliot, Chief Lynette Allston, Tribal Councilwoman Vivian Lucas (great-great-great-granddaughter of Nat Turner), Senator Louise Lucas, and Senator Yvonne Miller. Courtesy of NITOVA.

to the resolutions citing the tribe's failure to meet the council's criteria. But the response from the Senators, led by Senator Yvonne Miller, was a thorough tongue lashing. "The jig is up," Miller stated. She chided the VCI for having transformed the council's mission to assist all Native peoples into an exclusive club focused on assisting a select few. SJR 12 passed out of committee by unanimous vote. It arrived on the Senate floor for a full vote on February 15, 2010. Once again it passed by unanimous vote and was sent to the House. Despite the efforts of Delegate Harvey Morgan, a former VCI member, who tried in a last ditch effort to derail the House floor vote, SJR 12 passed by a vote of 91–5.

On February 26, 2010, the NITOV's efforts had finally paid off. The petitioner's dream of becoming a state recognized tribe had finally been fulfilled. The road to recognition had been long and hard. From the eighteenth century to the present, numerous "experts" had declared the

Nottoway people extinct. But they defied such premature proclamations as evidenced by their triumph in 2010. Their perseverance also benefited the Patawomeck and the Cheroenhaka Tribes, who also received state recognition during the same legislative session. Yet, the NITOV's legacy lies in its exposure of the VCI's abuse of power in the state recognition process, a process based on exclusion rather than inclusion.[68]

But there remains a greater legacy still. It is a legacy that refused to allow the unwritten criteria of racial purity to dictate what it means to be an Indian. As Assistant Chief Archie Elliott, responding to questions regarding the legitimacy of his Indian identity, quipped, "I am Indian and I am Black, so what's your point?"[69] Challenges to the dictates of pseudo-notions of racial purity that requires that the preservation of Indian identity demand the absence or denial of African American ancestry, can be best summed up by the phrase, "all of my relations." It is underscored by an identity that is based on who one is rather than who one is not as captured by Lynette Allston's impassioned assertion, "We are Indian people. We have always been Indian people. As such we intermarried with Blacks, Whites and other Indians and I won't deny any of it." That is what it means to be Indian. That is what it means to be Nottoway.[70]

Epilogue:
Afro-Indian Peoples of Virginia:
The Indelible Thread of Black and Red

First they [Blacks and Indians] made prayers, then they sang,
then they danced and then they made relatives.

—FRANCIS YELLOW

Jasper Battle never asked to join the Rappahannock Indian Baptist Church. He was content with attending Sunday services with his wife, Lori, and their young niece and nephew, who they were raising due to the untimely death of Lori's brother, Hayward Hedgeman on April 23, 2003. The children, Sarah, then fourteen, and Preston, then ten, loved attending the church. The church and its community of people were a reminder of the father whom they had lost. It was a part of him that the children could hold on to. Yet as Rev. Custalow stood before the congregation earnestly extending an invitation for whosoever will to come just as you are, there was another scene playing out in the back room of the church. Immediately after the sermon, Lori and the children were summoned by two deacons. They believed they had been brought into the room to be given additional instructions before they would be presented before the congregation and received as members. But the two deacons, John and

Daniel Fortune had something else in mind. Daniel, the more aggressive of the two, announced that the family would not be allowed to join the church because Lori was married to a Black man. The children were shocked and overcome with disappointment. They could not understand what Jasper's race had to do with the decision not to accept the family as members. Lori, seeing the children's reaction turned to the two men and asked, "Do you mean to hurt my children?" "You did this!" Daniel snapped while vehemently wagging his finger in Lori's face. "You should not have married outside of your race."[1]

The significance of the Battles' church denial cannot be overstated. Lori was not simply Rappahannock; her brother, Haywood Hedgeman, had served for a time as Chief of the Tri-County Rappahannock Tribe for which Nokomis Lemons attempted to gain state recognition in 1997 and 1999. Hedgeman's heavy travel schedule due to military responsibilities caused him to relinquish his tribal duties to the current chief Nokomis Lemons. Despite being a separate entity, they were all considered Rappahannock and a vital part of the community. Also, despite the tensions that almost tore the community apart in the late 1990s, the church was the glue that held it together. The situation, however, became irreconcilable when the Rappahannock Indian Baptist Church refused membership to the sister of a former tribal chief and to his children. From the viewpoint of those on the opposing side of the Battles' membership, Lori and the children, though of Rappahannock descent, were no longer a part of the Rappahannock community. Ironically, at the time of the incident, the Battles' daughter was a member of the church; she, however, had married a White man.

While the eight tribes that received recognition in the 1980s are adamant against close associations with the African American community, the Rappahannock appear to be the most vehement in its resolution to keep Blacks at bay. Helen Rountree suggested that this is because the tribe had to fight harder than the others to maintain its tribal identity. She argued that "the Rappahannock more than the others, lived scattered in an area that was unusually hostile to non-whites."[2] She also cited the World War II experience of Oliver Fortune, who was racially identified by the draft board as colored because his parents had been listed as colored and he had, unlike many of his counterparts, attended a colored school. Yet, this seems an oversimplification of the situation. As Chief Lynette Allston asserted regarding the strict adherence to the doctrine of racial purity by some within tribal communities throughout the state, "It seems that those who are most adamant about racial purity came along during the integration era, not the Plecker era."[3] For certain, as Daniel Fortune, who was born in 1928, demonstrated, there were indeed exceptions. Many of those most opposed to the church's refusal to extend membership to the Battles were elderly members who had indeed come of age during the Plecker years. One such person was an eighty-four year old woman who stated, "There were those in the church who didn't like Jasper simply because he was Black. I don't understand that. He is a good man. He comes from a good Christian home. My mother always taught me to be kind to everybody no matter who they were."[4] Generational divisions notwithstanding, a cursory review of the documentary evidence demonstrates a historical connection between the Rappahannock and the African American community from which they continually struggle to distance themselves with mixed results.

Lori Battle came of age in the Jim Crow era during the post-Plecker years. She was raised in Champlain, Virginia, an unincorporated rural community located in Essex County. She attended Central Point Elementary School and also attended the historic Saint Stephen's Baptist Church in Central Point, Caroline County. While growing up, Lori had encounters with both White and Black children. Relationships with the latter proved to be far more difficult than the former. She often had to defend herself against the physical assaults of her Black classmates who would pull her long ponytails and call her names. The name calling one day turned into a violent brawl when one of the children called Lori's mother "a squaw," a derogatory term used to describe Indian women. She took out her revenge on her mother's insulter that day and received no reprimand or reprisal from school administrators. As soon as she returned home from school, Lori informed her mother of the incident. After relating her story she looked up at her mother with bright innocent eyes and asked, "Mama, what's a squaw?"

As a result of her early encounters with Blacks, not to mention encounters with those within the tribal community who held anti-Black views, one would assume that Lori held animosity towards African

American people. Yet, nothing could be further from the truth. She, much like her elderly counterpart, believed that everyone, regardless of race, should be treated with human decency. She also refused to allow her childhood experiences with a few misguided Black classmates to influence her opinion of an entire community of people. After high school, Lori left Champlain and her early unfortunate encounters with her African American schoolmates behind.

Lori worked for a number of government agencies in the Washington, D.C. area. She met Jasper while working at the Pentagon. They wedded during an intimate ceremony at a friend's house in 1974. But as some saw it, Jasper was all wrong for Lori. Yes, he was African American; but that was the least of their worries. Jasper was seventeen years her junior and had been previously married with children. Lori certainly understood the concerns of family and friends, but she felt differently. "Me and Jay," she stated, "are from the same corner." In other words, they shared the same values and the same worldview. They were kindred spirits whose relationship was grounded in the stuff that's made to last.

Nevertheless, while Jasper's race may have taken a back seat to some of the other concerns raised by Lori's loved ones, it did not remain on the periphery. She was aware that there were those within the Rappahannock community who opposed her marriage to Jasper for no other reason but that he was Black. Such opposition could be ignored since the couple lived away from the tribal community for a time; but, during her visits home to Champlain she keenly felt the disapproval of her choice of a spouse. Opposition to her marriage was voiced by both rank and file members and senior members of the tribal council. As one senior council member poignantly stated, "Lori, you can take your rightful place in the tribe if you would simply divorce your husband."[5] Jasper's North Carolina Cherokee ancestry, which he inherited from his grandmother whom he affectionately called Mama Sally, did nothing to redeem him in the eyes of those who clung to the mores of racial purity like it was gospel. Throughout their thirty-year marriage, the Battles posed no trouble for the Indian community even when Lori (with Jasper) moved back to the family farm in Champlain in the late 1980s. It was the couple's attempt to join the Rappahannock Indian Baptist Church, which some feared would be detrimental to the tribe's effort for federal recognition, that caused things to come to a head. "That day was bad," stated one former member. "I knew things had gotten ugly in that back room when I saw the children coming out of there crying. It was truly a bad day."[6]

Despite the trauma and the subsequent chaos resulting from the ensuing media circus, one person at least did not see it as a bad day. Barron Nelson, a member of the Rappahannock Tribe and the church musician, was able to move beyond the tragedy of the ordeal to find a glimmer of hope. Nelson stated of Jasper Battle during an interview with a local reporter, "[He's] an angel in disguise. He's a black man, and God sent him here to show what kind of hearts people had."[7] That Nelson could envision Blackness as something symbolic of goodness and righteous conviction reflected a traditional Powhatan worldview which envisioned Blackness as sacred rather than profane. It also spoke back to the long centuries of European thought which only envisioned Blackness as synonymous with all that is evil and perverse. Moreover, it spoke back to the four centuries of Virginia's long obsession with racial purity whose legacy continues to haunt families and communities still victimized by its devastating consequences.

America's racial dictatorship has imposed racial identities on its citizenry that many have uncritically accepted. Numerous African Americans embrace the "one-drop rule" and believe that those who wish to acknowledge a multiracial heritage are self-hating traitors to the race. American Indians, many of whom are caught up in the chaos of tribal recognition and enrollment, embrace racial purity unaware, it seems, of how its racist underpinnings jeopardize the very existence of the native peoples they claim to protect. L. Scott Gould asserted that "The tribe that tries to hold the line on racial purity risks extinction."[8] Forsaking the tenets of racial purity will certainly be a formidable task for the majority of state recognized Virginia Indians who presently show no sign of abandoning this state and federally imposed mythology. To the contrary, the example provided by the Nottoway Indian Tribe of Virginia is indicative of what can be accomplished when one follows the path of social justice and challenges the illusion of racial purity and societal notions of American Indian identity.

The entire enterprise of racial classification is not only founded on long invalidated scientific categories, but it is also founded on an "either/

or" fallacy that states one can only belong to one racial group, a dilemma the Seminole Freedmen have faced: "The fact that the freedmen appear to identify themselves as both American Indian and African American has apparently caused some resentment. At least some 'blood' Seminoles apparently do not believe that the freedmen can be both Seminole and black . . . the opinion was voiced that 'blacks had to decide whether they were blacks or Seminole tribal members—they could not be both.'"[9] Such racial pigeonholing underpinned by the American racial project demands that one construct a singular imagined American Indian history which denies the confluence of a Black–Indian historical reality. Consequently, an uncritical adherence to racial purity, the denial of Black mixture and familial relations, is a deliberate attempt to maintain the tenets of White supremacy, an ever present, yet veiled reality, which now seeks to promote the illusion of a post racial society.

Resistance to such racial pigeonholing is gaining momentum as many Americans are actively challenging oversimplified definitions of racial identification based on the Jeffersonian sophism that two races cannot coexist for one will cancel out the other. Or that American Indian authenticity depends on the absence of Blackness. In addition, despite proscriptions against Black–Indian intermarriage in many tribal communities, many are defying such archaic anti-miscegenation sentiment and the racist ideology it underscores. Lori and Jasper Battle and those who stood with them are representative of this latter group. They also represent the historical confluence and kinship realities of African American and Native American peoples, interwoven within the intricate tapestry of the Commonwealth of Virginia.

The story of African American–American Indian relations in Virginia is indeed filled with controversy and pain. It is a reality that many would rather remain unspoken. Yet, as Tiya Miles aptly contended, we must overcome the temptation to remain silent in the face of such difficult dialogue, "For the void that remains when we refuse to speak of the past is in fact a presence, a presence both haunting and destructive."[10] To break the silence about Virginia's racial integrity campaign and its effect on Black–Indian relations in Virginia is not to demonize or pathologize those who adhere to society's racialized notions, but rather it is to provide a means to decolonize our minds and consider alternative ways of thinking about identity, community and, yes, even citizenship. This process of decolonization, according to Afro-Indian scholar bell hooks, is "a gesture of resistance to the dominant culture's ways of thinking about history, identity and community . . . to reclaim the word that is our history as it was told to us by our ancestors [and contemporaries] and not as it has been interpreted by the colonizer."[11] Power is intrinsically linked to the Western view of history. Colonized histories construct and disseminate structures of knowledge that are intended to subjugate, silence, and in the end, foster disremembering. This has indeed been the result of the master narrative constructed by powerful elites who reinforced America's racial hierarchy in an effort to maintain White supremacy.

Plecker's war was not simply against the Virginia Indians; it was waged because of the Virginia Indians' historic relationships with African Americans. Hence, according to the dictates of racial purity, Indians should be reclassified as colored to prevent the infusion of Black "blood" they may possess from contaminating the White gene pool. It was the attempts by "negroid Indians" to marry Whites that motivated Plecker's unsavory war of extinction against Virginia's indigenous population. These statements are not intended to downplay or deny the unbridled racism Virginia Indians have faced on a continual basis since their first contact with Europeans in 1607. They serve only to acknowledge the reality of a racial ideology underscored by myths of the one-drop rule and Black racial contamination to justify Plecker's war of extinction on Virginia Indians.

Consequently, Frank Speck and those seeking to save the Virginia Indians from paper genocide engaged in a type of paper genocide themselves by deliberately attempting to erase Black–Indian relations and Afro-Indian peoples from the annals of Virginia's history, as demonstrated by the salvage campaign. Although this strategy to deny the existence of Afro-Indian peoples in Virginia has been interpreted by some as resistance to state-imposed racial purity regulations, its result, however unintentional, was the opposite; it reinforced rather than eradicated the tenets of racial purity. Moreover, the disruption of kinship, friendship, and community ties helped further the work of divide and rule which began in the late eighteenth century with Thomas Jefferson's myth of Black–Indian incompatibility, a myth that remains pervasive to this day.

Nevertheless, while this story is what Tiya Miles, drawing on historian Nell Irvin Painter, described as, a "'fully loaded cost accounting' of who we have been . . . ,'" it is also a story of "who we can become, as peoples whose lives have been intertwined on this land for centuries."[12] Despite a deliberate effort to divide the two peoples and erase the historical and contemporary realities of African American and Native American relations, as well as the kinship ties that followed, such efforts have not been altogether successful. Couples like Lori and Jasper Battle, Charlotte and William Allen, Lynette and Allard Allston, in addition to tribal communities like the Nottoway Indian Tribe of Virginia, the United Cherokee Indian Tribe of Virginia, Nokomis Lemons and the Rappahannock Indian Tribe, as well as organizations such as the Weyanoke Association of Red/Black History and Culture lend credence to the continued alliances between African American and Native American friendship and kinship relations in the state of Virginia. The indelible thread of Black and Red stretches from the early days of Spanish exploration in the sixteenth-century Chesapeake, which first brought peoples of probable African descent to the shores of the Tidewater, to Armstrong Archer's mid-nineteenth century homage to the Afro-Indian heritage of the Powhatan people to the present day survival of Afro-Indian people of the Virginia Commonwealth. It is this indelible thread of Black and Red that brings together the pouring of libation and offering of tobacco in sacred communion honoring the past, present and future of Afro-Indian peoples of Virginia who were indeed once faced with erasure, but are now faced with endless possibilities, a fitting reward for those who have the audacity to survive.

APPENDIX:
THE RACIAL INTEGRITY ACT

Acts of the Assembly
Chap.371.—A. D. An ACT to preserve racial integrity [S B 219]
Approved March 20, 1924

1. Be it enacted by the General Assembly of Virginia, That the State Registrar of Vital Statistics may as soon as practicable after the taking effect of this act, prepare a form whereon the racial composition of any individual, as Caucasian, negro, Mongolian, American Indian, Asiatic Indian, Malay, or any mixture thereof, or any other non-Caucasic strains, and if there be any mixture, then the racial composition of the parents and other ancestors, in so far as ascertainable, so as to show in what generation such mixture occurred, may be certified by such individual, which form shall be known as a registration certificate. The State Registrar may supply to each local registrar a sufficient number of such forms for the purpose of this act; each local registrar may personally or by deputy, as soon as possible after receiving said forms, have made thereon in duplicate a certificate of the racial composition as aforesaid, of each person resident in his district, who so desires, born before June fourteenth, nineteen hundred and twelve, which certificate shall be made over the signature of said person, or in the case of children under fourteen years of age, over the signature of a parent, guardian, or other person standing *in loco parentis*. One of said certificates for each person thus registering in every district shall be forwarded to the State Registrar for his files; the other shall be kept on file by the local registrar. Every local registrar may, as soon as practicable, have such registration certificate made by or for each person in his district who so desires, born before June fourteen, nineteen hundred and twelve, for whom he has not on file a registration certificate, or a birth certificate.

2. It shall be a felony for any person wilfully or knowingly to make a registration certificate false as to color or race. The wilful making of a false registration or birth certificate shall be punished by confinement in the penitentiary for one year.

3. For each registration certificate properly made and returned to the State Registrar, the local registrar returning the same shall be entitled to a fee of twenty-five cents, to be paid by the registrant. Application for registration and for transcript may be made direct to the State Registrar, who may retain the fee for expenses of his office.

4. No marriage license shall be granted until the clerk or deputy clerk has reasonable assurance that the statements as to color of both man and woman are correct.
   If there is reasonable cause to disbelieve that applicants are of pure white race, when that fact is stated, the clerk or deputy clerk shall with-hold the granting of the license until satisfactory proof is produced that both applicants are "white persons" as provided for in this act. The clerk or deputy clerk shall use the same care to assure himself that both applicants are colored, when that fact is claimed.

5. It shall hereafter be unlawful for any white person in this State to marry any save a white person, or a person with no other admixture of blood than white and American Indian. For the purpose of this act, the term "white person" shall apply only to the person who has no trace whatsoever of any blood other than Caucasian; but persons who have one-sixteenth or less of the blood of the American Indian and have no other non-Caucasic blood shall be deemed to be white persons. All laws heretofore passed and now in effect regarding the intermar-riage of white and colored persons shall apply to marriages prohibited by this act.

6. For carrying out the purposes of this act and to provide the necessary clerical assistance, postage and other expenses of the State Registrar of Vital Statistics, twenty per cent of the fees received by local registrars under this act shall be paid to the State Bureau of Vital Statistics, which may be expended by the said bureau for the purposes of this act.

7. All acts or parts of acts inconsistent with this act are, to the extent of such inconsistency, hereby repealed.

Reproduced from original text.

NOTES

Preface

1. The Grooms family, whose surname is prevalent among the Cherokee and Lumbee tribes, migrated from North Carolina to Virginia sometime during the nineteenth century. By the late nineteenth century the family had moved to Ohio where Lillian was born on July 8, 1898. She later migrated to Baltimore, Maryland and resided with family members living in the area until her marriage to Leighton Sylvester Kyler, Sr., an African American. The couple had two children: Leighton, Jr., and Merriel. Lillian's racial identity on the census appears as Black (1900), mulatto (1910 and 1920), and Negro (1930). Lillian's sisters also married African American men and were absorbed into the African American community.

2. Booker T. Washington to Albert Ernest Jenks (Dec. 4, 1911), *Booker T. Washington Papers,* Vol. 11, 1911–12, eds. Louis R. Harlan and Raymond Smock (Urbana: University of Illinois Press), 387.

3. Stuart Hall, *Race the Floating Signifier* (Northampton, Mass.: Media Education Foundation, 1996), VHS; for more on the subject of race as a political construct see Dorothy Roberts, *Fatal Invention: How Science, Politics and Big Business Re-Create Race in the Twenty-First Century* (New York: The New Press), 2011.

Introduction

1. Michael Paul Williams, "Church Denies Entry to Couple," *Richmond Times-Dispatch,* Mar. 31, 2004, TimesDispatch.com, 1.

2. Ibid.; Jasper Battle passed away on Saturday, March 20, 2011.

3. United Rappahannock Indian Tribe, Articles of Incorporation Amendment, 1981.

4. Author interview with Rappahannock informant, Dec. 1, 2010.

5. Williams, "Church Denies Entry to Couple," 3.

6. Ibid.

7. Mark Holmberg, "A Church Divided Against Itself: Split Over Membership at Rappahannock Indian Church Widens," *Richmond Times-Dispatch,* Apr. 5, 2004, TimesDispatch.com, 1; James Tignor passed away on February 8, 2012. His funeral was held at the Bethlehem Baptist Church in Champlain, Virginia. During

a telephone interview on Aug. 22, 2012, his widow, Ann Tignor, denied having any knowledge of the 2004 incident at the Rappahannock Indian Baptist Church. She stated that she and her husband visited the church with no intention to join.

8. Williams, "Church Denies Entry to Couple," 3.

9. Ibid.

10. Ibid.

11. Holmberg, "A Church Divided," 2.

12. "The Racial Integrity Act," *Image Archive on the American Eugenics Movement* [Online] (New York: Cold Springs Laboratory), http://www.eugenicsarchive .org/eugenics/.

13. For a discussion of the etymology of the term "miscegenation," see Sidney Kaplan, "The Miscegenation Issue in the Election of 1864," *Journal of Negro History,* 34, no. 3 (July, 1949): 274–343.

14. For a discussion on the etymology of the term Caucasian, see Nell Irvin Painter, "Johann Friedrich Blumenbach Names White People 'Caucasian,'" in *The History of White People* (New York: W. W. Norton , 2010*)*.

15. Carter G. Woodson, "The Relations of Negroes and Indians in Massachusetts," *Journal of Negro History,* 3, no.1 (1920): 1

16. With very few exceptions, the field continues to be dominated by studies focused on Black–Indian issues regarding identity formation, slavery, and civil rights among the Five "Civilized" Tribes. These works include: Murray R. Wickett, *Contested Territory: Whites, Native Americans and African Americans in Oklahoma 1865–1907* (Baton Rouge: Louisiana State University Press, 2000); Patrick N. Minges, *Slavery in the Cherokee Nation: The Keetoowah Society and the Defining of a People 1855–1867* (New York: Routledge, 2003) and *Black Indian Slave Narratives* (Winston Salem, N.C.: John F. Blair Publishers, 2004); Tiya Miles, *The Ties that Bind: The Story of an Afro-Cherokee Family in Slavery and Freedom* (Berkeley: University of California Press, 2006) and *House on Diamond Hill: A Cherokee Plantation Story* (Chapel Hill: University of North Carolina Press, 2010); Claudio Saunt, *Black, White and Indian: Race and the Unmaking of an American Family* (New York: Oxford University Press, 2006); Kevin Mulroy, *The Seminole Freedman: A History* (Norman: University of Oklahoma Press, 2007); Gary Zellar, *African Creeks: Estelvste and the Creek Nation* (Norman: University of Oklahoma Press, 2007); Fay A. Yarbrough, *Race and the Cherokee Nation: Sovereignty in the Nineteenth Century* (Philadelphia: University of Pennsylvania Press, 2007); Celia E. Naylor, *African Cherokees in Indian Territory: From Chattel to Citizens* (Chapel Hill: University of North Carolina Press, 2008); and David Chang, *The Color of the Land: Race, Nation, and the Politics of Land Ownership in Oklahoma, 1832–1929* (Chapel Hill: University of North Carolina, 2010).

17. Ariela J. Cross, *What Blood Won't Tell: A History of Race on Trial* (Cambridge, Mass.: Harvard University Press, 2010), 141.

18. As a result of BIA sanctions, the tribes rescinded the decision to oust the freedmen; however, the Cherokee Freedmen struggle for full citizenship continues. The continued justification for disenfranchising the freedmen, descendants of former slaves of the Five Civilized Tribes, has been premised on the notion that they are not Indian by "blood." Not only does this deny historic Black–Indian familial

ties, it also denies the freedmen their treaty rights which established them as citizens in 1866. For more on the blood politics of citizenship in the Cherokee nation see Circe Dawn Sturm, *Blood Politics: Race, Culture and Identity in the Cherokee Nation of Oklahoma* (Berkeley: University of California Press, 2002) and *Becoming Indian: The Struggle Over Cherokee Identity in the Twenty-First Century* (Santa Fe, N.Mex.: SAR Press, 2011); for more on the Seminole nation, see Josephine Johnston, "Resisting a Genetic Identity: The Black Seminoles and the Genetic Test of Ancestry," *Journal of Law, Medicine and Ethics,* 31, no. 2 (2003): 262–271.

19. A few recent studies have moved beyond the parameters of what is traditionally referred to as Indian Country and have broadened the lens by which Red and Black intersections can be further examined. Karen Blu, *The Lumbee Problem: The Making of An American Indian People* (Lincoln: University of Nebraska Press, 2001); James F. Brooks, *Confounding the Color Line: The Black–Indian Experience in North America* (Lincoln: University of Nebraska Press, 2002); Tiya Miles, *Crossing Waters, Crossing Worlds: The African Diaspora in Indian Country* (Durham, N.C.: Duke University Press, 2006); Malinda Maynor Lowery, *Lumbee Indians in the Jim Crow South: Race, Identity and the Making of a Nation* (Chapel Hill: University of North Carolina Press, 2010); Kim Warren, *The Quest for Citizenship: African American and Native American Education in Kansas, 1880–1935* (Chapel Hill: University of North Carolina Press, 2010); Brian Klopotek, *Recognition Odysseys: Indigeneity, Race and Federal Recognition in Three Louisiana Indian Communities* (Durham, N.C.: Duke University Press, 2011); and Barbara Krauthamer, *Black Slaves, Indian Masters: Slavery, Emancipation and Citizenship in the Native American South* (Chapel Hill: University of North Carolina Press, 2013).

20. Annette Gordon-Reed, *Thomas Jefferson and Sally Hemings: An American Controversy* (Charlottesville: University of Virginia Press, 1999), viii.

21. Recent works on Virginia Indians have primarily focused on White–Indian relations during the colonial era. See Margaret Holmes Williamson, *Powhatan Lords of Life and Death: Command and Consent in Seventeenth Century Virginia* (Lincoln: University of Nebraska Press, 2003); Danielle Moretti-Langholtz, ed., *A Study of Virginia Indians and Jamestown: The First Century* (Williamsburg, Va.: National Park Service, 2005), http://www.nps.gov/history/history/online_books/jame1/moretti-langholtz/contents.htm; Seth Mallios, *The Deadly Politics of Giving: Exchange and Violence in Ajacan, Roanoke and Jamestown* (Tuscaloosa: University of Alabama Press, 2006); Linwood "Little Bear" Custalow and Angela L. Daniel "Little Star," *The True Story of Pocahontas: The Other Side of History* (Golden, Colorado: Fulcrum Publishers, 2007); and Karen Ordahl Kupperman, *The Jamestown Project* (Cambridge, Mass.: Belknap Press of Harvard University Press, 2009).

22. Gordon-Reed, *Thomas Jefferson and Sally Hemings,* viii.

23. Jack D. Forbes, "The Manipulation of Race, Caste, and Identity: Classifying Afro Americans, Native Americans, and Red-Black People," *Journal of Ethnic Studies* 17, no. 4 (Winter 1990):43.

24. Interview with Richard Bowman, Jan. 5, 2010.

25. W. E. B. Du Bois, "The Souls of Black Folk" in *The Norton Anthology of African American Literature,* eds. Henry Louis Gates and Nellie McKay (New York: W. W. Norton, 1990), 613.

26. Ibid.

27. Tiya Miles, "Uncle Tom Was an Indian: Tracing the Red in Black Slavery," in *Confounding the Color Line: The Indian–Black Experience in North America* (Lincoln: University of Nebraska Press, 2002).

28. For more on the subject of racial identity on trial see James Hugo Johnston, *Race Relations in Virginia and Miscegenation in the South, 1776–1865* (Amherst: University of Massachusetts Press, 1970); Annette Gordon-Reed, *Race on Trial: Law and Justice in American History* (New York: Oxford University Press, 2002); and Ariela J. Cross, *What Blood Won't Tell: A History of Race on Trial in America* (Cambridge, Mass.: Harvard University Press, 2010).

29. Charles Hudson, *Red, White, and Black: Symposium on Indians in the Old South* (Athens: University of Georgia Press, 1970), 3.

30. Forbes, "The Manipulation of Race, Caste, and Identity," 10.

31. While hooks used the phrase "from margin to center" in reference to feminism, her use of the term as it relates to African American–Native American encounters is used implicitly in the chapter "Revolutionary Renegade" in *Black Looks: Race and Representation* (Cambridge: South End Press, 1999).

Prologue

1. Armstrong Archer, *A Compendium of Slavery As it Exist in the Present Day in the United States of America* (London: J. Haddon Printers, 1844). The full title of Archer's text reads *A compendium of slavery as it exists in the present day in the United States of America* to which is prefixed, a brief view of the author's descent from an African king on one side, and from the celebrated Indian Chief Powhatan on the other: in which he refers to the principal transactions and negotiations between this noble chief and the English colony under the famous Captain Smith, on the coast of Virginia in the year 1608, as well as to his still more illustrious daughter, the Princess Pocahontas, who excited so much interest in England; The research for this chapter was supported by a University of Delaware General University Research Grant.

2. Abraham Chapman, *Steal Away: Stories of the Runaway Slaves* (New York: Praeger, 1971), 39–45.

3. Frederic W. Gleach, "A Traditional Story of the Powhatan Indians Recorded in the Early 19th Century," in *Papers of the Twenty-third Algonquian Conference,* ed. William Cowan (Ottawa: Carleton University, 1992), 234–43. Gleach also provided a brief discussion of Archer in his essay regarding representations of Powhatan identity; see "Powhatan Identity in Anthropology and Popular Culture (and Vice Versa)" in *Southern Indians and Anthropologists: Culture, Politics and Identity,* Lisa J. Lefler and Frederic Gleach, eds. (Athens: University of Georgia Press, 2002), 5–18.

4. Archer, *A Compendium,* 11; for more on abolitionists' perceptions of American Indians see Linda K. Kerber, "The Abolitionist Perception of the Indian," *Journal of American History* 62, no. 2 (Sept. 1975): 271–295.

5. Archer appeared on the Free Negro Registry in Norfolk County on Oct. 17, 1825. He was described as follows: "5'9" of light complexion with a scar on his right arm just above his wrist occasioned by a cut." Archer was identified as having been

born free. The term "Negro" referred to any non-White citizen regardless of ancestry. For more on racial terms see chapter 2.

6. Richard Newman, et. al., "Introduction: The Theme of Our Contemplation," *Pamphlets of Protest: An Anthology of Early African American Protest Literature, 1790–1860* (New York: Routledge, 2001), 1–31; William Apess of the Pequot nation was the first American Indian to publish a personal narrative in English, *A Son of the Forest* (1829) and others later followed; however, it appears that American Indian writers did not embrace the pamphlet tradition.

7. R. J. M. Blackett, *Building An Antislavery Wall: Black Americans in the Atlantic Abolitionist Movement, 1830–1860* (Baton Rouge: Louisiana State University Press, 1983), 4.

8. "New York, Registers of Vessels Arriving at the Port of New York from Foreign Ports Between 1820–1850," Microfilm Serial M237, roll 56, National Archives, Washington, D.C. A search for records at the National Archives and other research institutions in the United Kingdom yielded no records on Armstrong Archer.

9. Pocahontas Saving the Life of John Smith, colored print, Kellogg and Thayer, ca. 1830; recent scholarship suggest that the Pocahontas saga was a fabrication by John Smith as he had not mentioned the incident in his earlier writings on Virginia. In addition, he had made several prior claims of being rescued by a "native" princess while on earlier expeditions. For more on the question of the validity of the Pocahontas legend, see Rayna Green, "The Pocahontas Perplex: The Image of Indian Women in American Culture," in *The Massachusetts Review* 16, no. 4 (Autumn 1975): 698–714; Helen Rountree, "Pocahontas: The Hostage Who Became Famous," in *Sifters: Native American Women Lives*, ed. Theda Perdue (New York: Oxford University Press, 2001); and Clara Sue Kidwell, "What Would Pocahontas Think Now? Women and Cultural Persistence," *Callaloo* 17, no. 1 (Winter 1994): 149–159; for a biography of Pocahontas that interprets her life within an Algonquian cultural context, see Paula Gunn Allen, *Pocahontas: Medicine Woman, Spy, Entrepreneur, Diplomat* (San Francisco: Harper Collins, 2004). For more on native female culture from an indigenous viewpoint see Tarrell Awe Agahe Portman and Roger D. Herring, "Debunking the Pocahontas Paradox: The Need for a Humanistic Perspective," *Journal for Humanistic Counseling, Education and Development* 40, no. 2 (Fall 2001): 185–200.

10. Archer's pamphlet provided no firsthand information on slavery. Instead he relied on newspaper accounts collected from southern pro-slavery newspapers and published in Theodore Weld's *American Slavery As It Is: Testimony of a Thousand Witnesses* (New York: American Anti-Slavery Society, 1837).

11. The Emancipation Act in 1833 began the gradual emancipation of slaves in the British West Indies from 1834–1838.

12. Arnold Shankman, "Black on Green: Afro-American Editors on Irish Independence, 1840–1921," *Phylon* 41, no. 3 (3rd Qtr., 1980): 287–288; for more on Irish–Black relations see Gilbert Osofsky, "Abolitionist, Irish Immigrants and the Dilemma of Romantic Nationalism," *The American Historical Review* 80, no. 4 (Oct. 1975): 889–912; see also Noel Ignatiev, *How the Irish Became White* (New York: Routledge, 1996).

13. Archer, 2.

14. Black repatriation as a solution to slavery was taken up in the early nineteenth century by the American Colonization Society. The ASC founded the African country of Liberia. Numerous free African Americans, including Paul Cuffee a wealthy Afro-Indian, relocated there. But, the idea was highly controversial and not widely supported. For more on the issues pertaining to the American Colonization Society see George Frederickson. "Prejudice and Reformism: Colonization Idea and the Abolitionist Response, 1817–1840," *The Black Image in the White Mind: Debate on Afro-American Character and Destiny, 1817–1914* (Hanover, N.H.: Wesleyan University Press, 1971), 1–42; see also *David Walker's Appeal to the Coloured Citizens of the World,* "Articles IV and V."

15. Archer, 5–11.

16. "The Incident at Atorkor," in Anne C. Bailey, *African Voices of the Atlantic Slave Trade: Beyond the Silence and the Shame* (Boston: Beacon Press, 2005), 27–56.

17. One of the earliest ships which carried the name Penelope was built in 1714 in Virginia, but was registered in London.

18. David Geggus, "The French Slave Trade: An Overiew," *The William and Mary Quarterly,* 3rd ser., 58, no 1, New Perspectives on the Transatlantic Slave Trade (Jan. 2001): 126.

19. The *Code Noir* Article LV.

20. For an analysis that places the Haitian Revolution within the larger context of revolutions during the period see Franklin W. Knight, "The Haitian Revolution," *American Historical Review* Vol. 105, No.1 (Feb. 2000): 103–115. Napoleon re-instituted slavery in the French West Indies when he became emperor in 1804.

21. James Sidbury, "Saint Dominigue in Virginia: Ideology, Local Meaning and Resistance to Slavery, 1790–1800," *Journal of Southern History* 63, no 1 (Aug. 1997): 538.

22. Thomas C. Parramore,, et. al., *Norfolk: The First Four Centuries* (Charlottesville: University of Virginia Press, 1994), 108; for more on the impact of the Haitian Revolution on Norfolk see chapters 8 and 9 in Parramore; for more on Norfolk's West Indies grain trade see Carville Earle, *Geographical Inquiry and American Historical Problems* (Stanford California: Stanford University Press, 1992), 118–125.

23. John H. Russell, *The Free Negro in Virginia 1619–1865* (Baltimore: Johns Hopkins University Press, 1913), 10–15. For more on the free Black population of Norfolk see Tommy Bogger, *Free Blacks in Norfolk, Virginia 1790–1860: The Darker Side of Freedom* (Charlottesville: University of Virginia Press, 1997).

24. Thomas C. Parramore, et. al., *Norfolk,* 123.

25. Ibid., 127–128.

26. Archer's date of birth is difficult to determine because Virginia did not begin keeping vital records until 1853.

27. Archer, 21.

28. The Seminole's fought three wars with the United States. The first war was from 1817–1818, the second was from 1835–1842, and the third was from 1855–1858. The second Seminole War was the longest war engaged by the United States from the American Revolution to Vietnam. Public sentiment turned against the war when the U.S. Army brought in the use of bloodhounds, a method decried by the public. Archer's mention of the Seminole War further demonstrates an Indian sen-

sibility as Black abolitionists and Black newspapers of the day hardly mentioned it. Ironically, in Archer's analogies of American Indian removal and slavery, he was careful not to implicate his Indian brethren, some of whom were slave owners.

29. A number of Afro-Indian informants in Virginia have told me about their childhood growing up in the African American community and their visits to the reservation during summer vacation.

30. Archer, 22–24.

31. Vine Deloria, Jr., "The Concept of History," in *God Is Red: A Native View of Religion* (Golden, Colo.: Fulcrum Publishing, 1992), 98. For an explication of the Manotee story, see Gleach, "A Traditional Powhatan Tale," 239–242.

32. Deloria, "The Concept of History," 100.

33. Lawrence W. Levine, *Black Culture and Black Consciousness: Afro-American Folk Thought From Slavery to Freedom*, 30th Anniversary Edition (New York: Oxford University Press, 2001), 131–132; for more on the tradition of trickster in African American and Native American literature see Mary Ellison "Black Perceptions and Red Images: Indian and Black Literary Links," *Phylon* 44, no. 1 (1st Qtr., 1983): 44–55; see also, Jonathan Brennan, *When Brer Rabbit Meets Coyote: African-Native American Literature* (Urbana: University of Illinois Press), 2003.

34. *Free Man of Color: The Autobiography of Willis Augustus Hodges*, edited with an Introduction by Willard B. Gatewood, Jr. (Knoxville: The University of Tennessee Press, 1980), 22–23.

35. George A. Levesque, "Inherent Reformers—Inherited Orthodoxy: Black Baptist in Boston, 1800–1873," *Journal of Negro History* (Oct. 1975): 506. The First African Baptist Church of Boston was also known as The First Independent Church, The Belknap Street Church and The African Meeting House. It was built in 1806 and became the first Black Baptist Church North of the Mason and Dixon line. The building was sold by the Baptist Convention in 1898. In 1904 the building became the Jewish Congregation Anshi Libavitz. It was purchased by the African American Museum of History in 1972. Today it is a National Historic Landmark.

36. Quoted in Willard B. Gatewood, Jr., "Introduction," in *Free Man of Color*, xxx–xxxi; for more on Blacks in Williamsburgh, see Robert J. Swan, "Some Historic Notes on Black Williamsburgh and Bushwick" in *An Introduction to the Black Contribution to the Development of Brooklyn* (Brooklyn, N.Y.: The New Muse Community Museum of Brooklyn, 1977), 117–128. Archer is listed on the 1840 census as the head of household. There are two females from the ages of 24–35 and 55–99 residing with him. He is listed between the age of 24–35. There is no evidence that Archer was married at the time. The women may be his sister and mother. At this time Archer's is the only household of color residing in the Fourteenth Ward. He and the women are listed as mulatto.

37. "Proceedings of the Convention of the Colored Citizens of the State of New York," *The Colored American, August 22, 1840;* for more on the convention movement see Howard Holman Bell, *The American Negro Convention Movement, 1830–1861* (New York: Arno Press and the New York Times, 1969).

38. There were northern and southern communities of color where light skinned Blacks lived separate from dark skinned Blacks. Color separation in communities of color is discussed in further detail in chapter 6.

39. On the 1850 census Archer's wife is identified as Frances and her place of birth is identified as Spain. In 1860, she went by the name of Catherine and identified her birthplace as Madeira. Despite such discrepancies there is nothing to suggest that they are not the same person. Madeira is an archipelago off the Atlantic Ocean located approximately 300 miles off the African coast and 600 miles from Europe. Today it is considered one of the outermost regions of the European Union.

40. For more on the issue of passing see Daniel J. Sharfstein, *The Invisible Line: Three American Families and the Secret Journey from Black to White* (New York: Penguin Books, 2011). For more on the phenomenon of passing in the 19th century see James M. O'Toole, *Passing for White: Race, Religion and the Healy Family, 1820–1920* (Amherst: University of Massachusetts Press, 2003).

41. The name Acquacknouk also means where gum blocks were found for pounding corn. For more on Indian place names see "Indian Place Names in New Jersey," Morris County GenWeb, http://www.rootsweb.ancestry.com/~njmorris/general_info/indian.htm and Henry Gannett, *The Origin of Certain Place Names in the United States,* 2nd edition (Washington, D.C.: Department of the Interior United States Geological Society, 1905).

42. Libation is a ceremonial ritual used in numerous African cultures during auspicious occasions in which water, wine or milk is poured into the earth in honor to God and in veneration of the ancestors. There is no such thing as ancestor worship in traditional African religions. For more on this see John Mbiti, *African Religion and Philosophy,* 2nd edition (Portsmouth, N.H.: Heinemann, 1992). Similarly, tobacco, although used within varying contexts, is sprinkled among the ground to honor God, the ancestors and to mark a certain area as sacred. For more on the ritual of tobacco, see Arlene Hirschfelder and Paulette Molin, "Tobacco," "Tobacco Invocation," and "Tobacco Societies," in *Encyclopedia of Native American Religions,* Updated Edition (New York: Checkmark Books, 2001), 305–306.

1. Notes on the State of Virginia

1. All quotations pertaining to *The Notes* are taken from Frank Shuffelton and Thomas Jefferson, *Notes on the State of Virginia* (New York: Penguin Classic, 1991). For more on Jefferson's *Notes,* see the issue devoted to this publication in *Virginia Magazine of History and Biography* 112, no. 2 (2004).

2. Ibid., vii.

3. See letter to Marquis De Chastelleux, June 7, 1785, found under "Letters and Documents" in Jefferson, *Notes,* 266.

4. Winthrop Jordan, *White Over Black: American Attitudes Toward the Negro, 1550–1812* (Chapel Hill: University of North Carolina Press, 1968), 429.

5. Ibid., 477.

6. For more on the European rites of passage from British subject to American citizen see Philip Deloria, "Patriotic Indians and Identities of Revolution," In *Playing Indian* (New Haven, Conn.: Yale University Press, 1998).

7. Jefferson, *Notes,* 66–68; for more on Logan's Lament see Anthony F. C. Wallace, *Jefferson and the Indians: The Tragic Fate of the First Americans* (Cambridge, Mass.: Harvard University Press, 2001), 1–20.

8. See letter to Marquis De Chastellux under "Letters and Documents" in Jefferson, *Notes,* 26.

9. For more on the American policy of expansion with honor, see Robert Berkhofer, "Early United States Expansion With Honor," in *The White Man's Indian* (New York: Vintage Books, 1978), 134–144.

10. Merrill D. Peterson, *Thomas Jefferson Writings* (New York: Library Classics of the United States, 1984), 1115. The term "amalgamation" was incorporated in the rhetoric of blood to more fully describe what scientist believed biologically occurred as a result of racial mixing. The term was appropriated from the field of metallurgy, "where since the seventeenth century, it has indicated a substance composed of two or more metals mixed together when molten." Within the context of the rhetoric of blood, amalgamation connoted race, "as a biological trait in the blood and race blood was perceived . . . as a 'mathematical problem of the same class with those mixtures of different liquors or different metals.'" As a result, Jefferson believed that White–Indian amalgamation would yield Indians who were White-identified. "Jefferson cannot imagine that a person with both white and Indian ancestry might remain politically aligned with Indians, because, for him, the biology of blood and presumably white blood in particular is a stronger force than politics and culture." For more on this see Lemire, *Miscegenation: Making Race in America* (Philadelphia: University of Pennsylvania, 2002), 51–52. After the Civil War the term amalgamation was replaced by the term miscegenation which connoted "mistaken mixture." However, the term was used exclusively when referencing White and non-White admixture. When discussing the admixture of whites with each other, the term "melting pot" was used. For more on this see David A. Hollinger, "Amalgamation and Hypodescent: The Question of Ethnoracial Mixture in the History of the United States," *American Historical Review* 108, no. 5 (Dec. 2003): 1363–1390.

11. For more on the history of proscriptions against interracial sex and marriage see Peter Wallenstein, *Tell the Court I Love My Wife: Race, Marriage, and Law—An American History* (New York: Palgrave Macmillan, 2002); see also Werner Sollors, *Interracialism: Black–White Intermarriage in American History, Literature and Law* (New York: Oxford University Press, 2002).

12. William Waller Hening, *Hening's Statutes at Large: Being a Collection of All the Laws of Virginia, from the First Session of the Legislature in the year 1619* (Westminster, Md.: Heritage Books, 2003), CD-Rom, Vol. 1, 6.

13. Johnston, "Documentary Evidence of the Relations of Negroes and Indians," 21; despite Sir Thomas Daly's approval, which Rolfe sought in a letter to the then governor of the Virginia colony explaining his reason for marrying Pocahontas, the marriage was met with much disapproval. Although biblical laws forbade mixed marriages on religious grounds (i.e. Jews and gentiles, Christians and heathens, etc.) Rolfe believed that Pocahontas's new-found Christianity would be strengthened as a result of the marriage. Their marriage would serve as an exemplar to the Powhatan nation, which would in turn lead to an increase of conversions among the heathen. See John Rolfe Letter 1614 at *American Journeys: Eyewitness Accounts of Early American Exploration and Settlement. A Digital Library and Learning Center,* http://www.americanjourneys.org/aj-079/summary/index.asp.

14. Johnston, "Documentary Evidence," 23; for more on religion and proscriptions against intermarriage, see Fay Botham, *Almighty God Created The Races: Christianity, Interracial Marriage and American Law* (Chapel Hill: University of North Carolina Press, 2009).

15. Johnston, "Documentary Evidence," 24; Patrick Henry proposed that "every white man who married an Indian woman should have ten pounds paid and five for each child born of such a marriage; and that if any white woman shall marry an Indian she should be entitled to ten pounds with which the County Court should buy live stock for them; that once a year the Indian husband to this woman should be entitled to three pounds with which the County Court should buy clothes for him; that every child born to the Indian man and white woman shall be educated by the state between the ages of ten and twenty-one years."

16. Jefferson, *Notes,* 147.

17. Ibid., 146.

18. For more on the issue of Africans as beast see Jordan, "Negroes, Apes, and Beast," in Jordan, *White Over Black,* 228–234; see also George M. Fredrickson, "The Negro as Beast: Southern Negrophobia at the Turn of the Century," in *The Black Image in the White Mind: The Debate on Afro-American Character and Destiny* (Hanover, N.H.: Wesleyan University Press, 1971), 256–282.

19. Jefferson, *Notes,* 147–148.

20. The letter from Benjamin Banneker to Thomas Jefferson appears in "Letters and Documents" in Jefferson, *Notes,* 271–274.

21. John Chester Miller, *The Wolf By the Ears: Thomas Jefferson and Slavery* (New York: Free Press, 1977), 77.

22. Banneker Letter in Jefferson, *Notes,* 271–274.

23. Ibid., 275; see letter to Condorcet, 275.

24. Ibid., 280; see letters to James Monroe, Nov. 24, 1801 and James Barlow, Oct. 8, 1809, in "Letters and Documents." For opposing views to Jefferson's Black inferiority theory see Jordan, "Thomas Jefferson: Self and Society," in Jordan, *White Over Black,* 435–457. See also Henri Grégoire, *An Enquiry Concerning the Intellectual and Moral Faculties, and Literature of Negroes,* trans. David Bailie Warden (Armonk, N.Y.: M. E. Sharpe, 1997). Grégoire was a popular French abolitionist whose work originally titled *De la littérature des Negres* first appeared in English in the United States in 1810. The Frenchman challenged Jefferson's theory of Black inferiority by showcasing people of African descent who had distinguished themselves in the areas of art, science, and literature. Although Grégoire's work refuted Jefferson's theory, he had hoped to persuade Jefferson to endorse an English translation of his work. In a patronizing response to Grégoire, Jefferson stated , "no person living wishes more than I do, to see a complete refutation of the doubts I have myself entertained and expressed on the grade of understanding allotted to them by nature." However, in his 1809 letter to Joel Barlow, Jefferson dismissed Grégoire's work as inconclusive evidence of Black intellectual equality. See letter to Heni Grégoire, Febr. 25, 1809, in Merrill, *Thomas Jefferson Writings,* 1202.

25. Jefferson, *Notes,* 284. See letter to Edward Cole, Aug. 25, 1814, in "Letters and Documents."

26. Jefferson, *Notes,* 151.

27. Michael P. Zuckert, "Founder of the Natural Rights Republic," in *Thomas Jefferson and the Politics of Nature, ed.* Thomas S. Engeman (South Bend, Ind.: University of Notre Dame Press, 2000), 18. While Jefferson is credited as the primary author of the Declaration of Independence, creating the document was a collaborative effort.

28. J. P. Boyd, ed., *The Papers of Thomas Jefferson* (Princeton, N.J.: Princeton University Press, 1953), 2:556–558. The bill was bought to the floor during the October 1786 session and passed the second reading, but no further action was taken. It would take an entire century before the Assembly declared interracial marriages null and void.

29. W. E. B. Du Bois, *The Conservation of the Races,* The American Negro Academy Occasional Papers No. 2, The Gutenberg Project, webdubois.org, http://www.webdubois.org/dbConsrvOfRaces.html; In 1705, the General Assembly passed an act declaring that Christian conversion did not exempt slaves from bondage. See ACT XXXVII, Hening, 3:460.

30. Jefferson, *Notes*, 145–146.

31. Jordan, *White Over Black,* 7.

32. Ibid.; Blackness was, on exception, also used as a site for the exotic. See Karen Kupperman, *The Jamestown Project,* 127–129.

33. Ibid., 8.

34. Pauline Turner Strong and Barrik Van Winkle, "'Indian Blood:' Reflections on the Reckoning and Refiguring of Native North American Identity," *Cultural Anthropology* 11, no. 4, Resisting Identities (Nov. 1996), 551.

35. Jordan, *White Over Black,* 8.

36. Ibid.

37. Ibid., 238; for more on the notion of interracial sex and marriage as deviant see Peggy Pascoe, *What Comes Naturally: Miscegenation, Law and the Making of Race in America* (New York: Oxford University Press, 2009).

38. Lemire, *Miscegenation,* 32.

39. Ibid.

40. Lincoln underwent a similar assault during his bid for reelection as his opponents attempted to cast the president as a proponent of miscegenation coining the phrase, "emancipation equals miscegenation." After the Civil War, Democrats overwhelmingly used the issue of miscegenation as a political pawn asserting that social equality equaled miscegenation. As numerous newspaper accounts report, Virginia Democrats proved no exception in the use of this tactic. It remained a mainstay in southern politics up through the Civil Rights era. See Sidney Kaplan, "The Miscegenation Issue in the Election of 1864," 274–343.

41. Jefferson, *Notes,* 145.

42. Alden T. Vaughan, "From White Man to Redskin: Changing Anglo-American Perceptions of the American Indian," in *Roots of American Racism: Essays on the Colonial Experience* (New York: Oxford University Press, 1995), 10; for more on the comparison of Anglo-American perceptions of Africans and American Indians see also Jordan, "Indians, Africans and the Complexion of Man," in *White Over Black,* 239–252 and, John Chester Miller, "Blacks and Indians," in *Wolf By the Ears,* 60–73.

43. Ibid., 3.

44. Ibid., 11.

45. William G. McLoughlin, "Red Indians, Black Slavery and White Racism: America's Slaveholding Indians," *American Quarterly* 26, no. 4 (Oct. 1974): 372.

46. Vaughan, "From White Man to Redskin," 32; for more on the cultural change of the Algonquian tribes see Helen Rountree, "A Century of Cultural Change," *Pocahontas's People: The Powhatan Indians of Virginia Through Four Centuries* (Norman: University of Oklahoma Press, 1990), 144–186; See also Frederic Gleach, *Powhatan's World and Colonial Virginia: A Conflict of Cultures* (Lincoln: University of Nebraska Press, 2000).

47. Woody Holton, *Forced Founders: Indians, Debtors, Slaves and the Making of the American Revolution in Virginia* (Chapel Hill: University of North Carolina Press, 1999), 3–4.

48. Ibid., 38; Holton observes (20) that it was during this period of forming a Pan-Indian alliance that American Indians began to construct a collective racialized identity as Red people.

49. Vine Deloria, Jr., "The Red and the Black," in *Custer Died For Your Sins: An Indian Manifesto* (Norman: University of Oklahoma Press, 1988), 173.

50. Julie Schimmel, "Inventing the Indian," in *The West as America: Reinterpreting Images of the Frontier, 1820–1920,* ed. William H. Truettner (Washington, D.C.: Smithsonian Institution Press, 1991), 174; David Stannard, *American Holocaust: The Conquest of the New World* (New York: Oxford University Press, 1993), 120; for more on Jefferson's Indian policy see Anthony F. C. Wallace, *Jefferson and the Indians,* 2001.

51. Jefferson, *Notes,* 98–113.

52. Ibid., 102–103.

53. James Mooney, "Powhatan," Bulletin 30; Du Ponceau to Jefferson, July 12, 1820, Nottoway Indian Tribe, Inc. Petition.

54. Rountree makes brief mention of Jefferson's comments regarding the Mattaponi and Pamunkey Indians in *Pocahontas's People,* 161. While she stated that his comments cannot be proved or disproved due to lack of county records for the period, I find her reliance on written records to ascertain the extent of racial amalgamation among the Indians problematic. With the exception of court cases that charged individuals of violating anti-miscegenation laws, the practice was never extensively documented. Hence, there would be far less written evidence of its occurrence.

55. Deloria, *Playing Indian,* 20.

56. Peter Onuf, "'To Declare Them a Free and Independent People': Race, Slavery, and National Identity in Jefferson's Thought," *Journal of the Early Republic* 18, no. 1 (Spring 1998), 26.

57. Jefferson, *Notes,* 145.

58. Lemire, *Miscegenation,* 52.

59. Michael Dorr. "Segregation's Science: The American Eugenics Movement and Virginia, 1900–1980," (PhD diss., University of Virginia, 2000), 68. This is a massive work that provides extensive detail on the social, political and cultural role of science and its relationship to public policy; for more on Jefferson's influence on racial

integrity see Dorr's chapter "The Sacrifice of a Race,"47–70; for an abridged version of these issues see Michael Dorr Segregation's Science: Eugenics & Society in Virginia (Charlottesville: University of Virginia Press, 2008). Senate Bills Nos. 1–224 Virginia 192, Library of Virginia.

60. Onuf, *To Declare Them*, 26.

61. The term "sexual colonialism" was coined by Arthur Einhorn. See Valerie L. Philips, "Epilogue: Seeing Each Other through the White Man's Eyes," in *Confounding the Color Line: The Indian–Black Experience in North America*, ed. James F. Brooks (Lincoln: University of Nebraska Press, 2002), 369–385.

62. Dorr, "Segregation's Science," 51.

63. *The Jeffersonian Cyclopedia: A Comprehensive Collection of the Views of Thomas Jefferson*, ed. James Foley (Charlottesville: University of Virginia Library Electronic Text Center), http://etext.lib.virginia.edu/jefferson/quotations/foley/.

64. Dorr. "Segregation's Science," 51; for more on Jefferson's tri-racial metaphor White, Red, and Black see Vaughan, *Roots of American Racism*, 4; for more on David Walker see *David Walker's Appeal To The Coloured Citizens of the World*, ed. Peter Fink (University Park, Pa.: The Pennsylvania State University Press, 2000).

2. Redefining Race and Identity

1. Ralph Ellison, "Hidden Names and Complex Fate: A Writer's Experience in the United States," In *The Collected Essays of Ralph Ellison*, ed. John F. Callahan (New York: Modern Library, 1995), 201–202.

2. Michael Omi and Howard Winant, *Racial Formation in the United States from the 1960s to the 1990s*, 2nd ed. (New York: Routledge. 1994), 55–56, 66.

3. Ibid., 66.

4. Jack D. Forbes, "The Manipulation of Race, Caste, and Identity: Classifying AfroAmericans, Native Americans, and Red-Black People," *Journal of Ethnic Studies* 17, no. 4 (Winter 1990): 22.

5. Karen I. Blu, *The Lumbee Problem: The Making of An American Indian People* (Lincoln: University of Nebraska Press, 1980), 25.

6. Jack Forbes, "The Manipulation of Race," 24.

7. Quoted in Sandra F. Waugaman and Danielle Moretti-Langholtz, "Prologue: The Indelible Thread of Red," in *We're Still Here: Contemporary Virginia Indians Tell Their Stories* (Richmond, Va.: Palari Publishing, 2000), 7.

8. Wright, *The Only Land They Knew: The Tragic Story of the American Indians in the Old South* (New York: Free Press, 1985), 43.

9. Forbes, *Africans and Native Americans: The Language of Race and the Evolution of Red-Black People*, 2nd ed. (Urbana: Illinois University Press, 1993), 66.

10. Ibid.

11. Ibid., 66–67.

12. Ibid., 68–72. The pejorative "nigger" was also used broadly; see Forbes, *Africans and Native Americans*, 74–75; see also James R. Barrett and David Roediger, "How White People Became White" in *White Privilege: Essential Readings on the Other Side of Racism*, ed. Paula S. Rothenberg (New York: Worth Publishers, 2002).

13. John Smith, *The Generall Historie of Virginia, New England and the Summer Isles,* vol. 1 (New York: Macmillan Company, 1907), 247.

14. Helen Tunnicliff Catterall, *Judicial Cases Concerning American Slavery and the Negro,* vol.1 (District of Columbia: Carnegie Institute of Washington, 1926) 55–56.

15. Forbes, *Africans and Native Americans,* 84.

16. Ibid.

17. William Waller Hening, *The Statutes at Large Being a Collection of All the Laws of Virginia from the First Session of the Legislature in the year 1619,* vol. 3, CD-ROM (New York: Heritage Books, 2003), 333.

18. Ibid., vol. 4, 133.

19. Forbes, *Africans and Native Americans,* 83.

20. Hening, *Statutes at Large,* vol. 3, 449–450.

21. Forbes, *African and Native Americans,* 84.

22. Ibid., 65.

23. Forbes, *Africans and Native Americans,* 86.

24. Ibid.

25. Ibid., 88; although not identified as a Negro, a runaway advertisement dated Aug. 4, 1768, described Thomas Greenwich as "an East India Indian." The Geography of Slavery in Virginia Online, University of Virginia, 2005. http://www2.vcdh .virginia.edu/saxon/servlet/SaxonServlet?source=/xml_docs/slavery/ads/rg68.xml &style=/xml_docs/slavery/ads/display_ad.xsl&ad=v1768080277.

26. Engel Sluiter in his article "New Light on the '20 and Odd Negroes' Arriving in Virginia, August 1619," in *William and Mary Quarterly,* 3rd ser., 54, no. 2 (Apr. 1997): 395–398, proposed a new theory that suggests the original twenty came from Angola, West Africa. He based his assertion on one primary source cited from a Vera Cruz account book which stated, "The story of the one slave ship that was attacked en route to Mexico is told in barest outline" (397). According to Sluiter, the only ship to be attacked during the fiscal years 1618–1619 was the slaver "*San Juan Bautista* off Campeche in late July or early August of that year." In addition, Sluiter asserts that it was not Dutch, but "English corsairs" that attacked the ship. Sluiter took many liberties in his interpretation. His assertion is also based on the work of William Thorndale whose appraisal of the 1619–1620 census placed Africans in the Virginia colony prior to the arrival of the famous 20. While, the evidence Sluiter provided is intriguing, it does not offer conclusive evidence. In addition, the continuance contact between Brazil and West Africa was not established until the 1630s onward. Jack Forbes contends, "Angola was more closely connected to Brazil than Portugal"; see *Africans and Native Americans,* 58. For more on the 1619 census, see William Thorndale, "The Virginia Census of 1619." *Magazine of Virginia Genealogy* no. 33 (1995), 155–170. For a reprisal see Martha W. McCartney, "An Early Virginia Census Reprised," *Quarterly Bulletin of the Archeological Society of Virginia* 54, no. 4 (1999), 178–196. Note that Thorndale's published census of Manuscript A list 32 "Negroes." McCartney in her summary lists the thirty-two as "African," an erroneous assumption given the broad use of the term Negro in the early seventeenth century.

27. Hening, *Statutes at Large,* vol. 3, 252.

28. Forbes, *Africans and Native Americans,* 195.

29. Hening, *Statutes at Large,* vol. 12, 184.

30. Forbes, *Africans and Native Americans,* 200.

31. James Hugo Johnston, *Race Relations in Virginia and Miscegenation in the South, 1776–1860* (Amherst: University of Massachusetts Press, 1970), 191.

32. Miles, "Uncle Tom Was an Indian," 138.

33. Vine Deloria, *Custer Died for Your Sins: An Indian Manifesto* (Norman: University of Oklahoma Press, 1988), 7–8.

34. Allan Gallay, *The Indian Slave Trade: The Rise of the English Empire in the American South 1670–1717*(New Haven, Conn.: Yale University Press, 2002).

35. Forbes, *Africans and Native Americans,* 62.

36. Lauber, *Indian Slavery,* 105. See chapter I, "Enslavement by the Indians Themselves," 25–48; chapter IV, "The Number of Slaves," 105–119; and chapters V, VI, VII, and VIII, "The Process of Enslavement," 119–210.

37. Hening, *Statutes at Large,* vol. 1, 396.

38. "Indian Slaves," *William and Mary College Quarterly Historical Magazine* 6, no.4 (Apr. 1898): 215.

39. "Indian Slaves," *William and Mary College Quarterly Historical Magazine* 8, no.3 (Jan. 1900): 165.

40. Hening, *The Statutes at Large,* vol. 2, 280–281.

41. Ibid., 283.

42. Ibid.

43. Ibid, 346, 404, and 440.

44. Ibid., 380.

45. Ibid., 440.

46. Ibid., 491–492.

47. Ibid., vol 3., 69, 468, 333; vol. 4, 182.

48. Herbert Aptheker, *American Negro Slave Revolts, Deluxe Edition* (New York: International Publishers, 1993), 169–170; Aptheker provides a number of anecdotes regarding African American-Native America alliances and conflicts during slave insurrections.

49. Allan Gallay, *The Indian Slave Trade,* 305–306; for more on the Indian slave trade in the American South, see Robbie Ethridge and Sheri M. Shuck-Hall, eds., *Mapping the Mississippian Shatter Zone: The Colonial Indian Slave Trade and Regional Instability in the American South* (Lincoln: University of Nebraska Press, 2009); for a pre- and post-contact examination of slavery with Indian nations, see Christina Snyder, *Slavery in Indian Country: The Changing Face of Captivity in Early America* (Cambridge, Mass.: Harvard University Press, 2010).

50. The Geography of Slavery in Virginia Online, retrieved Aug. 25, 2011; for additional examples of Indian references in runaway slave notices during the colonial period for Virginia, North Carolina and South Carolina see Forbes, *African and Native Americans,* 207–209.

51. Daniel E. Meaders, ed., *Advertisements for Runaway Slaves in Virginia 1801–1820* (New York: Routledge, 1997), 6, 205, 282, 286, 308, 314. There are a number of references to Negro and mulatto men wearing their hair long and tied back which was used as a mark for Indian identity and freedom; Kanawha County became a part of West Virginia during the Civil War.

52. Catterall, *Judicial Cases,* 64.

53. Ibid., 91–92.

54. Ibid., 94–95.

55. Ibid., 99–100.

56. Ibid., 114.

57. Ibid.

58. Ibid., 117.

59. Ibid., 147, 66–67.

60. Ibid., 148, 163–166.

61. Charles L. Perdue, Jr., Thomas E. Barden, and Robert K. Philips, *Weevils in the Wheat: Interviews with Virginia Ex-Slaves* (Charlottesville: University of Virginia Press, 1976), 90–91. While Featherstone stated several times that she was Indian, she also identified herself as a free Negro.

62. Ibid., 130.

63. Russell, *The Free Negro in Virginia,* 130; see also Ira Berlin, *Slaves Without Masters: The Free Negro in the Antebellum South* (New York: The New Press, 2007).

64. Will of Thomas Nelson recorded in King William County, Sept. 25, 1804, Virginia Land Office, Wills from Land Office Records, LOI-10, Box 2, document. Many thanks to reference librarian Thomas Crew for his assistance in finding the document; HR 5130 "To extend Federal recognition to the Rappahannock Tribe, and for other purposes," Apr. 6, 2006. The exact quote from the bill reads, "During the 1760s 3 Rappahannock girls were raised on Thomas Nelson's Bleak Hill Plantation in King William County. One girl married a Saunders man, one married a Johnson man, *and the third had 2 children, Edmund and Carter Nelson, fathered by Thomas Cary Nelson*" (italics mine). Jenny, as indicated in the will had eight children (Billy, Henry, Jack, Bob, Edmund, Carter, Lucy and Lewis) whom Nelson freed and all of which no doubt belonged to him. Jenny's ancestry has been lost to history. The genealogy forum for Spurlock descendants of King William County assert that their ancestors were Black, White, and Native American; http://www.census.gov/population/www/documentation/twps0056/tab61.pdf.

65. Paul Spruhan, "A History of Blood Quantum in Federal Indian Law to 1935," *South Dakota Law Review* 51, no. 1 (2006): 2.

66. Ibid.

67. Petition of Inhabitants, Northampton County (Nov. 11, 1785). Northampton County Land Records Relating to Gingaskin Indian Lands. The Library of Virginia.

68. Ibid.

69. Ibid.

70. Petition of Thomas Littleton Savage, Northampton County (Oct. 26, 1787), Northampton County Land Records Relating to Gingaskin Indian Lands, 1795–1815, Library of Virginia.

71. Statement of George Parker, Northampton County Petition (Nov. 12, 1812). Northampton County Land Records Relating to Gingaskin Indian Lands, Library of Virginia.

72. Ibid.

73. Ibid.

74. Petition of William Bozeman, Southampton County, 1824. Library of Virginia.

75. Lynette Allston, Nottoway Petition Cover Letter to the Virginia Council on Indians, Oct. 17, 2006, 4, http://www.nottowayindians.org/petitioncoverletter.html.

76. Ibid.

77. King William County Legislative Petitions B 1208 (Jan. 12, 1843), Microfilm Reel 104, State Library of Virginia.

78. King William County Legislative Petitions B 1208 (Jan. 12, 1843), Microfilm Reel 104, State Library of Virginia.

79. J. H. Johnston, "Documentary Evidence," 29.

80. Forbes, *Africans and Native Americans,* 90.

81. Acts of the Assembly.

82. John Garland Pollard, "The Pamunkey Indians of Virginia," Bulletin 17 (Washington, D.C.: The Smithsonian Institution Bureau of American Ethnology, 1894), 17.

83. Ibid., 10, 11; Pollard also expressed similar sentiments regarding Virginia Indians as Jefferson had earlier done for the frontier Indians. Pollard stated, "The average intelligence of these Indians is higher than that of the Virginia negro. In view of their limited advantages they are strikingly well informed."

84. Ibid., 17.

85. Marie Anna Jaimes Guerrero, "Civil Rights versus Sovereignty: Native American Women in Life and Land Struggles," in *Feminist Genealogies, Colonial Legacies, and Democratic Futures,* ed. M. Jacqui Alexander and Chandra Talpade Mohanty (New York: Routledge, 1997), 109.

86. Ward Churchill, "The Crucible of American Indian Identity: Native Tradition vs. Colonial Imposition in Post Conquest North America," *American Indian Culture and Resource Journal* 23, no. 9 (1999): 43.

87. Johnston, *Race Relations in Virginia,* 216.

3. Race Purity and the Law

1. Forbes, *Africans and Native Americans,* 258.

2. J. David Smith, *The Eugenics Assault on America: Scenes in Red, White and Black* (Fairfax, Va.: George Mason University Press Trade, 1992), 16–17.

3. Walter Plecker to Senator Sheppard Morris (Mar. 12, 1925), John Powell Collection, University of Virginia Special Collections; Morris sponsored similar legislation by the same title in Washington, D.C.; Afro-Virginian newspapers remained ambivalent towards racial integrity legislation reasoning that Black Virginians cared little about disrupting Virginia's color line in the sand. Nevertheless after its passage, editorials from such papers as the Norfolk *Journal and Guide* complained that Virginia's effort to preserve White racial integrity came at the expense of the Negro; see editorial (Mar. 15, 1924), 12.

4. John Powell, Untitled Article, *Richmond News-Leader* (June 5, 1923), John Powell Collection.

5. Ibid.

6. A reproduction of the back cover of *White America,* John Powell Collection, University of Virginia; Cox remained an ardent supporter of Black repatriation until his death in 1966. In his will dated Dec. 15, 1965, he left his executors instructions to use any excess monies towards the effort to repatriate Blacks to Africa.

7. Walter A. Plecker, "Virginia's Attempt to Adjust the Color Problem," *American Journal of Public Health* 15, no. 2 (1925):114; for more on Virginia's involvement in the eugenics movement see Dorr, *Segregation's Science,* 2008.

8. See letter to R. F. St. James (Sept. 1, 1926), Charles Davenport Papers, American Philosophical Society.

9. A. Leon Higginbotham and Barbara K. Kopytoff, "Racial Purity and Interracial Sex in the Law of Colonial and Antebellum Virginia," *Georgetown Law Review* 77, no. 6 (1989): 1980.

10. Ibid., 1977.

11. Ibid., 1984.

12. See letter to Francis C. Gray (Mar. 4, 1815) in Barbara Chase-Riboud, *Sally Hemings* (New York: St. Martin's Griffin, 1979), 18; also in Libscomb and Bergh, *Writings, Thomas Jefferson* [Monticello Edition], vol. XIV, 267–271.

13. Ira Berlin, *Slaves Without Masters: The Free Negro in the Antebellum South,* New York, New Press, 1992, 162.

14. Higginbotham and Kopytoff, "Racial Purity and Interracial Sex," 1980.

15. Ibid.

16. "Fellow-Caucasians," *Nation* 118, no. 3066 (Apr. 9, 1924): 388.

17. Trinkle served as Governor of Virginia from 1922–1926; According to a Feb. 25, 1925, letter from John Powell to George H. Roberts of the Ohio House of Representatives, Trinkle sent copies of the proposed RIA to every governor. Of the 31 replies he received, 19, most from the south, were noncommittal; 11 from the north and west strongly approved; and Minnesota disapproved, stating they had no such problem; the RIA's sister bill SB281, "An Act to provide for the sexual sterilization of inmates in State institutions in certain cases" was signed into law on the same day, unleashing abusive power for the state to involuntarily sterilize racial minorities and poor Whites, whom eugenics proponents determined were menaces to society (i.e. the "insane, idiotic, imbecile, feebleminded or epileptic"). The law also targeted anyone with the slightest malady including alcoholics, those with syphilis, prison inmates, and those with physical disabilities. From 1924 to 1979 approximately 8,300 Virginia residents were victimized by what is now referred to as Virginia's Sterilization Act. On Feb. 14, 2001, the Virginia General Assembly passed House Joint Resolution No. 607 "Expressing the General Assembly's regret for Virginia's experience with eugenics." For the full text of the resolution see http://leg1 .state.va.us/cgi-bin/legp504.exe?011+ful+HJ607ER; for more on the issue of sterilization see Dorr's *Segregation's Science* (2008).

18. "A Bill to Preserve the White Race," Senate Bill 219, Senate Bills Nos. 1–224 Virginia (1924), Library of Virginia.; quoted in Brian William Thomson, "Racism and Racial Classification: A Case Study of the Virginia Racial Integrity Legislation," (PhD Diss., University of California, Riverside, 1978), 127–128.

19. Ibid., 128.

20. Ibid., 132.

21. An Act to Preserve Racial Integrity, Senate Bill 219, Acts of Assembly (Virginia 1924), Library of Virginia, 534–535.

22. Quoted in Shari Huhndorf, "From the Turn of the Century to the New Age: Playing Indian Past and Present," in *As We Are Now: Mixblood Essays On Race and Identity*, ed. William S. Penn (Berkeley: University of California Press, 1997), 184.

23. Ibid.

24. The Racial Integrity Act, Library of Virginia; see full text in the Appendix of this book.

25. Marcus Garvey, "A Special Note On Intermarriage and Racial Purity," *Marcus Garvey: Life and Lessons,* ed., Robert A. Hill (Berkeley: University of California Press, 1987), 204; see also "Miscegenation" and "Purity of Race" in *Philosophy and Opinions,* vol. 1, 17–18, 37; other Black Nationalist organizations which supported Black repatriation were Mittie Maude Lena Gordon's Peace Movement of Ethiopia (PME) (ca. 1934–1958) and Benjamin Gibbons's Universal African Nationalist Movement, Inc. (UANM) (ca. 1947–1963).

26. John Powell, "Answer to the Appeal To White America," Speech presented Oct. 28, 1925, before the UNIA reprinted from the *Negro World* in *Philosophy and Opinions of Marcus Garvey,* vol. 2, 339–349; see also Amy Jacques Garvey, *Garvey and Garveyism* (New York: Octagon Books, 1986), 177.

27. Letter from Marcus Garvey to Earnest S. Cox (Aug. 8, 1925), Marcus Garvey Archive Online, www.marcusgarvey.com.

28. Garvey, *Philosophy and Opinions,* vol. 2, 342; see advertisement for *White America* on p. 414. The UNIA also advertised Cox's pamphlet "Let My People Go," which advocated for the removal of Blacks from the United States. Cox dedicated the pamphlet to Garvey.

29. See "Garvey Wife Heard By Large Audience: White Speakers Also Make Addresses on Racial Integrity," *Richmond Times-Dispatch,* Aug. 14, 1925, John Powell Collection.

30. Letter from Marcus Garvey to Earnest S. Cox (June 10, 1925), Marcus Garvey Archive Online; letter from Walter Plecker to President Calvin Coolidge (Mar. 19, 1927), John Powell Collection; Plecker received a response from John Finch, United States Pardon Attorney. Finch stated that Garvey was not imprisoned for his work within the Black community, but for mail fraud in which he swindled upwards of $1,000,000 from his followers. See letter from Finch to Plecker (Mar. 24, 1927), marcusgarvey.com, http://www.marcusgarvey.com/wmview. php?ArtID=326&term=james%20finch; Garvey lost support among many Blacks including the chief editor of the *Negro World,* the organ of UNIA, who openly scolded the leader for his association with Powell, Plecker and Cox. While Garvey was no doubt a staunch supporter of racial integrity and repatriation, his pursuit of a friendship with the Virginia trio may have had an ulterior motive as it appears that he may have used the men's influence as an avenue by which to obtain a pardon. Garvey's sentence was commuted by President Coolidge on Nov. 18, 1927. He was immediately deported to Jamaica and died in London on June 10, 1940. While Du Bois was a staunch opponent of Garvey's Back to Africa Movement, he also strongly opposed the treatment the Jamaican native received at the hands of the U.S. government.

31. W. E. B. Du Bois, "A Lunatic or a Traitor," In *W. E. B. Du Bois, A Reader,* 341; for an overview of Du Bois's life and career, see David Levering Lewis, "Introduction" in *W. E. B. Du Bois, A Reader,* 1–12.

32. Quoted in Paula Giddings, *When and Where I Enter: The Impact of Black Women on Race and Sex in America* (New York: William Morrow, 1984).

33. Letter from Madison Grant to John Powell (Feb. 1, 1924), John Powell Collection; in a letter to Plecker dated Oct. 5, 1925, leading eugenicist Charles Davenport advised the registrar to get a law passed that would deny the rights of inheritance to mixed raced children. "When a man of colored blood is married to a white woman . . . especially the inheritance of the land might be prevented. This would stop passage of the lands of Virginia into the hands of mulattoes and their descendants." Charles Davenport Papers.

34. Untitled, Papers of the NAACP, Part II: Special Subject Files, 1912–1939, Series B. Harding, Warren G through YWCA, Reel 3. University Publications of American, Bethesda, Md. (Jan. 12, 1915).

35. Letter to Arthur Capper from James Weldon Johnson (Jan. 24, 1923), Papers of the NAACP.

36. Letter from Plecker to the Undertakers and Coffin Dealers of Virginia, Fitzhugh Lee Sutherland Papers (May 1924), Library of Virginia.

37. Warren Fiske, "The Black and White World of Walter Plecker, Part 2" *The Virginia Pilot* Online (Aug. 20, 2004), http://home.hamptonroads.com/stories /print.cfm?story=74490&ran=160379.

38. Letter to NAACP from Dr. L. L. Shelton (Mar. 17, 1925), Papers of the NAACP.

39. Letter from James Weldon Johnson to James J. Davis (Mar. 25, 1925); Letter from James Davis to James Weldon Johnson (Mar. 28, 1925); letter from James Weldon Johnson to James Davis (Apr. 2, 1925); "The NAACP Wins Another Trophy," *The St. Luke Herald* (Apr. 11, 1925.), Papers of the NAACP.

40. Letter from Florence Kelley to James Weldon Johnson (Apr. 17, 1925), Papers of the NAACP.

41. Letter from Walter White to Florence Kelley (Apr. 18, 1925), Papers of the NAACP.

42. Letter from Lucy Mason to Florence Kelley (May 14, 1925), Papers of the NAACP.

43. Ibid.

44. Letter from Walter White to Maggie Walker (Apr. 22, 1925), Papers of the NAACP.

45. "Virginia Race Purity Law Tested in Court: Marriage License Is Refused White Man and Woman of Mixed Blood," *Washington Post* (Sept. 8, 1924), 11.

46. Ibid.; Letter from Plecker to M. B. Booker (Feb. 15, 1924), John Powell Papers.

47. "The Rockbridge Comedy of High-Powered Blood" (Nov. 22, 1924), Papers of the NAACP. This article was copied from the collection at the Library of Congress. Unfortunately, the name of the newsletter in which it appeared is obscured. However, a running head on page 2 indicates the article was published in Richmond, Va.

48. Smith, *The Eugenic Assault on America,* 71–72.

49. Atha Sorrells v. A. T. Shields, Clerk. Petition for Mandamus. n. d. John Powell Collection. While Judge Holt's decision bears no date, from newspaper accounts it can be inferred that the date of the decision was Nov. 17, 1924.

50. John Powell, "Breach in the Dike," Draft, John Powell Collection.

51. Ibid.

52. Ibid.

53. Thomson, "Racism and Racial Classification, 233.

54. Ibid, 234.

55. Ibid., 235.

56. Ibid.

57. "Virginia Will Fight Racial Integrity Bill: Law Would Affect Many Distinguished Persons, Say Patriotic Bodies," *Washington Post* (Feb. 9, 1926), 2; the White–Indian marriages referenced in the *Post* article were those of John Bass and Elizabeth a woman of the Nansemond Tribe (1638) and Sue and a Indian Servant (1688); see Rountree, *Pocahontas's People,* 141.

58. "Virginia Will Fight," 2; Thomson, "Racism," 236.

59. Thomson, "Racism," 236.

60. Ibid., 237.

61. Ibid., 240–241

62. Ibid., 241; for a fictional account of the legislative attempt to secure a separate Indian racial category see Roy Flannagan's *Amber Satry,* First Edition (Garden City, N.J.: Double Day Doran,1932), Part II, chapters 11 and 12.

63. Thomson, "Racism and Racial Classification," 241.

64. Ibid, 242.

65. Ibid.

66. Ibid, 244.

67. "An Act to amend and re-enact section 67 of the Code of Virginia defining colored persons and American Indian and tribal Indians," Senate Bill No. 49, Acts of Assembly 1930, 96–97.

68. W. E. B. Du Bois, "Virginia," In *Writings in Periodicals: Selections from the Crisis* (New York: Kraus International Publishers, 1983), 580.

69. Letter from Davenport to Plecker (Aug. 13, 1925), Charles Davenport Papers.

70. Letter from Plecker to Davenport (Aug. 17, 1925), Charles Davenport Papers.

71. Letter from Plecker to Davenport (Nov. 24, 1925), Charles Davenport Papers; after a 32-year struggle, the Shinnecock Indians were granted federal acknowledgement in 2010.

72. Letter from Plecker to John Powell (June 7, 1933), John Powell Collection.."

73. Fiske, "The Black and White World of Walter Plecker, Part 2."

74. Ibid.

75. For more on Plecker's compromise see "Bureau of Vital Statistics Finds Solution Puzzle," *Richmond News Leader* (Aug. 4, 1923; see also "At an Interview Between William Archer Thaddeus Jones And Hon, Albert O. Boschen Held in the Office of Vital Statistics The Following Questions Were Asked and Answered (Jan. 31, 1925; in addition see "Stenographic report of an interview regarding the so-called "Indians" of Charles City County between Dr. Walter Plecker and Mr. E. H. Marston, Feb. 1925; also see "Letter handed Honorable A. O. Boschen by W. A. T. Jones

and read to me by Mr. Boschen during an interview" (Jan. 31, 1925); letter from Plecker to Mrs. A. Bohannon (May 3, 1938), John Powell Collection.

76. Letter from Plecker to Mrs. A. Bohannon (May 3, 1938), John Powell Collection.

77. Ibid.

78. Letter from Estabrook to Davenport (June 28, 1923), Charles Davenport Papers.

79. Brochure advertisement for *Mongrel Virginians* from Image Archive on the American Eugenics Movement.

80. Ibid.

81. Ibid.

82. Arthur Estabrook, *Mongrel Virginians* (Baltimore, Md.: William & Wilkins Company, 1926), 199.

83. Abraham Myerson, Book Review, Image Archive of the American Eugenics Movement. http.www.eugenicsarchive.org/images/eugenicsnormal/1301–1350/1329.jpg.

84. See Letter from Plecker to Estabrook (Sept. 9, 1924). Plecker indicated in this letter that he received a correspondence from Estabrook on September 5.

85. Letter from Davenport to Estabrook (Jan. 16, 1925); letter from Estabrook to Davenport (Jan. 17, 1925), Charles Davenport Papers.

86. Letter from Plecker to Davenport (Dec. 21, 1926); letter to Plecker from Davenport (Jan. 4, 1927), Charles Davenport Papers.

87. Quoted in Smith, *Eugenics Assault on America*, 96.

88. Ibid., 97; letter from Plecker to Powell (Oct. 13, 1942), John Powell Collection.

89. Letter from Plecker to Davenport (Sept. 21, 1925), Charles Davenport Papers.

90. Letter from Plecker to John Collier (Apr. 6, 1946), John Powell Collection.

91. Carter G. Woodson, *Free Negro Heads of Families in the United States in 1830: together with a brief treatment of the free Negro* (Washington, D.C.: The Association for the Study of Negro Life and History, 1925). Woodson, known as the father of Black History, received his PhD in History from Harvard in 1912. He was a prolific writer and founder of several scholarly journals. In 1926 he began Negro History Week which is now celebrated as African American Heritage Month.

92. Letter to Senator Lloyd M. Robinette (May 4, 1944), John Powell Collection; West Virginia was formed from the western region of Virginia in 1863 due to the regions desire to secede from Virginia in support of the Union during the Civil War.

93. Quoted in Smith, *Eugenics Assault on America*, 99.

94. Letter from Plecker to Dr. I. C. Riggin (May 27, 1946), John Powell Collection.

95. Letter from Plecker to Powell (June 29, 1946), John Powell Collection.

96. Fiske, "The Black–White World of Walter Ashby Plecker"; other reports state that Plecker was hit by a truck; see Rountree, *Pocahontas's People*, 237; a search on Ancestry.com yielded no results for Kenneth R. Berrell or Burrell.

4. Denying Blackness

1. Vine Deloria Jr., "Anthropologists and Other Friends," In *Custer Died for Your Sins: An Indian Manifesto* (Norman: University of Oklahoma Press, 1988); Frederic Gleach, "Professionalization and the Virginia Indians at the Turn of the Century," *American Anthropologist* 104, no. 2 (June 2002): 500; for additional in-

digenous critiques of anthropology see Jack D. Forbes, "Anthropologists and Native Americans," http://cougar.ucdavis.edu/nas/faculty/forbes/personal/comments .html; Devon Mihesuah, *Natives and Academics: Researching and Writing About Native Americans* (Lincoln: University of Nebraska Press, 1998); Linda Tuhiwai Smith, *Decolonizing Methodologies: Research and Indigenous People* (London: Zed Books, 1999); for an overview of the Indian–Anthropologist divide see *Indians and Anthropologists,* Thomas Biolsi and Larry Zimmerman, ed. (Tuscon: University of Arizona Press, 1997); for other critiques see Robert Bieder, *Science Encounters the Indian, 1820–1880: The Early Years of American Ethnology* (Norman: University of Oklahoma Press, 1986); and selections in *When They Read What We Write: The Politics of Ethnography,* Caroline B. Brettel, ed. (West Port, Conn.: Praeger, 1996).

2. Gleach, "Professionalization and the Virginia Indians," 500.

3. Samuel R. Cook, "Anthropological Advocacy in Historical Perspective: The Case of Anthropologists and Virginia Indians," *Human Organization* (Summer 2003): 192.

4. Ibid., 193.

5. Ibid.

6. Edward Said, *Orientalism* (New York: Vintage Books, 1978), 20–21.

7. Deloria, "Anthropologists and Other Friends," 92.

8. Said, *Orientalism, 5.*

9. James Clifford and George E. Marcus, eds., "Contemporary Problems of Ethnography in the Modern World System," *Writing Culture: Poetics and Politics of Ethnography* (Berkeley: University of California Press, 1986), note 1, p. 165; for further comments on salvage anthropology, see James Clifford, "On Ethnographic Allegory," 112–113, 115 in the same volume; Said, *Orientalism, 5.*

10. Georg Henriksen, "Anthropologists as Advocates-Promoters or Makers of Clients," in *Advocacy and Anthropology,* ed. Robert Paine (St. John's, Newfoundland, Canada: Institute of Social and Economic Research Memorial University of Newfoundland, 1985), 125.

11. For more on the history of anthropology see Lee D. Baker, *From Savage to Negro: Anthropology and the Construction of Race 1896–1954* (Berkley: University of California Press, 1998); for more on the two schools of anthropology see Lee D. Baker, *Anthropology and the Racial Politics of Culture* (Durham, N.C.: Duke University Press, 2010), 9–13; for more on Niggerology see Jabari Asim, *The N Word: Who Can Say It, Who Shouldn't, and Why* (New York: Mariner Books, 2008).

12. Peggy Pascoe, "Miscegenation Law, Court Cases, and Ideologies of Race in Twentieth-Century America," *Journal of American History* 83, no. 1 (June 1996): 53.

13. Ibid.

14. Ibid., 54.

15. Ibid, 55.

16. Ibid.; For more on the anthropological concept of culture see George W. Stocking, Jr., "Matthew Arnold, E. B. Tylor, and the Uses of Invention," *American Anthropologist* 65, no. 4 (Aug. 1963), 783–799; On Boas's contribution to the culture concept see George W. Stocking, Jr., "Franz Boas and the Culture Concept in Historical Perspective," *American Anthropologist* 68, no. 4 (Aug. 1966), 867–882; African American folklorist Zora Neale Hurston and American Indian scholar Ella

Cara Deloria collected folklore under the guidance of Franz Boas during the 1920s and 30s; see Roseanne Hoefel, "'Different By Degree': Ella Cara Deloria, Zora Neale Hurston, and Franz Boas Contend with Race and Ethnicity," *American Indian Quarterly* 25, no. 2 (Spring 2001): 181–202.

17. Lee D. Baker, *Anthropology and Racial Politics,* 115–116.

18. Ibid.; Ashley Montagu, another Boas protégé, was the first to provide a full length work challenging the scientific basis of race; see his 1942 classic *Man's Most Dangerous Myth: The Fallacy of Race,* 6th ed. (Walnut Creek, Calif.: Altamira Press, 1997).

19. Rountree, *Pocahontas's People: The Powhatan Indians of Virginia through Four Centuries* (Norman: University of Oklahoma Press, 1990), 215.

20. Ibid.

21. James Mooney, "The Powhatan Confederacy, Past and Present," *American Anthropologist,* n. s., 9, no. 1 (Jan. 1907): 45.

22. Letter to Mooney from Speck (Feb. 15, 1916), Nanticoke Indians, Frank Speck Papers, American Philosophical Society.

23. Frank Speck, "The Ethnic Position of the Southeastern Algonkian," *American Anthropologist,* n.s. 26, no 2 (April–June 1924): 196.

24. Ibid., 194.

25. Ibid., note 6, p. 188.

26. Frank Speck, *The Rappahannock Indians of Virginia* (New York: Museum of the American Indian, Heye Foundation, 1925), vii–viii.

27. James Clifford, *The Predicament of Culture: Twentieth Century Ethnography, Literature and Art* (Cambridge, Mass.: Harvard University Press, 1988), 231.

28. Ibid.

29. Ibid.

30. Frank Speck, *Chapters on Ethnology of the Powhatan Tribes of Virginia* (New York: Museum of the American Indian Heye Foundation, 1928), 236.

31. Rountree, *Pocahontas's People,* 222.

32. Said, *Orientalism,* 7.

33. Rountree, *Pocahontas's People,* 222.

34. Letter from Plecker to John Powell (June 7, 1933), John Powell Collection, University of Virginia Special Collections; letter from Plecker to Davenport (Sept. 21, 1925), Davenport Papers.

35. Letter from Ivan McDougle to Arthur Estabrook (July 5, 1925), *Image Archive on the American Eugenics Movement,* http.www.eugenicsarchive.org/images/eugenicsnormal/1251-1300/1298.jpg.

36. Ibid.

37. C. A. Weslager, "An Unexpected Champion," in *Delaware's Forgotten Folk: The Story of the Moors & Nanticokes* (Philadelphia: University of Pennsylvania Press, 1943), 82–111.

38. "Barring Red-Haired Indians From the Pow-Wow: Why the Chief of the Nanticokes Refuses Membership in His Tribal Association to Neighbors Whose Ruddy Heads Figure in a Romantic Legend," *Philadelphia Inquirer* (1937), Nanticoke Indians, Frank Speck Papers.

39. Rountree, *Pocahontas's People,* 224.

40. Ibid.

41. Rountree, *Pocahontas's People,* 224.

42. Ibid., 228.

43. Clifford, *The Predicament of Culture,* 232.

44. Ibid., 230.

45. Letter from B. H. Van Oot to Frank Speck (Dec. 14, 1932); Frank Speck Papers.

46. Virginia-Race and Hispanic Origin, 1790–1990, Census Bureau Online.

47. Frank Speck, "Testimonials for Indians of Virginia Approving their Claim for Indian Classification" (Dec. 8, 1944), Frank Speck Papers.

48. Letter from Speck to Dr. Willard M. Beatty (Dec. 9, 1945), Frank Speck Papers.

49. Letter from Coates to Speck (Dec. 12, 1945), Frank Speck Papers; for more on the conflict concerning the racial classification of the Virginia Indians during World War II see Paul T. Murray, "Who Is An Indian? Who Is A Negro? Virginia Indians in the World War II Draft," *Virginia Magazine of History and Biography* 95, no. 2 (Apr. 1987): 215–231.

50. John Garland Pollard, *Pamunkey Indians of Virginia,* 15.

51. Letter to James Coates from Tecumesh Cook (Dec. 18, 1944), Frank Speck Papers.

52. Letter from Coates to Speck (Jan. 17, 1945), Frank Speck Papers.

53. Petition Untitled (Mar. 1, 1945), James R. Coates Papers, Library of Virginia.

54. Letter from Coates to Speck (May 7, 1945), Frank Speck Papers.

55. Letter from James Coates to Virginia Tribes (undated), James R. Coates Papers.

56. Karrenne Wood, "Virginia Indians: Our Story," *Virginia Heritage Trail* (Charlottesville: Virginia Foundation for the Humanities, 2008), 20.

57. Letter from Willard Beatty to Frank Speck (Jan. 21, 1946), Frank Speck Papers.

58. Cook, "Anthropological Advocacy in Historical Prospective," 194. Speck secured enrollment for Nanticoke tribal children to attend the Haskell Indian School in Lawrence, Kansas, which they attended from 1946 to 1960 so that they would not have to attend the local school for Black children.

59. Kim Douglass, "A Rich Past, A Divided Future," *Freelance Star,* June 11, 1997.

60. Ibid.; Trinchett was among those who were outspoken opponents of the United Rappahannock Tribe's anti-Black policies. In 2004, she also resigned her membership from the Rappahannock Indian Baptist Church in protest of the Battle decision.

61. Jack D. Forbes, "Tribes Must Bring Their List Up to Date," *Attan-akamik News* 1, no. 4 (Rancocas, New Jersey: Native American Publishers, n. d.): 1; Nemattanew (Chief Crazy Horse) was chief of the Powhatan-Renape Tribe of New Jersey until his untimely death in November 2004.

62. Idem, "Indians, Blacks, and Whites: A Tale of Three Races," *Attan-Akamik News* 1, no 4 (n. d.): 4.

63. Ibid.; while Crispus Attucks is often cited as the first "Negro" to die for the cause of American independence, Attucks was of African and Natick Indian de-

scent. Hiram Rhoades Revels, the first "Negro" to sit in the U.S. Senate was born in North Carolina in 1822 of African and Croatan Indian descent.

64. Rountree, *Pocahontas's People*, 246.

65. Frederick Douglass, "The Claims of the Negro Ethnologically Considered," In *Frederick Douglass: Selected Speeches and Writings,* ed. Philip Foner (Chicago: Lawrence Hill Books, 1999), 289.

66. Rountree, *Pocahontas's People*, 160.

67. Ibid., note 208, p. 333.

68. Speck, *Chapters on Ethnology*, 266; Minutes of the Joint Subcommittee Studying Relationships between State and Indian Tribes (HJR97), Aug. 9, 1982, 2.

69. Adamstown Indian Tribal Roll, James Coates Papers.

70. Rountree, *Pocahontas's People*, 173.

71. Ibid.

72. Ibid.

73. *Virginia Gazette,* Mar. 12, 1772, *The Geography of Slavery in Virginia,* The University of Virginia, http://www2.vcdh.virginia.edu/saxon/servlet/SaxonServlet ?source=/xml_docs/slavery/ads/rg72.xml&style=/xml_docs/slavery/ads/display_ad .xsl&ad=v1772030809; an additional advertisement was posted for Dick on Nov. 26, 1782 alleging that he was possibly harbored by the Pamunkey.

74. Ibid., Nov. 16, 1782, http://www2.vcdh.virginia.edu/saxon/servlet/ SaxonServlet?source=/xml_docs/slavery/ads/vg1782.xml&style=/xml_docs/slavery/ ads/display_ad.xsl&ad=v1782110014.

75. John Mercer Langston, *From the Virginia Plantation to the National Capital,* New York: Arno Press and the New York Times, 1969, 13; Langston identified Lucy's mother as full-blooded Indian.

76. Rountree, *Pocahontas's People*, 174.

77. Ibid.

78. Johnston, *Race Relations in Virginia,* 270.

79. Rountree, *Pocahontas's People*, 155.

80. William Strachey, *The Historie of Travell Into Virginia Britania (1612),* ed. Louis B. Wright and Virginia Freund (London: Hakluyt Society, 1953), 71.

81. Frederic Gleach, *Powhatan's World,* 57–58; for an extensive analysis of color symbolism in Powhatan cosmology see Margaret Holmes Williamson, Powhatan Lords of Life and Death: Command and Consent in Seventeenth-Century Virginia (Lincoln: University of Nebraska Press, 2008), 247–254.

82. Strachey, *Historie of Travell,* 71; note the author's use of the term "Moore" to describe what appears to be African people.

83. Quoted in Kenneth W. Porter, "Contacts as Allies," *Journal of Negro History* 17, no.3 (July 1932): 314. Europeans equated the Powhatan deity Okee with the devil probably because he had black skin or was painted black; there is no evidence to support the notion of anti-Black discrimination among the Virginia tribes in the colonial period.

84. Rountree, *Pocahontas's People*, 227.

85. Christian Feest asserted that "those not of our tribe" were not Negroes, but other Indians, including, Catabaw Indians from South Carolina. But this seems to have occurred after the 1843 petition. Rountree states that some Catawba arrived

on the reservation sometime between 1836 and 1839 with the purpose to "entrench the Indian blood," (194). But the Catawba did not stay, as they along with their Pamunkey spouses soon returned to South Carolina. Thus, the Pamunkey lost rather than gained population. See Christian Feest, *The Indians of North America: The Powhatan Tribes* (New York: Chelsea House Publishers, 1990), 73.

86. Rountree, *Pocahontas's People*, 205.

87. Ibid., 275.

5. Beyond Black and White

1. Simeon Booker, "The Couple That Rocked Courts," *Ebony*, Sept. 1967; a previous version of this chapter was published under the title "Tell the Court I Love My [Indian] Wife: Interrogating Race and Self-Identity in *Loving v. Virginia*," *Souls: A Critical Journal of Black Politics, Culture, and Society* 8, no. 1 (Spring 2006): 67–80.

2. "The Crime of Being Married: A Virginia Couple Fights to Overturn an Old Law Against Miscegenation," *Life*, Mar. 18, 1966, 85.

3. Peter Wallenstein, *Tell the Court I Love My Wife: Race, Marriage and Law— An American History* (New York: Palgrave Macmillan, 2002), 216.

4. Victoria Valentine, "When Love Was A Crime," *Emerge*, July 1997, 61.

5. Phyl Newbeck, *Virginia Hasn't Always Been for Lovers: Interracial Marriage Bans and the Case of Loving v. Virginia* (Carbondale: Southern Illinois University Press, 2004), 17.

6. Robert Pratt, "Crossing the Color Line: A Historical Assessment and Personal Narrative of Loving v. Virginia," *Howard Law Journal* 41 (Winter 1998): 244. Robert Pratt, interview by author, Feb. 17, 2012.

7. Mildred Loving of Virginia, interview by author, July 14, 2004; marriage license obtained from Superior Court of the District of Columbia.

8. ACLU letter appears in Newbeck, *Virginia Hasn't Always been For Lovers*; original Social Security application received from Social Security Administration, Baltimore, Maryland.

9. Gordon-Reed, *Thomas Jefferson and Sally Hemings: An American Controversy*, 136.

10. Joshua D. Rothman, *Notorious in the Neighborhood: Sex and Families across the Color Line in Virginia 1787–1861* (Chapel Hill: University of North Carolina Press, 2003), 53.

11. Newbeck, *Virginia Wasn't Always for Lovers*, 17.

12. Ralph Emmett Fall, *People, Post Offices and Communities in Caroline County, Virginia, 1729–1969* (Roswell, Ga.: WH Wolfe Associates, 1989), 185, 187.

13. Ibid., 91.

14. Booker, *The Couple That Rocked Courts*, 78.

15. Newbeck, Virginia Hasn't Always been for Lovers, 21.

16. Original Social Security application for Sidney C. Jeter dated Feb. 2, 1973. Obtained from the SSA in Baltimore, Maryland.. It appears that a concerted effort was made to conceal Sidney's actual age during the period leading up to the Supreme Court decision. Sidney used a secondary birthdate Sept. 1, 1958. A caption under a picture of the Lovings' children taken for the *Life Magazine* feature article

lists the children's ages as Sidney 8, Donald 7, and Peggy 6; however, Sidney at that time was 9.

17. Booker, "The Couple That Rocked Courts," 80.

18. Judge Leon M. Bazile, Commonwealth v. Richard Perry Loving and Mildred Delores Jeter (Jan. 6, 1959), Loving v. Virginia Papers, Central Rappahannock Heritage Center, Fredericksburg, Va.

19. Philip T. Nash, "When Marriage Was Illegal: 25 Years Ago, a Triumph of Love and Law Over Racism," *Washington Post,* June 14, 1992, C5.

20. Judge Leon M. Bazile, Commonwealth v. Richard Perry Loving and Mildred Delores Jeter (Jan. 1965), Loving v. Virginia Papers, Central Rappahannock Heritage Center, Fredericksburg, Va.; for an analysis of Bazile's statement, see Fay Botham, *Almighty God Created the Races: Christianity, Interracial Marriage, and American Law* (Chapel Hill: University of North Carolina Press), 2009, 159–165.

21. Peter Wallenstein, "Interracial Marriage on Trial: Loving v. Virginia," in *Race on Trial: Law and Justice in American History,* ed. Annette Gordon-Reed (New York: Oxford University Press, 2002), 182.

22. In March 1967, in anticipation of the Supreme Court decision, Maryland repealed its anti-miscegenation law. Sixteen states including Virginia, however, maintained their stance against interracial marriage: Alabama, Arkansas, Delaware, Florida, Georgia, Kentucky, Louisiana, Mississippi, Missouri, North Carolina, Oklahoma, South Carolina, Tennessee, Texas, and West Virginia. On Nov. 7, 2000, by a vote of 60 to 40 percent, citizens of Alabama became the last state in the Union to strike anti-miscegenation language from its constitution.

23. Booker, "The Couple That Rocked Courts," 82.

24. Ibid., 79.

25. Ibid., 80.

26. Ibid.

27. Ibid.

28. Wingfield, *A History of Caroline County Virginia,* 170; Wingfield asserted that there was little racial tension between Blacks and Whites in Caroline County.

29. Booker, "The Couple That Rocked Courts," 79, 80.

30. Ibid.

31. Pratt, "Crossing the Color Line," 235.

32. Letter from Otho Nelson to Frank Speck (Oct. 3, 1942), Frank Speck Papers.

33. Letter from Mills P. Neal to Lloyd G. Carr (Nov. 2, 1942), Frank Speck Papers.

34. Murray, "Who is an Indian? Who is a Negro?," 227–228.

35. "Powhatan Confederacy Reorganized," *Attan-Akamik* 1, no 3 (n. d.), 1.

36. Anonymous Informant, interview by author, Nov. 15, 2011.

37. Mildred Loving of Central Point, interview by author, July 14, 2004; Kim Douglass, "Is Mildred Loving Considered Black or Indian? Both She Says," *The Free Lance-Star,* June 12, 1997, A1.

38. Anonymous resident of Caroline County, interview by author, Mar. 4, 2005. Due to the volatile nature of the African American and Native American identity dilemma, several interviewees asked that their names not be released for fear of retaliation.

39. Anonymous resident of Central Point, interview by author, Mar. 5, 2005.

40. Ibid.; for more on the dilemma of African American ancestry within tribes seeking federal recognition, see Brian Klopotex, *Recognition Odysseys: Indigeneity, Race and Federal Recognition in Three Louisiana Indian Communities* (Durham, N.C.: Duke University Press, 2011).

41. Bernard Cohen of Alexandria, Virginia, interviewed by the author, Mar. 6, 2005.

42. "Loving v. Virginia," The Oyez Project at ITT Chicago-Kent College of Law, accessed Jan. 2, 2013, http://www.oyez.org/cases/1960-1969/1966/1966_395#chicago.

43. *Richmond News Leader,* "Pair Files Suit to End State Ban," Oct. 28, 1964, 23; "Anti-Miscegenation Case Move Rejected," Oct. 29, 1964, 21; "Brief Filed On Mixed Marriages," Dec. 28, 1964, 21; "Court Won't Rule On Mixed Marriage," Feb. 12, 1965, 17; "VA. Mixed Marriage Ban Killed," June 12, 1967, 1.

44. *Washington Post,* "Judge Denies Suit Against Marriage Ban," Oct. 30, 1964, A9; "Mixed Marriage Ban in Virginia Attacked," Dec. 20, 1964, A27d; "Ban On Interracial Marriages Defended," Dec. 9, 1965, D18; "High Court to Hear Miscegenation Case," June 12, 1965, B1; "Interracial Union Case to be Heard," Jan. 8, 1966, B4"; Supreme Court Asked to Give Ruling On State Interracial Marriage Bars," July 30, 1966, A17; *New York Times,* "Supreme Court Agrees to Rule on State Miscegenation Laws," Dec. 13, 1966, 40; "Excerpts from the Supreme Court's Ruling on Virginia Ban on Miscegenation," June 13, 1967, 29.

45. Margolick, "A Mixed Marriage's 25th Anniversary of Legality," B20.

46. Georgia Heneghan, "The Crime of Being Married: Caroline County Woman Recalls Fight Against Virginia Law," *Free Lance-Star,* Aug. 1, 1992.

47. Lynne Duke, "Two Separated By Death," *Washington Post,* June 12, 1992; Nash, "When Marriage Was Illegal," C5.

48. Ibid.

49. Ibid.

50. H. Res. 431 (110th): Recognizing the 40th anniversary of *Loving v. Virginia* legalizing interracial marriage within the United States, May 23, 2007; according to a Mar. 12, 2001 census report, only 2.4 percent of the American population took advantage of the option to identify as multiracial. Many Americans who identified themselves by more than one race checked the White category and another category such as Black, Asian, or American Indian. Although anyone who reported two or more races is included in the tally for each of those races when using the "alone or in combination" concept, anyone who checked a White category and some other race were counted as a minority.

51. Newbeck, *Virginia Hasn't Always Been For Lovers,* 215; anonymous resident of Central Point interview by author, Mar. 5, 2005.

52. Peggy Fortune interview with author, Apr. 10, 2011; Lewis Jeter interview with author, July 11, 2011.

53. Dionne Walker, "Pioneer of Interracial Marriage Looks Back," *USA Today* [Online], June 10, 2007, http://www.usatoday.com/news/nation/2007-06-10-loving _N.htm; Idem., "Mildred Loving: Matriarch of Interracial Marriage Dies," *USA Today*[Online], May 5, 2008, http://www.usatoday.com/news/nation/2008-05-05 -334349848ox.htm; "Mildred Loving Dies at 68," *Richmond Times-Dispatch* [Online], May 5, 2008, http://www2.timesdispatch.com/news/2008/may/05/-rtd_2008_05

_05_0189-ar-130821/?referer=http://www.google.com/url?sa=t&rct=j&q=mildred%20
1oving%20dies%20richmond%2; Edie Gross, "Caroline Heroine Dies," *Free Lance-Star,* May 5, 2008, http://fredericksburg.com/News/FLS/2008/052008/05052008/3768
25; Douglass Martin, "It Changed Laws Nationwide: She Called Case 'God's' Work," *Virginian-Pilot,* May 6, 2008, A4; "Quiet Va. Wife Ended Interracial Marriage Ban," *Washington Post,* May 6, 2008, A01; Douglas Martin, "Mildred Loving, Who Battled Ban on Mixed-Race Marriage Dies at 68," *New York Times,* May 6, 2008; "Mildred Loving," *Times* (London), May 19, 2008, 49; Andrew Gumbel, "U.S. Mourns Black Woman Who Dared to Love a White Man," *Independent,* Frist edition (London), May 7, 2008, 22; Phyl Newbeck, "Mildred Loving," *Guardian* [Online], May 6, 2008, http://www.guardian.co.uk/world/2008/may/07/usa.humanrights; "Mildred Loving Obituary," *Daily Post* (Liverpool), May 20, 2008).

54. "Mildred Loving, Law Changer," *The Economist* [Online], May 17, 2008, http://www.economist.com/node/11367685.

55. Margolick, "A Mixed Marriage's 25th Anniversary of Legality," B20.

56. Ibid.; during his interview with Kim Douglass in 1997, Brooks recanted his earlier statement insisting that his arrest of Mildred Loving was not a matter of race, but a matter of upholding the law.

57. Ibid.

6. The Racial Integrity Fight

1. Story related by Mr. Richard Bowman, Joseph's son; interview, Jan. 5, 2010; the 1920 census listed the Bowman family as mulatto. By 1930, the term mulatto was discontinued on the census and the family was listed as Negro.

2. Sara Lawrence Lightfoot, Balm in Gilead: Journey of a Healer (Reading, Mass.: Addison-Wesley Publishing Company, 2006), 119.

3. Ibid.

4. For more on the Chickahominy see chapter 7.

5. Charles City County History online. http://www.charlescity.org/history .shtml; Daryl Cumber Dance, *The Lineage of Abraham: The Biography of a Free Black Family in Charles City County, VA* (self-published, 1998), 3.

6. Ibid.; The Harrison's owned Berkeley Plantation. Benjamin Harrison was one of the signers of the Declaration of Independence and William Harrison became the ninth president of the United States; the Harrisons also had ties to Northbend, Westover, and Evelynton Plantations; John Tyler, America's tenth president, owned Sherwood Forest Plantation. Some believe Sally Hemings, the slave mistress of Thomas Jefferson, was born in Charles City County. Sally was the half sister of Jefferson's wife; of the sixteen tourist attractions offered by the county during the 400th anniversary of Jamestown, eight were plantation tours.

7. James P. Whittenberg, "Present and Past in Charles City County," In *Charles City County: An Official History,* James P. Whittenberg and John M. Coski, eds. (Salem, West Virginia: Don Mills, Inc., 1989), 9.

8. Charles City County History Online.

9. Dance, *The Lineage of Abraham,* 3–4.

10. Michael J. Puglisi, "'A Lustie and a Daring People': The Indians of Colonial Charles City County," In *Charles City County: An Official History*, 22–23.

11. Ibid, 23.

12. Ibid., 23–24; the Tuscarora are an Iroquoian speaking people whose original territory was in North Carolina.

13. Thomas Stern, "Chickahominy: The Changing Culture of a Virginia Indian Community," *Proceedings of the American Philosophical Society* 96, no.2 (Apr. 21, 1952), 162.

14. Ibid.

15. Ibid., 162–163.

16. Puglisi, "'A Lustie and a Daring People,'" 24. Gleach stated regarding the red coat, copper chain and copper engraving of King James that these reflected Powhatan color symbolism. Noticeably absent, however, is the color black which reflects a European rather than Powhatan worldview. See *Powhatan's World*, 138.

17. Stern, "Chickahominy," 168.

18. Puglisi, "'A Lustie and a Daring People,'" 24.

19. Ibid.

20. Ibid.

21. David Lazarus Jones, "Chickahominy Indians of Charles City County, Virginia: Past! Present?," unpublished undergraduate thesis (Williams College, 1974), 9. Many thanks to Mr. Bowman for sharing his copy of the thesis with me.

22. Stern, "Chickahominy," 201; genealogical information was also provided by Mr. Richard Bowman in a letter to author, Nov. 12, 2010.

23. Ibid, 204.

24. Puglisi, "Controversy and Revival," 98.

25. Charles City County Registration of Free Negroes and Mulattoes Database Online, http://charlescity.org/fnr/index.shtml.

26. Puglisi, "Controversy and Revival," 99; genealogy was confirmed by Richard Bowman Dec. 2010.

27. Ibid.

28. Interview with anonymous informants of Charles City County, Sept. 25, 2010 and Nov. 20, 2010.

29. Interview with Richard and Marian Bowman, Jan. 5, 2010.

30. Mary Ann Shadd Cary, *A Plea for Emigration or Notes of Canada West* (Detroit: George W. Pattison, 1852), 21.

31. Some of the Bradby's from Charles City resided for a time in Windsor, Ontario. R. L. Bradby, who was born in Canada in 1877 and resided in Windsor, migrated to Toledo, Ohio and became a "colored" Baptist minister; Ancestry.com. *Border Crossings: From Canada to U.S., 1895–1956* [online database]; Rountree, *Pocahontas's People*, 198.

32. Documents regarding Spotswood Adkins's claim were obtained from his paternal great-granddaughter Sherida Bradby. Many thanks to her for providing this information.

33. Stern, *Chickahominy*, 208.

34. "Cedar Grove Baptist Church Official History," researched and compiled by Joyce Christian 1975. Special thanks to Rev. F. Wayne Henley for providing a copy of the history.

35. Puglisi, "Controversy and Revival," 99.

36. William Archer Thaddeus Jones Deposition (Jan. 31, 1925), John Powell Collection.

37. Letter from Plecker to D. E. Harrower (Apr. 27, 1925), John Powell Collection.

38. Letter from Plecker to Elizabeth Tyler (Apr. 16, 1936), John Powell Collection.

39. Ibid.; Plecker's origin story of the Chickahominy Indians was told to him by Charles City resident E. H. Marston in a deposition given at the state registrar's office. For more on this see "Stenographic report of an interview regarding the so-called 'Indians' of Charles City County between Dr. Walter Plecker and Mr. E. H. Marston," Feb. 1925, John Powell Collection.

40. Marian Bowman, the wife of Richard Bowman stated that her father Lazarus Wallace drove a number of Charles City couples to Washington, D.C. so that they could have their race identified as Indian on their marriage licenses. Interview, Jan. 5, 2010.

41. Stern, "Chickahominy," 204; for more on the erasure of Blacks from Indian genealogies see Claudio Saunt, *Black, White and Indian: Race and the Unmaking of an American Family* (New York: Oxford University Press, 2005).

42. Sherida Bradby, e-mail message to the author, Jan. 31, 2012; Levy's father, William Bradby's racial identity on his death certificate was listed as "Red."

43. Telephone interview with Mr. Richard Bowman, Jan. 28, 2012; for more on Andrew Warren Adkins and the history of the Alfred Street Baptist Church see Alton S., Wallace, *I Once Was Young: History of Alfred Street Baptist Church, 1803–2003* (Littleton, Mass.: Tapestry Press, 2003); for more on Rutherford Hamlet Adkins see http://www.answers.com/topic/rutherford-h-adkins.; for more on Andretta Adkins see http://obit.lafuneral.com/obitdisplay.html?task=Print&id=447135 &listing=Current; interestingly, Andretta's parents who are described in her obituary as a Chickahominy Indian (Andrew) and the mixed race daughter of a William and Mary professor (Mattie) may be a modern day attempt to distance her from her African American roots.

44. Red/Black Symposium Session Five, Charles City County Virginia, n. d., tape of symposium obtained from the Weyanoke Association.

45. Lorraine Blackwell, "Ties That Don't Bind in Charles City, Identity Often Divides Blacks and American Indians," *Richmond Times Dispatch.com,* July 23, 1995.

46. Ibid.

47. In Feb. 2004, during a genealogical forum held at the Hampton, Virginia Public Library, several attendees presented census data which documented their ancestral ties to the Chickahominy tribe, yet stated that their admission application was denied. They unanimously agreed that the denial was due to their having noticeable African American ancestry.

48. Blackwell, "Ties That Don't Bind." Chief Adkins displayed a similar case of historical amnesia during his talk on Virginia Indian Tribes at the Virginia Museum of Science on Jan. 27, 2012. Adkins claimed that intermarriage with Blacks and Whites were equally discouraged by tribal leadership. He stated, however, that although he had urged his daughters to marry "their own kind," to prevent the dilu-

tion of the Indian blood, one had married a Black man while the other had married a White man. Both were equally welcomed by the tribe. As a result his family had become a rainbow coalition. Adkins's Black son-in-law, however, does not erase the long history of anti-Black-miscegenation sentiment within the Chickahominy establishment.

49. Idem., "Hampton Couple Look to Build Center," *Richmond Ties Dispatch.com* (Mar. 1994).

50. Devon Mihesuah, *Indigenous American Women: Decolonization, Empowerment, Activism* (Lincoln: University of Nebraska Press, 2003), xvii.

51. Alice Walker, "If the Present Looks Like the Past, What Does the Future Look Like," in *In Search of Our Mother's Gardens: Womanist Pose* (New York: Harcourt Brace Jovanovich, 1982), 290.

52. Kathy Russell, et. al., *The Color Complex: The Politics of Skin Color Among African Americans* (New York: Harcourt Brace Jovanovich, 1993).

53. Dance, *The Lineage of Abraham*, 14.

54. Interview with Elam Baptist Church informant, Sept. 26, 2010.

55. Russell et. al., *The Color Complex*, 27; Colorism diminished much during the era of the Civil Rights and Black Power Movements; it continues, however, to be an issue in African American and other communities of color. Numerous studies have shown that dark skinned Blacks have a harder time with upward mobility than light skinned Blacks because Whites are more likely to hire and promote the latter rather than the former. For an in depth look at the legal aspects of colorism, see Trina Brown, "Shades of Brown: The Law of Skin Color," *Duke Law Journal,* 49, no.6 (Apr. 2000), 1487–1557.

56. bell hooks, "Revolutionary Renegade," in *Black Looks: Race and Representation* (Boston, Massachusetts: South End Books, 1992), 185; traditional Indian societies dating back to the Mississippian era (900–1600 AD) used hair styling as a marker for nationality and political affiliation. For more on this see Snyder, *Slavery in Indian Country,* 17.

57. Rountree, "The Indians of Virginia" In *The Southeastern Indians Since the Removal Era,* ed. Walter L Williams (Athens: University of Georgia Press, 2009), 36; Speck, *Chapters on Ethnology,* 267.

58. Rountree, "The Indians of Virginia," 36.

59. A Statement as to the Origins of the "so-called Indians" of Charles City County, as given by Mr George H. Marston, brother of Mr. E. H. Marston both of Whom have lived in Charles City all their lives (Feb. 1925), John Powell Collection.

60. Interview Harold Caldwell, Nov. 20, 2010.

61. Shonda Buchanan, "Being a Black Indian at a Chickahominy Powwow," *Indian Country Today* (Oct. 29, 2010).

62. Kenneth Bradby, Jr., *Pamunkey Speaks: Native Perspectives* (Charleston: BookSurge Publishing, 2008), 62.

63. There are indeed exceptions to this. During the same powwow in which Caldwell's Indian identity was challenged a "White Indian" woman of Shoshone descent was ejected from the dance circle because she did not have a tribal card. This woman is well known in the Virginia Indian community and had been dancing at powwows for two decades. Some believed she was pulled out of the circle to

serve as a sacrificial lamb in order to avoid cries of racism when "Black Indians" were ejected. The expulsion resulted in much protest among tribal members. Some even left the powwow in protest. There appears to have been no protest, however, regarding Ms. Buchanan's expulsion; also, on a recent visit to the Pamunkey Indian Museum located on the Pamunkey reservation, a visitor asked the museum worker if her son, who was working on a book report on Algonquian speaking nations, could see a "real" Indian. The worker with pale skin and deep red curly hair explained to the visitor that she was a Pamunkey Indian, a product of an Indian father and Irish mother. "I look more like my mother, she kindly stated, "but I am just as Indian as all the rest."

64. Julienne K. Coleman, "Reflections of a Black Indian at a Nottoway Powwow, Another Perspective, Sept. 17, 2010, unpublished paper.

65. Despite his undeniable ancestral connection to the Chickahominy, William Allen has nevertheless not petitioned the tribe for membership. Neither has the tribe extended an invitation for membership.

7. Nottoway Indians, Afro-Indian Identity, and the Contemporary Dilemma of State Recognition

1. The NITOV should not be confused with the Cheroenhaka Nottoway of Southampton County, Virginia.

2. "Report of the Joint Subcommittee Studying Relationship Between the Commonwealth and Native Indian Tribes," House Document No. 10 (Richmond: Commonwealth of Virginia,1982), 6; the VCI became effective on July 1, 1983; for more on the VCI see "Report on the Commission on Indians to the Governor and General Assembly 1983."

3. Howard M. Cullum, "Report on the State Recognition Petition of the United Cherokee Indian Tribe of Virginia, Inc." Secretary of Health and Human Resources Office of the Governor, Jan. 1993, 2.

4. Ibid.; The council vote was "5 yays, 0 nays, and 1 abstention" to deny the UCITOVA state recognition.

5. James Mooney, "The Powhatan Confederacy, Past and Present," *American Anthropologist,* n.s., 9 (1907):45; Horace Rice, *The Buffalo Ridge Cherokee: A Remnant of a Great Nation Divided (*Berwyn Heights, Md.: Heritage Books, 1995), 131.

6. Rice, *The Buffalo Ridge Cherokee,* 220.

7. On Jan. 12, 2011, House Delegate William Abbott submitted House Joint Resolution 644, which would extend state recognition to the UCITOVA; on February 1, the House Rules Committee tabled the resolution.

8. VCI Minute Book Dec. 3, 1998, 3; On Feb. 4, 2002, The Occaneechi became the eighth tribe to received state recognition in North Carolina.

9. VCI Minute Book Apr. 20, 1999. The VCI did not keep records of its meetings until 1998 and continued through 1999. They were once again taken intermittently from 2000 to 2002. Meeting minutes from 2003 to 2010 are archived on the VCI website, http://indians.vipnet.org/councilMeetings.cfm.

10. Kim Douglass, "Rich Past, Divided Future," *Free Lance-Star,* June 11, 1997, A10.

11. *Testimony Before the Joint Subcommittee Studying the Relationship Between the State and Indian Tribes Rappahannock Tribe, Inc.* Submitted By the United Rappahannock Tribe, Inc, Nov. 5, 1982, 2. Testimony is in the possession of the author.

12. Kim Douglass, "Rich Past, Divided Future," A10.

13. Ibid.

14. The Tri-County Tribe's name change resulted in a lawsuit brought by the United Rappahannock who argued that Lemon's use of the Rappahannock name would cause confusion and result in an unfair competition for grant monies. The suit was later dropped. Reporter Kim Douglass continued to refer to Lemons's group as the "newer tribe." See "Tribal Dispute in Court: Rappahannock Indians Divided," *Free Lance-Star,* Feb. 27, 1998, C4; see also "Suit Dropped Over Indian Tribe's Name," *Free Lance-Star,* Aug. 16, 1998, C11.

15. VCI Minute Book, Nov. 1999, 9.

16. Ibid., 7.

17. Ibid.,12; VCI Minute Book, Aug. 17, 1999, 7.

18. Nokomis Fortune Lemons served on the 1982 subcommittee to study Virginia-American Indian relations and was an original member of the committee to form the VCI. She was instrumental in assisting the eight tribes in gaining state recognition in 1983.

19. Bill Wright letter to the VCI, Mar. 18, 2008.

20. In 2004 I made inquiry via email to the VCI asking how I could obtain a copy of the state recognition criteria. I was told that the only way to obtain the information was to identify my tribal affiliation with a letter of intent to petition for state recognition. When I reminded the VCI representative that the information was protected under the FOIA, she sent the same reply. I asked a family member and an acquaintance, both residents of Virginia, to make the same inquiry. They were given the same response. Failure to comply with the FOIA was a constant complaint of the NITOV throughout the recognition process.

21. Federal recognition can be obtained through several ways: Administrative Recognition through the Bureau of Indian Affairs, Legislative Recognition through an Act of Congress, and Judicial Recognition obtained by court order. Six Virginia tribes (Chickahominy, Chickahominy Eastern Division, Upper Mattaponi, Rappahannock, Nansemond and Monacan) are seeking federal recognition by an act of Congress. The two reservation groups, the Pamunkey and the Mattaponi decided not to join the six in seeking recognition through congressional means. On Oct. 14, 2010, The Pamunkey Tribe of Virginia became the first Virginia tribe to submit a formal documented petition to the BIA for federal recognition. Because the BIA process is laden in bureaucratic red tape, it may take over two decades before the Pamunkey receive a decision. For an excellent analysis of the federal recognition processes see Brian Klopotek, *Recognition Odysseys: Indigeneity, Race and Federal Tribal Policy in Three Louisiana Indian Communities* (Durham, N.C.: Duke University Press, 2010). Klopotek's work inadvertently provides parallels between the Virginia and Louisiana tribes regarding anti-Black sentiment within tribal communities.

22. Virginia Council on Indians, Tribal Recognition Criteria, http://indians.vipnet.org/resources/tribalRecognitionCriteria.pdf; for the BIA criteria see 25 CFR

Part 83. Procedures for Establishing That an American Indian Group Exist as an Indian Tribe, http://www.bia.gov/cs/groups/public/documents/text/idc-001115.pdf.

23. Alexa Koenig and Jonathan Stein, "Federalism and the State Recognition of Native American Tribes: A Survey of State Recognized Tribes and State Recognition Processes across the United States." Santa Clara Law Review 48 (Jan. 2007), 140–141; for an updated version of this work see K. Alexa Koenig and Jonathan Stein, "State Recognition of American Indian Tribes: A National Survey of State-Recognized Tribes and the Federalist Process," In *Sovereignty Struggles and Native Rights in the United States: State and Federal Recognition,* eds. Amy E. Den Ouden and Jean O'Brien (Chapel Hill: University of North Carolina Press, 2013).

24. Rountree letter to VCI, Apr. 21, 2009.

25. VCI Business Meeting Minutes, Feb. 19, 2008.

26. VCI Minute Book, July 20, 1999, 8.

27. Letter from Allard A. Allston, III to Chief William Miles, VCI Chairperson, Mar. 18, 2008. Mr. Allston, the husband of Chairperson Lynette Allston, served as one of the tribe's legal counsels during the recognition process.

28. R. L. Fleming telephone interview with author, Jan. 25, 2010.

29. In addition to the NITOV, the VCI received letters of intent from The Cheroenhaka (Nottoway) Indian Tribe of South Hampton, Virginia (Apr. 18, 2006), the Appalachian Intertribal Heritage Association (Sept. 9, 2006), the UCITOVA/ Buffalo Ridge Cherokee (Oct. 17, 2006). The VCI received two additional letters from Tauxenent Indian Nation of Virginia (Jan. 16, 2007), and Bear Saponi Tribe of Clinch Mountain Southwest Virginia (Jan. 27, 2009).

30. Mitchell Bush interview by author, Jan. 25, 2010.

31. VCI Minutes, Jan. 18, 2007: this was the first of three committees to be appointed during the process. Members included Reggie Tuppance Sr. (Upper Mattaponi), Chairman, Paige Archer (Meherrin), Powhatan Owen (Chickahominy), Frank Richardson (Rappahannock) and Delegate Chris Peace. Helen Rountree and Mitchell Bush served as consultants.

32. Ibid.

33. Chairperson Lynette Allston also serves as the NITOV's tribal chief. She holds a BA in History from Duke University.

34. Byrd also described the Nottoway as being "the only Indians of consequence now remaining within the limits of Virginia." See William Byrd, *History of the Dividing Line Betwixt Virginia and North Carolina,* Diary entry Apr. 7, 1728 (Dover Publications, 1967), 113–114.

35. Allard Allston, a native South Carolinian, identifies as African American; but like most African Americans, his ancestral lineage is African, European, and American Indian, the latter of which includes three lines of American Indian ancestry: Catawba, Saponi and Cherokee.

36. Lynette Allston, "Nottoway Indian Tribe of Virginia Measure in Time: A View of Our History after First Contact," in *Dotratung (New Moon): Our Story-Nottoway Indians,* Vol. 1 (Southampton: The Virginia Circle and Square Foundation, 2010), 7. This is an excellent general overview of Nottoway history and contemporary tribal life and culture.

37. Ibid., 8.

38. For more on the treaty of Middle Plantation see Martha W. McCartney, "Narrative History," In *A Study of Virginia Indians and Jamestown: The First Century,* ed. Danielle Moretti Langholtz (Williamsburg, VA: Colonial National Historic Park, National Park Service, 2005).

39. Allston, "Nottoway Indian"; Parramore, *Southampton County, Virginia* (Charlottesville: University of Virginia, Press, 1978), 1–18.

40. Parramore, *Southampton County,* 6.

41. Ibid., 1–18. Lynette Allston, "The Nottoway Indian," 9–10; Petition Cover Letter, Oct. 17, 2006, 3–4; the Nottoway were traditionally an Iroquois speaking people. Thomas Jefferson studied the Nottoway language and compiled a list of Nottoway words and phrases that were combined with a second list and published in 1836; for more on this see Lynette Allston, "The Nottoway Indians," 15.

42. Ibid., 5–6; Lynette Allston, Petition Cover Letter, 4. Not all Indians found sanctuary at the Nottoway reservation. During the Tuscarora War, the Nottoway, having signed a treaty with Governor Alexander Spotswood in 1714, became a buffer zone between the colonial powers and enemy Indians; hence, Tuscarora Indians seeking refuge at the reservation were turned over to colonial authorities.

43. Parramore, *Southampton County,* 65–68; Vivian Lucas interview with author, Sept. 23, 2010 and Nov. 2, 2010.

44. Parramore, *Southampton County, 81–112; Nat Turner's Rebellion,* PBS.org Resource Bank. http://www.pbs.org/wgbh/aia/part3/3p1518.html.

45. Vivian Lucas telephone interview with author, Nov. 2, 2010.

46. Parramore, *Southampton County,* 81–112; *Nat Turner's Rebellion,* PBS.org Resource Bank. http://www.pbs.org/wgbh/aia/part3/3p1518.html; Vivian Lucas telephone interview with author, Nov. 2, 2010.

47. Lynette Allston conversation with author, Nov. 25, 2006.

48. By Apr. 2007, two committee members, Reggie Tuppance and Chris Peace, resigned and were replaced by Mitchell Bush and Gene Adkins, Chief of the Chickahominy Tribe Eastern Division. Dr. Carole Nash replaced Mitchell Bush as committee consultant, but she attended only one meeting. NITOV Chairperson Lynette Allston in a prepared statement read before the VCI expressed concern about the slowness of the process. She provided suggestions regarding how to jumpstart and refocus the process. See VCI Business Meeting Minutes Apr. 17, 2007.

49. Committee member Powhatan Owens was inactive on the committee after its initial meeting in June 2007.

50. The NITOV once again raised questions regarding the accuracy of the official Feb. 19, 2008, meeting minutes as presented by Rountree. According to the VCI minutes dated Mar. 18, 2008, "Chairman Bass conferred with Jane Hickey from the attorney general's office about the tape recording made by Rountree. Ms. Hickey stated that if the recording made by Rountree was used to help prepare the Feb. 19 minutes, its use would fall within the guidelines of FOIA. Rountree stated they were "for her personal use." She refused Ms. Hickey's request for a copy of the recorded minutes.

51. Quoted in letter from Allard Allston to Chief William Miles.

52. VCI meeting minutes, Feb. 19, 2009; Rountree is an honorary member of the Nansemond Tribe and has served as its secretary since 1982.

53. Letter from Arlene Milner to Recognition Committee, Apr. 2, 2008 and presented to VCI Recognition Committee on Apr. 15, 2008.

54. Rountree, "Position paper on Criteria 1," read before the VCI Recognition Committee on Apr, 15, 2008.

55. Narrative in Support of Petitioner Vivian Claud Lucas, Nottoway Indian Tribe of Virginia, Inc., VCI Recognition Petition, Genealogy, Aug. 21, 2007.

56. Arica L. Coleman, "Against All Odds: The Nottoway Indian Tribe of Virginia and the Triumph of State Recognition," *DoTratung (New Moon),* 66.

57. The Dawes General Allotment Act of 1887, named for Henry L. Dawes of Massachusetts, substituted communal land ownership for individual land ownership as a way to "civilize" American Indians by making them farmers. Individual heads of households were granted 80 to 160 acres. Ownership of the land, however, was withheld for twenty-five years to avoid the sale of property to land speculators. But, by 1932 approximately two-thirds of Indian land was owned by Whites; The Termination and Relocation Acts were BIA initiatives to terminate federal services and trust responsibility over Indian affairs for certain tribes whose lands and economy were not profitable to the U.S. economy. These policies were enforced by Public Law 280 (1953) and Public Law 959 (1956). For more on termination and relocation, see Rebecca L. Robbins, "Self Determination and Subordination: The Past, the Present and the Future of American Indian Governance," in *The State of Native America: Genocide, Colonization and Resistance,* ed. M. Annette Jaimes (Boston, Mass.: South End Press, 1992), 98–100.

58. Helen Rountree, "Minutes: Meeting of Nottoway Descendants and Others" at the cottage of Francis and Mary Kello, Courtland, Va., Feb. 2, 2002.

59. Allard Allston Letter to the VCI; The Powhatan-Renape people who began migrating to New Jersey sometime during the late eighteenth century engaged a similar strategy as the Nottoway in maintaining Indian identity. They settled in a place called Morrisville, New Jersey, which was first inhabited by people of "part Mohican/part Black" ancestry. Virginia's RIA drastically increased migration to Morrisville and surrounding areas in the twentieth century. Their effort to maintain identity did not prevent them from socializing across racial lines. The Powhatan-Renape strategy was to "keep a low profile. Be proud to be Indian, but don't tell anyone." The Powhatan-Renape went public in 1962 and gained state recognition in 1980. For more on the Powhatan-Renape, see Nemattanew, *Morrisville: A Native Hidden Community* (Rancocas, N.J.: Powhatan Press, 2002), 8, 13, 47, and 23; for more on the Powhatan-Renape migration, see Jack D. Forbes, "The Renape People: A Brief Survey of Relationships and Migration," *Wicazo Sa Review* (Spring 1986): 14–19.

60. VCI, Recognition Committee Report, Apr. 17, 2009.

61. Karrenne Wood, "Virginia Indians: Our Story," 20.

62. The requirement to demonstrate continuous existence is the most controversial of all of the requirements because the question was not considered by the Virginia General Assembly when passing the resolutions for the Virginia Eight. It is this BIA requirement the tribes seeking to obtain federal recognition via legislation want to avoid.

63. See Recognition Committee Report, Apr. 17, 2009, 18.

64. Email from Eric Gregory to Allard Allston titled "The Ag's response to Senator Lucas's June 2008 Letter &VCI FOIA Compliance.

65. The final committee vote was as follows: Bush—yes, Bass, Milner, and Rountree, no, Richardson, abstain.

66. On Jan. 11, 2010, Rountree sent Senator Lucas an email requesting that she vote against SJR 12. It was apparent that she was unaware at the time that Lucas had written to the AG's Office requesting that she be investigated and that Lucas was the sponsor of the bill the retired professor had asked her to vote against.

67. I testified on behalf of the NITOV at this hearing. Also testifying at this hearing was Las Vegas entertainer Wayne Newton, of Cherokee/Patawomeck descent. He testified on behalf of the Patawomeck who first attempted to gain recognition in 1999.

68. Coleman, "Against All Odds,"68; House Joint Resolution 150 granted state recognition to the Patawomeck and House Joint Resolution 171 granted state recognition to the Cheroenhaka (Nottoway) of Southampton, Virginia (CITOSV). The resolution submitted on behalf of the Cheroenhaka at the eleventh hour resulted in much confusion regarding the two groups as legislators debated whether they were splinter groups with the same genealogy or competing groups. First, they are not splinter groups according to the definition of a splinter group as outlined in the VCI guidelines. The NITOV and CITSV each submitted separate letters of intent to petition for recognition, Feb. 2006 and Apr. 2006 respectively; but only the NITOV followed through submitting a formal petition in Oct. 2006. If the VCI viewed the NITOV as a splinter group, they would have never moved forward with the recognition process. Second, there is no proof that the two shared the same genealogies as the CITSV tribal members have never undergone formal review. Hence, the group has not submitted genealogical information which validates their claim that they are descendants of the historic Nottoway Indians of southeastern Virginia. To the contrary, the genealogical information of the NITOV was reviewed over a six month period and all ten family lines were verified as having a direct connection to the historic Nottoway, some dating back to 1805. Third, legislators who believed the two were competing groups misread the situation entirely. They were not competing with one another, but rather one group (the CITSV) was piggybacking on the other (NITV) to gain state recognition. While the NITOV went through a three year vetting process, the CITSV was never vetted. The CITSV's connection to the historic Cheroenhaka was assumed rather than formally validated. Although Chief Walt Brown recently claimed that the road to state recognition for the Cheroenhaka was a long, twisted process which took eight years, never in the duration of that time did the tribe submit a formal petition, and in fact refused to do so. Hence, it was erroneous to place the two groups on par with one another as one had demonstrated that they are descendants of the historic Nottoway while the other has yet to do so. Therefore, the question is not how are the NITOV and CITSV distinct, but rather, who are the members which comprise the CITSV and what are the ancestral links of this group to the historic Cheroenhaka?

69. Elliott became the salient focus among opponents seeking to derail Nottoway efforts to gain state recognition via the Virginia General Assembly because newspapers and other media referred to him as the first "Black" judge in the city of

Portsmouth. As demonstrated by the above quote Elliot embraces both ancestries and has traced his lineage back to the Nottoway Reservation.

70. In protest of the three newly recognized tribes, VCI members refused to attend monthly meetings and business was halted due to a lack of a quorum. On Nov. 28, 2011, tribal leaders received an email from Doug Domenench, Virginia Secretary of Natural Resources, notifying them that the Governor's Office had decided to eliminate the VCI as an advisory body. See Governor McDonnell's Commission on Government Reform and Restructuring Report to the Governor (Nov. 21, 2011), 23; The dissolution of the VCI was supported by a majority of the state recognized Indian tribes who, according to Pamunkey Chief Kevin Brown, believed that the general assembly's recognition of the three tribes against "the wishes of the Council" demonstrated that the VCI had "outlived its usefulness . . . I think everyone felt it was just ineffective in some ways, and the tribes could be more effective establishing their own relationship with the commonwealth." See Michael Paul Williams, "Making Gains, but Losing an Advocate, RichmondTimesDispatch.com, Apr. 13, 2012, http://www2.timesdispatch.com/news/columnists-blogs/2012/apr/13/tdmet01-michael-paul-williams-making-gains-but-los-ar-1839032/

Epilogue

1. Lori Battle interview with author, Nov. 29, 2010.

2. Helen Rountree, *Southeastern Indians,* 40; Rountree provides no evidence to support the claim that the tri-county area inhabited by the Rappahannock was more antagonistic to people of color than any other county within the Commonwealth. In fact, in *Eastern Shore Indians of Virginia and Maryland* (1997), she identified Northampton County as being the most hostile towards people of color than any other county.

3. Chief Lynnette Allston interview with author, Nov. 15, 2010.

4. Interview with anonymous informant, Nov. 29, 2010.

5. Lori Battle interview with author, Nov. 29, 2010.

6. Interview with anonymous informant, Nov. 10, 2010.

7. Michael Paul Williams, "Church Denies Entry to Couple," 4.

8. L. Scott Gould, "Mixing Bodies and Beliefs: The Predicament of Race," *Columbia Law Review* 101, no. 4 (May 2007): 772.

9. Josephine Johnston, "Resisting a Genetic Identity: The Black Seminoles and Genetic Test of Ancestry," *Journal of Law, Medicine & Ethics* 31 (2003): 262–271.

10. Tiya Miles, *The Ties That Bind: A Story of an Afro-Cherokee Family in Slavery and Freedom* (Berkeley: University of California Press, 2006), xvi.

11. bell hooks, "Revolutionary Renegade," in *Black Looks: Race and Representation* (Boston: South End Books, 1987), 184.

12. Tiya Miles, *The Ties that Bind,* xvi.

SELECTED BIBLIOGRAPHY

PRIMARY SOURCES

Manuscripts and Archives

Attan-Akamik Newspaper Collection. State Library of Virginia, Richmond, Va.
James R. Coates Papers. State Library of Virginia, Richmond, Va.
Charles Davenport Papers. The American Philosophical Society, Philadelphia, Pa.
Loving v. Virginia Papers. The Central Rappahannock Heritage Center, Fredericks-
    burg, Va.
Papers of the NAACP Part II Special Subject Files, 1912–1939 Series B. Warren G.
    Harding through YWCA. Microfilm. University of Delaware, Newark, Del.
John Powell Collection. University of Virginia Special Collections, Charlottesville, Va.
Frank Speck Papers. American Philosophical Society, Philadelphia, Pa.

Interviews

Allard and Lynette Allston
Lori Battle
Richard and Marion Bowman
Sherida Bradby
Bernard Cohen
Peggy Fortune
Hugh and Anita Harrell
Philip Hirschkopf
Lewis Jeter
Mildred Jeter Loving
Vivian Lucas
Robert Pratt
Ann Tignor
Peter Wallenstein

Magazines and Periodicals

Booker, Simeon. "The Couple That Rocked Courts." *Ebony,* September 1967, 78–84.
Valentine, Victoria. "When Love Was a Crime." *Emerge,* July, 61, 1997.

———. "The Crime of Being Married: A Virginia Couple Fights to Overturn An Old Law Against Miscegenation." *Life*, March 18, 1966, 85–91.

Newspapers Surveyed

(Fredericksburg) *Free Lance-Star*
New York Times
Richmond News Leader
Richmond Times-Dispatch
(Norfolk) *Virginian Pilot*
Washington Post

Pamphlets

Archer, Armstrong. *A Compendium of Slavery as It Exists in the Present Day in the United States of America*. London: J. Haddon Printers, 1844.
Cox, Earnest Sevier. *Let My People Go*. Richmond, Va.: The White American Society, 1925.
———. *Lincoln's Negro Policy*. Richmond, Va.: William Byrd Press, 1938.
Plecker, Walter. *Eugenics and the New Family in Relation to the Law of Racial Integrity*. Richmond, Va.: Bureau of Vital Statistics State Board of Health, 1924.
———. *Racial Improvement*. Reprint. Paper Presented Before the 56th Annual Meeting Medical Society of Virginia. October, 1925.
———. *The New Family and Race Improvement*. Virginia Health Bulletin. November, 1925.
Pollard, John Garland. *The Pamunkey Indians of Virginia*. Bulletin 17. Washington, D.C.: The Bureau of American Ethnology, 1894.

Government Documents

Acts of Assembly. 1924. Va.
Acts of Assembly. 1930. Va.
Legislative Petitions 1843 King William County, Va.
Report of the Joint Subcommittee Studying Relationship between The Commonwealth and Native Indian Tribes. House Document No. 10, 1982.
Report on the Commission on Indians to the Governor and General Assembly, 1983.
Report on the State Recognition Petition of the United Cherokee Indian Tribe of Virginia, Inc. Secretary of Health and Human Resources Office of the Governor, 1993.
Senate Bills Nos. 1–224. 1924. Va.
Social Security Death Index
United States Census Data 1790 to 2000.
Virginia Council on Indians Tribal Recognition Criteria 1989 and 2006.
Virginia Council on Indians Recognition Committee Report on the Nottoway Indian Tribe of Virginia, Inc., April 17, 2009.

Secondary Sources

Baker, Lee D. *Anthropology and the Racial Politics of Culture.* Durham, N.C.: Duke University Press, 2010.

Berkhofer, Robert. *The White Man's Indian: Images of the American Indian from Columbus to the Present.* New York: Vintage Books, 1979.

Blackett, R. J. M. *Building an Antislavery Wall: Black Americans in the Atlantic Abolitionist Movement, 1830–1860.* Baton Rouge: Louisiana State University Press, 1983.

Bothan, Fay. *Almighty God Created the Races: Christianity, Interracial Marriage, and American Law.* Chapel Hill: University of North Carolina Press. 2009.

Brennan, Jonathan, ed. *When Brer Rabbit Meets Coyote: African-Native American Literature.* Urbana: University of Illinois Press, 2003.

Catterall, Helen T., ed. *Judicial Cases Concerning American Slavery and the Negro.* Vol. I. Washington, D.C.: Carnegie Institute of Washington, 1926.

Clifford, James. *The Predicament of Culture: Twentieth-Century Ethnography, Literature, and Art.* Cambridge: Harvard University Press, 1988.

Cook, Samuel R. "Anthropological Advocacy in Historical Perspective: The Case of Anthropologists and Virginia Indians." *Human Organization* 63, no. 2 (2003):191–201.

Cox, Earnest Sevier. *White America.* Richmond, Va.: White American Society, 1937.

Deloria, Philip. *Playing Indian.* New Haven, Conn.: Yale University Press, 1998.

Deloria, Vine. "The Red and the Black." *Custer Died for Your Sins: An Indian Manifesto.* Norman: University of Oklahoma Press, 1988.

———. "The Concept of History." *God Is Red: A Native View of Religion.* 98–113. Golden, Colo.: Fulcrum Publishing., 1992.

Dorr, Michael. *Segregation's Science: Eugenics and Society in Virginia.* Charlottesville: University of Virginia Press, 2008.

———. "Segregation's Science: The American Eugenics Movement and Virginia, 1900–1980." PhD diss., Charlottesville: University of Virginia, 2000.

Douglass, Frederick. "The Claims of the Negro Ethnologically Considered." In *Frederick Douglass: Selected Speeches and Writings,* ed. Philip Foner. Chicago: Lawrence Hill Books, 1999.

Du Bois, W. E. B. "Virginia." In *Writings in Periodicals: Selections from the Crisis,* 580. New York: Kraus International Publishers, 1983.

———. "A Lunatic or a Traitor." *W. E. B. Du Bois, A Reader,* ed. David Levering Lewis, 341. New York: Henry Holt, 1995.

———. "Back to Africa." *W. E. B. Du Bois, A Reader,* ed. David Levering Lewis, 335. New York: Henry Holt, 1995.

Ellison, Mary. 1983. "Black Perceptions and Red Images: Indian and Black Literary Links." *Phylon* 44, no. 1 (1983): 44–55.

Ellison, Ralph. "Hidden Names and Complex Fate: A Writer's Experience in the United States." In *The Collected Essays of Ralph Ellison,* ed. John F. Callahan, 189–209. New York: The Modern Library, 1995.

Estabrook, Arthur. *Mongrel Virginians.* Baltimore: William & Wilkins Co., 1926.

Fall, Ralph Emmett. *People, Post Offices and Communities in Caroline County, Virginia, 1729–1969.* Roswell, Ga.: W. H. Wolfe Associates, 1989.

Feest, Christian F. "Virginia Algonquins." In *Northeast,* Vol. 15 of *Handbook of North American Indians,* ed. Bruce G. Trigger. 253–270. Washington, D.C.: Smithsonian Institution, 1978.

Forbes, Jack D. *Africans and Native Americans: The Language of Race and the Evolution of Red-Black Peoples.* 2nd ed. Urbana: University of Illinois Press, 1990.

———. "The Manipulation of Race, Caste, and Identity: Classifying AfroAmericans, Native Americans, and Red-Black People." *Journal of Ethnic Studies* 17, no. 4 (Winter 1990):1–51.

Gallay, Allan. *The Indian Slave Trade: The Rise of English Empire in the American South, 1670–1717.* New Haven, Conn.: Yale University Press, 2003.

Garroutte, Eva Marie. "The Racial Formation of American Indians: Negotiating Legitimate Identities within Tribal and Federal Law." *American Indian Quarterly* 25, no. 2 (Spring 2001): 224–239.

Garvey, Marcus. "A Special Note on Intermarriage and Racial Purity." In *Marcus Garvey: Life and Lessons,* ed. Robert A. Hill, 204. Berkeley: University of California Press, 1987.

———. *Philosophy and Opinions of Marcus Garvey or Africa for the Africans.* Vols. 1 and 2. Dover, Mass.: Majority Press, 1989.

Gatewood, Willard B, Jr., ed. *Free Man of Color: The Autobiography of Willis August Hodges.* Knoxville: University of Tennessee Press, 1980.

Giddings, Paula. *When and Where I Enter: The Impact of Black Women on Race and Sex in America.* New York: William Morrow, 1984.

Gleach, Frederic, W. "Anthropological Professionalization and the Virginia Indians at the Turn of the Century." *American Anthropologist* 104, no. 2 (June 2002): 499–507.

——— "A Traditional Story of the Powhatan Indians Recorded in the Early 19th Century." In *Papers of the Twenty-Third Algonquian Conference,* William Cowan, ed., 234–243. Ottawa: Carleton University, 1992.

———. *Powhatan's World and Colonial Virginia: A Conflict of Cultures.* Lincoln: University of Nebraska Press, 2000.

Gordon-Reed, Annette. *Thomas Jefferson and Sally Hemings: An America Controversy.* Charlottesville: University of Virginia Press, 1999.

Gould, L. Scott. "Mixing Bodies and Beliefs: The Predicament of Tribes." *Columbia Law Review* 101, no.4 (May 2001): 702–772.

Gross, J. Ariela. *What Blood Won't Tell: A History of Race on Trial in America.* Cambridge, Mass.: Harvard University Press, 2010.

Guerrero, Marie Anna Jaimes. "Civil Rights versus Sovereignty: Native American Women in Life and Land Struggles." In *Feminist Genealogies, Colonial Legacies, and Democratic Futures,* ed. M. Jacqui Alexander and Chandra Talpade Mohanty, 101–124. New York: Routledge, 1997.

Guild, June Purcell. *Black Laws of Virginia.* 1936. Fauquier County, Va.: Afro-American Historical Association, 1995.

Hedlin, Ethel Wolfskill. "Earnest Cox and Colonization: A White Racist's Response to Black Repatriation, 1923–1966." Ph D diss., N.C.: Duke University, 1974.

Hening, William Waller. *The Statutes at Large Being a Collection of All the Laws of Virginia from the First Session of the Legislature in the Year 1619.* 13 Vols. CD-ROM. Westminister, Md.: Heritage Books, Inc., 2003.

Henriksen, Georg. "Anthropologists as Advocates-Promoters or Makers of Clients." In *Advocacy and Anthropology,* ed. Robert Paine, 119–129. St. John's, Newfoundland, Canada: Institute of Social and Economic Research Memorial University of Newfoundland, 1985.

Higginbotham, A. Leon, Jr., and Barbara Kopytoff. "Racial Purity and Interracial Sex in the Law of Colonial and Antebellum Virginia." *Georgetown Law Journal* 77 (Aug. 1989): 1967–2029.

Hollinger, David A. "Amalgamation and Hypodescent: The Question of Ethnoracial Mixture in the History of the United States." *American Historical Review* 108, no. 5 (Dec. 2003): 1363–1390.

Holton, Woody. *Forced Founders: Indians, Debtors, Slaves, and the Making of the American Revolution in Virginia.* Chapel Hill: University of North Carolina Press, 1999.

Hudson, Charles. Introduction to *Red, White, and Black: Symposium on Indians in the Old South.* Athens: University of Georgia Press, 1971.

Huhndorf, Shari. "From the Turn of the Century to the New Age: Playing Indian Past and Present." In *As We Are Now: Mixblood Essays On Race and Identity,* ed. William S. Penn, 181–198. Berkeley: University of California Press, 1997.

Huggins, Nathan. *The Harlem Renaissance.* New York: Oxford University Press, 1991.

Hutchinson, Earl Ofari. *The Assassination of the Black Male Image.* New York: Touchstone Books, 1997.

"Indian Slaves." *William and Mary College Quarterly Historical Magazine* 6, no. 4 (1898): 214–215.

"Indian Slaves." *William and Mary College Quarterly Historical Magazine* 8, no. 3 (1900): 16.

Jefferson, Thomas. *Notes on the State of Virginia.* Edited by Frank Shuffleton. New York: Penguin Books, 1999.

Johnston, James, Hugo. "Documentary Evidence of the Relations of Negroes and Indians." *The Journal of Negro History* 14, no. 1 (1929): 21–43.

———. *Race Relations in Virginia and Miscegenation in the South, 1776–1860.* Amherst: University of Massachusetts Press, 1970.

Johnston, Josephine. "Resisting a Genetic Identity: The Black Seminoles and Genetic Test of Ancestry." *Journal of Law, Medicine & Ethics.* 31, no. 2 (2003): 262–271.

Jordan, Winthrop. D. *White Over Black: American Attitudes Toward the Negro, 1550–1812.* Chapel Hill: University of North Carolina Press, 1968.

Kerber, Linda, K. "The Abolitionist Perception of the Indian." *Journal of American History.* 62, no. 2 (1975): 271–295.

Koenig, Alexa, and Jonathan Stein. "Federalism and the State Recognition of Native American Tribes: A Survey of State Recognized Tribes and State Recognition Processes Across the United States." *Santa Clara Law Review.* 48 (2007): 79–153.

Langholtz, Danielle Moretti, ed. *A Study of Virginia Indians and Jamestown: The First Century.* Williamsburg, Va: Colonial National Historic Park, 2005.

Lauber, Almon Wheeler. *Indian Slavery in Colonial Times within the Present Limits of the United States.* New York: Columbia University, 1913.

Lemire, Elise. *Miscegenation: Making Race in America.* Philadelphia: University of Pennsylvania Press, 2002.

McLoughlin, William G. "Red Indians, Black Slavery and White Racism: America's Slaveholding Indians." *American Quarterly* 26, no. 4 (Oct. 1974): 367–385.

Meaders, Daniel. *Advertisements for Runaway Slaves in Virginia, 1801–1820.* New Jersey: Routledge, 1997.

Mihesuah, Devon Abbott. *Indigenous American Women: Decolonization, Empowerment, Activism.* Lincoln: University of Nebraska Press, 2003.

Miller, John Chester. *Wolf by the Ears: Thomas Jefferson and Slavery.* New York: The Free Press, 1977.

Mooney, James. "The Powhatan Confederacy, Past and Present." *American Anthropologist* n.s. 9, no. 1 (1907): 129–152.

Morgan, Edmund. *American Slavery, American Freedom: The Ordeal of Colonial Virginia.* New York: W. W. Norton, 1975.

Murray, Paul T. "Who Is an Indian? Who Is a Negro? Virginia Indians in the World War II Draft." *Virginia Magazine of History and Biography* 95, no. 2 (1987): 215–231.

Nemattanew (Chief Roy Crazy Horse). *Morrisville: A Native Hidden Community.* Rancocas, N.J.: Powhatan Press, 2002.

Newbeck, Phyl. *Virginia Hasn't Always Been for Lovers: Interracial Marriage Bans and the Case of Loving v. Virginia.* Carbondale: Southern Illinois University Press, 2004.

Nottoway Indian Tribe of Virginia, Inc. *Dotratung (New Moon): Our Story—Nottoway Indians,* Vol. 1. Southampton: The Virginia Circle and Square Foundation, 2010.

Omi, Michael and Howard Winant. *Racial Formation in the United States from the 1960s to the 1990s.* 2nd ed. New York: Routledge, 1994.

Onuf, Peter S. "'To Declare Them A Free and Independent People': Race, Slavery, and National Identity in Jefferson's Thought." *The Journal of the Early Republic.* 18, no. 1 (1998): 1–46.

Parramore, Thomas, C, et. al. *Norfolk: The First Four Centuries.* Charlottesville: University of Virginia Press, 1994.

Parramoore, C. Thomas. *Southampton County, Virginia.* Charlottesville: University of Virginia Press, 1978.

Pascoe, Peggy. "Miscegenation Law, Court Cases, and Ideologies of Race in Twentieth-Century America," *Journal of American History* 83, no. 1 (1998): 44–69.

———. *What Comes Naturally: Miscegenation Law and the Making of Race in America.* New York: Oxford University Press, 2009.

Perdue, Charles L., Thomas E. Barden, and Robert K. Philips, eds. *Weevils in the Wheat: Interviews with Virginia Ex-Slaves.* Charlottesville: University of Virginia Press, 1976.

Peterson, Merrill, ed. *Thomas Jefferson, Writings*. New York: Library Classics of the United States, 1984.

Philips, Valerie. L. "Epilogue: Seeing Each Other Through the White Man's Eyes." In *Confounding the Color Line: The Indian-Black Experience in North America*, ed. James F. Brooks, 369–385. Lincoln: University of Nebraska Press, 2002.

Porter, Kenneth. "Relations between Negroes and Indians: Contacts as Allies." *Journal of Negro History* 17, no. 3 (1932): 307–320.

Pratt, Robert. 1998. "Crossing the Color Line: A Historical Assessment and Personal Narrative of *Loving v. Virginia*." *Howard Law Journal* 41 (Winter 1998): 229–244.

Rice, Horace. *The Buffalo Ridge Cherokee: A Remnant of a Great Nation Divided*. Westminister, Md.: Heritage Books, Inc., 1995.

Rothman, Joshua. D. *Notorious in the Neighborhood: Sex and Families across the Color Line in Virginia, 1787–1861*. Chapel Hill: University of North Carolina Press, 2003.

Rountree, Helen. *Pocahontas's People: The Powhatan Indians of Virginia through Four Centuries*. Norman: University of Oklahoma Press, 1989.

Russell, John H. *The Free Negro in Virginia, 1619–1865*. Baltimore, Md.: Johns Hopkins University Press, 1913.

Russell, Kathy, et al. *The Color Complex: The Politics of Skin Color among African Americans*. New York: Harcourt Brace Jovanovich, 1993.

Said, Edward. *Orientalism*. New York: Vintage, 1978.

Salmon, Emily J., and Edward D. D. Campbell, Jr., eds. *The Hornbook of Virginia History*. Richmond: Library of Virginia. 1994.

Selden, Stephen. *Inheriting Shame: The Story of Eugenics and Racism in America*. New York: Teachers College Press Columbia University, 1999.

Sidbury, James. "Saint Dominique in Virginia: Ideology, Local Meaning and Resistance to Slavery, 1790–1800," *Journal of Southern History*. 63, no. 1 (1997): 531–552.

Smith, John. *The General Historie of Virginia, New England and the Summer Isles: Together With The True Travels, Adventures and Observations, and A Sea Grammar. Vol. 1*. John MacLehose and Sons, 1907.

Smith, J. David. *Managing White Supremacy: Race, Politics and Citizenship in Jim Crow Virginia*. Chapel Hill: University of North Carolina, 2002.

———. 1993. *The Eugenics Assault on America: Scenes in Red, White, and Black*. Fairfax, Va.: George Mason University Press, 1993.

Smith, Linda Tuhiwai. *Decolonizing Methodologies: Research and Indigenous People*. London: Zed Books, 1998.

Smits, David D. "'Abominable Mixture': Toward the Repudiation of Anglo-Indian Intermarriage in Seventeenth-Century Virginia." *Virginia Magazine of History and Biography*. 95, no. 2 (1987): 157–192.

Snyder, Christina. *Slavery in Indian County: The Changing Face of Captivity in Early America*. Cambridge, Mass.: Harvard University Press, 2010.

Speck, Frank. "The Ethnic Position of the Southeastern Algonkian." *American Anthropologist*. n.s. 26, no. 2 (1924): 184–200.

———. *The Rappahannock Indians of Virginia*. New York: Museum of the American Indian, Heye Foundation, 1925.

———. *Chapters on the Ethnology of the Powhatan Indians of Virginia*. New York: Museum of the American Indian, Heye Foundation, 1928.

Stern, Thomas. "Chickahominy: The Changing Culture of a Virginia Indian Community." *Proceedings of the American Philosophical Society*. 96, no. 2 (1952): 157–225.

Strachey, William. *The Historie of Travell Into Virginia Britania (1612)*. Edited by Louis B. Wright and Virginia Freund. London: Hakluyt Society, 1953.

Thomson, Brian William. "Racism and Racial Classification: A Case Study of the Virginia Racial Integrity Legislation." PhD diss., University of California, Riverside, 1978.

Tucker, Saint George. *A Dissertation on Slavery: With a Proposal for the Gradual Abolition of It in the State of Virginia*. Philadelphia: Matthew Carey Publishers, 1861.

Vaughan, Alden T. *Roots of American Racism: Essays on the Colonial Experience*. New York: Oxford University Press, 1995.

Wallace, Anthony, F. C. *Jefferson and the Indians: The Tragic Fate of the First Americans*. Cambridge, Mass.: Belknap Press of Harvard University Press, 2001.

Wallenstein, Peter. "Interracial Marriage on Trial: Loving v. Virginia." In *Race on Trial: Law and Justice in American History*, ed. Annette Gordon-Reed, 177–196. New York: Oxford University Press, 2002.

———. *Tell The Court I Love My Wife: Race, Marriage and Law—An American History*. New York: Palgrave Macmillan, 2002.

Whittenburg, James P., and John M. Coski, eds. *Charles City County: An Official History*. Salem, W.Va.: Don Mills, Inc., 1989.

Williams, Walter, L., ed. *The Southeastern Indians Since the Removal Era*. Athens: University of Georgia Press, 2009.

Williamson, Margaret Holmes. *Powhatan Lord of Life and Death: Command and Consent in Seventeenth-Century Virginia*. Lincoln: University of Nebraska Press, 2008.

Wingfield, Marshall. *A History of Caroline County Virginia*. Richmond, Va.: Press of Trevvet Christian and Co., 1924.

Wright, J. Leitch. *The Only Land They Knew: American Indians in the Old South*. Lincoln: University of Nebraska Press, 1981.

Zuckert, Michael. 2000. "Founder of the Natural Rights Republic." *Thomas Jefferson and the Politics of Nature*. Edited by Thomas Engerman. Notre Dame, Ind.: University of Notre Dame Press, 2000.

INDEX

ARICA L. COLEMAN is Assistant Professor of Black American Studies at the University of Delaware. Her research interests include American History (African American, Native American, and the American South), identity formation, eugenics, and intersections of race and gender. Her current research focuses on the family histories of Richard and Mildred Loving, the plaintiffs of the Supreme Court case *Loving v. Virginia*.